Polish-US Industrial Cooperation
in the 1980s

Contributors

JAN ANUSZ — Senior Research Associate, Foreign Trade Research Institute, Warsaw

JERZY BOROWSKI — Associate Professor of Marketing, Central School of Planning and Statistics, Warsaw

JOSEF C. BRADA — Associate Professor of International Business, Arizona State University, Tempe

ROBERT W. CAMPBELL — Professor and Chairman of Economics, Indiana University, Bloomington

JOHN S. GARLAND — Assistant Professor of Business, University of Kansas, Lawrence

JAN GIEZGALA — Deputy Director, Foreign Trade Research Institute, Warsaw and Associate Professor, Central School of Planning and Statistics, Warsaw

JANUSZ KACZURBA — Director, Foreign Trade Research Institute, Warsaw

ZYGMUNT KOSSUT — Professor and Dean of the Faculty of Foreign Trade, Central School of Planning and Statistics, Warsaw

JANUSZ KOZINSKI — Research Associate, Foreign Trade Research Institute, Warsaw

PAUL MARER — Professor of International Business, School of Business, Indiana University, Bloomington

JOSEPH C. MILLER — Associate Professor of Marketing, School of Business, Indiana University, Bloomington

SCHUYLER F. OTTESON — Professor and Dean, School of Business, Indiana University, Bloomington

HOWARD V. PERLMUTTER — Professor of Social Architecture, The Wharton School of Commerce and Finance, University of Pennsylvania, Philadelphia

ANDRZEJ RUDKA — Research Associate, Foreign Trade Research Institute, Warsaw

JOZEF SOLDACZUK — Professor and Chairman of Department of International Economic Relations, Central School of Planning and Statistics, Warsaw

ADAM SZEWORSKI — Professor of International Economics, Warsaw University

JERZY SZUMSKI — Former Deputy Director, BUMAR Foreign Trade Organization, Warsaw

EUGENIUSZ TABACZYNSKI — Associate Professor and Head of Department, Foreign Trade Research Institute, Warsaw

BRONISLAW WOJCIECHOWSKI — Associate Professor and Head of Department, Foreign Trade Research Institute, Warsaw

THOMAS A. WOLF — Associate Professor of Economics, Ohio State University, Columbus

EDWIN ZAGORSKI — Senior Research Associate, Foreign Trade Research Institute, Warsaw

Polish-US Industrial Cooperation in the 1980s
Findings of a Joint Research Project

Edited by

PAUL MARER
Indiana University
Bloomington

EUGENIUSZ TABACZYNSKI
Foreign Trade Research Institute
Warsaw

INDIANA UNIVERSITY PRESS
BLOOMINGTON

Studies in East European and Soviet
Planning, Development, and Trade
International Development Institute
Indiana University, Bloomington, Indiana
Paul Marer, Editor
No. 30

Manufactured in the United States of America

Library of Congress Cataloging in Publication Data
Main entry under title:

Polish-US industrial cooperation in the 1980s.

    1. Poland—Industries.   2. United States—Industries.   3. Technology transfer—Poland.   4. Technology transfer—United States.   5. Poland—Foreign economic relations—United States.   6. United States—Foreign economic relations—Poland.   I. Marer, Paul.   II. Tabaczyński, Eugeniusz.   III. Title: Polish-U.S. industrial cooperation in the 1980s.
HC340.3.P66   338.91′73′0438   81-47884
ISBN 0-253-34529-4   AACR2
1 2 3 4 5 85 84 83 82 81

Contents

Contributors   2304008   ii
List of Tables   ix
Foreword
    E. Raymond Platig   xi
    Janusz Czamarski   xii
Preface
    Schuyler F. Otteson   xv
    Janusz Kaczurba   xvii
Acknowledgements   xix
About the Project   xxiii

PART I: SUMMARY, CONCLUSIONS, RECOMMENDATIONS

    US and Polish Teams   1

PART II: INTERNATIONAL HARVESTER-BUMAR COOPERATION: The Manufacture and Marketing of Construction Machinery, a Case Study

    US and Polish Teams   41

PART III: CONFERENCE IN BLOOMINGTON: Papers by the Polish Team and Discussion

The Foreign Trade System in Poland
    Jan Giezgala   87
    Comment: Robert W. Campbell   92
    Reply   96

East-West Industrial Cooperation and Specialization in Polish Production
    Eugeniusz Tabaczynski   98
    Comment: Thomas A. Wolf   104
    Reply   107

Problems of Polish-US Economic Relations: A Polish Perspective
    Zygmunt Kossut   109
    Comment: Josef C. Brada   117
    Reply   119

US-Polish Industrial Cooperation: Achievements, Problems,
  Prospects
  Edwin Zagorski   121
  Comment: *Paul Marer*   131
  Reply   136

Technology Transfer in US-Polish Industrial Cooperation
  Janusz Kozinski   140
  Comment: *Robert W. Campbell*   154
  Reply   157

The International Harvester-BUMAR Cooperation
  Experience: Practical Problems and How They Are Being
  Solved
  Jerzy Szumski   159
  Comment: *John Garland*   171
  Reply   174

Summary of the Discussion
  The Editors   175

PART IV: CONFERENCE IN WARSAW: Papers by the
           US Team and Discussion

The Future of East-West Industrial Cooperation:
  A Social Architectural Perspective
  Howard V. Perlmutter   187
  Comment: *Eugeniusz Tabaczynski*   204
  Reply   206

Technology Transfer by Means of Industrial Cooperation: A
  Theoretical Appraisal
  Josef C. Brada   207
  Comment: *Jan Anusz*   224
  Reply   226

Import Protectionism in the US and Poland's Manufactures
  Exports
  Paul Marer   228
  Comment: *Adam Szeworski*   251
  Reply   255

Marketing Polish Industrial Goods in the United States
  Joseph C. Miller   259
  Comment: *Jerzy Borowski*   266
  Reply   270

Determinants of Polish Exports of Manufactured Products to
the West and the Strategy of Industrial Cooperation
Thomas A. Wolf 272
Comment: *Zygmunt Kossut* 293
Reply 295

Organizational Constraints on Industrial Cooperation
John Garland 298
Comment: *Bronislaw Wojciechowski* 312
Reply 316

Summary of the Discussion
The Editors 318

PART V: JOINT VENTURES IN POLAND

Today's Approach to Joint Ventures in Poland
Eugeniusz Tabaczynski 343

Polish Legal Documents Relating to Foreign Investment
and Joint Ventures in Poland, 1976-79 349

Appendix 1: Questionnaire on US-Polish Industrial Cooperation 399

Appendix 2: List of Conference Participants
Bloomington (December 1978) 404
Warsaw (March 1979) 406

List of Tables

International Harvester-BUMAR Cooperation
1. Share of the Major Export-Oriented Manufacturers in the World Exportation of Construction Equipment, 1975   77
2. Leading North American Companies, Construction Equipment Industry, 1977   77
3. Poland's Exports and Imports of Equipment and Machinery, 1976-78   78
4. BUMAR Union Production and Export, 1978   80
5. International Harvester Sales by Major Project Groups, 1978   80

Kossut, "Problems of Polish-US Economic Relations"
1. Polish-US Trade and Trade Balance 1972-77   115
2. Polish-US Trade and Trade Balance 1977-78   115
3. Polish Exports to the United States in 1977-78   116
4. Polish Imports from the United States in 1977-78   116

Kozinski, "Aspects of Technology Transfer"
1. Poland's Trade with all Western Countries and with the US and the Share of IC Deliveries in 1978   151
2. Analytical Framework of Phases and Elements of Technology Transferred Through Industrial Cooperation Agreements   152
3. Main Features of Three ICAs Between Poland and the US   153

Perlmutter, "Future of East-West Industrial Cooperation"
1. Key Elements in Alternative Politico-Economic Scenarios for East-West Industrial Cooperation in the 1980s   201
2. Social Architectural Parameters of East-West Industrial Cooperation (illustrative)   201
3. Proposed Model for a Successful ICA Between a US Corporation and a Polish Firm (abbreviated)   202

Brada, "East-West Technology Transfer"
1. Firm Characteristics Influencing Participation in East-West Technology Transfer Via Industrial Cooperation   220
2. East-West Industrial Cooperation Agreements from 1974 to 1976 by Sector and Characteristics of US Industry   221

Marer, "Import Protectionism"
1. US Import-Protective Laws and Procedures   246
2. Market Disruption   248
3. Antidumping   249

Wolf, "Determinants of Polish Exports"
1. Leading Polish Exports to the Industrialized West, 1976 (SITC Divisions 5-8)   284
2. Seven-Digit Product Groups Investigated   286
3. Summary Data on Polish Exports, Market-Shares, and Relative Prices   287
4. Econometric Results   288

Foreword

This volume represents the final report of a group of US and Polish scholars who have analyzed commercial relations between their respective countries in order to gauge the potential for East-West industrial cooperation in the 1980s. It is one of a number of research projects undertaken by academic and other research institutions supported in part by the Department of State as part of its external research program. This particular project was also supported by the East-West area of the International Trade Administration in the Department of Commerce. External research projects are designed to supplement the research capabilities of State and to provide expert views to policy officers and analysts on key questions with important policy implications.

The idea for this study of US-Polish commercial relations was contained in an unsolicited proposal submitted to the government by Professor Paul Marer of Indiana University. The first of two joint seminars was arranged by Marer and held in December 1978 at Bloomington, Indiana. Poland's research team, made up of experts from the Foreign Trade Research Institute (FTRI) in the Ministry of Foreign Trade and Shipping, presented a series of six papers. Comments on the papers by members of the U.S. research team, based at Indiana University and composed of experts from there and other universities, launched a full discussion in which the other attending U.S. businessmen, academicians and government officials took part. At the second seminar, arranged by FTRI Director Janusz Kaczurba and held in March 1979 at Warsaw, the U.S. team presented six additional papers. These too evoked comments by the Polish team and discussions by participating officials from Polish banks, academic Institutions, the Polish Government, and the American Embassy.

Both teams revised their respective papers as a result of the seminars, incorporating new data derived from interviews conducted independently in Poland with employees at various levels at the International Harvester-BUMAR facility, where Poles and Americans cooperate in the manufacture and marketing of construction machinery. The final versions of the papers also benefited from interviews with Polish Government officials whose supervising activities are related to the negotiating and implementing of international industrial cooperation agreements. The two teams enriched still further the report's findings and recommendations when they met in the Spring of 1979 with the Polish-US Economic Council in Krakow. This council is comprised of executives of U.S. firms doing business in Poland and their Polish counterparts.

This publication was co-edited by Professor Marer and Dr. Eugeniusz Tabaczynski of the FTRI. Warren H. Reynolds of this Office attended the seminar at Bloomington. He and Allen Lenz, former Director of Commerce's Office of East-West Policy and Planning, were the chief government monitors for the project.

The Office of Long-Range Assessments and Research plans and manages this program for drawing on the independent expertise of the private research community. Queries about the Programs or comments on this study may be addressed to:

E. Raymond Platig
Director
Office of Long-Range Assessments and
Research
Department of State
Washington, D.C. 20520

Industrial cooperation plays an especially important part in international relations between countries with different economic and social systems. From the Polish point of view, industrial cooperation is very important because it introduces an element of stability into our economic relations. Industrial cooperation agreements—whether in the form of joint ventures in production, in investment, in scientific-technical cooperation, or in the sale of goods—clear the way for increased commercial turnover and make possible the acquisition of a wider assortment of goods.

A natural result of increasing cooperation between Polish and Western industrial firms is the creation of productive enterprises with mixed capital. Several years ago Poland provided the legal basis for

Western partners to set up such enterprises on Polish soil. Further regulations issued since then have tried continuously to improve the legal environment for such ventures and to provide for increased flexibility of operations.

Our efforts to create a more suitable economic environment for prospective partners will be enhanced by the realization of one of the most important tasks in our country, that of implementing comprehensive economic reforms. The reforms will include changes in the management system, restraining direct influences on enterprises by planners in order that the economy be increasingly guided by economic rules. The reforms will also change the principles of enterprise operations. Firms will have more freedom to determine the level and structure of their production and more independence in establishing backward and forward linkages with other enterprises. Their decisions will be based on such economic criteria as cost calculations and price signals. Such changes, if implemented, are expected to make Polish enterprises more suitable partners for Western firms.

Thus, the Polish economy today is undergoing changes which will surely affect its economic relations with firms in other countries. For this reason, too, we cannot consider as fully complete the research findings contained in this interesting volume, even though it contains pioneering contributions by experts from Indiana University in the USA and from the Foreign Trade Research Institute in Poland, each side cooperating with many participants from the scientific and business communities in the two countries.

The rapid evolution of the international economic situation should be grounds for further cooperation between American and Polish research teams. Their work should be continuously improved and updated.

Janusz Czamarski
Director
Department of Foreign Trade
Planning Commission
Warsaw, Poland

Preface

It is a particular pleasure to write a foreword to this volume because the participation of the Indiana School of Business in this joint US-Polish project fits so well with the mission of our university and with the increasing international orientation of our school.

One of the missions of any university is to train young men and women to understand and appreciate the languages, history, culture, and economic systems of other countries. For this reason, supporting international programs has long been one of Indiana University's highest priorities and notable academic strengths. One of the foremost areas of international specialization at Indiana University—which has an approximate enrollment this year of 70,000 students—is in its East European program area. There is a strong and growing interest in East European studies in the United States, not only because we have more and more scientific, governmental, commercial, and tourist contacts with the people in Eastern Europe, but also because more than 15 million Americans—many living in the Midwest—have an East European heritage. The largest group is, of course, Americans of Polish descent.

Indiana University has placed a special emphasis within its East European studies on Poland. This is symbolized by the 1975 agreement between the President of Indiana University and the Rector of Warsaw University to establish an American Studies Center at Warsaw University and a Polish Studies Center in Bloomington. Both centers are staffed jointly by professors from the two universities and both centers host students from the other country.

Within the larger university community, our School of Business has the specific mission to train young men and women as professionals to perform the multiple functions and services characteristic of modern business. We recognized some time ago that preparation for a business career requires more and more familiarity with the international dimensions of business. This fact was obvious, I am sure, much sooner and to a much greater extent in a European country such as Poland. But today, with the increasing dependence of the United States on imports and exports, the growing involvement of our multinational firms in productive activities worldwide, and the fluctuating value of the dollar in terms of other currencies, the importance of the international dimension of business is also being recognized by our faculty, by each of our more than 6,000 Business School students, and by the business constituencies we serve.

To inculcate an international perspective, we have introduced into the curriculum an international business component. We are also making special efforts to attract faculty and students from other countries. For example, this year we have a visiting professor of international business from Poland and last year we had a Fulbright-grantee graduate student from Poland. The School has been involved for many years with overseas projects. We have worked closely with the National Institute for Development Administration in Thailand, the Institute of Business Administration in Dacca, Bangladesh, and the Faculty of Economics at the University of Ljubljana, Yugoslavia. For ten years, the School has administered an Executive Development Program in Venezuela which has graduated more than four hundred persons, an endeavor often cited as the most successful professional education program in Latin America. Under the auspices of the School's International Business Research Institute, we have encouraged and supported our faculty's involvement in teaching and research activities involving foreign countries.

It is in this context that we were especially pleased to sponsor and support a joint research project on US-Polish industrial cooperation between a team organized by the School of Business and composed of experts from the School and from other academic centers, and a team organized by the Foreign Trade Research Institute in Warsaw. We were fortunate to have the opportunity to work closely with scholars from this Polish institute and from collaborating Polish universities.

I was able to see first-hand the immediate, practical utility of the work carried out by the two teams when I talked at some length with the many business, academic, and government participants who attended the first conference in Bloomington in December 1978. But I am convinced that the long-term benefits of this project—in terms of teaching and stimulating further research—will be still greater, thanks in large measure to the publication of this book, which makes it possible to combine immediate, practical relevance with a lasting scientific achievement.

I congratulate and thank all of those who initiated, financially supported, successfully carried out, and contributed to this pioneering joint project between a group of Polish and American scholars in the field of business and commerce.

Schuyler F. Otteson
Dean, School of Business
Indiana University
Bloomington, Indiana

A joint research project on US-Polish industrial cooperation, for which this book is the end product, was initiated in 1977 by two teams of research scholars affiliated with Indiana University in Bloomington and the Foreign Trade Research Institute in Warsaw. The main objectives of the project were to identify and to discuss problems in US-Polish economic relations and to improve understanding of the substance of US-Polish industrial cooperation against the broad background of the economic environments in both countries.

I wish to congratulate the members of the two teams on the success of their efforts to implement this project.

Words of sincere appreciation are addressed to the representatives of the academic, business, and government communities in both countries for their kind support and contribution to this undertaking. I wish to acknowledge with particular satisfaction the assistance of International Harvester Company in the US and BUMAR Industrial Association in Poland for so generously supplying information for the case study and for their active participation in our joint seminars and discussions. I wish to express my thanks and appreciation also to the organizers of the Bloomington and Warsaw conferences; they were critically important components of our collaborative effort.

The participation of the Foreign Trade Research Institute in the US-Polish joint project was not accidental. Undertaking this kind of research is one of the essential tasks of the Institute's activities. Subordinated to the Ministry of Foreign Trade and Shipping, the Institute employs 125 scientific workers and support staff. The Institute maintains very close links with the academic community in Poland and with specialists in many foreign countries. Many of our leading researchers hold academic appointments. Moreover, the Institute consults regularly with leading experts from our universities. The close link between the Institute and the academic community is illustrated by the composition of the Polish team for this project, which included not only experts from our Institute, but also distinguished professors from the Warsaw Central School of Planning and Statistics and Warsaw University.

Research programs undertaken by our Institute cover a wide spectrum of topics, including East-West trade, East-West and tripartite industrial cooperation, analysis and projection of the geographic and commodity composition of Poland's foreign trade, the economic integration of the CMEA countries, the international transfer of technology, foreign trade development strategy, and systems and methods of economic calculus and planning of foreign trade.

This volume contains basic research materials contributed by both teams. I find it most encouraging that the true partnership established by Polish and American colleagues involved in the project is reflected in wide consensus on many essential issues, without restraining the presentation of individual points of view.

May I express my sincere hope that these writings will be of interest to the business and academic communities of both countries in their search for new channels and more effective forms of international economic relations.

Janusz Kaczurba
Director, Foreign Trade Research Institute
Warsaw, Poland

Acknowledgments

It is our privilege to acknowledge the financial and other support of numerous organizations and the help of many individuals who have contributed to this project.

Each side obtained funding for its participation in the project from organizations in its own country. On the US side, the principal financial support came from the US Department of State and the US Department of Commerce. Further financial support was obtained from a Ford Foundation grant to Indiana University to support a problem-oriented interdisciplinary training and research program on Eastern Europe, from the International Research and Exchanges Board (IREX) for travel to and from Poland, and from the following units of Indiana University: the School of Business, which provided overall sponsorship, released time for faculty, research assistants, secretarial assistance, and other overhead support; the International Development Institute, which made available its facilities and personnel to help prepare for publication both a bibliography and this book; the Polish Studies Center, which funded a US team member's travel to Poland; the Russian and East European Institute, which co-sponsored the project and co-hosted the Bloomington Conference; International Programs, which financially supported the publication of this book; and the University Press which produced and is distributing this book.

On the Polish side, the principal financial support came from the Ministry of Foreign Trade and Shipping. Further contributions were made by the Chamber of Foreign Trade of Poland which provided its facilities for the Warsaw Conference and hosted the US team in Cracow.

Further institutional support was received by the US side from the

American Embassy in Warsaw. Our special thanks to former Ambassador Richard T. Davies; Carroll Brown, Deputy Chief of Mission; Messrs. Arthur Smith, Chief, Economic & Commercial Section; Donald E. Grabenstetter, Second Secretary; William F. Schraage, Commercial Attache; and former Cultural Attache Robert Gosende for their advice and support and/or participation in the Bloomington or Warsaw conferences. Our parallel thanks are extended to the Embassy of the Polish People's Republic in Washington, D.C., especially to former Ambassador Professor Witold Trampczynski and former Economic Counselor Professor Josef Soldaczuk. Our appreciation also goes to Mr. Lech Dzikiewicz, Commercial Attache, for participation in the Bloomington Conference as well as to the Commercial Consulate of the People's Republic of Poland in Chicago, especially to Mr. Ireneusz Kubiczek, for their support and representation at the Bloomington Conference.

We would like to express, further, our thanks to the cooperating universities in the US and Poland which encouraged the participation of their faculty members and provided support for them: Arizona State University, Ohio State University, and the Wharton School of the University of Pennsylvania in the US, and the Central School of Planning and Statistics in Warsaw and Warsaw University in Poland.

Several corporations in the US and in Poland provided inestimable help, which ranged from making their executives available for interviews with members of our teams, providing and explaining copies of relevant documents, and hosting members of the "other" team on more than one occasion, to participating in the Bloomington and Warsaw conferences. In the US, our special thanks must go to *International Harvester Corporation*, at its headquarters in Chicago especially to Mr. W. B. McIlvaine, Jr.; at its *Payline Division* in Schaumburg, Illinois, to Messrs. H. L. Lehman and Wesley D. Lee; at their affiliate in Heidelberg, the Federal Republic of Germany, to Mr. Alfons Weber; and to its personnel in Poland, particularly Messrs. John Simpson, Technical Representative, and Howard G. Sandilands, Director of Operations in Poland. In Poland, our parallel thanks are extended to the executives of BUMAR FTO, especially to Messrs. Ryszard Mikoda, General Director, Wojciech Konecki, Director, Jerzy Szumski, Director of BUMAR operations in Chicago, and Waldemar Niemotko, counsel. Our appreciation goes also to the executives of the industrial plant "Stalowa Wola Steelworks" in Stalowa Wola: Messrs. Tadeusz Skrzat and Jerzy Czopinski, Deputy Directors, and Mr. Janusz Piotrowski, Chief Technical Representative of the "Stalowa Wola Steelworks" in Warsaw.

Several other corporations and academic institutions assisted us by providing tours of their facilities for the visiting team and by making their executives and staff members available for in-depth discussions. In the US, our thanks go to *Cummins Engine Co.* (especially to Messrs. Laurie R. Hoagland, Vice President for Finance and Treasurer; Vartkes J. Ehramjian, Assistant Treasurer, International; Thomas R. Lieberman, Manager of Major Accounts; Steven Gaal, Chief Engineer; Karl Kuehner, Executive Engineer; John R. Schrink, Senior Manufacturing Engineer; Ruth M. Kawecki, Manager of Employee Relations; Paul A. Wendowski, Manager of Corporate Compensation; and Peggy A. Charipar, Manager of Public Relations Services).

In Poland, our thanks for the reciprocal hosting of the US team go to *Polimex-Cekop* (especially to Messrs. Henryk Medlewski & Jerzy M. Genello), the *Gdynia Shipyards* (especially to its Deputy General Director, Dr. Jurand Graniczny, for personally hosting the team), *Promasz* (Mr. Marcin Szyszkowski, Head of Division); *Pezetel* (especially Feliks Bialozor, Deputy General Manager), and several other corporations for hosting us during the 1979 visits to Poland; the Chamber of Foreign Trade in Warsaw (especially to Mr. Stanislaw Stala, Director, and Mr. Michal Bukowski, Chief Analyst); and the Chamber of Foreign Trade in Cracow (especially Mr. Jan Lukasik, Director). Members of the US team were also hosted by the University of Gdansk (where our special appreciation goes to Professor Zygmunt Dmowski, Dean, and Professor Krystyna Zoladkiewicz); by the Central School of Planning and Statistics (especially to its former Dean, Pawel Sulmicki, Professor Zygmunt Kossut, Dean and Professor Josef Soldaczuk); and by Warsaw University (Professors Romuald Kudlinski and Jacek Kochanowicz).

We would like to acknowledge, further, the contribution of the US-Polish Economic Council, for inviting us to present our preliminary findings to their members, in writing and in person, at its May 1979 session in Cracow.

Many individuals at our respective home institutions provided valuable support. At Indiana University, our appreciation goes to the Dean of the School of Business, Schuyler Otteson, for hosting the Polish team and for participating in the Bloomington Conference. Our special thanks also must go to the Director of Indiana University's Polish Studies Center, Professor Mary Ellen Solt, and to her daughter, Susie Solt, for helping in so many practical ways with the implementation of this project. Our further thanks to the Director of the International Development Institute, Professor William J. Siffin, for providing financial and staff support in connection with the publication of the bibliography and the preparation of this volume, and to Mrs. Barbara Dutton, Publications Manager, for preparing the camera-ready copy of this book for printing. We would also like to thank Professor Alexander Rabinowitch, Director of the Russian and East European Institute, for his participation, and for the Institute's co-sponsorship of the project.

Special thanks to Mrs. Leah Nunn, Office Manager, for helping with the conference and travel arrangements and for managing the accounts; to Mrs. Heather Hall, Mrs. Judy Heinmiller, and Ms. Debby Cummings of the International Business Department of the School of Business who at various times provided secretarial and typing assistance and were helpful in so many other ways; and to our student assistants: Gayle Sherman and Andrea Stevenson for help on the bibliography, Craig Capehart for hosting the Polish team at Indiana and at his family's farm, and to Marianne Platt, Cathy Sokil, and Janet Robinowitch for editorial assistance.

At the Foreign Trade Research Institute in Warsaw our special thanks go to its Director, Dr. Janusz Kaczurba, and to its former Director, Professor Witold Trzeciakowski for helping to initiate and develop the project, for their participation in the Warsaw Conference and for their continuous support.

We are pleased to acknowledge the major contribution of Mr. Tadeusz Kaminski, Director of Polimex-Cekop, who was the first architect of the IH-BUMAR cooperation. Special thanks are extended to Mr. Jan Dygut, Deputy Director of the FTRI, and Boleslaw Meluch, FTRI Foreign Relations Officer, for helping with the conference, hotel and travel arrangements and for managing the accounts, to Mrs. Czeslawa Szczepanska, for her editorial contribution to the Polish papers, to Mrs. Danuta Debska and Jolanta Widermanska for their secretarial and typing assistance, and to Mr. Janusz Kozinski and Mr. Roland Pac for editing and proofreading the manuscript.

About the Project

This book is the product of a three-year joint research project between a team of American and a team of Polish specialists on East-West commerce. Before describing the project and the purpose of this volume, we would like to explain some of the considerations which prompted the two teams to undertake a joint research project.

East-West economic relations—commercial transactions between industrialized market economies and the planned economies of the Council for Mutual Economic Assistance (CMEA)—have expanded rapidly, although from a relatively low level, during the 1970s. This expansion resulted from two independent but complementary trends: the growing need of Western firms and governments to find new export markets to reduce unemployment, improve the balance of payments, and increase corporate sales and profits, and the decision by the planned economies to participate more actively in the international division of labor. The gradual relaxation of East-West political tensions during the 1970s facilitated this expansion. To be sure, the growth of East-West commerce—which accounts for only about 5 percent of the total trade of the OECD countries and a third of the trade of the CMEA countries—took place despite the difficulties firms in market economies have faced in doing business in planned economies and the problems planned economies have encountered in penetrating Western markets.

These difficulties in part reflect a lack of clear understanding about the political, economic, managerial, and even purely psychological environments in which enterprises on the other side make commercial decisions. So long as East-West economic relations were only of marginal importance to both sides and predominantly took the form of simple export and import transactions, the "information gap" about the other side was not critical. But as commercial intercourse between planned and market economies increased in importance and a growing share of this commerce took the form of industrial cooperation (IC), the information gap increasingly limited the expansion of commerce.

One principal purpose of this project was to reduce this information gap. To do so, each team carried out original research both in the US and in Poland and then hosted members of the other team for extensive periods to discuss—and synthetize when possible—their findings. The information gap was further reduced by the two teams' joint setting up of parallel conferences in the US and in Poland to exchange views and findings with a larger community of academic, business, and government specialists. Finally, the publication and distribution of this book in both countries is intended to improve mutual understanding about the political, economic, and managerial environments in which "the other side" makes IC decisions.

A second principal purpose of this project was to seek a better understanding of the evolving nature of IC. What is IC? Although the term has no precise, internationally agreed-upon definition, it refers to that increasingly important component of East-West commerce which entails more than simple, arm's-length export or import transactions or even simple licensing agreements (see: Summary, Conclusions, Recommendations).

Our joint research project found, and other experts agree, that much of the new business between East and West in the 1980s will take the form of IC projects. The East bases this conclusion on its growing recognition that through international trade it will find it advantageous to acquire not only products but also related technical, managerial, and marketing know-how. This conclusion is reinforced by the urgent need of the Eastern countries to increase their export capabilities, which in the long run is the only sound basis for a continued expansion of imports and sound management of debt service. On the Western side, the same conclusion results from an increased recognition that successful efforts to penetrate the markets of planned economies will require more and more that the seller help generate the means to pay for Western exports and Eastern debt service. In most cases, this help will take the form of IC agreements involving counterpurchase, coproduction, joint ventures, and so on. IC is often also the preferred form when the Western partner wishes to rely on an Eastern firm to source components or finished products. The growing importance of more complex forms of business arrangements in East-West commerce requires decisionmakers on both sides to learn more about each other's decisionmaking environment.

This need was perceived by a group of American and Polish specialists a few years ago and prompted them to undertake this pioneering joint research on East-West economic relations focusing on IC between US and Polish firms. We decided to collaborate on the design and implementation of the project in the belief that such joint research would lead to a more in-depth understanding and yield a more balanced perspective on the issues. The joint research project was organized by Indiana University's School of Business and by the Warsaw-based Foreign Trade Research Institute. The US team was composed of experts on East-West commerce from Indiana University, Ohio State University, the Wharton School of the University of Pennsylvania, and Arizona State University. The Polish team also included experts from the Warsaw Central School of Planning and Statistics, Warsaw University, and the BUMAR Foreign Trade Organization.

The main goals of the project were:

1. To bring together representatives of the research communities in the two countries to share perspectives and information and to facilitate access to decisionmakers in the respective countries;

2. To assess the extent to which the principle of mutual advantage exists in the industrial cooperation agreements (ICAs) already begun by US and Polish firms;

3. To conduct in-depth research on ongoing cases of IC by identifying specific problems and making recommendations on their solution and by determining what types of ICAs have the best chance of success.

4. To identify issues of long-term importance to both sides and to reach conclusions that would be concretely useful to businessmen, bankers, government officials, and the academic communities in our two countries.

The project has produced the following tangible research results, listed chronologically:

1. Both research teams have compiled comprehensive, annotated, and cross-referenced bibliographies of the literature, both in English and in Polish, on IC and related topics.[1]

2. The two teams jointly developed a set of research questions on East-West IC which were used in designing their joint case study and in preparing some of the individual contributions to this volume. (The set of questions can be found in Appendix 1).

3. The two teams jointly prepared a detailed case study of US-Polish IC, focusing on the International Harvester (IH)-BUMAR

---

1. Paul Marer, *An Annotated and Cross-Referenced Bibliography of East-West Commerce* (Bloomington: International Development Institute, Studies in East European and Soviet Planning, Development and Trade, 1978 and 1980) (2nd ed.) and Edwin Zagorski and Janusz Kozinski, *An Annotated Bibliography on East-West Trade and Industrial Cooperation* (Warsaw: Foreign Trade Research Institute, 1978).

cooperation for the manufacture and marketing of construction machinery. This case was selected because in terms of size and complexity, it is one of the most important examples not only of US-Polish IC but of East-West IC in general. Moreover, as this project has evolved over nine years (1972-81) from a relatively simple to a much larger and more complex arrangement, it has encountered and by and large successfully handled many of the problems that are typical in negotiating and implementing such projects.

Using the joint questionnaire as a point of departure, both teams reviewed the literature on IC and interviewed executives of IH and BUMAR in their own countries. Omitting information which IH or BUMAR considered proprietary or confidential, drafts of preliminary findings were exchanged and discussed at length by representatives of the two teams. Subsequently, arrangements were made for the Polish team to visit IH headquarters in Chicago and a manufacturing plant nearby and, reciprocally, for the US team members to interview executives of BUMAR in Poland. The US team visited the main plant of Huta Stalowa Wola where the actual manufacturing under the agreement takes place and talked at length with the managers of that enterprise. Our individual findings were then revised and discussed further and finally combined to form the joint case study presented in its entirety in Part II of this volume.

4. We organized two joint seminars, the first one in Bloomington in December 1978, the second in Warsaw in March 1979, each with participation by our respective business, banking, academic, and government communities. At the Bloomington seminar the findings and views of the Polish team were presented in six papers, each of which was commented on by a discussant from the US team, and replies were given by the authors. A general discussion by the two teams and invited participants followed. The revised papers, comments, replies, and the main points of the general discussion, summarized by the editors, can be found in Part III of the volume. The seminar in Warsaw followed the same format: the findings and views of the US team were presented in six papers, each followed by comments by a discussant from the Polish team, which were in turn answered by the author. A general discussion among all participants followed. Part IV of the volume contains the papers and the edited discussion; Appendix entries 2A and 2B give a list of invited participants at the Bloomington and Warsaw seminars, respectively.

5. After the two seminars, the two teams prepared their joint preliminary conclusions and recommendations which Professor Tabaczynski presented to the Polish-US Economic Council at its May 1979 meeting in Crakow, Poland.

6. The two groups worked together to prepare the results for publi-

cation. The editors first worked independently with members of their own teams on their respective contributions and then worked jointly, first in Warsaw in June 1979 and in Bloomington in September 1979, to select, clarify, and when necessary compress the studies, conclusions, and recommendations presented in this volume.

7. During 1980-81, while the book was being edited and typeset, the two teams continued to work together to selectively update their summary, conclusions, and recommendations, taking into consideration recent developments in their countries up to April 1981. This summary comprises Part I of this volume.

We have tried to organize this book so that it would be useful to businessmen and policymakers and to others who might be interested only in the main findings, at the same time also making available the longer research papers, the case study, the discussion, and the supporting materials that should be of interest to scholars of East-West IC and related topics.

Because the material in this volume is not arranged according to topic, a brief guide to the contributions may be helpful.

Immediately following the Summary, Conclusions, and Recommendations (Part I), we present a detailed case study of the most important IC project between the two countries: the IH-BUMAR cooperation for the manufacture and marketing of construction machinery (Part II). We believe that the most informative way to describe East-West IC is to present a concrete case analysis of this highly significant project. The case study is supplemented by a detailed analysis of some of the practical problems faced and solutions found. This selection was written by J. Szumski, Director of BUMAR operations in Chicago, who for several years played a key role in implementing the project (p. 159). Other examples of US-Polish IC can be found in the contributions by Kozinski (p. 140) and in the general discussion (see especially pp. 182-184).

Many businessmen have stated repeatedly that they could better assess the possibilities for IC in Poland if only they understood the operation of the Polish economic and foreign trade systems and the changes that are now being introduced. The contributions by Giezgala (p. 87) and Garland (p. 298) focus on that topic.

Another topic of great interest to Western businessmen and to students of economic systems and international business is the relationship between production specialization in a planned economy and prospects for IC with Western firms. How and on what basis are decisions made in this area in a centrally planned economy? The contributions by Tabaczynski (p. 98) and Zagorski (p. 121) and the ensuing discussion (p. 176) contain much practical information on this topic. Wolf (p. 272) approaches the same topic from a different perspective, undertaking an econometric analysis of Polish foreign trade to obtain new insights into Poland's foreign trade specialization.

Just as Western students and businessmen are interested in the decisionmaking process in a planned economy, so their counterparts in Poland and in other planned economies want to know more about the decision process of Western corporations, especially the global multinational corporations which play such a predominant role in East-West IC. On what basis do these firms decide to enter into IC in Poland and in other Eastern countries? How does Poland, and the CMEA region in general, fit into the global strategies of MNCs? The contribution by Perlmutter (p. 187) summarizes the results of a US research project on this topic.

Two papers focus specifically on the achievements and problems of IC between American and Polish firms and on prospects for its future development. The contribution by Kossut (p. 109) reviews the history of US-Polish IC and summarizes relevant statistics, while the chapter by Zagorski (p. 121) takes the perspective of Polish firms deciding about IC with US and Western partners.

One of the key issues in East-West IC is the economics and politics of technology transfer. Two contributions examine some of the issues both from a theoretical and a practical perspective, e.g., the papers by Kozinski (p. 140) and Brada (p. 207).

One form of IC of special interest to Western businessmen, government officials, lawyers, and students involves entering into equity- and non-equity joint ventures in the planned economies. Since the 1972 joint venture legislation introduced by Romania and Hungary, and a few years earlier by Yugoslavia (which is not a member of the CMEA), other planned economies, including Poland, have seriously considered this matter. Poland has taken the first steps toward allowing joint ventures on its territory. The evolution of Poland's approach to joint ventures (p. 343) and relevant legal documents (p. 349) are presented in a special contribution by Tabaczynski in Section V.

Another topic of relevance to IC is marketing. What role can IC play in facilitating the efforts of US firms to penetrate the Polish and other CMEA markets and the efforts of Polish producers to market their products more successfully in Western countries? This is the focus of Miller's paper (p. 259); much specific information on marketing also can be found in the IH-BUMAR case study (especially p. 41).

Linked very closely to marketing are the difficult questions of real and alleged protectionism in the US and other Western markets—its extent, its affect on potential Polish exporters, and the role, if any, which IC can play to overcome protectionist barriers. This topic is frequently raised by Polish specialists who feel that Western protectionism remains one of the great impediments to a more rapid expansion of East-West commerce (see, for example, the discussion at the Warsaw Conference, pp. 329-339, and comments by Kossut, p. 293). Some Western specialists, on the other hand, argue that while protectionism is a problem, its importance should not be exaggerated (Brada, p. 117). The technical details of import protectionism in the US and its effect on potential Polish manufactures exports are examined by Marer (pp. 228-250 and 329-337).

—The Editors

Polish-US Industrial Cooperation
in the 1980s

PART I
SUMMARY,
CONCLUSIONS,
RECOMMENDATIONS

CONTENTS

SUMMARY

Importance of Industrial Cooperation   3

The International Harvester-BUMAR Case Study   6

    The Partners   6
    The Initial Approach   7
    The Motives   7
    The Initial Agreement and Extensions   8
    Pricing Policies and Payment Flows   9
    Quality Control Procedures   9
    Integrated Sourcing of Components and Products   10
    Marketing and Buy-Back Arrangements   10
    Problems and Solutions   11
    Conclusions   12

Generalizing the IH-BUMAR Experience   14

Industrial Cooperation Opportunities in Poland   17

Long-Term Benefits of Cooperation with Poland
    for US Firms   19

Joint Ventures   21

Technology Transfer   23

Impact of Economic Systems on Trade and
    Industrial Cooperation   24

Prospects for the 1980s   29

CONCLUSIONS AND RECOMMENDATIONS

Possibilities for Industrial Cooperation and
    the Selection of Partners   32

The Environment for Industrial Cooperation in
    the US and in Poland   36

Suggestions for Further Research   37

Summary, Conclusions, Recommendations

US and Polish Teams

SUMMARY

Importance of Industrial Cooperation

In a world of expanding industrial production, increased international competition for export markets, rising protectionism, growing concern with many countries' balance of payments, and increased East-West economic interdependence, it is time to examine seriously and systematically the possibilities for expanded trade and industrial cooperation (IC) between US and Polish firms.

What is IC? Although the term has no internationally agreed upon standard definition, it refers to that increasingly important component of East-West commerce which involves more than simple export or import transactions or even simple licensing agreements. IC refers to licensing and know-how agreements which are combined with turnkey projects, subcontracting, subdeliveries and certain types of counterpurchase deals, coproduction agreements, and joint ventures of all types (whether based on equity participation or contract). Although nearly all IC deals also involve exports or imports, under IC the partners enter into more complex arrangements and have a relatively longer time horizon for cooperation than they do under simple import or export deals.

The essential feature of IC is an arrangement between Eastern and Western firms to coproduce manufactured products. Such arrangements are, typically, long term; they involve the one-way or two-way transfer of technology in the form of products, licenses, know-how, training, or cooperation in research and development, and result in a one-way or two-way flow of components and finished products. Each partner hopes to gain access to the other's and to third-country markets; to improve its technological and organizational expertise; to secure a reliable, less expensive, new, long-term source of components and finished products; and to enlarge its world-wide production, marketing, or technical development capability but with a smaller investment and lower operating costs than would be needed to achieve these same tasks individually.

How do Poland and the US fit into the East-West commercial scenario? Trade between the US and Poland has increased rapidly during the 1970s and has been one of the most dynamic components of East-West trade. At the same time, economic trends in our two countries and in the world at large are generating pressures for US and Polish enterprises to enter into cooperative undertakings with each other and with firms in third countries. While conventional trade will remain important in the 1980s, more complex forms of business—IC that is—may become increasingly significant in East-West commerce during the 1980s and 1990s.

This conclusion is based on the growing recognition by Eastern and Western countries that it would be to their advantage to acquire in international trade not just products but also related technical, managerial, and marketing know-how and that IC can increase the efficiency of operations. Another reason for the Eastern countries is their urgent need to increase export capabilities, to provide a sound basis in the long run for continued import expansion and sound management of their debt service. On the Western side, the same conclusion results from its recognition that successful efforts to penetrate the markets of planned economies will require the seller's increased participation in helping to generate the means to pay for the East's imports.

It is necessary, however, to add that the events in Poland since the summer of 1980 (workers' protest against management and the price system) have posed short-term problems to the development of IC with foreign partners. The reasons are: difficulties with Poland's balance of payments, inadequate supply of certain raw material, and the priority that must be given to satisfy Poland's domestic needs.

"But," concluded the Polish team, "the very nature of IC requires a longer term perspective. In spite of today's shortages we are and we remain in favor of an 'open economy' principle for our country. Having in mind our production structure and the inadequate scale of the home market, no improvement and no development is possible without international cooperation. Taking into account the reforms already introduced and still under way in Poland, it is our view that the prospects for IC will be improved to a much greater extent than before because it will now be based on the actual interests of enterprises."

There is a growing body of literature on East-West IC describing the forms, motives, conditions and economic and political significance of East-West IC.[1] This literature includes case studies,[2] surveys of the experience of individual countries,[3] and attempts to quantify this phenomenon.[4] Quantification, however, has proved to be exceedingly difficult because no official statistics are published by countries on the number or size of their industrial cooperation agreements (ICAs). Researchers must gather their own raw data on IC under particularly difficult circumstances, due to the commercial and political sensitivity of the material. Even international organizations such as the United Nations rely primarily on press reports, supplemented by some interview data. Moreover, the available data typically is only on numbers of ICAs; the monetary value of each is almost impossible to determine, given the diverse and intangible transactions involved in ICAs.

Nonetheless, by carefully sifting published information, a recent survey[5] concluded that (1) the extraordinarily rapid growth in East-West trade during the 1970s was matched by an equally explosive growth in East-West IC; (2) the most active Eastern participants were those countries more open to trade with the West and/or more reform-minded, such as Hungary and Poland, followed by Romania; (3) in value terms, Poland probably ranked first among the East European countries, if the Soviet Union is excluded;[6] (4) the most active participants in the West were the larger West European countries, led by the FRG; (5) the industry pattern of ICAs depends on the extent to which joint projects in third countries and joint equity ventures located in Western countries are included. Among the general and substantive agreements involving IC activity in Eastern Europe, the producers' goods sectors, especially the engineering industries, tend to dominate; (6) within a relatively short time the US has established a significant position in Polish IC with the West. Of the 200-odd significant ICAs Poland had in effect with Western countries in 1980, about 20 are of major importance; of these, four have been concluded with American firms (Zagorski).

Polish studies have indicated that many of the contracts, especially those with West Germany, are for sub-contracting (sub-deliveries) by Polish enterprises. Licenses play a part in more than half of the Polish agreements. Some Polish foreign trade organizations (FTOs) participate actively in joint tendering with Western firms in third, especially developing, countries, e.g., *Polimex-Cekop*. Like other East European countries, Poland's more complex ICAs have been concentrated in the non-electrical machinery industries, followed by chemicals, electrical machinery and electronics, transport equipment, and metallurgy, while many of its simpler-level ICAs have been in textiles and clothing.

The International Harvester-BUMAR Case Study

An important example of successful IC is the IH-BUMAR agreement signed in 1972 to manufacture crawler tractors. The agreement eventually provided that the partners supply each other with components and finished products; subsequently it has been extended to include the joint development, testing, and production of new types of construction machinery. IH gains better access to Polish and CMEA markets and a competitive source of components and enlarges its worldwide production, marketing, and technical development capability. The Polish partner gains technological and organizational expertise, improves its convertible currency export potential and gains a competitive edge in foreign markets.

The Partners. IH is the twenty-eighth largest US corporation and the thirteenth largest US industrial exporter, with manufacturing operations in 18 countries and markets in 160. IH is a multiproduct corporation: trucks account for approximately 45 percent of its sales; agricultural equipment for 40 percent; construction equipment for 12 percent; and miscellaneous other products for 3 percent. Its agreement with Poland is in the construction equipment branch in which IH is in contention for being the distant second in production in US and world markets. Five manufacturers in the US and a few in other countries have found worldwide acceptance for the construction equipment they produce.

Poland ranks sixth among the countries of the world in the manufacture of construction machinery. Among the most important producers are BUMAR Union and the plant Huta Stalowa Wola (HSW),[7] both under the Ministry of Machine Industry. They produce 80 percent of Polish heavyduty construction machinery. The enterprise which primarily cooperates with IH is HSW, one of the largest vertically integrated machine building complexes in Poland. The cooperation with IH affects approximately 20 percent of the production of HSW. BUMAR and HSW have won several international awards for the technical excellence of their products. The HSW plant we visited has a fully modern infrastructure and one of the largest concentrations of technically up-to-date machine tools in all of Europe. BUMAR's foreign trade organization (FTO) is the exclusive exporter and importer of construction machinery for Poland. BUMAR FTO has pioneered ICAs by Polish enterprises with Western firms—including Clark Equipment (US), Stetter and Menck (FRG), Coles Cranes and Jones Cranes (UK), Kockums (Sweden), and Nicholas (France).

Even before cooperation with Western firms was started, HSW had experienced cooperating with enterprises in the CMEA countries, especially in the USSR. An example is an agreement with the USSR to coproduce large cranes: at one time the undercarriage was manufactured by BUMAR and the superstructure by a firm in the USSR. This is significant because the experience gained in cooperating within the CMEA may have fostered an attitude on the part of BUMAR and HSW that made it more receptive to complex agreements with Western firms also.

The Initial Approach. During the 1960s, trade relations between the partners were insignificant and practically irrelevant as far as the present ICA is concerned. The entrepreneurial initiative was taken by BUMAR FTO when it approached American and other construction equipment manufacturers in search of cooperation possibilities. Its initiative reflected Poland's commitment since the early 1970s to an extensive modernization program in general and to an expansion of the construction equipment sector in particular. In approaching various US firms, BUMAR FTO often encountered either the attitude that a Polish manufacturer would not be able to serve as an equal partner to an American firm, or the fear that today's partner may one day become a threatening competitor. This is important to stress because such lack of confidence on the part of either American or Polish firms can prevent serious negotiations which could develop into mutually profitable IC.

BUMAR's first contact with IH was in 1968; intensive negotiations started in 1972. Preliminary discussions were necessary not only for each to become convinced of the other's capabilities to implement an agreement successfully, but also to allow the gradual development of mutual understanding and trust. We cannot underscore strongly enough that the development of understanding and trust among the top executives of IH and BUMAR Union, BUMAR FTO, and HSW played a decisive role in placing difficult issues and short-term problems in their proper perspective, not allowing them to undermine the negotiations and, subsequently, the implementation of the agreement.

The Motives. The interests of IH and BUMAR were similar:

1. *Better access to markets.* IH wanted to gain entry to those CMEA and less developed country (LDC) markets in which its market penetration was limited. BUMAR wanted to gain a competitive edge within the CMEA, especially in the Soviet market, and obtain specialization rights for construction machinery under a CMEA specialization agreement.[8] "If you want assured sales there," stated an executive of the BUMAR group, "you must offer machines of the highest quality, a renowned trademark, and good service. We could develop exports to the socialist countries even more if we offered a

greater number of machines built in cooperation with American partners.''

That Poland has become the largest exporter of construction machinery within the CMEA has benefited IH in the following ways: through royalties, the export of components essential to the production of these machines, and the introduction of their own trademark in the other CMEA countries. BUMAR also wanted to gain a competitive edge in LDCs with which Poland has bilateral clearing agreements and, very importantly, to increase its convertible currency earnings potential in Western markets.

2. *Obtaining advanced technology.* Initially, this was an important consideration only for BUMAR, which wanted to acquire and successfully absorb the most advanced world technology, including organizational and managerial know-how. BUMAR also wished to employ more productively the existing technological expertise of the Polish scientific community. Subsequently IH realized that it, too, could benefit from BUMAR's design, engineering, and technical development capability.

3. *Mutual sourcing of components and products.* IH wanted to obtain a competitive source of supply for its West European and Middle Eastern production and marketing operations, which could not be supplied economically from the US, as well as for its US operations. BUMAR wished to source components from IH for incorporation into its final products.

4. *Enlarging capacity with minimum investment.* From the point of view of IH, adding BUMAR as a partner enlarged the market and enabled IH to limit the initial investment costs while expanding production capabilities. These are important considerations for a company which is attempting to expand by filling out its worldwide product line and by extending the geographic scope of operations, both of which require large investment outlays. From BUMAR's point of view, gaining access to IH's technology as well as distribution and service networks also saved substantial investment and time.

The Initial Agreement and Extensions. The initial 1972 agreement provided for the transfer of technology for the manufacture and assembly in Poland of five types of crawler tractors and attachments to allow the tractors to be adapted to pipe-laying, loading, and other jobs. The technology package included the provision of ongoing technical assistance and training, as well as information concerning specification, tooling and machine techniques, assembly methods, and quality control procedures. In 1973 an agreement was reached for BUMAR to supply skids (the basic frame of the machine without the engine, wheels, or attachments) to the IH subsidiary in England. In 1975 the agreement was expanded to define BUMAR's role in a

cooperative effort to develop a large pipe-laying tractor to be manufactured in Poland. Another protocol specified that IH would provide a technology package for nine types of front-end, rubber-tired
loaders. Another agreement was signed to jointly design and manufacture a machine, under the following terms:

IH to design and engineer the new product;

BUMAR to produce prototype units according to the IH design;

IH to test and evaluate the prototypes and issue final approval for
production;

BUMAR to tool and manufacture the product;

BUMAR to remain the exclusive source of the product for an
agreed period;

IH and BUMAR to share marketing responsibilities.

Finally, an agreement signed in 1978 lays the basis for the joint development of torque converters.

Pricing Policies and Payment Flows. The initial license, know-how,
and technical assistance part of the agreement called for a "front
money" payment, payable in four annual installments. In addition, IH
receives royalties on each IH-labelled machine produced by BUMAR.
There is a ceiling, however, beyond which total annual royalty payments may not go, so that sales by BUMAR beyond that level are not
subject to royalty.

Pricing of IH component sales to BUMAR is contractually established at cost plus X percent, though the markup percentage may vary
from product to product and from year to year. Pricing of BUMAR
component sales to IH is negotiable. From IH's point of view, the
price reflects such considerations as the cost advantage it must have
over in-house production or over outside suppliers in the US and the
present operating capacity of IH. In other words, there is no fixed
price formula; BUMAR's pricing methods apparently follow the price
policies generally found in this industry. The pricing of components
sold in either direction is facilitated by BUMAR's having, under the
terms of the agreement, a current list of IH standard manufacturing
costs, a fixed point of departure for the negotiations. BUMAR's pricing of complete machines sold to IH or to third markets must take
into account competitive pressures.

Quality Control Procedures. Before the IH trademark may be attached to a BUMAR-produced machine, the machine must satisfy a
sequence of parts certification requirements established by IH. Testing of randomly selected products occurs first in the Polish plant and
then at IH's testing facilities in Arizona. BUMAR-labeled products
are not required to meet these certification and testing procedures. In
IH's view, continuous quality stems primarily from workers' and
managers' attitudes, which is an ongoing learning process. Quality

levels can be achieved, as BUMAR has demonstrated, but the maintenance of quality and its necessary further development require a continuous effort. BUMAR has demonstrated its strengths in the manufacturing process and in engineering design, through the quality of its equipment and instruments. Problems, however, still arise in materials handling, scheduling, coordination of activities, and some other areas. Our impression was that progress was being made in the solution of these problems.

Integrated Sourcing of Components and Products. For several years, BUMAR has been a source of skids (comprising approximately 40 percent of the value of the complete machine) for two models of crawler tractors produced by the IH subsidiary in the UK. Initially, this arrangement satisfied all, for it allowed the UK plant to widen its product line, BUMAR to gain substantial hard-currency receipts, and IH to become, at least potentially, more competitive in the European market. Unfortunately, the European market in these particular models failed to develop to expectations.[9]

With respect to integrating IH into BUMAR's sales and cooperation with partners within the CMEA, there are achievements and further possibilities, but also important limitations. IH receives a royalty on each IH-labeled machine sold by BUMAR within the CMEA or elsewhere. However, in the long run, insufficient convertible currency within the CMEA restricts the extent to which a Polish firm can expand sales within the CMEA of products that incorporate world-level technology and components directly imported or acquired through cooperation with a Western firm, for hard currency, unless the Polish firm can generate substantial sales on Western markets, too.

Marketing and Buy-Back Arrangements. According to the agreement, BUMAR and IH have divided world markets into three categories. BUMAR has exclusive marketing rights in the USSR, Poland, the German Democratic Republic, Czechoslovakia, Hungary, Romania, Bulgaria, Albania, Mongolia, and Vietnam. In these countries, BUMAR may sell any product it produces under a BUMAR or IH label, with no obligation to IH besides royalty payments. BUMAR has non-exclusive marketing rights in Pakistan, Egypt, Syria, Libya, Sudan, Iraq, Algeria, India, Yugoslavia, Bangladesh, and the People's Republic of China. If there is a BUMAR distributor in any of these countries, a BUMAR or HSW-labeled product may be sold to that distributor, with no commission payable to IH. The sale of an IH-labeled product in these countries must go through the IH distributor, to whom BUMAR also pays a commission. All countries not specifically mentioned above constitute IH's exclusive territory in which BUMAR may sell an IH-labeled machine only through an IH distributor.

IH has a contractual commitment to buy back products from BUMAR at a value of at least 50 percent of the royalties paid to IH by BUMAR. IH has more than fulfilled this obligation.

Problems and Solutions. Being strongly committed to the cooperation, both partners have shown flexibility in seeking solutions to the problems which have arisen during the implementation of the ICA. The principal difficulties have been:

Unclear initial understanding of the technology to be transferred. Under the original 1972 agreement, BUMAR expected to receive a considerable amount of peripheral information on technology which IH did not intend to transfer. This misunderstanding stemmed from one party's interpreting the technology transfer clauses much more broadly than the other. For example, BUMAR's metallurgical specialists sought knowledge on the composition and quality of steel products to be used as inputs, and its computer specialists expected to receive detailed information about IH's computer support systems. The problem of transferring and translating much unwritten know-how also arose. IH was as accommodating as possible and encouraged the exchange of specialists, provided that the expense was not prohibitively high. If very costly, IH transferred peripheral technology on a cash basis, under separate contracts.

Inadequate production and service infrastructure in Poland. This problem was encountered mainly in assembly operations and especially in materials handling procedures. The case study supports a point often made in the literature, that while Poland (and other East European planned economies) have a sound technology base and good theoretical engineering, they have occasional difficulties in applying that knowledge on the shop floor. Management information systems, communication facilities, servicing networks and general product support systems tend to be neglected. Today, increased attention is being given to these areas, as suggested by the fact that in 1980 IH increased from 3 to 9 the number of technical specialists it has stationed in Poland, although part of the expansion was due to the increased activities of the cooperation.

Skepticism about an ICA within the organizations. Initially, both partners exerted much effort to assure their respective constituencies of the ICA's desirability. At first, IH perceived certain reservations among its stockholders, lower level management, and employees; such reservations are no longer significant today. On the other side, BUMAR in some cases insisted that sometimes inadequate domestically produced substitutes be used in place of the IH-designated component. This particular problem no longer arises. Furthermore, some influential people in the ministries and elsewhere believed, mistakenly, that IH had a specific contractual buy-back commitment beyond that already mentioned which it had not lived up to (perhaps because

ICAs between BUMAR and other Western firms had often included detailed buy-back provisions), whereas no such specific commitment had been signed, except as noted above. Others, knowing the terms of the contract, criticized the absence of a contractual buy-back provision. The overriding concern about Poland's balance-of-payments problems has exacerbated these concerns and has put pressure on BUMAR to improve its hard-currency balance. Both partners are now very concerned with the problem and are taking steps to increase components and parts supplied from Poland.

Conclusions. IH and BUMAR (HSW) have achieved a highly integrated level of cooperation. IH has seen market opportunities for new products but lacked sufficient human and physical capital to exploit them; BUMAR has been able to widen its capabilities, drawing on technical resources and engineering know-how to create a more powerful production and export base. The cooperation has enabled both partners to save substantial investment funds and time, to undertake activities which may have been too expensive for each without the cooperation. To be sure, BUMAR had undertaken heavy investment in physical facilities, including a few foundries to produce high-quality steel and satellite plants to support the fabrication of parts. These investments and the assembly of the machines have required some hard-currency imports. But the new facilities also have applications in operations not directly connected with the cooperation, as well as technical and managerial spill-over effects. Although IH has not found it necessary to invest in additional plant or equipment to support the cooperation, it has made substantial investment in terms of personnel, travel, and the training of Polish specialists.

The network of agreements between them has increased worldwide manufacturing capacity for IH and access to previously unavailable technology and markets for BUMAR. It appears that by 1980, IH and BUMAR had begun to move toward the highest possible form of cooperation between independently-owned firms in two countries: joint planning for integrated global strategies involving crawler tractors. Evidence of this is the continuous discussion between the two firms on the kinds of products to be designed and produced in the future, as well as the ongoing cooperation in the design, development, testing, production, and marketing of certain new models. In spite of the difficulties enumerated, this ICA is considered one of the most successful large-scale ventures by an American multinational in Eastern Europe.

What has made this ICA, on balance, successful, in spite of the problems encountered? One of the most important factors is the strong initial commitment, on both sides and at the highest levels, to the idea of cooperation. In that setting, initiatives have been taken and solutions to problems found by people implementing the ICA at the critical middle-management level. Without top-level encouragement and backing, fewer initiatives would have been taken to overcome the difficulties encountered. The fact that IH has continuously assigned some of its best people to work on the project is also very important.

One reason why IH has made a strong, long-term, strategic commitment to IC in Eastern Europe was the personal interest in Poland of IH's Brooks McCormick, a descendant of the company's founder and its President and subsequently Chief Executive Officer until 1978. Other reasons may be found in the nature of the industry's technology and IH's global competitive position. IC tends to be more feasible in industries in which competition is based on process rather than product-technology (see discussion below, under technology transfer). Moreover, our survey of US multinationals interested in Eastern Europe revealed a tendency (with important exceptions) for those with a relatively small global market share to seek ICA more aggressively than the industry leaders. Notably, IH has only about a 6% market share of construction machinery in the West.

Turning to factors on the Polish side, we cannot stress strongly enough the importance of the entrepreneurial qualities and problem-solving attitudes displayed, first by those who initiated the ICA at BUMAR and then by the key people implementing it at HSW. We want to underscore especially the entrepreneurial risk and initiative taken by Mr. Sykstus Olesik, General Director of BUMAR FTO during 1970-76. This is a critically important intangible aspect which bears significantly on the question of whether other Polish enterprises would be able to replicate successfully the experience of IH with BUMAR.

Other supportive factors include the preferred position of heavy industry in general and of the construction machinery sector and the HSW complex in particular in Poland's economic strategy. The strong bargaining position of the principals has enabled the Polish partner to obtain the scarce investment and hard-currency resources needed. Today, given Poland's serious balance-of-payments problems, projects requiring large initial hard-currency outlays may be more difficult to implement, even in high-priority sectors.

Another important factor is that the HSW complex is a highly vertically integrated operation. This enables the Polish partner to avoid or at least manage more easily the domestic supply problems which often constrain Polish enterprises that are less integrated and have less bureaucratic influence.

Another consideration is the importance within Poland of the construction equipment sector in general, and HSW in particular, as a supplier of machinery and parts in heavy demand in the USSR and in Eastern Europe. On the one hand, this can facilitate cooperation with Western multinationals because high priority is given for the factories and because of pressure to export modern, high-quality goods. On the other hand, specialization for the CMEA market and IC with a Western multinational can be competitive if large export commitments to the CMEA constrain the ability of a Polish partner to cooperate with a Western firm. Further, exporting to the CMEA market is easy if an enterprise can supply modern, high-quality products, such as Poland's construction machinery. But selling within the CMEA, OECD, and domestic market today requires a great deal of product support, such as preventive maintenance and corrective service and repair systems. Although Poland has the engineering capability to produce construction machinery technically comparable to machinery sold in the West, it still lacks sufficient total capability to penetrate world markets as rapidly as desired. Because Poland must increase hard-currency earnings via manufactures exports, the long-term success of its export-drive will be affected significantly by the outcome of efforts in this area.

Generalizing the IH-BUMAR Experience

The IH-BUMAR cooperation is not the only example of successful IC between an American and a Polish firm, nor is it the only type of agreement that can be advantageous to both sides. Several dozen US firms have ICAs in Poland, of which four or five are of significant complexity, value, and scope. These include the IH-BUMAR ICA detailed above; the agreement between Clark Equipment and BUMAR for the manufacture of heavy-duty drive axles; Honeywell's ICA (through its subsidiary in Scotland) with MERA Union in industrial process control systems; Singer company's agreement with Universal for the assembly of sewing machines; and the recent agreement between Piper Aircraft and Detroit Diesel Allison with the Polish aviation industry. Several of these agreements are discussed in some detail in the contributions by Kossut, Zagorski, and Kozinski.

The major US-Polish ICAs tend to have the following in common. They typically extend over the entire product—which is usually a machine or instrument system (Clark's ICA is an exception). They all operate in the sphere of investment goods (except for the Singer ICA). Under each ICA, advanced technology has been transferred to the Polish partner. The envisaged duration of IC is, typically, at least ten years. Both partners have well-established positions in their industries. The Polish partners are the leading manufacturers at home and are experienced exporters; some even have previous experience in cooperating with Western firms. In Poland, the Ministry of Machine

Industry and its subordinate enterprises dominate IC activity; in fact, all the Polish enterprises involved in the above-mentioned ICAs are subordinated to that Ministry, which accounts for over 80 percent of Poland's IC-related trade turnover with partners from all countries. The main motive for IC on the Polish side is the acquisition of technology to modernize industry and to gain a competitive edge in the CMEA, Western and LDC markets. The American counterparts are well-known world-wide, possess advanced technology and organizational know-how, have highly esteemed trademarks, global sales and service networks, and are pioneers in entering into IC ventures in Eastern Europe.

Although the ICAs are typically negotiated and signed by the US parent, the implementation is often by the corporation's European production or marketing subsidiaries. Consequently, US-Polish IC often would be more appropriately labeled a "cooperation triangle" (Kozinski).

The length and difficulty of negotiating an ICA in Poland varies. Some US firms have found the negotiations no more difficult than a comparable agreement with a Western partner; others have been frustrated by long and expensive negotiations. The most successful ICAs involve almost continuous negotiations on an informal basis; as the partners become more familiar with each other's capabilities they tend to seek and as a rule find new opportunities for extending the existing agreement or negotiating additional ones.

Typically, the Polish partner receives the technical documentation and organizes the production at his own facilities, usually involving a substantial investment on the Polish side, while the American partner supplies some of the components and buys sub-assemblies, components, or final products. The two-way flow of goods between the partners is not organized on the basis of clearing; rather, the commitment of the US side is to buy Polish-made products either under separate short-term contracts or under buy-back arrangements set as a percentage of the Polish partner's annual output. The Polish side also obtains the right to use its partner's registered trademark, contingent upon meeting specific quality standards.

The partners typically divide the world market, with the Polish side having exclusive access to the CMEA countries and selected developing countries, and the US partner to markets elsewhere. However, the Polish side often can sell products to the West through the partner's sales network or directly supply the latter's manufacturing plants (often West European subsidiaries). The fact that the independent sales of Polish-made machines is usually restricted to the CMEA market reflects, in the view of the Polish team, the stronger bargaining position of the US partner while, in the view of the American team, perhaps also the Polish partner's limited marketing capability in the West.

From the point of view of quality standards, in the majority of ICAs mentioned, the Polish side was successful in receiving the partner's trademark. To be sure, there have been some delays in production start-up as well as in deliveries. The US side sometimes complains about the low elasticity of supply on the Polish side in responding rapidly to changing Western demand. The US team attributes this to the absence of reserve production capacity in Polish plants and to various organizational and incentive barriers. Viewed from the Polish perspective, however, the problem is that the Western partners may only be interested in short production runs. Thus, the US side may want to rely on the Polish partner for reserve production capacity for periods of boom in the world market, leaving the Polish enterprise with excess capacity in times of stagnating Western demand.

To place IC in perspective, one should note that within a relatively short time the US has taken a significant position in Polish trade and IC with Western countries. Trade turnover jumped from a quarter of a billion US dollars in 1972 to over $1.2 billion in 1978, and over $1.3 billion in 1980. The US now accounts for about 10 percent of Polish trade with developed market economies. IC has proved to be one of the most dynamic forms of economic relations between the US and Poland. In the early 1970s mutual deliveries in the framework of ICAs were insignificant, but since 1976 the US has ranked third or fourth, after Italy, the Federal Republic of Germany and Austria (in some years) in terms of the value of deliveries under ICAs between Poland and the industrial Western countries. Admittedly, however, these percentage shares are dominated by deliveries under a few key ICAs.

Considering the benefits of IC and the experience of US firms in Poland, why have only a half a dozen or so large US multinationals had significant IC involvement in Poland? One reason is that most US corporations, even those that have a significant export or import business in the region, have no clearly-defined long-term business strategy in Eastern Europe.[10] The approach of most US companies to Eastern Europe may be called "opportunistic." That is, realizing that the potential East European market is too large to be neglected (if only out of concern that a competitor may pre-empt it), many US firms are "interested" in commercial relations but are not devoting a great deal of top-management time and talent to developing long-term business opportunities in the region.

There are several reasons why Eastern Europe (including the Soviet Union) typically represents only a small fraction of US firms' worldwide sales or purchases. Uncertainty regarding East-West political relations, and about US policy on East-West commerce, is a factor. Also very important is top management's unfamiliarity with the economic systems and business environments of the planned economies. Organizational considerations are a further contributing factor. Most US multinationals are organized along worldwide product divisions and tend to be quite decentralized so as to allow flexibility in dealing with diverse market situations. (West European companies tend to be more centralized partly because they typically serve a more limited market.) Decentralized corporate organization is not conducive to the nurturing of long-term business opportunities in a centrally planned economy such as Poland's where most manufacturing, trade, and IC decisions are centralized, and top government officials are directly involved. Moreover, East European government, industry, and trade officials prefer long-term working relationships with foreign corporations and want to deal with their top management personnel. Many US firms, however, send to Eastern Europe their product-oriented sales representatives or purchasing agents whose perspectives are typically not strategically long-term.

Not surprisingly, therefore, we find that companies successful in negotiating and implementing ICAs in Poland and elsewhere in Eastern Europe are those willing to adapt their organizational structures to the special requirements of the East European market. This organizational adaptation typically involves the centralization of activities related to Eastern Europe, most often by forming ad hoc top management teams that have strategic, functional, or coordinating responsibilities for operations in Eastern Europe. IH, for example, relies on this approach. Clark Equipment has a two-tier approach to Eastern Europe: direct sales are handled by a West German sales office, but the firm's IC activities are managed from the headquarters in the US (Garland). Perlmutter's contribution to this volume summarizes the results of a survey of US corporate leaders regarding the role of East-West linkages in the global strategies of US multinational corporations, enumerating the current "driving and restraining forces" toward ICAs by US firms in Poland.

Industrial Cooperation Opportunities in Poland

Executives of US companies interested in IC in Poland typically ask:

> *Since Poland is a planned economy, what are its strategic plans and preferences? Is there a best formula for exploring business opportunities, either through trade or IC? With whom, and how, should we explore concrete IC opportunities? What is the approval process on projects, and what considerations will dominate decisions on the Polish side?*

The Polish team's answers may be summarized as follows.

We have described in our contributions in some detail what has been done to date. Several key sectors—shipping, mechanical engineering, transportation equipment, industries based on Poland's natural resources (including coal, copper, sulphur) and the machinery and equipment branches supporting these sectors—have already been developed so extensively that it is safe to assume that they will remain high-priority sectors in which IC will continue to be particularly welcome. Yet, priorities are not permanently fixed but are continually changing. One thing, however, is certain: IC proposals that give us firm prospects to earn hard currency are going to receive high priority.

ICAs are planned similarly to foreign trade. Since they involve long-term commitments and domestic supply lines and deliveries, ICAs have to be incorporated into the national economic plan.

ICAs may be initiated both at the central level, that is, by the Central Planning Commission and the branch ministries (e.g., in the automotive industry) or by the executive units of industry, that is, by enterprises or production associations, e.g., for construction equipment. IC opportunities can be created in almost any sector.

Poland has some special regulations and institutions governing IC. ICAs can be negotiated by FTOs in their own name or in behalf of the interested industrial unit, or directly by the latter but with participation by personnel from the relevant FTO. The FTOs must notify the Central Statistical Office in Poland regularly of the volume of trade conducted under ICAs. Production associations usually have their own FTOs through which member enterprises are able to enter into ICAs with foreign firms. This was the case, for example, in the IH-BUMAR agreement signed by BUMAR FTO. The latter is a unit of BUMAR Union, a production association.

The role the various central planning authorities play in IC depends on the size of the project, the scale of additional investments required, the nature of supply lines used to support the ICA, forms of financing, and the marketing arrangements. If an ICA requires large-scale investment, that investment must be included in the central plan. By contrast, if an ICA uses mainly existing facilities, then only the approval of the local planning unit is required. Generally, the greater the need for coordination among branches of the economy and the need for hard currency outlays, the higher the level at which a project must be approved. The more important ICAs must be approved by the Ministry of Foreign Trade and Shipping, which is responsible for Poland's balance of payments and foreign trade policy. The Ministry has a special IC division to facilitate prompt decisions. In some cases, of course, the Ministry may not approve an IC proposal. In practice, for an agreement involving the manufacturing, say, of suits to the specifications of a foreign partner, using existing premises and staff, the factory manager and his immediate superior may make a quick decision; no lengthy, formal approval is required.

No special incentives for IC are in effect. FTOs and industry units are to weigh the advantages of cooperation, as they do in the case of exports and imports, by the usual profitability criteria.

Long-Term Benefits of Cooperation with Poland for US Firms

Poland is part of Eastern Europe, whose economies have grown rapidly during the 1970s and are expected to continue to grow during the 1980s, though at a much slower pace. Until mid-1980, the region had been considered one of relative stability: contracts were observed; laws and regulations, if changed, were modified to attract rather than to discourage US corporations; and Western firms were not overly concerned about unforeseen price increases or breaks in production due to labor walkouts or other causes.

The Polish team wishes to underscore that in spite of the events that have occurred in Poland since the summer of 1980, its fundamental attitude toward Poland's East-West relations remains unchanged. The well-known events resulted from some obvious and considerable mistakes in Poland's investment and price policies. It is the consensus of Polish economists that the necessary measures and reforms which are being introduced currently (in 1981) into Poland's economic and decision-making system will help to re-establish stability in the country and in Poland's East-West relations. The difficulties encountered in Poland should be considered short-term. Their long-run consequences, in the view of the Polish team, will definitely have a positive effect on international industrial cooperation. The Polish team hopes that "our foreign partners will show patience and understanding regarding the current situation and confidence in Poland's future prospects."

An important advantage of having a commercial base in Poland is its geographical location, which may facilitate export penetration by American firms of the other East European countries and may serve as a convenient production base for marketing in Western Europe.

Several sectors of the Polish economy, including shipbuilding, aviation, and machine tools, have long traditions. As a result of a modernization drive undertaken during the early 1970s, these and other sectors have been reconstructed and equipped with the most modern machinery. The number and quality of skilled workers and engineers in Poland provide a further basis for achieving technical excellence, as is shown by the experience of IH in cooperating with BUMAR's main unit in HSW. Once the labor and material supply situations have stabilized, the strong desire in Poland to improve the productivity and performance of these newly modernized enterprises should make these enterprises increasingly attractive partners for American firms.

With the development and modernization of many industries in Poland, the areas of potential long-term US-Polish cooperation have been enlarged because the cooperation potential grows as countries become more similar in their industrial structure and technical potential. The Polish side cites the following industries and sectors as being particularly suitable for IC with Western firms: shipbuilding, machine tools, computers, computer peripherals and other electronics, automotives, construction equipment, aircraft, consumer durables, household appliances, food processing, and safety and environmental equipment. Of course, enterprises in other sectors also can take initiatives to enter into ICAs with US partners.

Long-Term Benefits of Cooperation with US for Polish Firms

Cooperation with American companies has always been attractive. US firms generally have modern machinery and equipment as well as up-to-date technical, managerial, and organizational know-how. The huge American market provides a great opportunity for Polish exports of parts and components or final products manufactured under ICAs. Conditions leading to profit from large scale cooperation deals have improved since 1972 when the US Eximbank was authorized to support American machinery exports to Poland. Several large US-Polish ICAs were made possible by the financial support of the Bank.

An important step increasing the attractiveness of cooperating with American firms was the gradual easing of the US government's control of the transfer of technology by US firms to Poland. To be sure, further steps in this direction would be helpful. The Polish side has emphasized that, for instance, the procedures for issuing export licenses for technical documentation and know-how in the aviation and electronic industries are still too complicated and lengthy.

Another positive factor is the performance of the US economy. In the mid-1970s, many Western economies were more or less stagnant, while the US economy continued to grow, although at a lower rate than earlier. As a result, the component of US-Polish IC which involved deliveries to the US was not affected much by recession. The fundamental strength and growth potential of the US economy also suggests that, cyclical fluctuations notwithstanding, the US will continue to grow and play a leading role in scientific and technical developments.

Other attractive features are the immense experience of large American companies—often multi-branch or multinational—in doing worldwide business in various political and economic environments, and the variety of planning and organizational methods they routinely apply in their operations and in the development of strategies for dealing with future uncertainty. The location of many American affiliates in Western Europe and in other parts of the world increases the chances for Polish firms to find an appropriate unit within an American corporation to enter, through ICAs, into worldwide sourcing and marketing arrangements.

Poland is also the ancestral homeland of many millions of Americans. This fact, combined with the generally-appreciated relative flexibility of Polish businessmen and decisionmakers, makes it easier for American partners to understand and to work within the "rules of the game" in Poland.

Joint Ventures

In the early 1970s, following the publication of joint venture decrees in Hungary and Romania, the Polish government examined the desirability and practicability of joint ventures in Poland. It concluded that no special legislation was required and that any foreign proposal for such arrangements would be considered. In 1976, however, special regulations were issued (see Section V for the English translation of all relevant joint venture laws, regulations and related decrees). The 1976 decree (not limited to joint ventures) permitted foreigners and foreign firms to invest in Poland, in the form of wholly-owned companies, in such sectors as handicrafts, hotels, restaurants, and other consumer services, with regional councils having the authority to approve the required investment. The decree was designed primarily to attract hard-currency funds from Polish communities in the West and was linked to parallel measures to encourage more domestic private activity in consumer services.[11] In 1979 a new decree was issued which extended the scope of activity permitted by the earlier regulation, permitting not only wholly-owned but also mixed companies, and in different sectors of small-scale, non-basic industries (see Tabaczynski).[12]

The Polish legislation on equity participation is one of several different types of joint venture models introduced in Eastern Europe. One is the fully integrated Yugoslav model, in which the joint venture is essentially no different from any other domestic enterprise; its accounts are maintained in local currency and the valuation of inputs is based on domestic market prices and on foreign prices converted to domestic prices according to the official exchange rate. At the other extreme is the enclave-system Romanian model, in which the accounting and settlement are in a foreign currency, as is the valuation of inputs. Thus, even purchases from and sales to domestic firms are calculated in foreign prices and currency. The joint venture determines its own economic plan, which is then incorporated into the national economic plan; otherwise the joint venture is not well integrated into the national economic mechanism. In between the Yugoslav and Romanian models is the calculation-system Hungarian model, in which accounting and settlement is undertaken in both foreign and local currencies. Financial transactions with domestic enterprises are based on domestic prices; exports and imports on foreign currency prices converted to domestic prices according to the official non-convertible exchange rate. According to the Polish 1976 (wholly-owned companies) and 1979 (mixed companies) legislation, the accounting system and the settlement are in Polish currency, based either on Polish domestic prices or on foreign prices converted to domestic prices according to the official, non-convertible exchange rate. These joint ventures are subject to the existing Polish economic and legal order but so far they are restricted to activities in certain non-basic industries.

How attractive is the possibility of entering into a joint venture for US and other Western firms? The attitudes of the top management of US and other Western companies differ on this issue. Some take a categorical stand against participating in joint ventures anywhere unless they can have majority ownership and full managerial control. Others believe that equity is not at all important if the same results can be achieved through a contract. But a third group is very much interested in joint venture possibilities. To them, the fact that joint ventures are permitted symbolizes the strong commitment of the East European country to cooperation with Western firms. It also helps to explain—and in a sense, justify—to the stockholders why the firm is willing to make a commitment in Eastern Europe. For some firms it also satisfies the conditions under which they are willing to make a long-term commitment to a country, or a project, including transfer of its most advanced technological and managerial know-how on a continuous basis (Marer's comment on Zagorski). For such firms, the key factors in their decision on whether to enter—once the technical and marketing questions have been answered—are the stability of the host country's economic, political, social, and legal environments. Right now the above-noted stability conditions do not prevail in Poland. However, we consider the current period transitional.

Several US executives stated that too much legal experimentation tends to be a strong disincentive, even if successive changes tend to make entry or operating conditions more favorable to the Western partner. Frequent changes in rules and regulations create the impression that the country had not made up its mind about what it wants to do. Members of the Polish team, however, underscored that this "experimentation" is aimed at finding more workable solutions, which should attract Western cooperation partners in the long run.

An even more fundamental issue corporate executives are concerned about is the satisfactory integration of a joint venture with the rest of the economy in a planned economy like Poland. The essence of a joint venture is the intermingling of foreign and local financial contributions—initial capital, inputs, outputs, profits. How can this financial intermingling be accomplished in a country that has an inconvertible currency? Most executives, therefore, agreed with the statement by one of the Polish team members that one of the greatest obstacles to equity joint ventures is the inconvertibility of the zloty, which makes the calculation of production costs and profits complicated and not necessarily reliable (Zagorski). Other possible problems involve the managerial distribution of decision-making authority between the partners with respect to the sourcing of inputs, the hiring and compensation of labor, the marketing of output, and so on.

Technology Transfer

Technology transfer is a key aspect of East-West IC. Two contributions focus on that issue, one from the point of view of Polish firms (Kozinski) and the other from the perspective of multinational corporations (Brada).

Technology transfer may be conceptualized as a three-phase process: phase one, exploration and selection, during which the appropriate technology and the mechanism of its transfer are chosen; phase two, duplication and adaptation, during which the technology is acquired, adapted to local conditions, and applied in the manufacturing process; and, finally, phase three, reproduction and innovation, during which the imported technology is diffused and further developed so that a stream of benefits accrues to the importing country even after the original technology has become obsolete. This "reproduction" is achieved, ideally, through R & D cooperation between the IC partners. Unless the importing Polish enterprise successfully moves to phase three, no lasting benefits have accrued, in the author's opinion (Kozinski). The author examines three US-Polish ICAs, one between General Motors and Polmo for the coproduction of vans and trucks (an ICA which has been suspended); another between Corning Glass Works—RCA with UNITRA on the sale of technology and equipment for the manufacture of color picture tubes; and IH-BUMAR. Kozinski finds that only the IH-BUMAR ICA has successfully reached phase three and discusses why the other cases fell short of reaching the final phase.

Another contribution develops the hypothesis that the willingness of a Western multinational firm to transfer technology through ICAs may be inferred from the way the firm organizes and conducts its world-wide production and exploitation of technology (Brada). The technology that a firm employs may be divided into two basic types: product technology and process technology. Product technology involves the development of new, unique products which have few close substitutes, so that the firm's competitive advantage derives primarily from its ownership rights over the proprietary technology embodied in the new product. In contrast, process-technology involves the ability to successfully produce and market a product even though many firms may have the manufacturing know-how to put on the market similar or close-substitute products, as is the case, for example, in the construction machinery sector. Competitive advantage is then based on the efficiency of organizing and financing complex, large-scale production and marketing networks, which requires the disembodied technologies of the organization and management of production, marketing, and after-sales service.

One reason for IH's willingness to transfer technology on a continuous basis to its Polish partner is that the technology IH possesses is essentially process technology. Contrasting the technology in the construction equipment industry with that in the pharmaceutical industry, tentative support is found for this hypothesis (Brada). Further empirical verification of the hypothesis would have two major implications for IC. First, it would facilitate the process of partner and project selection for the Polish side by suggesting which types of products and firms would make IC partners most willing to transfer technology. Second, the theory would help identify the obstacles to IC in the case of firms which compete on the basis of unique products.

Impact of Economic Systems on Trade and Industrial Cooperation

Several contributions discuss Poland's planning and management system, focusing on the role of large economic organizations and the planning of foreign trade (Giezgala), the policy and pattern of Poland's foreign trade specialization (Tabaczynski), and how the ministries, large economic organizations, FTOs, and enterprises are organized from the point of view of decisionmaking affecting trade and IC with Western countries (Garland).

Concerning the planning and management system, the contributions by the Polish team stress that a significant portion of industry has been effectively decentralized to support the strategy of export-oriented development and to encourage IC (Giezgala). In the view of the US team, however, this decentralized sector appears to have some of the characteristics of an export-oriented enclave with its associated interface problems. Successful development requires integrating this enclave with the other parts of the economy that supply materials, components, and parts. This may present difficulties unless the Polish IC partner is almost fully vertically integrated, as is the case with IH's IC partner, BUMAR. In the view of the US team, there are two ways to deal with the problem: to bring more of the domestic economy into this enclave, requiring comprehensive economic reforms; or to turn the export enclave more and more to the outside world, which means a greater reliance on hard-currency imports to solve supply difficulties. According to the US team, as of the late 1970s Poland had adopted neither of these alternatives, with the result that the rapid expansion of investment, trade, and IC during the previous decade has not led to the intended macro-economic results (Campbell). Questions also have arisen regarding the extent to which the decentralization decrees have been implemented in practice. Obstacles to de facto decentralization include bureaucratic inertia and a worsening of Poland's external financial position which appears to have prompted the continuance, if not the increase, of administrative intervention in IC-related activities of enterprises (Garland).

Poland's modernization drive of the 1970s created a rapidly-growing potential market for US and other Western firms, especially for their investment-sector export products, as well as a growing willingness on the part of Polish enterprises to enter into ICAs with Western firms. Yet, Poland's investment drive was clearly excessive, resulting in a dilution of priorities and severe strain on the Polish economy to implement simultaneously all the projects that were started. One of the most frequent complaints among Poland's Western IC partners was the long delay in investment projects coming on stream. Delays affect not only the given project but, through extensive backward and forward linkages with the economy's other sectors, the implementation of other ICAs as well.

Poland's development strategy has led to large hard currency debts. Poland hopes to resolve these by expanding rapidly her exports of manufactured goods to the West, efforts that have been made difficult by the slow growth of Western economies, growing protectionist trends, rising competition from newly industrialized nations, and—most importantly—by inadequate past Polish export performance in producing and marketing goods to the West. This in turn contributed to bringing about the current economic crisis.

There are numerous economic, financial and even political reasons for the Polish crisis at the beginning of the 1980s. The main economic reasons are:

—Shortcomings in the centralized management of the Polish economy;
—Decisionmaking at various levels in the economic hierarchy disregarding major goals and directives;
—Deficiency of objective economic accounting for the use of in-

vestment resources and production operations, resulting in major inefficiencies in many areas of production.

The outcome was an uncontrolled explosion of investment projects throughout the country, many of them involving foreign finance and imported plants and equipment.

For all these reasons, the point of departure for any new approach must be a more realistic economic policy in the future.

In January 1981 the Polish Government proposed a plan of economic reforms which is very important for the improvement of the situation in Poland. The main reform points are the following:

— The Central Planning Commission should no longer issue directives for the economy but retain only its "strategic role."

— Under the new system, individual enterprises would be entitled to decide independently production and trade and would finance from their own resources their current operations and investments.

— One aspect of industrial decentralization would be to secure for worker councils a larger role in control over the factory and its administration.

— Rationalization of the domestic price structure, especially for imported products, and of the rate of exchange of the Polish zloty. Prices should be calculated according to rational production costs; raw material prices should be based on price ratios in effect on the world market.

— Modernization of the private sector in agriculture. The private farms should be granted access to machinery and fertilizers on the same terms as state farms.

— For the advantageous implementation of the reform it was necessary to decide that only some of the investments begun during the 1970s should be continued; namely, those in food production, certain others designed to produce and export raw materials, and finally some projects supporting the introduction of energy-saving technology.

The Government decided to stop work on 49 major projects in 1981 and to cut investment spending. Many other investment projects were suspended by branch ministers and regional governors. However, the largest investment projects involving Western companies will not be halted, and ongoing successful operations such as the IH-BUMAR ICA are not intended to be affected.[13]

Several contributions focus on Poland's foreign trade specialization, export strategy, and the relationship between foreign trade and IC. The role of marketing strategies in expanding exports and the difficulties encountered by Polish enterprises in marketing in the US are also described (Miller and comments by Borowski). A significant difference between Polish and Western determination of products for export specialization is that Polish product policy has been designed mainly to satisfy domestic demand, relegating the generation of hard currency through export specialization to a subordinate role. On the other hand, Western corporations view exports as a means to expand their operations (Borowski).

Although IC has recently taken on a new importance in Polish trade with the West, most Polish hard currency exports are still accounted for by conventional trade or at least by more "traditional" forms of IC. One of the studies presented in this volume examines econometrically the export determinants for a sample of the most important Polish non-agricultural exports to West Germany, Poland's largest Western trade partner (Wolf). The study shows that as late as 1977 IC accounted for a significant share of exports only in the clothing sector. These ICAs have tended to be more in the nature of subcontracting arrangements, in which most of the product development and marketing is undertaken by the Western partner, although some important technology transfer has taken place. The existence of these agreements did permit extremely rapid increases in the Polish share of West German clothing imports in the early 1970s, however, and their success suggests that IC can have a considerable impact on trade if there are sufficient microeconomic motivations on both sides and if there is a favorable trade policy climate.

What pattern should future Polish specialization follow? Members of the Polish team stress that Poland is not looking to specialize in progressive industrial branches necessarily, which are difficult to identify, but in progressive products in all sectors (Tabaczynski). The US side stressed how difficult it is to forecast precisely which are the progressive products in the long run, in view of the fact that all actual and potential producers in all of the countries in the world are looking at basically the same set of data and opportunities. There is a danger of being seduced by the fallacy of composition: if a producer is the only one embarking on a given strategy, it would be sound and profitable, but if many competitors are thinking along the same lines, it may not be. The Polish team underscored that even when looking at the same set of data and opportunities, different countries and producers may reach different conclusions. The Japanese pattern of specialization is quite different, for example, than the West European pattern. Moreover, even potential competitors can decide to agree upon some fundamental international division of labor in order to increase the scale and efficiency of production.

The point was repeatedly made by both sides that much depends both on initiative by the Polish enterprise manager and perseverance by the Western partner in seeking and implementing specialization and IC opportunities. No better example can be found to illustrate the catalytic role of initiative and entrepreneurship than the IH-BUMAR case study.

Many participants in the Warsaw Conference were concerned about the impact of increasing protectionism in the US and in Western Europe on Poland's manufactures exports (see Szeworski and Summary of Discussion). One contribution describes in considerable detail the impact of US import-protective laws and regulations on Poland's manufactures exports (Marer). The essential point made is that enterprises operate according to different concepts and "rules of the game" in the US and in Poland which causes inevitable difficulties, such as the question: What constitutes "fair" competition? An import competing producer in a market economy like the US feels he is competing against Polish enterprises which do not face the same constraints as he does in a market economy, such as having to make a profit to stay in business. This view is based on the observations that (1) there are large and often apparently quite arbitrary differences in relative prices, especially of raw materials and fuels, between market and planned economies; (2) prices of raw materials and fuels in Poland are fixed by the state and generally remain unchanged for long periods regardless of shifts in supply and demand; (3) exchange rates, established and published by the state, do not appear to be meaningful for converting Polish prices or costs into US dollars.

For all these reasons, in US investigations of alleged dumping by Poland, the "fair value" of imports from Poland must be established by reference to prices and costs in a market economy country. In some cases it is extremely difficult to select a surrogate producer in a market economy that will produce results considered fair and equitable by all parties. Such was the situation in the case of Polish golf cart exports to the US. To the Polish participants, the golf cart case illustrates a lack of basic logic in recent East-West trade developments. The West is ready to finance Eastern imports on credit but at the same time puts up protectionist barriers that seriously limit access to Western markets and impede the repayment of Western credits. The unpredictible character of US trade regulations undermined Poland's effective long-range trade agreements and planning. This concern looms especially large when Polish enterprises purchase costly US technology on credit and want to pay for it later with resulting products. There is uncertainty as to how these goods will be treated under any number of provisions of the US trade law. Poland and other East European countries experiencing large trade deficits and severe shortages of convertible currency cannot continue to purchase US exports if the products they attempt to sell to the US in return are challenged at every point. In the words of one Polish participant:

We can fully respect the right of the American government to determine the list of sensitive goods and exclude from our export expansion program these commodities. But we must be certain that if we develop production capacities in other commodities, these new areas of our export specialization will not become 'sensitive' tomorrow. Some 'fair play' rules should be jointly elaborated and then respected by both sides. Of course we do not expect guarantees from the US government that our exports will be sold, only guaranteed access to the US market on equal terms with other competitors (see Trzeciakowski in the Summary of Warsaw Conference Discussion).

A US team member then commented that in response to the complaint of the Polish golf cart exporter (aided by Poland's willingness to provide detailed information about the production process so that "costs" could be reconstructed on an alternative basis), US dumping investigation procedures were altered during 1978-80, resulting in a new outcome more favorable to Poland in the golf cart case (for details, see Summary of Warsaw Conference Discussion). The US team concluded that the circumstances surrounding the initial dumping finding in the golf cart case were so extreme as to make it a unique case. The coincidence of (1) highly visible rapid penetration of the US market; (2) inability to find a surrogate producer outside North America; (3) an interpretation of legislative intent regarding how fair value should be "constructed" that was most unfavorable to Poland; and (4) inadequate initial legal advice, all combined to yield a decision that seemed unfair to Poland. While the case was by no means typical of the reception of other Polish exports in the US, the wide publicity it received in Poland created the greatly exaggerated impression that the US is a strongly protectionist country.

Prospects for the 1980s

Both teams agree that if the planned comprehensive economic reforms are implemented soon, the long-term potential for the further development of East-West IC during the 1980s is very good (fundamentally for the reasons spelled out in the earlier section on "Long-Term Attractiveness of Cooperation"); however, we also see numerous practical short-term difficulties and constraints.

East-West IC is particularly sensitive to the political climate of East-West relations, and in this respect the decade did not begin auspiciously. For example, the importance of IC as a channel for the transfer of Western technology makes it vulnerable to politically-motivated embargoes on high-technology processes and products. But even since the inception of the recent sanctions against one particular

Eastern country, the United States has maintained that its licensing policy toward Eastern Europe would remain unchanged provided that no diversion of licensed goods and technology occurred to that particular country. It is too early to tell, given a new Administration in Washington (1981), whether there will or will not be a more restrictive licensing policy toward Eastern Europe.

The executives of US multinationals are also concerned about the fragility of East-West economic cooperation. Many recognize that a straightline extrapolation of the growth rate of East-West commerce during the 1970s would be unrealistic for the 1980s. We confronted them with three possible scenarios: a divergent competitive environment, wherein political and economic relations between East and West become increasingly tense; an emergent-pragmatic environment, wherein relatively short-term pragmatic considerations take precedence over political and economic differences; and an integrative-cooperative environment, wherein the long-term view prevails, and an explicit commitment is made by both sides to an international division of labor in many East-West industrial sectors. At the end of 1979, most US executives considered the emergent-pragmatic scenario as most likely for the 1980s. They also stressed that because of the hard-currency shortages in Poland and elsewhere in Eastern Europe, during the 1980s there would be increasing pressures to buy back products produced in the East. The executives reacted differently to pressures for counterpurchase. Some advocated an aggressive counterpurchase policy, which for many firms will be a new type of business; others concluded that such pressures would be a major constraint on business opportunities in Eastern Europe (Perlmutter).

The third scenario, an integrated international East-West system, was considered improbable in the short term, but not for the 1990s. There appeared to be little indication that such a process would be legitimized in the present and foreseeable international political climate, although it seems more plausible than the divergent-competitive scenario. Many US executives questioned the willingness of the East European planned economies to engage in long-term planning with Western countries and firms and to increase exchanges of information and personnel between the blocs, a problem that may not be resolved easily in the short and middle term.

The concern is partly over the reconciliation required between the institutions of planned and market economies. Detailed planning must be carried out by firms rather than by governments. Because Eastern firms are state owned, US executives question whether their East European counterparts have the independence to engage in long-term strategic planning with Western firms. No central planning model blueprints increasingly comprehensive linkages with non-CMEA economies. But some executives believe that this issue will become increasingly important in the late 1980s and that chances are at least a few CMEA countries will move toward legitimizing this joint planning process. Everyone recognized that some balance must be struck between independence and planning for interdependence.

Because IC typically involves investment goods, its prospects are influenced by the investment outlook in Poland. The current decline and prospective slowdown in the rate of growth of investment in Poland (and in the other East European countries) suggests, *ceteris paribus*, a slowdown in East-West IC also. However, ICAs in new priority sectors, such as energy industries, energy-saving projects, infrastructure improvements, environmental protection, and export industries in general, may receive a new impetus during the 1980s. Further constraining IC in the short run are Poland's chronic hard currency balance of payments problems which force planners to curb imports from the West and may prompt them to approve only ICAs that are self-financing in the short run. At the same time, balance of payments problems may give a new impetus to certain types of IC, such as foreign direct investment which finances the Western contribution via equity participation. Moreover, Poland as well as the other East European countries must become strongly export-oriented, and IC can be an excellent vehicle toward achieving that objective. But, in the view of the American team, the extent to which IC can promote Poland's export orientation depends largely on the ability of Poland (and of other East European countries) to overcome the systemic factors that impede the implementation of ICA arrangements and the diffusion of the organizational, technological, service, marketing, and managerial benefits of ICAs throughout the economy. In the opinion of the US team, East-West IC is not a substitute for economic reform; it must be accompanied by complementary changes in the domestic economic and foreign trade mechanism.

The Polish team shares the above opinion. In their view the new economic reforms in Poland should insist on the significance of the financial calculation and financial results of enterprise activity. IC is, first of all, a vehicle for improving the performance of the participating firms by lowering unit production costs and saving on investment and R & D outlays. In some circumstances export promotion can be achieved without IC (e.g., Japan) provided that the country is able to produce competitive, high quality goods.

It is the view of the Polish team that the new economic climate in Poland in the 1980s will be conducive for IC. Moreover, a new impetus for IC in the years ahead is considered a vital necessity for the Polish economy.

With respect to the economies of the Western countries, 1981 appears to be the year of slow recovery from the 1980 slump. The concensus of experts is that the upturn should gain momentum during the next couple of years, even though the recovery will be modest by historical standards. Generally speaking, the more rapid the economic expansion in the US, and in the West generally, the more it tends to promote IC because firms are then more willing to establish permanent links with foreign suppliers and because protectionist tendencies are easier to keep at bay. Slow expansion or stagflation does the opposite, although a partial offset is that some firms then become more eager to expand abroad, and IC with the Eastern countries is one avenue to do so. Financing for East-West IC, *ceteris paribus*, also tends to be easier to obtain during periods of Western economic slowdown.

CONCLUSIONS AND RECOMMENDATIONS

Possibilities for Industrial Cooperation and the Selection of Partners

1. After examining carefully the IH-BUMAR agreement and its implementation, looking at other case studies, consulting with the business communities in the US and Poland, and the often frank and open discusssions during the two seminars, we conclude that there are many more opportunities for US and Polish firms to enter into ICAs than have been realized up to now. IC between US and Polish firms represents an increasingly important additional strategy for expanding trade between our two countries and with third countries beyond the level that would be possible through conventional exports alone.

2. We believe that US and Polish firms should explore more seriously the possibilities for IC. The IH-BUMAR case exemplifies strong, mutual commitment to strategic international cooperation between a large American and Polish firm; the case also shows that motives and conditions can be mutually compatible. Therefore, once Poland solves the problems which have caused the recent interruptions—in foreign trade, transportation, domestic supply distribution, and labor services—and also eliminates the main shortcomings in its planning and management system, it would be useful to look systematically, industry-by-industry, for IC opportunities. The most likely candidates for IC would be in the Polish machine building sectors, especially enterprises whose top management, supported by technical and organizational capability, is inclined to want IC. The potential partner might also think systematically about different forms of IC (i.e., licensing only, subcontracting, coproduction of completely standardized items, joint marketing, and so on) and the conditions under which they would be recommended, and then try to identify particularly promising situations.

3. Focusing on IC between large American and Polish firms, we find

that partner selection may proceed basically in one of two ways. Usually IC evolves from successful previous technical-commercial contacts between firms. This is the predominant form of partner selection between Polish and West European enterprises. The alternative is for a Polish or Western firm to decide independently that IC is a desirable development strategy, and then search for a suitable and willing foreign partner. The IH-BUMAR case is an example of this latter approach to partner selection.

The long distance between the US and Poland and the lack of extensive previous commercial contacts between US and Polish manufacturing firms suggest that, as far as cooperation between large enterprises is concerned, this second approach may hold more promise in Polish-US than in Polish-West European relations. This suggests that a systematic search for IC opportunities might be undertaken if a large Polish or American firm makes a policy decision that IC with a Western (Eastern) partner is a desirable strategy. If so, an important governmental body, such as the US-Polish Economic Commission, or a private organization such as the US-Polish Economic Council, may be able to help in the match-making process.

4. If we take a long-range view on IC between the US and Poland, one of the most effective ways of promoting IC and smoothing the implementation of agreements would be to set up a transnational management exchange program. Junior and middle-level managers from manufacturing enterprises in one country would benefit particularly from the opportunity to spend six to twelve months with a large firm in the partner country.

5. The following preconditions must exist for successful coproduction-type IC between large US and Polish firms:

a. The partners should have a reasonably similar scale of operations in the relevant product line and adequate levels of technical and organizational capability.

b. The partners should have an outward-oriented rather than simply import-substitution-oriented production and development strategy. That is, they should produce or plan to produce not only for the domestic but also for foreign (East European or Western) markets.

c. Top managers and other decisionmakers on both sides should be strongly interested in and committed to the success of IC. Previous successful IC experience with firms in other East European, Western, or Third World countries presumably fosters a favorable managerial attitude toward IC and a heightened awareness of its potential.

d. From the point of view of US firms seeking an appropriate Polish partner, it is critical to investigate carefully the prospective partner's ability to cope with ICA-related commitments, especially with respect to the quality and timing of deliveries by supplying firms. (Such potential problems have been minimized in the IH-BUMAR ICA because HSW is a highly vertically-integrated manufacturing unit. Full vertical integration should not, however, be considered an absolute precondition for a successful ICA.) US business executives stressed at the Bloomington conference that the reduction and eventual elimination of interface problems for a manufacturing operation based in Poland are tied very closely to further changes in Poland's economic organization and management system.

e. Coproduction ICAs which are based on a two-way flow of components, final products, services and technology generally have better prospects than ICAs without a counterpurchase or buy-back commitment. Buy-back arrangements (payment with resulting products) should be considered a possible mechanism for overcoming difficulties in Poland's balance-of-payments. Buy-back agreements may remove at the outset critically important payment problems, and may strengthen the commitment of the US partner to helping the Polish producer achieve quality excellence throughout the manufacturing process. US business executives at the same time stressed that a precondition for coproduction and buy-back agreements is a strong commitment on the part of Polish firms to improving quality and meeting schedules, and the acceptance of more rigorous requirements than the Polish economic environment has hiterto imposed on them. Further research is needed to determine which buy-back arrangements may be of interest to both sides.

6. Subdeliveries (subcontracting-type) ICAs are based on the principle of a one-way flow of components, services and technology, though in some cases they may involve buy-back commitments. These kinds of ICAs seem to be dominant in today's East-West IC links. It would be desirable gradually to replace them by more complex coproduction schemes.

7. Mutually advantageous IC opportunities between small and medium-sized American and Polish firms can also be found. In addition to coproduction possibilities in the manufacturing sector, there are numerous "special situation" opportunities for the delivery of components to large or small US firms. IH has thousands of independent subcontractors in the US and a smaller number outside the US, as do most other large US manufacturers. Although the distance between the US and Poland is a very important factor, a systematic exploration of subcontracting opportunities could involve small and medium-sized firms in our respective countries (see footnote 12). The advantage of small size is flexibility. The fact that Eximbank has a small business program could facilitate such efforts.

8. With respect to IC between small and medium-sized firms, it is important to note the evolution of recent Polish law on equity joint ventures on Polish territory. A decree of May 14, 1976, by the Council of Ministers allowed foreign citizens to invest in Poland (100 percent ownership) in such sectors as handicrafts, hotels, restaurants, catering, and other services. On February 7, 1979, the Council of Ministers issued another decree which also permits joint stock companies to be set up in Poland, in small-scale, non-basic industrial activities. Polish state and cooperative firms are allowed to conclude agreements with foreigners, but the equity share of the Polish partner must be not less than 51 percent. Joint stock companies should manufacture goods for the local market and for export, particularly to the hard currency markets. The provisions of the new law especially encourage small and medium-sized firms to participate in US-Polish ICAs. Detailed guidelines with regard to tax exemption, transfer of profits, rate of exchange, and other financial regulations were issued by Poland's Minister of Finance during 1979. Joint research between US and Polish experts on problems that could arise during the operation of a joint venture would be extremely useful, as would be the joint preparation of model contracts (see Tabaczynski).

9. A potential new area of cooperation between US and Polish firms in the 1980s is tripartite IC under bilateral or multilateral projects. US firms occupy the first place in the world in exports of complete industrial plants. This type of export is also growing rapidly in Poland; in particular, the Polish organization Polimex-Cekop has considerable experience in the exporting of complete plants. American and Polish companies could extend this form of delivery cooperation to third markets, primarily in developing countries. For example, American companies may serve as prime contractors or participate in various consortia with Polish partners or with Polish and host country enterprises. This concept of multilateral cooperation is based on the assumption that, in a world of growing competition and political preferences of an increasing number of developing countries to diversify their commercial and technical contacts, even large US firms cannot afford to "go it alone" in all markets.

Tripartite cooperation, which may take the form of a joint stock company with agreed contributions and proportionate sharing of profits, should always be based on the specialization of partners. In this respect, Polish lines of specialization are widely known in the developing countries, particularly those relating to coal mining, sugar mills, chemical plants, and other industrial projects. Poland can offer many technologies which are especially suitable for third world markets; it also has good political relations with many developing countries.

The Environment for IC in the US and in Poland

1. Our joint research and the two conferences have made clear the need for a much better understanding by each side of the internal economic environment and the basic legal and organizational frameworks for IC. Of great interest to the US side is an improved understanding of the informational, organizational, incentive, and decisionmaking environments in Poland. Of particular interest and concern to the Polish side is an improved understanding of US corporate strategies and decisionmaking regarding IC in Eastern Europe, and how IC might help to alleviate for Polish firms the problem of protectionism in the US.

2. One of the conclusions of the Bloomington conference was that future prospects for increased IC are linked closely to further changes in the planning and management system in Poland. In improving the planning system in Poland, it is essential to take into account the specific requirements of IC, particularly with respect to achieving an appropriate balance between long-term planning and short-term flexibility. This is important in view of the fact that successful IC requires both partners to adapt quickly and efficiently to continually changing world technical and marketing conditions.

3. One of the conclusions of the Warsaw conference was that the legal and procedural environment in the US affecting Polish exports and IC deliveries is different from those typical in Western Europe. For example, the Executive Branch of the US government has much more limited discretionary power to adjudicate controversies between US and Polish interests than is the case in Western Europe or Japan. Polish firms and decisionmakers should be acquainted with these differences.

Critically important to Polish firms is the so-called "injury test" employed by the US International Trade Commission under which Polish manufactures exports face special barriers. We recommend that the criteria for finding injury be spelled out more clearly in order to aid Polish enterprises in making investment, production, and marketing plans. IC may help overcome trade barriers to the US because it is unlikely that the specific components or semifinished products delivered to the US under ICAs or subcontracting would be subject to dumping, market disruption or similar charges.

4. US businessmen are sometimes concerned that ICAs with Polish firms may create more competition; but these fears, though understandable, should not be exaggerated. The movement toward IC between firms in different countries is a long-term trend which increases the efficiency of both partners and creates new market opportunities in the respective countries and on third markets. US concerns with creating new competition due to the transfer of technology to Poland

can be alleviated if this transfer takes place within the context of long-term coproduction agreements, possibly linked with worldwide marketing arrangements.

5. To improve the environment for IC, reporting in the US and Polish media about the economic situation in both countries should be more detailed and less biased. Reports stressing repeatedly, for example, only the problems of the other economy create an important psychological barrier for firms that might otherwise be willing to consider commercial or industrial cooperation agreements.

Suggestions for Further Research

1. We believe that further theoretical and practical research on IC would be extremely useful to our academic, business, banking, and government experts and decisionmakers. The collaborative research between American and Polish scholars that this project has pioneered should be continued, for it provides significant payoffs to both sides. Close research cooperation facilitates access to the literature and expertise available in the other country on IC and related topics, guards against one-sidedness in the research perspective and recommendations, and stimulates better identification of important problems, better choice of appropriate research methodology, and a balanced interpretation of findings.

2. Further studies are needed to identify and help eliminate obstacles to IC found on both sides. Additional case studies of both successful and unsuccessful ICAs would help identify specific factors that account for successful negotiations and implementations of ICAs and factors that can explain the failures.

3. Specific problems on which joint or parallel research would be very useful include:

a. The influence of the Western business cycle on the attitudes and policies of US firms (perhaps by size of firm, by industrial sector, or by type of product or technology) and of government and private financial institutions toward IC may be investigated.

b. The influence of the status of America's and Poland's global and bilateral balance of payments on the attitudes and policies of the respective governments toward IC. On the US side, a possible impact could be on the availability and terms of credit; on the Polish side, the type of IC project which would be approved by the Polish government.

c. The impact of various political bodies and organized interests on government and business policy affecting IC may be investigated. In the US, the discretionary powers of the executive and legislative branches of government and those of the independent agencies (such as the US International Trade Commission), and the position and importance of labor unions and other powerful lobby groups could be better understood. In Poland, of interest would be to understand better the attitude toward IC of the various levels in the administrative hierarchy of the country and the position and influence of the trade unions.

d. What is the role of the CMEA, and especially CMEA specialization agreements, in promoting Polish-US IC? Our joint research has established that one of the important motives of large American firms for East-West IC is to facilitate penetrating other CMEA markets. US firms need to understand better both how the current and prospective mechanisms of CMEA integration may promote US-Polish IC and how such agreements may contribute to the regional or subregional integration of CMEA members.

e. Commercial interface problems need to be investigated when the rules and practices of market and planned economies differ. An important problem area is the protection of domestic industries against foreign competition. US firms would like to understand better the role that the new economic reforms will play in the Polish economy; Polish enterprises would like to understand better the criteria in the US for invoking dumping, market disruption, and other import-limiting procedures affecting their exports.

f. The more complex ICAs become and the closer the horizontal and vertical integration between US and Polish firms, such as under coproduction or joint venture projects, the greater will be the importance of financial and accounting issues, which need to be carefully investigated. A key issue in joint ventures, for example, is the appropriate exchange rate; the absence of a meaningful exchange rate for the zloty prevents the full integration of a joint venture into the Polish economy and creates a host of other issues, such as profit repatriation and salary equity between US and Polish employees of a firm. Inflation and fluctuations in Western currency values also raise difficult issues which affect IC prospects and contracts and these will need to be studied.

Notes

1. Excellent summaries and synthesis of this literature can be found in C. T. Saunders (ed.), *East-West Cooperation in Business: Interfirm Studies* (Vienna: Springer-Verlag, 1977); Carl H. McMillan, "East-West Industrial Cooperation," in *East European Economies Post Helsinki: A Compendium of Papers Submitted to the Joint Economic Committee, Congress of the United States* (Washington, D.C.: GPO, 1977); F. Levcik and J. Stankovsky, *Industrial Cooperation Between East and West* (White Plains, N.Y.: M. E. Sharpe, Inc., 1979); Carl H. McMillan, "Trends in East-West Industrial Cooperation," paper presented at the Second World Congress of Soviet and East European Studies, Garmisch, Federal Republic of Germany, October 1980; W. Trzeciakowski, *Indirect Management in a Centrally Planned Economy* (Amsterdam; North-Holland, 1978); and E. Tabaczynski, *Wspolpraca inwestycyjna Wschod-Zachod*

[East-West Investment Cooperation] (Warsaw: Panstwowc Wydawnictwo Ekonomiczne, 1981).

2. For example, Paul Marer, "US-CMEA Industrial Cooperation in the Chemical Industry," in C. T. Saunders, *op.cit.;* H. Radice, "Experiences of East-West Industrial Cooperation: A Case Study of UK Firms in the Electronics, Telecommunications and Precision Engineering Industries," in *op.cit.*

3. For example, Paul Marer and Joseph C. Miller, "US Participation in East-West Industrial Cooperation Agreements," *Journal of International Business Studies,* Fall/Winter, 1977; E. Tabaczynski, *Kooperacja przemyslowa z zagranica* [Industrial Cooperation with Abroad] (Warsaw: Panstwowe Wydawnictwo Ekonomiczne, 1976).

4. For example, UN, Economic Commission for Europe, *Analytical Report on Industrial Cooperation Among ECE Countries* (Geneva: 1973) and *East-West Industrial Cooperation* (same author and publisher, 1979).

5. Carl H. McMillan, "Trends . . ." *op. cit.*

6. Carl H. McMillan, "East-West . . ." *op. cit.*

7. HSW has been an independent organization, not affiliated formally with the BUMAR Union structure, since July 1, 1979. BUMAR FTO, however, remains responsible for its foreign transactions, as before.

8. By 1974, Poland (i.e., mainly BUMAR) had been granted specialization rights within the CMEA for eleven types of loaders, four types of excavators, three types of crawler tractors, twelve types of self-propelled cranes, and 40 other types of construction machinery and equipment.

9. IH had also hoped to integrate BUMAR into its West German operations, using Polish components for its Payloader (front-end wheel loaders) line. This did not materialize. It was largely a matter of meeting the very high technical requirements of IH and of having to spread over too long a time the essential but highly capital-intensive investments in BUMAR facilities. This is why BUMAR did not reach the desired results as quickly as it wanted to.

10. Business International, *Corporate Strategy, Planning, Organization and Personnel Practices for Eastern Europe* (Geneva: Business International, 1977) and G.P. Lauter, "East-West Trade Organizational Structures and Problems of U.S. Multinational Corporations," in M.R. Jackson and J. Woodson (eds.), *New Horizons in East-West Economic Relations* (Boulder, Co.: East European Quarterly Press, forthcoming).

11. In 1979 Poland further liberalized legislation governing foreign equity investment in the country, as did Hungary in the same year. In 1980 Bulgaria also joined the ranks of countries permitting foreign equity participation in domestically-based enterprises. As a result, the majority of the seven East European countries now permit foreign direct investment based on equity participation. For a comparative analysis of joint venture legislation in Eastern Europe, see Deborah Lamb, "Potential for Western Direct Investment in Centrally Planned Economies." Paper presented at the International Conference on Multinational Corporations in Latin America and Eastern Europe, Indiana University, Bloomington, March 5-8, 1981. See also E. Tabaczynski, *East-West Cooperation, op. cit.*

12. In February 1979, the Polish Central Union of Work Cooperatives tentatively identified industries and products where its affiliated cooperatives would have the capability and interest to enter into subcontracting of ICAs with American firms. These include: leather, sport, and travel articles: candles, cosmetics, brushes, household articles; ready-made clothing of all kinds; folk articles, such as kilims, regional tapestries, furniture; electric blankets; electroinstruments; saunas; non-ferrous metal castings; steam and gas sterilizers; plastic and rubber articles produced by injection and press moulding; latex gloves; soft plush, textile, floating, and wooden toys; all kinds of items in the glass and tile industries; fireplaces made of semi-precious minerals; restaurant fittings in folk or rustic style; constructing and equipping small industrial plants in developing countries.

13. Such projects, for instance, as those with Massey Ferguson (Perkins tractor plant in Ursus), the Polish airlines hotel complex being built by Cementation Ltd (British) in Warsaw, the PCV complex under construction at Wloclawek (British), the fertilizer factory in Police (France), the paper plant in Kwidzyn (Canada) are intended to be continued.

PART II
INTERNATIONAL HARVESTER-BUMAR COOPERATION

CONTENTS

BACKGROUND FOR THE CASE STUDY   43

Introduction   43

A. Industrial Cooperation: Definitions and Significance   45
    1. Definitions   45
    2. Significance of IC in East-West Commerce   46
    3. IC in US-Polish Economic Relations   47
B. The Construction Equipment Industry in the US and
    Poland   48
    1. The Industry: An Overview   48
    2. Competitive Structure of the Industry   51
        The Industrial West Region   51
        The Construction Equipment Industry in Poland   52
C. The US Partner: International Harvester   53
    1. Overview   53
    2. History   53
    3. Foreign Operations   54
    4. Postwar Organization, Strategy, and Performance   55
    5. The Pay Line Group   55
        Reorganizatin   56
        Marketing   57
        Overseas Investment Patterns   57
        Product Line Expansion   58
D. The Polish Partner: BUMAR   59

NEGOTIATING AND IMPLEMENTING
  THE AGREEMENTS   60

A. Negotiations   60
B. The Series of Agreements, 1972-79   61
C. Motives   62
D. Principles of Payment for License and Know-how   65
E. Industrial Cooperation with a Western Partner and
    CMEA Specialization   66
F. Investments Required   66
G. Marketing Arrangements   67
H. Quality Control   68
I. Pricing IH Sales to and Purchases from BUMAR   69
J. Two-Way Flow of Payments   71
K. Technical, Commercial, and Financial Risks   71
L. BUMAR's Integration with IH European Operations   74
    1. Great Britain   74
    2. West Germany   75
    3. France   76

Notes

INTERNATIONAL HARVESTER— BUMAR COOPERATION

The Manufacture and Marketing of Construction Machinery, A Case Study

US and Polish Teams*

BACKGROUND FOR THE CASE STUDY

Introduction

After several years of exploratory discussions and negotiations, in 1972 a ten-year industrial cooperation agreement (ICA) was signed between International Harvester (IH) and BUMAR Foreign Trade Organization (FTO) to manufacture in Poland crawler tractors designed and engineered by IH. Since the original agreement, the product line covered by the agreement has been expanded to include addi-

*Members are: J. Brada, R. Campbell, J. Garland, J. Giezgala, J. Kaczurba, Z. Kossut, J. Kozinski, P. Marer, J. Miller, H. Perlmutter, J. Szumski, E. Tabaczynski, T. Wolf, and E. Zagorski. To illustrate the meaning and content of industrial cooperation, this statement describes in some detail the International Harvester-BUMAR coproduction project. Although we discussed the negotiations and implementation of the agreement with executives of International Harvester and the BUMAR group, the assessment herein reflects our understanding and interpretation and not necessarily that of either International Harvester or BUMAR.

tional types of construction machinery, the duration of the agreement has been extended, and new joint activities have been initiated. This series of agreements has increased IH's worldwide manufacturing capacity and given BUMAR FTO previously unavailable access to technology and markets.

In preparation for the research on this case study, the two teams made a thorough analysis of the literature on East-West industrial cooperation (IC), and then drew up an annotated list of critical issues to be investigated (see Appendix 1, p. 399). This was not a formal questionnaire, but an internal document to guide the two teams in their interviews with IH and BUMAR. New issues arising during the course of the interviews were also pursued.

A series of interviews was conducted independently by both teams, with many people at different levels at IH and BUMAR as well as at those supervising organs in Poland whose activities may have an influence on negotiating or implementing the ICA. Reciprocal visits permitted the US team to interview executives of BUMAR and other relevant bodies in Poland, and the Polish team to conduct discussions with executives of IH in the US. For example, in Poland both teams independently interviewed people at the production plant, association, union, FTO, industrial ministry, and the Ministry of Foreign Trade and Shipping; in the US, both teams conducted interviews with IH personnel ranging from shop floor foremen to top executives.

Because the interviews were conducted over a two-year period (1978-79), it was possible to arrange follow-up meetings to clarify certain issues and to check on the progress of projects. The cross-interviewing was interspersed with periodic meetings of members of the two teams. After each team's independent evaluation of its interview results, their non-confidential findings were jointly discussed.

Because the two sides started with an agreed set of questions and developed the answers in a somewhat parallel fashion, we concluded that only one case study should be published. The two case studies were, therefore, "merged," using the US case study as a point of departure.

*   *   *

Is the IH-BUMAR ICA typical of the type of agreements entered into by American and Polish firms and of the future potential for cooperation between enterprises in the two countries? In attempting to answer this question, it must be recognized that until recently only about a half dozen ICAs, somewhat comparable to the IH-BUMAR project in terms of current size, complexity, and duration, had been signed. However, each of these agreements was signed with a Polish partner subordinated to the Ministry of Machine Industry; enterprises under that Ministry account for approximately 80 percent of Poland's IC-related trade turnover with all Western partners.[1]

Because the IH-BUMAR ICA has evolved from a simple license agreement to a complex joint project, much can be learned that is relevant for other projects. It is our view that this case study's findings—regarding the motives and initial approaches of the partners, the negotiations, how the ICA is being implemented, the problems that have arisen, and how they are being solved—offer practical insights for other projects. The study as a whole reflects quite well the "environment" for US-Polish IC at the end of the 1970s and at the beginning of the 1980s. If read in conjunction with the other contributions to this volume, the case study should provide a comprehensive and balanced perspective on US-Polish commercial relations and industrial cooperation.

Industrial Cooperation: Definition and Significance

1. Definitions

There is no internationally agreed upon definition of industrial cooperation (IC). One reason is that IC has emerged only since 1965 as an increasingly important dimension of East-West commercial relations. Furthermore, defining IC has been made difficult by the failure of most Western countries to keep formal registers of cooperation agreements or resultant transactions, while Council for Mutual Economic Assistance[2] countries have their own definitions of IC.

In the broadest sense of the term, IC connotes any commercial arrangement more complex than exports and imports, such as licensing, subcontracting, the building of turnkey plants involving repayment with resulting products, production or marketing cooperation in third countries, coproduction, joint research and development, and joint ventures. Such a broad definition was used in one of the most comprehensive studies of US involvement in East-West IC because it facilitates the consideration of a wide range of embodied and disembodied technology transfers, which is a key dimension of IC.[3]

International organizations, such as the UN's Economic Commission for Europe (ECE), have been systematically gathering data to determine the nature and forms of IC. The ECE has defined IC in an East-West context as

> the economic relationships and activities arising from (a) contracts extending over a number of years between partners . . . which go beyond the sale or purchase of goods and services to include a set of complementary or reciprocally matching operations (in production, in the development and transfer of technology, in marketing, etc.) and from

(b) contracts between such partners which have been identified as industrial cooperation contracts by Governments in bilateral or multilateral agreements.[4]

Part (b) of the definition has little operational significance and reflects,
we believe, the preference of some European countries for broad,
government-to-government "umbrella" agreements. While such
agreements help set the stage for IC, our primary concern is the operational activities of individual firms and enterprises. Because there
is no internationally accepted definition of IC, individual countries
and researchers have used their own.

It should be noted that the generally accepted Polish definition is
compatible with the UN concepts mentioned above. IC is defined in
Poland as

> economic cooperation between two or more partners in which: (a) the
> cooperating parties are producers (trade organizations may act as in-
> termediaries); (b) the cooperation consists in the supply of parts of final
> products or know-how or services according to technical specifications
> and time-table agreed upon by the cooperating parties; (c) the duration
> of the cooperation is planned for several years.[5]

2. Significance of IC in East-West Commerce

Having developed in an East-West context since 1965, the number
of ICAs is estimated to have reached more than 1,000 by the late
1970s.[6] No accurate measure exists, however, of the global value or
significance of IC, for several reasons. Commercial activities under IC
cannot be easily separated from exports and imports under current
methods of reporting trade statistics. Also, there is no common de-
nominator for valuing the different forms of IC. They vary, not only
with respect to duration, but also in terms of the composition of partner contributions (which can be tangible or intangible, such as
technology, machinery, entrepreneurship, brand name, access to a
worldwide marketing organization) as well as derived benefits (which
may not be easily quantifiable, such as improved penetration of third
country markets and technological and organizational spillover effects). Therefore, the significance of IC cannot be measured by a
single indicator, such as value of total turnover, duration of the
agreements, or hard currency exports generated. The conventional
approach has been to count the number of ICAs. Based on that approach, Hungary leads all East European countries in IC with the
West; but because Hungarian IC projects are typically smaller than
those in Poland, Poland's IC-related turnover is almost certainly
larger than Hungary's. On the other hand, the USSR, having fewer
ICAs with the West than Poland, typically prefers large turnkey proj-

ects to the more complex forms found in Poland, so it has a larger value of IC turnover with the West.

Quite apart from these difficulties, an entirely different approach to the question of significance may be taken by focusing on the role that the two partners assign to IC. For the Eastern partner, the point of departure must be the foreign economic policy of the state. Poland is typical of the centrally planned economies (CPEs) in that its foreign economic policy is subordinated to such national objectives as modernizing the economy, fostering specialization through the international division of labor, and maximizing exports to increase imports and reduce balance-of-payments pressures.[7] The state desires and promotes IC with Western partners to help fulfill these objectives. IC facilitates the transfer, absorption, and diffusion of technology; often diminishes investment outlays; provides access to Western markets through improved quality and via the partner's marketing channels; decreases production costs; and encourages specialization in manufactures, which in turn can improve the structure of exports. The state, therefore, attempts to create an environment and a system of incentives under which the industrial ministries and producing enterprises will find it attractive to seek out and implement ICAs with Western firms. This approach held in the mid-1970s when emphasis shifted from building new productive facilities to modernizing existing facilities. It is necessary to underscore, however, that IC, irrespective of the state economic policy, does not as a rule provoke new tensions in international payment flow. On the contrary, it may contribute to the lessening of tension in the balance-of-payments of cooperating countries.

On the Western side, the concerns of the individual firms are dominant. For a typical Western firm, IC may represent a viable strategy to gain better access to the CMEA market, to obtain a competitively priced source of components and finished products, to expand production capacity with minimal investment, and to gain from the research and development activities of the Eastern partner.

3. IC in US-Polish Economic Relations[8]

It is difficult to assess the US competitive position vis-à-vis Western countries in regard to East-West IC because of the definitional problems referred to above, the lack of accurate statistical data, and foreign subsidiaries' role in implementation. Nevertheless, it has been concluded that the US no longer lags significantly behind its competitors in penetrating the CMEA market through ICAs.[9] Among the East European countries of the CMEA (omitting the USSR), Poland is clearly the number one partner of American firms. At the end of 1976, according to a US study using a very broad definition of IC, US firms had concluded 74 ICAs with Polish enterprises and had several dozen other agreements under negotiation or exploration.

Of the 74 US-Polish ICAs, 7 were primarily know-how agreements; 26 were basically direct licensing and 9 indirect (i.e., implemented through foreign subsidiaries) licensing agreements; 22 were turnkey projects; 4 involved subcontracting; and 6 were coproduction agreements.[10]

These ICAs have played a significant role in increasing the trade turnover between Poland and the US, which increased fourfold between 1972 and 1977. During that five-year period, Polish exports to the US tripled and Polish imports from the US rose fivefold.[11] This trend continued in 1978, when Polish exports to the US rose by 20 percent and imports from the US rose by 25 percent. Nevertheless, US-Polish trade represents less than .5 percent of total US trade, and representatives of both countries feel that there is considerable room for improvement.

In 1976 and 1977 the US ranked third in coproduction agreements, and in 1978 it ranked fourth in cooperation between Poland and Western countries. Some of the largest Polish ICAs have been with American firms.[12] Successful ICAs have been concluded with International Harvester (IH), Clark Equipment, Singer Corporation, and RCA and Corning Glass Works. Of these, the ICA IH concluded with BUMAR is one of the oldest (Clark's ICA was also initiated in 1972), apparently one of the most successful, and without question one of the most complex and comprehensive. As the case study indicates, the IH-BUMAR ICA has a wide range of products and involves many functional areas, such as production, product support, product service, marketing, and joint design activities. Due to an increasing commitment to enter into increasingly complex arrangements since 1972, the IH-BUMAR ICA now covers every major activity usually associated with manufacturing and marketing a line of products, from product development to final marketing and after-sales service. Consequently, it is an excellent illustration of the essence of IC.

B. The Construction Equipment Industry in the US and Poland

1. The Industry: An Overview

Since the IH-BUMAR ICA involves the joint production of construction machinery, it will be helpful to have some idea of the general characteristics of the industry and its competitive structure. The major exporting countries in the industry are indicated in table 1.

The world's construction and industrial equipment industry had sales of approximately $14 billion in 1978. Projections indicate that within five years, the volume will climb to $18 billion. Three factors are considered fundamentally important bases for these projections.[13]

1. Growing world population demands more natural resources, the supply of which depends in part on using more construction equipment.

2. Many developing countries and CPEs have undertaken large-scale development programs. Their success largely depends on a fundamental upgrading of the economic infrastructure, which in turn requires extensive use of construction equipment.[14]

3. The energy crisis has stimulated the development of new energy sources in many countries. This in turn stimulates the production of coal mining machinery, pipe-laying equipment for oil and gas, and excavating equipment.

There is a great diversity of products in the industry, which has recently been complemented by a large number of product innovations. This trend is due, in part, to the switch from gasoline to diesel power sources and to the engineering refinements being made to conserve fuel and limit noise emissions.[15] But in spite of this diversity, 85 percent of the worldwide unit volume in construction and industrial machinery is accounted for by four basic types of machines: industrial wheel tractors, crawler tractors, hydraulic excavators, and wheel loaders.[16]

It is diffult to distinguish precisely between construction and industrial equipment. The distinction is based more on the specific use of the machinery than on the types of machinery involved. Originally, construction machinery was associated with earth-moving activities, and industrial equipment with a variety of jobs connected with construction services, grounds keeping, public works installations, forestry, material handling, and other industrial applications. But the term "industrial market" is misleading. For example, a farmer who in his spare time used his tractor with a backhoe attachment to dig irrigation ditches was once the prime customer of the industrial equipment market. At one time, "industrial equipment" referred to machinery up to 100 hp, and size was used to distinguish it from construction equipment. This distinction is no longer valid. Today's industrial equipment often goes beyond 100 hp, while construction machinery reflects a trend toward smaller machines as the market (in the US) changes from road construction to urban development projects.[17]

There are thousands of manufacturing firms in the industry worldwide, but none produce the complete product line. The industry is dominated by Caterpillar Tractor Co., which has half of the Western market, and a half dozen giant firms competing for second place (see pp. 00-00). During the last three decades there has been a noticeable trend toward consolidation and integration in the US, and in the last decade the same phenomenon can be observed worldwide. This trend, reflected in part by a series of acquisitions of subsidiaries by the major producers, is the result of intensified competition and is related to the huge capital requirements of the industry.

The dominant producers are all multi-industry firms; that is, they are involved in other lines of machinery production as well as construction equipment. Historically, the US construction equipment industry has been closely associated with the farm equipment industry, which partly explains its geographic concentration in the Midwest. However, its major firms have also produced railroad equipment (Westinghouse), trucks (GM and White Motors), machine tools (Warner and Swasey), materials handling equipment (Clark), and diesel engines (Caterpillar in 1972 committed itself to contend in this sector through internal diversification).[18]

A large and growing demand has made possible a scale of production large enough for standardization and mass production.[19] Economies of scale are important because volumes are relatively small. However, the scale required for such economies varies according to the individual products. It ranges from mere hundreds (in the case of graders or off-highway dump trucks) to 3 or 4 thousand (in the case of hydraulic excavators or wheel loaders).

With so many firms in the industry (more than 800 in Europe), the strategic choice of product is crucial. The range of equipment is so wide that no single producer could hope to meet every need, which leaves room for small and medium-sized companies to compete. Most of the smaller companies specialize in only one or two products, while the larger companies have relatively full lines. In other words, a company may try to create its own niche with a highly specialized product in which few others are interested; it may select one product and try to achieve higher quality in that class than its competitors; or it may try to compete across a broad line. The advantage of the full-line supplier is primarily in stronger distributorships, which usually have strong service facilities.

The diversity of the industry is reflected not only in the product lines, multi-industry affiliations, and size of firms, but also in the tendency of distributors to handle the products of more than one company. Only a small percentage of the approximately 1,500 US dealers handle one manufacturer's products exclusively. This stems not only from the economies of distribution, but also from the traditional practice of selling specialized attachments separately from the basic machines.[20]

Competitive advantage in the industry stems not from product technology, but from process technology.[21] That is, the disembodied technology of organizational know-how and production processes seems to be more important for competitive position than the uniqueness of a firm's product. The finished products are often comprised of thousands of individual pieces, few of which are technologically unique.[22] IH's 300 hp crawler tractor has only one patent, sublicensed from Caterpillar, and it involves a seal.[23] The critical difference among firms, consequently, lies in manufacturing know-how (such as heat tolerance, metallurgical practices, and tooling) and in the efficiency of operations, including distribution and service.

2. Competitive Structure of the Industry

*The Industrial West Region.*Caterpillar Tractor Company holds approximately half of the Western World's market in the construction equipment industry. Behind Caterpillar worldwide comes Komatsu Ltd., with about 10 percent of the market. Competing for third place are J. I. Case, IH, John Deere, Clark Equipment, and Fiat-Allis, each with approximately 6 percent of the market. It is important to note, however, that the leading competitors are multi-industry firms (see Table 2). At least four of the six industry leaders listed have entered (IH, Clark, and Massey-Ferguson) or are negotiating (Case) ICAs with Poland.

Caterpillar Tractor Company's size and the sophistication of its manufacturing processes are unrivaled. It has a large competitive advantage, due mainly to its early decision to specialize in construction equipment, to its distributive networks, and to its multinational activities, which were first seriously promoted during the 1950s. Nevertheless, it faces serious problems, the most fundamental of which is the question of diversification into new product lines in view of changing environmental conditions, which seem to favor smaller machines.

J.I. Case's 40 percent acquisition of Poclain of France in 1977 has given both companies expanded marketing outlets and a broadened product line. Since 1972, Case has acquired majority stakes in several smaller European construction equipment manufacturers and is trying to strengthen and diversify its international operations. In 1979 the company was still (after 2 years) trying to successfully negotiate an ICA with BUMAR for the production of cranes.

A detailed description of IH's organization and construction equipment activities will be presented in the next section. Its construction equipment line is handled by the Pay Line Group, which is one of five worldwide product groups comprising the company. Construction equipment sales account for only 12.8 percent of company sales. Consequently, although IH is one of the largest multinational companies in the US, its construction equipment branch is less than one-fifth the size of Caterpillar. The IH line is primarily loaders and crawlers and industrial equipment; Caterpillar has a much broader line.

John Deere, considered by some industry observers to be Caterpillar's most important competitor, is rapidly expanding its capacity for construction equipment in the US and intensifying its marketing efforts in Europe. Deere's strategy seems to be directed toward using farm tractors, in which its competitive strength lies, and to fit them with attachments for construction work—a strategy well adapted to changing environmental requirements.

Clark Equipment Company has just completed a five-year campaign to strengthen its traditional lines of lift trucks and construction equipment. Like IH, Clark entered into an ICA with BUMAR in 1972, but the ICA involves only heavy driving axles for wheeled construction machines.

Massey-Ferguson, primarily a producer of farm equipment, has recently divested itself of its unprofitable construction equipment business. The company has an ICA with Poland for farm tractors, as well as supplementary licensing agreements for bearings and diesel engines.

There is limited cooperation among Western European firms, and several are particularly strong in their own domestic markets. However, except for narrow product lines, none is particularly strong in the industry as a whole. Recently, however, they have begun to promote exports. Similarly, the large domestic market of the Japanese provides a solid base for exports, and several Japanese companies, led by Komatsu, have made significant inroads in the Far East and Africa. Until the early 1960s, US manufacturers led in both producing and selling construction equipment throughout the world; in recent years, European manufacturers have narrowed the lead. Yet certain areas of the European market are swamped by both foreign and domestic companies who make similar machines, who are fiercely competitive, and who exist on smaller profit margins than had been the case earlier. The resulting limited profitability has tended to inhibit the expansion of sales and service networks.[24]

*The Construction Equipment Industry in Poland.*The BUMAR Union of Construction Machinery Industry, subordinate to the Ministry of Machine Industry, is primarily responsible for the manufacture and sale of construction equipment in Poland. The branch of construction equipment includes two other organizations, although they are oriented to the domestic market and are much smaller than the BUMAR Union: the ZREMB Building Industry Mechanization Union, subordinate to the Ministry of Construction Work and Construction Materials Industry, and the MADRO Building Machinery Construction and Repair Works, subordinate to the Ministry of Transportation.

As the leading producer of construction equipment in Poland, BUMAR Union has chosen a strategy of development based on exports. Table 3 reflects the strong CMEA orientation in its exports, which is supported by numerous specialization rights. Exports for a country the size of Poland are crucial in this sector, due to the economies of scale they provide. The value of BUMAR machines supplied to the USSR amounts to 50 percent of all Union exports to CMEA countries.[25]

In 1978, BUMAR's export offerings included hydraulic excavators, wheeled loaders, crawler tractors (fitted with bulldozer blade, loader attachment, and pipelayer sideboom), self-propelled and truck-mounted cranes, truck-mounted concrete mixers, truck-tippers, and various components. Most of these lines have been developed through ICAs with Western firms (see p. 000). Table 4 indicates the heavy export orientation of the Union.

C. The US Partner: International Harvester

1. Overview

With 1978 sales totaling $6.66 billion, IH ranked on the *Fortune* 500 list as the 28th largest US industrial corporation.[26] But because IH is a multi-branch corporation, the industry position of its branches varies. Table 1 indicates its position in the construction equipment branch; table 5 shows the share of the four major industrial branches in IH's total 1978 sales. IH's 8 percent of the total US truck market is dwarfed by GM's 42 percent. Even in the manufacturing of heavy trucks in the US, a sector in which IH enjoys industry leadership, competitors make trucks more profitably. When GM and Ford increased their efforts aimed at this segment in the 1960s, IH's market share dropped from 30 percent to 24 percent. In farm machinery sales, Deere has a comfortable lead over IH.

In 1971, one year before the ICA with BUMAR was signed, IH reportedly had reached a point where it was virtually all sales and no profits.[27] Although the company ranked 35th among US companies in total sales, it ranked only 202nd in net profits. IH was bigger overall than most of its competitors, but it was smaller in each of its major lines, although this alone does not explain the low profitability of its operations.

2. History

IH and its predecessor companies have been in business for almost 150 years, nearly always under the direction of the McCormick family. Operations began in 1831 when Cyrus Hall McCormick perfected the reaper (a harvesting machine)—one of the most important technological advances in the world at the time—which started the transition to mechanized farming.[28] In the 1880s IH experimented with internal combustion engines to motorize farm equipment. Experimental work on the first IH tractor began in 1905, and the first all-IH tractors were produced in 1908. There was also experimental work on a farm truck, and by 1915 the prototype of the present IH truck was produced. It was not until 1944 that the IH Construction Equipment Division was created.

In 1902 McCormick's organization joined with the other leading manufacturer of agricultural equipment, Deering Harvester Company, and three smaller concerns to form the International Harvester Company. The objectives of the merger were to develop new products, to bring about a more diversified line, and to give more attention to the foreign market.

3. Foreign Operations

IH had been active in international trade since 1851, but it was only in 1909 that factories were established in several European countries to supplement its many sales outlets around the world. IH had a long history of exports to Russia before World War I, and had export as well as concession operations in the USSR between the two world wars. With $660 million of exports in 1977, IH was the 13th largest US industrial exporter that year. Today, IH markets in more than 160 countries and has major manufacturing subsidiaries in Great Britain, West Germany, France, Mexico, and Australia, and smaller manufacturing operations in 13 other countries. Continued expansion of foreign production capacity is indicated by the establishment in May 1978 of a joint venture in Mexico (IH has 40 percent equity, Fasa 60 percent) to manufacture medium and heavy-duty diesel trucks. This venture is in addition to the IH subsidiary in Mexico that manufactures agricultural equipment. Joint ventures have also been established in Japan, India, Turkey, and Venezuela.

Since the early 1970s, IH has also been involved in the CMEA countries. In 1972 it sold $40 million worth of bulldozers and pipelayers to the USSR, followed in 1974 with $115 million worth of equipment sales for the BAM Siberian rail line. IH's total business with the USSR during the 1970s reached about $250 million in 1977.[29] In 1976, IH signed an umbrella agreement on scientific and technical cooperation with the USSR, which provided for potential industrial cooperation in research and development, design, and manufacture of agricultural tractors and equipment, trucks, and construction equipment. The protocol represented a framework for negotiating subsequent specific agreements.

In March 1977, IH signed a 10-year agreement with a Hungarian enterprise to coproduce several IH farm implements.[30] But IH's longest and strongest postwar ties in the CMEA have been in Poland, where in 1972 it signed a complex ICA with BUMAR for the production of construction equipment. In addition, according to US sources, in 1977 IH's Truck Group began negotiations with Pol-Mot of Poland regarding a joint truck program.

4. Postwar Organization, Strategy, and Performance

Since the Second World War, IH had been a leader in sales but a poor profit performer. During 1966-71, it increased sales by 3.1 percent per annum while profits declined by 16.3 percent per annum, on average. By the early 1970s it needed new capital badly, but could find virtually no outside sources. It had a relatively large corporate debt that it could not reduce by raising an adequate amount of capital through new stock offerings, so that retained earnings became virtually its only capital source.[31] This severe judgment of the financial markets finally prompted IH to introduce a comprehensive program to reverse its profit performance. The objective was to attack the persistent problems of overstaffing, excessive production costs, and lack of corporate direction and control.[32] The program had four major features:

1. Decentralization of authority by delegating greater operating responsibility and profit accountability to component units.

2. Greater participation of middle and lower management in long-range planning.[33]

3. A revised managerial incentive program.

4. A complete reorganization of the company into five basic business groups, each with worldwide scope, which further delegated authority and responsibility.[34]

As background for the case study, our immediate concern is with the fourth measure, which resulted in dividing IH into five basic business groups, delineated by the uniqueness of its products, markets, and the requirements to achieve profitability: agricultural equipment, trucks, construction and industrial equipment, turbo machinery, and components. Each group was given relative autonomy and worldwide scope to utilize the advantages of IH's global distribution system and sourcing capability. Decentralization was coupled, however, with an improved method of financial control.

As part of the campaign since 1971 to introduce a new era of efficiency, in September 1977 IH broke tradition and for the first time reached outside the company to appoint a new chief executive officer (CEO). Within six months, the new CEO had reduced employment by 3,000 through terminations, hiring freezes, and early retirements— steps quite different from the paternalistic practices that characterized the company in earlier years.[35]

After the reorganization, the company's new construction and industrial equipment group was named Pay Line. This group accounts for approximately 12 percent of company-wide sales and is the IH unit that implements the ICA with BUMAR.

5. The Pay Line Group[36]

Pay Line's predecessor, the Construction Equipment Division of

IH, was created in 1944 with three principal factories (two in Chicago and one in Milwaukee). In 1952, IH acquired as a subsidiary the Hough Company, which became the Hough Division of IH in 1965, specializing in rubber-tired loaders. These divisions were consolidated into the Pay Line Division in 1974, which became an autonomous group after a new corporate reorganization in 1977. The Pay Line Group specializes in construction and industrial equipment. Were it a separate company, it would rank as the 281st largest US industrial corporation.

Today, Pay Line Group has US-based plants and units in Libertyville, Illinois (pay loaders, pay movers, pay haulers, pay scrapers, and material handling equipment); Melrose Park, Illinois (crawler tractors); Gulfport, Mississippi (Pay Line Product Distribution Company; wheeled industrial tractors); and Springfield, Missouri (Pay Line ReNEW Center, for the remanufacture of components for Pay Line products). It also manufactures pay loaders in Candiac Quebec, Canada. Pay Line Group has major subsidiary operations in Doncaster, Great Britain (crawler tractors and wheeled industrial tractors); Chauffailes and Genas, France (excavators); and Heidelberg, Germany (pay loaders and engines). It has smaller subsidiaries in Mexico and New Zealand. Pay Line has over 600 distributors worldwide (approximately 70 in the US). Its construction equipment distributors tend to supply the larger pieces of equipment and to have multiple outlets, whereas its industrial equipment distributors tend to supply smaller vehicles and to have single outlets.

Pay Line Group set an objective for itself in 1979: to become, within the next five years, the number two construction equipment producer in the world (behind Caterpillar). The group has set its medium-term goal at doubling worldwide sales to $2 billion annually, anticipating that profits should rise at an even faster rate. Pay Line's strategy focuses on coordinated adjustment in four areas: reorganization, marketing, overseas investment patterns, and expansion of the product line.

Reorganization. When a new president took control of the Pay Line Group early in 1977, he initiated a worldwide reorganization aimed at increased efficiency through the better utilization of facilities and standardization of the product line. The actions taken have affected the relationship of the group's headquarters to its subsidiaries as well as to its suppliers.

Better utilization of facilities was deemed necessary because the factories were operating at less than capacity; a larger volume of production would reduce unit production costs. To eliminate unnecessary functions and to consolidate others for cost efficiency, the operations of each factory, including each support system (material scheduling, production scheduling, purchasing, and so on), were put under close scrutiny and revamped as necessary. The efforts have already paid off to some extent. Within one year Pay Line has increased average plant utilization from 55 to 65 percent; 80 percent utilization is its present goal.

Moreover, Pay Line Group is in the process of implementing a new purchasing strategy: (1) buy at the best possible price anywhere in the world and build a product at the lowest possible cost; and (2) shift from outside vendors to in-house production if economical. The strategy is designed to trim purchasing costs between 7 and 10 percent and increase market share by 1 percent annually.[37]

It is interesting that IH's decentralization, making the Pay Line Group a relatively autonomous unit, has been accompanied by centralization within the Pay Line Group itself to solve the problem of inefficient duplication.[38] In the past, when an IH subsidiary manufactured two or more products belonging to more than one industry (for example, combines and crawler tractors), one was given priority as the "host" product and the other was designated "guest," with the subsidiary being subordinated to the group responsible for the "host" product. This meant that in certain cases, Pay Line Group did not have direct line authority over units that manufactured part of its product line.[39]

Marketing. Increased volume of production is essential to Pay Line's improved profitability. The new "marketing thrust," calling for increased marketing efforts directed at specific geographical targets, was partly responsible for Pay Line's sales increase from $731 million in 1977 to $852 million in 1978. Much effort has been concentrated in the heavily populated Pacific island area (mainly Thailand, Indonesia, and the Philippines), whose market growth exceeds world average, and also in West Africa and South America. In these three areas, Pay Line forecasted a 35 to 40 percent increase in sales in 1978 over 1977. Intensified marketing efforts are also being undertaken in the Middle East and in North America. The medium-term goal is to improve market penetration worldwide by 5 or 6 percent by 1983, which implies an average annual growth of 20 percent. Only in Europe has the market been relatively flat for Pay Line, although even there sales were up slightly in 1978.

Overseas Investment Patterns. To supplement its fully owned foreign subsidiaries, Pay Line is entering into joint ventures or licensing, especially in countries where the possibilities of direct foreign investment are limited, such as Poland and Japan. A joint venture with Komatsu, for example, now gets about 40 percent of the Japanese market for rubber-tired loaders and also opens up new export markets in other Pacific countries.

Product Line Expansion. The broadening of Pay Line Group's product line primarily affects construction equipment, where there is a need for bigger machines with more horsepower to offset rising labor costs. Pay Line is introducing larger excavators and backhoe loaders. IH's Solar Group, producing gas turbines that, it is hoped, can eventually be installed in every piece of IH equipment, is working closely with Pay Line Group. Although nearly all Pay Line vehicles are diesel-powered, the Group's long-range strategy takes into consideration potential technological and energy-related developments.

D. The Polish Partner: BUMAR

In Poland, the sixth largest exporter of construction machinery in the world, three industry associations produce construction machinery and equipment:

1. BUMAR Union of Construction Machinery Industry, subordinate to the Ministry of Machine Industry.

2. ZREMB Union of Building Mechanization, subordinate to the Ministry of Building and Building Materials Industry.

3. MADRO Board of Road Building and Repair Works, subordinate to the Ministry of Transportation.

The three groups combined have 70 plants. The BUMAR Union produces 80 percent of the heavy-duty construction machinery in Poland and has its own research and development base. BUMAR is one of 18 industry unions that report directly to the Ministry of Machine Industry. As of June 1979, the BUMAR Union includes, in addition to its foreign trade organization (FTO), the giant Huta Stalowa Wola (HSW) machine building complex,[40] an enlarged construction equipment complex, BUMAR-Warynski in Warsaw (with a 150-year tradition in the industry), BUMAR-Labedy (a new combine producing hoisting and handling machines), Fadroma (a construction equipment factory in Wroclaw with an affiliated factory in Katy Wroclawski), Bipro-BUMAR (a design office for construction equipment in Lodz), and a research and development center in Warsaw with a testing lab at Ossow near Warsaw. There are smaller satellite plants attached to the larger factories. BUMAR's activities with US firms are aided by a section in the Polish Commercial Consulate in Chicago. BUMAR is planning to establish a wholly owned subsidiary office in Chicago by 1980, due in part to increased commercial contacts with American firms. BUMAR Union's production program includes general purpose excavators, wheeled loaders, crawler tractors, heavy and self-propelled light cranes, rollers, forklifts, conveyers, and machinery and equipment for the minerals and building-materials industries.

Subordinate to the BUMAR Union is the BUMAR FTO, the exclusive exporter and importer of all construction machinery built in or coming to Poland (that is, it imports and exports machinery even for associations and factories outside the jurisdiction of the Ministry of Machine Industry, to which it is attached). It exports to 50 countries and has trade and service stations in 29. In 1974 it was awarded the International Promotion Prize (*Prix de Promotion Internationale*) for the dynamic production development of construction and road building machinery and for its general emphasis on technical progress. In 1976 it was granted the Gold Mercury International Award for the expansion of international economic relations. As one of the most enterprising of Polish FTOs in establishing cooperation ties with Western firms, BUMAR FTO is partner to at least 19 foreign licensing and cooperation agreements, including: Clark Equipment Company, US (drive axles for wheeled construction machines and mobile cranes, with Huta Stalowa Wola); Jones Cranes, UK (mobile cranes, with Huta Stalowa Wola); Coles Cranes, UK (mobile cranes, with Huta Stalowa Wola); Stetter, FRG (concrete mixers and related equipment, with Huta Stalowa Wola); Kockums, Sweden (off-highway dumpers, with Fadroma); and International Harvester, US (construction machinery, primarily with Huta Stalowa Wola). Each of these ICAs was concluded during the 1970s, with the exception of the one with Jones Cranes concluded in 1966.

It was not until 1971 that BUMAR FTO became subordinated to the BUMAR Union and the Ministry of Machine Industry. In that year, a major reorganization of Poland's foreign trade shifted half of the FTOs from the ministry of Foreign Trade to industrial organizations or industrial ministries. Until then, what is presently known as BUMAR FTO was the construction equipment division of Polimex-Cekop, which was (and is) one of the giant FTOs attached to the Ministry of Foreign Trade and Shipping and which handles products of numerous industrial ministries. The strong commitment to industrial cooperation remained with the division when it was transferred to the Ministry of Machine Industry. That commitment was fostered by the entrepreneurial spirit of BUMAR executives.

HSW, the main implementor of the IH-BUMAR ICA, is a huge industrial combine with a 40-year history, dating back to its hurried establishment in 1938 in "safe" central Poland to produce armaments with which Poland could defend itself against the gathering Nazi aggression. Its establishment was also an effort to industrialize one of the poorest and least developed regions of Poland. Initially it produced high quality steels and artillery equipment. But it began to specialize in the production of construction equipment in 1967 and has become the dominant enterprise in this sector. The range of products delivered by HSW has changed as national economic requirements have developed, from military equipment through plows through mining equipment and trucks to the heavy earth-moving machinery, its main specialization today.

Poland has enjoyed a rapid growth of its construction equipment sector. The destruction in Poland during World War II left the country in need of a large number of different types of construction machinery and equipment. Moreover, under the CMEA integration program, Poland has been granted specialization rights for the production of at least 11 types of loaders, 4 types of excavators, and 3 types of crawler tractors with dozer equipment, as well as 12 types of self-propelled cranes and 40 other types of building-transport machines or equipment.[41]

NEGOTIATING AND IMPLEMENTING THE AGREEMENT

A. Negotiations

During the 1950s and early 1960s, trade relations between BUMAR and IH were insignificant and largely irrelevant as far as the present ICA is concerned. The initiative was taken by BUMAR, whose representative approached several American construction equipment manufacturers in 1968 in search of cooperation possibilities. This reflected Poland's commitment to an extensive modernization program in general and to an expansion of its construction equipment sector in particular.

IH and BUMAR began their discussions in 1968 as a result of the initiative of the Polish commercial representative in Chicago. By 1972, after four years of preliminary discussions, including many IH and BUMAR personnel fact-finding trips, the stage was set for the final, intensive phase of negotiations.[42] Long exploratory discussions were necessary not only to become familiar with each other's operations and to become convinced of the other's capabilities to successfully implement any agreement, but also to allow the gradual development of mutual understanding and trust.[43]

Cooperation under the original 1972 contract (signed on September 18) was to continue for ten years, with an agreement that the parties would review their positions after seven years and decide whether to renew for a further term or to terminate after three years. In fact, however, negotiations have been continual. More recent agreements provide for automatic extensions of the cooperative relationship as each new product is brought on stream as a result of joint development efforts. Moreover, continual negotiation has been the practice even beyond the scope of joint development efforts, reflecting not only the dynamic nature of the ICA, but also the firm commitment each partner has made to strengthen the relationship. With these extensions, the cooperative venture as of mid-1979 was expected to continue until at least 1995.

B. The Series of Agreements, 1972-79

The most distinctive feature of the IH-BUMAR relationship is that it is not one agreement but a series of interlocking and increasingly complex agreements. These agreements include general protocols (nonbinding statements of principles and intent to cooperate) as well as legally binding contracts. Their evolution and substance can be traced as follows:

1. The initial ten-year agreement in 1972 provided for the transfer of technology for the assembly and manufacture in Poland of five types of crawler dozers and loaders: the 300 hp TD-25C, the 192 hp TD-25E, the 210 hp TD-20E, the 140 hp 175-C, and the 140 hp TD-15C, and various attachments (e.g., side booms and ripper blades) that allow the crawler tractors to be adapted to pipelaying, loading, and other jobs. The technology package included the provision of technical assistance and training, as well as information concerning dimensions, metallurgical specifications, tooling and machining techniques, assembly methods, and quality control procedures.

2. In 1973 an agreement was reached between BUMAR and IH of Great Britain for the supply of skids[44] from Poland to the IH subsidiary in Doncaster to initiate a new crawler tractor manufacturing program [TD-15C and 175C].

3. In the fall of 1975, a protocol defined BUMAR's cooperation with IH in the development of a large pipelaying tractor, also to be manufactured in Poland.

4. A protocol in the fall of 1975 concerned front-end, rubber-tired loaders, a technology package of nine such loaders, in which IH provided technical specifications and assistance and BUMAR cooperated in producing machines [through 1990].

5-6. These agreements in the fall of 1975 called for joint design, development, and prototype construction of a large crawler tractor (agreement 5) and big diesel engine (agreement 6) under an expanded agreement called "Cooperation Agreement on Development, Manufacturing and Marketing of New Products."

7. An agreement, signed in March 1978, laid the basis for another joint development project involving torque converters for heavy construction equipment.

Although the 1972 contract contained no requirements that IH buy back specific quantities of products from BUMAR, a general mutual-benefit clause in the 1972 contract made provisions for IH's purchase of machines, components, and service parts at a competitive price within the limits of BUMAR's production capacity. The rapid development of BUMAR's capability to produce a quality crawler tractor, plus IH's need for these machines, components, and service parts, led the parties to exercise this contract clause.

There were two contingency clauses in the 1972 contract. The first, a short-term or start-up provision, required IH to post an irrevocable letter of credit against the disclosure fee paid by BUMAR to ensure a refund of the fee if BUMAR were unable to manufacture the crawler tractors according to IH specifications. The second clause referred to the standard procedure for arbitration, but rather than provide that arbitration take place in a neutral third country (e.g., Switzerland), the contract specified that arbitration should be in the defendant's home country.[45]

The reference for the seven protocols is the 1972 contract; each protocol refers to this contract and extends its scope. Neither the 1972 contract nor the subsequent protocols provide for a transfer of contract obligations to any third party. The tenor of the entire agreement is that the production technology used or jointly developed is the property of the two partners and is not to be shared with others. However, the opportunity for transfer of technology to a third party may be raised in each case.

C. Motives

Although the motives of the respective partners concerning the various protocols and agreements overlap, it is of interest to list some of them:

1. The 1972 transfer of technology for the assembly and manufacture of crawlers, dozers, and loaders: IH saw this as a way to gain entry into the CMEA market, that is, to share at least indirectly in meeting CMEA demand for heavy construction equipment. IH received front-end fees as well as royalty payments and benefited from the sale of components as well as of complete machines.[46] BUMAR was motivated in part by the fact that Poland had been assigned some types of heavy construction equipment under CMEA specialization agreements and also by additional types in this sector. In addition, BUMAR saw this as an opportunity to enhance its potential for earning convertible currency. BUMAR anticipated benefits from spillover effects; that is, that the technology demands of the ICA would help upgrade the technology of the supplier industries outside BUMAR's jurisdiction within Poland.

2. The 1973 agreement for BUMAR to supply skids to the IH subsidiary in Doncaster: IH wanted BUMAR to become a competitive source of skids and components, thereby improving IH's competitive

position in Europe. For BUMAR, this was a major opportunity to increase hard currency earnings.

3. The 1975 protocol for the joint development of large, pipelaying tractors: IH had a North American market for such tractors, which was too small to justify production economically, and could look to Poland as a possible supplier. Furthermore, BUMAR was likely to develop this product with the help of an IH competitor if IH did not agree to joint design and development. An important consideration for BUMAR was that these large pipelaying tractors were particularly marketable in the USSR. BUMAR saw its joint development program with IH as a means of gaining a competitive edge in the USSR and in some other CMEA countries, specifically vis-à-vis a comparable product developed by the Japanese. Technical and other specifications being comparable, a CMEA country like Poland generally has a competitive edge within the CMEA because bilateral clearing arrangements make it possible for the buyer to save convertible currency (see Section E). The joint design project was also seen as an opportunity to better utilize the technological expertise of the Polish scientific community, which might not favor simply buying foreign technology, especially in view of the large number of highly qualified design engineers available in this industry to Poland. Moreover, the cooperation opened up new avenues for the practical application of the theoretical design capability of Polish specialists.

4. The 1975 protocol on front-end loaders: An IH subsidiary in the FRG needed competitively priced supplies of transmissions and axles for front-end loaders. The Polish loader produced at that time was obsolete, and the engineering improvements made in cooperation with IH would improve the performance of the Polish machines. Moreover, this protocol was aimed at broadening the interface between IH and BUMAR of product lines for which BUMAR would provide components of machines marketed in the West by IH and its subsidiaries. After the increase in world oil prices and the induced increased demand for coal, the Poles were particularly interested in improving the quality of loaders used in their domestic coal-mining operations. Moreover, the growing Soviet mining industry represented a promising market for Polish front-end loaders if BUMAR could incorporate recent world technology. Finally, potential exports of these products to the West were an additional source of convertible currency earnings.

5-6. The 1975 agreement for joint research and development and prototype construction of a large crawler tractor (5) and diesel engines (6): By sharing development costs with BUMAR, IH could round out its product line in the crawler tractor area at one-half the cost of doing it alone. At the time, Pay Line was not in a position to fund the project by itself. BUMAR, in turn, saw this as a means to enhance its competitive position in other markets. IH had the same motives for the diesel engine. In addition, this would give IH the ability to develop an engine source "within the family" rather than giving the business to competitive Western firms. BUMAR saw that these engines were needed in the large vehicles being manufactured under the ICA, and felt that it was easier and probably less costly to obtain the necessary technology "inside the family" than to acquire it from an IH competitor.

7. The March 1978 agreement on joint development of torque converters for heavy construction equipment: IH had previously relied on the assistance of outside suppliers for the development of this component, but because the product was IH-specific and not used by other firms in the industry, IH incurred the development costs. By sharing the research and development tasks with BUMAR, IH could develop an in-house research/development/production capacity at approximately half the cost. IH would then have a potential European supplier producing under IH documentation, enabling IH to further round out its product line.

8. Both partners are motivated to better capitalize on the potential for coordinated marketing in third countries.

To recapitulate, IH's main motives for cooperation were:

1. To gain entry into those CMEA and developing country (LDC) markets in which its normal market penetration was limited.

2. To achieve a lower-cost source of supply for its West European and Middle Eastern production and marketing operations and to some extent for the US market.

3. To expand its product line by sharing the costs of development and production with BUMAR. Adding BUMAR as a partner increases the market and enables IH to limit capital costs. These are important considerations for a company that is attempting to expand by filling out its worldwide product line and by extending the geographic scope of operations, which require large investment outlays.

BUMAR's motives for cooperation were:

1. To enlarge and speed up the investment and modernization program of some BUMAR plants.

2. To increase the country's convertible currency earnings potential.

3. To gain a competitive edge within the CMEA market by acquiring and successfully absorbing the more advanced world technology.

4. To gain a competitive edge in those LDCs having bilateral clearing agreements with Poland.

D. Principles of Payment for License and Know-how

The initial license, know-how, and technical assistance part of the ICA called for a front money payment payable in four annual installments. In addition, IH receives royalties on each machine BUMAR produces using IH technology.[47] There is a ceiling, however, beyond which total annual royalty payments may not go, and beyond which any additional sales by BUMAR are not subject to royalty payments. Royalties are paid even when BUMAR sells the machine to IH. The only exception is in the case of IH buy-back of some specific jointly developed products.

The precise amount involved in the sale of know-how is not known, but we have reason to beleive that the six basic revenue items US firms customarily receive under licensing and coproduction arrangements were also applicable in this particular case:

1. Disclosure fees for the initial transfer of documentation, the right to use it, and royalty fees payable on units produced.

2. Payment for the assistance of IH technical and management personnel assigned to the project, on a man-day basis.

3. Sales of components.

4. Sales of complete machines.

5. Purchase of components at advantageous prices.

6. Purchase of complete machines for resale.

A firm usually begins negotiations with a discussion of what is going to be sold, leaving the disclosure and technology fee discussions for the last; otherwise the negotiators would be talking about the price of something that had not been defined. There are usually opposing views on the value of the technology and know-how. The buyer argues that the technology already exists, you have it, you used it, so the price charged should be minimal. The seller argues that it took a large amount of money to develop, and that its sale, usually for a fraction of the development cost, helps the seller generate funds for continued research and development in the same or in different product lines.

The seller partitions the actual cost into two components: *variable costs,* which are the cost of the paperwork, the negotiations, and the time of the people involved in transferring the technology (usually a relatively small amount); and *fixed costs,* which are basically indeterminate, although certain approaches are useful in trying to establish a reasonable range. First, the seller usually has some preliminary idea of the scope and level of the production he will help establish. At the end of a certain period, how many units will be produced? The seller then takes the value of that production and calculates a certain percent as a first estimate of what can be charged. The percent varies from industry to industry and from firm to firm. Generally, a 5 percent figure may be considered reasonable. The seller's second approach is: What would it cost the buyer to create the facilities to produce this product? Then it takes something like 10 percent of the value of the capital facilities as another estimate. Such a fee would be comparable to that charged by a consultant who may design such facilities and advise on how to set it up. There are two kinds of adjustments to the resulting figures: first, are they big enough for the seller to make it worthwhile even to think about serious negotiations; and second, are the resulting figures too large for the buyer to be seriously interested?

E. Industrial Cooperation with a Western Partner and CMEA Specialization

The relationship between IC with a Western partner and CMEA integration can be complementary because the inflow of Western goods, technology, and managerial know-how can give an additional impetus to product specialization within the CMEA. Some of the imports and industrial cooperation agreements with Western firms can strengthen a CMEA country that wants to become a specialized supplier of certain types of machinery or other products under CMEA specialization agreements.[48] For Western corporations, the possibility of penetrating other CMEA markets through IC with an East European partner can also be an important commercial motive.

This kind of complementarity is illustrated by this case study. One of IH's motives was to gain entry to those CMEA markets in which its penetration was limited. One of BUMAR's motives was to gain a competitive edge within CMEA. IH benefits from Poland's CMEA arrangements directly, through royalties and the export of components essential to the production of these machines, and indirectly because it can help promote its sales in the other CMEA countries.

F. Investments Required

The cooperation has enabled both partners to save substantial investment funds and time to undertake certain productive activities that otherwise may have been too expensive. Nevertheless, both sides have undertaken indispensable investments to support the cooperation.

BUMAR has invested heavily in physical facilities, including new foundries necessary to produce the high quality steel to IH specifications, one of the largest gear shops in Europe, and satellite plants to support the fabrication of tractor parts. These undertakings have often involved hard currency technology imports. Approximately 50 percent of the initial investment requirements involved hard currency outlays, according to Szumski (see p. 159 for his analysis). The new facilities have uses and applications for operations not directly connected with the cooperation, as well as technical and managerial spillover effects. The early heavy investment in physical facilities made financing a key issue for the Polish partner. A $2.7 million credit from the Export-Import Bank covered 45 percent of the value of tractors and components supplied by IH to BUMAR. Another 45 percent was provided by private sources and guaranteed by Eximbank, and the remaining 10 percent came from a Polish bank. This is a fairly typical financial package.

Although IH has not found it necessary to invest in additional equipment or plants in the US to support the cooperation, it has made a substantial investment by revealing technical know-how, in terms of its personnel, travel, and the training of Polish specialists. Moreover, the cooperation has made it possible to expand the capacity and the product line in England at a much lower cost than if IH had relied on its own resources. In fact, it might have been too expensive for IH to tool up alone for the expanded capacity, given the market volume in Europe. Since IH has a relatively high debt-to-equity ratio, it often faces a capital constraint when it contemplates developing new products or markets. Cooperation with BUMAR helps ease this constraint.

G. Marketing Arrangements[49]

When the original cooperation agreement was signed in 1972, a separate agreement concerning BUMAR's use of the IH trademark was also signed. The trademark arrangements were based on a clear distinction among three groups of countries.

First, BUMAR has unrestricted marketing rights in the USSR, Poland, the GDR, Czechoslovakia, Hungary, Romania, Bulgaria, Albania, Mongolia, and Vietnam.[50] In these countries, BUMAR may sell any product it produces (BUMAR or IH label) with no obligation to IH except to make royalty payments for all licensed products produced. IH may also sell directly to this market in the event that BUMAR is not able to satisfy the demand.[51]

Second, BUMAR has been granted non-exclusive marketing rights in Pakistan, Egypt, Syria, Libya, Sudan, Iraq, Algeria, India, Yugoslavia, Bangladesh, and the People's Republic of China. Within this area, BUMAR may sell in three ways: If there is a BUMAR distributor in the country concerned, a BUMAR labeled product may be sold to that distributor with no commission payable to IH. Alternatively, BUMAR may sell an IH-labeled product directly to an IH distributor, in which case BUMAR must pay, in addition to royalty, a negotiated commission to Pay Line to develop and maintain a worldwide marketing organization that BUMAR is utilizing. Finally, BUMAR may sell directly to Pay Line Group, which then resells to the IH distributor or (rarely) to the end user;[52] in this case, the commission is not payable since Pay Line is acting as a principal in the transaction. Whenever BUMAR uses an IH distributor, the machine must bear the IH trademark, signifying that the machine meets all standards.

In the second category of countries, neither BUMAR nor IH has its primary market strength. Although Poland has bilateral clearing arrangements with some of them, the ties are clearly not as strong as within the CMEA. Political circumstances in these countries are often not conducive to IH market penetration. In some instances, tenders for equipment purchases have been private instead of open, and BUMAR but not IH was invited to bid. Thus, the provision of "nonexclusive" territories seems to be an attempt to enter the markets from either side, each partner doing what it can.

The third category, consisting of all countries not specifically listed above, is IH's exclusive territory. Here, any BUMAR sale of an IH trademarked machine, components, or spare parts is made solely with the permission of IH and only through Pay Line Group or an IH distributor. Although this category of countries is IH's exclusive territory, during the course of the ICA, IH recognized more clearly BUMAR's capability in manufacturing and decided to use BUMAR as an exclusive manufacturing source of two products (an agricultural tractor and a side pipelaying tractor) that IH buys for marketing in its exclusive territories. The rationale of that decision is based on design peculiarities as well as production volume of the two models in question. In at least one case, a country's bilateral trade agreement with Poland made a sale possible only for BUMAR. Although the IH distributors in this third marketing area are obligated to buy from IH, logistical problems, usually involving delivery delays when IH is oversold, can warrant IH permission for the distributor to buy from BUMAR.

In 1979 negotiations began concerning the possibility of more closely aligning BUMAR and IH marketing efforts for third country sales. If those efforts are successful, the marketing arrangements described above could be altered. The relationship between IH and BUMAR is dynamic, and thus changes continually.

H. Quality Control[53]

Under the terms of the trademark agreement, before the IH trademark can be attached to a BUMAR-produced machine, it must satisfy a sequence of parts certification steps in a qualifying process established by IH. Testing occurs first in the Polish plant, then at IH's testing facilities in Phoenix, Arizona, where a machine undergoes approximately 1,500 hours of testing.

The inference drawn from discussions about quality control is that problems still exist but they have become less severe. In the six years that IH and BUMAR have worked together, first in the transfer of IH crawler tractor technology and later in the joint development of new products, both partners have learned about each other's methods of operation and quality standards. BUMAR has seen three of its IH-licensed products successfully pass the strict IH certification procedures.

BUMAR's strengths lie in its experience in the manufacturing process. The quality of its products is high because of good engineering design, modern equipment, and top quality measuring and testing instruments. BUMAR machinists are well-trained and they use their equipment well. Moreover, BUMAR has introduced in five and a half years six models of crawler tractors, a task which would have taken IH five to seven years.

Problems arise, however, in the areas of materials handling, quality inspection, and other quality control procedures. Scheduling and coordinating a complex system of activities pose especially difficult problems. In the attempt to assure quality, any departure from the highest standards anywhere on the shop floor or in the chain of activities can offset the excellent work done in the manufacturing stage. Consequently, IH found it desirable recently to assign its own product support manager and manager of manufacturing coordination in Poland.[54]

Quality, once attained, cannot be considered permanent; it requires continual attention even to maintain given levels of quality, and thus avoid backslides. The IH quality control is a continuous formal procedure, standardized for all IH and affiliated manufacturers throughout the world, and includes scheduled or surprise visits to plants. Inspections are made at various points throughout the entire manufacturing process-from materials testing, to heat treatment, to materials handling procedures, to the final product. The IH view is that quality stems from the workers' and managers' attitudes, and that it is a learning process. Quality levels can be achieved, as indeed BUMAR has demonstrated, but the maintenance of quality and its necessary further development are dynamic, never-ending processes.

I. Pricing IH Sales to and Purchases from BUMAR

The selling of IH components and finished products is agreed by contract, fixed at cost plus X percent. The same pricing principle has been used year after year. The prices are fixed in relation to the standard manufacturing cost determined annually by IH, and the price list for all components is sent to BUMAR. With respect to the pricing of IH purchases of components and complete machines from BUMAR, the original 1972 agreement did not stipulate exactly (types and quantity) what would be purchased from BUMAR, but merely that BUMAR would sell at a competitive price within its production capability.

More recently, the general practice has been to agree on a price for a one-year period in combination with a stipulated quantity of components or machines. For example, if IH and BUMAR would agree that within one year IH would buy 100 machines at a specific price, and BUMAR finds itself able to deliver only 80 of those machines, then the remaining 20 would still be delivered by BUMAR at the agreed upon price, regardless of the new price established for the following year through annual re-negotiation. This price, fixed for a year, is negotiated, and on the IH side, it is influenced by many things, including the price advantage over in-house production as well as over other offshore suppliers and the current and projected capacity utilization of IH.

As noted, prices are negotiated annually. Even where multi-year contracts exist (there is at least one three-year contract, for example), an escalation clause to cushion against inflationary pressures provides that a price increase may be negotiated every 12 months. Included in the agreement is a framework that establishes under what conditions and by what amounts the prices may be raised.

BUMAR has traditionally had to price its exports to Western countries on the basis of world market prices. Lack of a convertible currency and other factors make this necessary. To be sure, Poland and other CPEs perform internal calculations to decide the profitability of actual and potential exports, and these calculations usually become a factor when export prices are negotiated with Western importers.[55] In the case of complete machines, BUMAR relies heavily on watching competitive pricing on world markets to determine the general price range. The price at which IH previously purchased the machine is also important. In the case of components, the procedure is different. By contract, IH must inform BUMAR of the IH standard manufacturing costs. Accordingly, BUMAR begins its negotiations on pricing at X percent below the given costs. Even here, however, there is no set formula; the discount price varies not only according to the complexity of the product, but also with the individual negotiator, opportunity costs for IH, and other factors.

J. Two-Way Flow of Payments

According to the stipulation of the ICA, IH has no contractual commitment to buy anything from BUMAR, even though the general provisions indicate IH's intention to do so.[56] There is, however, a related clause stipulating that BUMAR's annual payment of REM fees[57] will not be greater than one-half of the value of IH's purchases from BUMAR. In other words, if IH buys $1 million worth of components or machines from BUMAR, IH's REM payments from BUMAR cannot exceed $500,000. This requirement has never affected the two-way flow, because IH purchases have far exceeded the minimal conditions. In fact, between 1973 and 1976, IH bought 50 percent of BUMAR's production of two tractors (the skids that were being shipped to Doncaster; see p. 74). This amounted to roughly 35 times more than required by the agreement. When the Doncaster project began to dwindle in 1977, IH used BUMAR as a source of certain components for domestic manufacturing operations in the US.

As far as the westward flow of complete machines is concerned, progress has been much slower. This is understandable in view of the relatively short time that the ICA has been under implementation.

Between IH and BUMAR alone, not taking into consideration any other flows prompted by or related to the ICA, the westward flow of hard currency payments is not only substantially larger than the eastward flow, it is also gaining relatively. This fact itself reveals little, of course, regarding BUMAR's overall position vis-à-vis hard currency markets.

K. Technical, Commercial, and Financial Risks

1. By technical risk we mean the possibility that the transferred technology will be too difficult to absorb and manage. The main risk seems to be the longer-than-planned time it takes to achieve the proper technological standard in Poland. Once the standard has been achieved, the Polish partner is a very reliable producer. There do seem to be some minor problems concerning the delivery of supplies to Huta Stalowa Wola from Polish enterprises outside of BUMAR Union.

As far as materials are concerned, 147 of the approximately 158 various steels and irons specified by IH for machine production have been successfully replaced by Polish equivalents, with the remainder now being made in Poland specifically in accordance with IH requirements. One of the most time-consuming tasks has been the translation, metrication, and adaptation to Polish standards of the extensive documentation transferred through the agreement.[58] IH has been favorably impressed by their Polish counterparts' ability to absorb the technology within a relatively short time.

In addition, two types of government regulation have been mentioned as impeding or slowing the transfer of technology:

a. US strategic export controls. The approval time on applications for validated licenses on technology transfer has not been appreciably reduced since cooperation began. In fact, it may be that the additional requirement for US Defense Department screening, embodied in 1974 legislation, has slowed up the process. In important cases, however, IH has found that it can expedite approval by directly contacting the Commerce Department and presenting its case.

b. Travel restrictions. Polish restrictions and changing guidelines for obtaining travel permits for Polish personnel can disrupt well-planned IH schedules for visits by Polish technical delegations. IH has responded by waiting to make definite plans until immediately before the expected arrival of the Polish visitors. Also, IH insists on several confirming Telexes at relatively high levels to ensure that planned trips will in fact take place. IH personnel have yet to be granted multiple-entry visas for their frequent travels to Poland in connection with the cooperative ventures. This results in spending valuable time and energy in reapplying for visas and represents an additional monetary expense. In fact, it appears that these travel restrictions have impeded cooperation much more than US strategic export controls.

There have also been examples of an initial unwillingness by BUMAR to base decisions on IH's own trial-and-error experience. When decisionmakers in Poland realized that they had a domestically produced engine with generally the same specifications as the IH engine, they insisted on putting the domestic engine into the co-produced equipment. IH advised them that for a machine to be used mainly for short hauls, an engine developed for a different use would not work. Initially HSW did not accept the advice, built prototypes with its own engine for export, and then found out that it had the same experience as IH. The problem has since been corrected.

2. By commercial risk we mean the problem that the resulting product may not be readily marketable, or creating competition through the transfer of technology. The IH-BUMAR ICA provides, as noted earlier, that BUMAR has special selling conditions for each of the three basic market areas. It appears that such an arrangement substantially reduces the risk of creating competition. Yet occasionally there are unintentional problems. For example, not all Polish commercial consulates in the various countries are fully aware of the details of the IH-BUMAR agreement, and because they are under strong pressures to promote hard currency exports, they occasionally promote the sale of Polish construction machinery at a very attractive

price to the buyer in a country where IH has a dealer or a representative. When IH hears about such cases, it works through its channels to make sure the initial agreement is not contravened, and the problem is usually settled quickly. IH stresses that the few such cases have resulted because of a lack of information on the part of the Polish commercial agents.

The ultimate risk for IH (as we perceive it, not one that IH seems to worry about) is the possibility of BUMAR severing the agreement once Poland reaches a certain level of technological development in the construction equipment sector. With the substantial investment already undertaken by BUMAR, Poland could become a leading competitor on world markets for construction equipment. The likelihood of that risk materializing, however, seems small. First, there is still a considerable degree of Western content in the form of technology that Poland does not yet have the expertise to produce itself. Second, IH provides a significant market to BUMAR, which of course would be lost if the agreement were severed.

3. By financial risks we mean that costs and sales price relationships will be less favorable than planned. The only such risks noted involved the costs of training and other dimensions of the technology transfer process, which turned out to be more expensive than IH had anticipated. For example, neither party had a clear initial understanding of the meaning of technology transfer (TT). This refers to the initial 1972 agreement and the subsequent protocol concerning front-end loaders. A considerable amount of peripheral information relating to technology was expected by the Poles, but it was not expected to be transferred by IH.[59] For example, the Poles sent metallurgical specialists to find out about the composition and quality of steel products to be used as inputs, and they sent computer specialists to find out about computer support systems. A further problem was that technology is not always embodied in documentation or in written form but may well be specific to a particular plant where there may be unwritten practices and rules. For example, workers at an IH plant, if told to drill a certain kind of hole, would know how it would be drilled, how deeply, how quickly, and so forth. So there was the problem of having to translate a great deal of unwritten know-how and technology into written form and somehow conveying it to the Polish side. IH was as accommodating as possible and encouraged the exchange of specialists, provided that the expense of doing so was not prohibitively high. Ways were found to transfer such peripheral technology on a cash basis, under a separate contract. For example, when an incompatibility occurred in computer software between the Polish and IH computer systems, IH agreed to correct the incompatibility for a minimum fee.

L. BUMAR's Integration with IH European Operations

1. Great Britain

During the 1950s and 1960s, IH of Great Britain was the major British manufacturer of crawler tractors; in 1972 the company was ranked 40th among the country's manufacturing exporters. In 1973 the company was granted its second Queen's Award to Industry for export performance. Net sales in 1972 reached a record £ 45½ million (cca. $96 million), and after seven months of the 1973 fiscal year, were 35 percent ahead of the 1972 record.

In 1973 IH of Great Britain and BUMAR FTO reached an agreement that became, in effect, an extension of the original ICA between IH and BUMAR. The negotiations for this agreement were carried out jointly by IH (US) and IH of Great Britain. Under the agreement, BUMAR FTO was to supply heavy construction equipment components for assembly into powershift crawler loaders and crawler dozers in the IH subsidiary in Doncaster, England, thereby extending the line of construction equipment then offered by IH of Great Britain for both home and export sale. (Diesel engines for these machines were supplied by IH of the US.) The two models of equipment under question would not have been economically viable either as total-UK or part-UK, part-US manufacture. It allowed the parent company and Doncaster to utilize more fully their productive facilities, and opened marketing opportunities heretofore not available.

Because the venture was supplementary to Doncaster's production program, it did not disturb Doncaster's other sourcing arrangements; nor did the Doncaster subsidiary consider that the arrangement posed any threat to its own sales. To the contrary, it was felt that the two models, larger than previously available, would expand marketing opportunities. In addition, IH of Great Britain was at the time hopeful that it could rely on BUMAR to alleviate certain problems with particular quality engineered components for which the Doncaster subsidiary occasionally lacked adequate capacity; these problems had in the past resulted in shortages, which in turn had reduced output and resulted in disappointing deliveries to certain customers. Moreover, the agreement between IH of Great Britain and BUMAR FTO provided for the reciprocal exchange of components and machines, thereby opening up the Polish market to the subsidiary.

Through the agreement, BUMAR became for several years a source of skids (approximately 50 percent of the value of the complete machine) for two models of crawler tractors produced by the IH subsidiary in Doncaster. Initially, this was a satisfactory arrangement, for it allowed the Doncaster subsidiary to widen its product line,

BUMAR to gain substantial hard currency receipts (approximately $5 million per year), and IH to become, at least potentially, more competitive in the European markets. Unfortunately, the European market for those particular model sizes failed to develop to expectations, and in fact declined abruptly and significantly after four years. In 1979 the market was still soft.

Incidentally, the agreement was successful in spite of the local problems experienced at the Doncaster plant. Less than six months after the "Doncaster extension" to the ICA, a major crisis befell the IH subsidiary at Doncaster. In the midst of a fundamental clash between Prime Minister Heath and strike-prone coal miners and railwaymen and at a peak of the energy crisis, lack of fuel supplies forced the entire town of Doncaster into a three-day workweek. The timing of the crisis was particularly unfavorable to IH's British operations, which had finally moved into the black (in the year ending October 31) after a loss of $4.3 million the previous year. With a history of bad labor relations the Doncaster subsidiary of IH was now not only involved in "a rat race for materials," but also found it necessary to let go about 230 (5½ percent) of its 4,200 employees.[60]

2. West Germany

IH's West German subsidiary in Heidelberg is primarily an assembler and fabricator (rather than a complete manufacturer) of rubber-tired loaders. The Heidelberg plant buys most of its major assemblies (transmissions, axles, etc.) from outside Germany. It imports components from Japan and the US as well as from other West European operations. In an effort to establish a more synergistic effect, IH pursued an agreement through which BUMAR would supply payloader components (primarily transmissions and axles) to the German subsidiary, thereby more closely integrating BUMAR into IH's European operations. IH supplied the technology to BUMAR for the production of a complete small wheel loader in 1976 and a larger loader in 1977, and at that time indicated its intention to use BUMAR as a source of components for its German subsidiary.

Contrary to IH's expectations, no components have been supplied by BUMAR. By 1979, in fact, production of those models had not yet begun in Poland. The plant involved is Huta Stalowa Wola, which is expanding rapidly to keep pace with its many commitments. These delays have had serious consequences for all parties concerned. IH had planned to rely heavily on BUMAR as a source of components for the German operations, and consequently has had to change its long-range strategy. BUMAR, at least temporarily, lost the opportunity to be a supplier to the German subsidiary, which would have provided a hard currency market. The German subsidiary is still searching for a viable alternative to the highly impractical importing of components from Japan. Apparently the only flow between the Heidelberg plant and Poland currently involves components supplied by the Heidelberg subsidiary to BUMAR in support of the ICA.[61]

3. France

Although BUMAR has had no trading relations with the IH subsidiary in France, the possibility of an exchange of components and attachments for excavators was being explored in mid-1979. The discussions, although moving slowly, are especially noteworthy for three reasons:

1. For the first time, it would bring IH's French subsidiary into active participation in the larger cooperative venture.

2. It would introduce a fully new product line into the cooperation.

3. It is at the initiative of IH instead of BUMAR.

The subject of the negotiations is the potential marriage of excavator lines of BUMAR and IH's French subsidiary. BUMAR's line of excavators, produced in the Warynski facilities in Warsaw, is not complete; moreover, its four or five models, although in some aspects fairly modern, are in other aspects somewhat obsolete. Thus, to satisfy the growing market, BUMAR needs to not only update its technology, but also to expand its product line. On the other hand, there is a void in the excavator line produced by IH's French subsidiary, which lacks the very small and very large machines that BUMAR produces. Consequently, there was perceived a natural marriage of product lines, with IH supplying the modernity for BUMAR's middle-of-the-line and receiving in return an expansion of its own product line to include smaller and larger models.

Discussions reached a stalemate when IH found the BUMAR technology in this line not modern enough for easy adaptation. Instead of dropping the discussion, however, the focus was simply shifted. The two partners are now trying to develop an exchange of excavator components and attachments. IH has a wide variety of attachments (buckets, shovels, and magnets) that BUMAR needs. In return, BUMAR would probably either produce some excavator components for the French subsidiary or sell unrelated goods to IH. Although still in the pre-negotiation stage, the potential for further integration of BUMAR into IH European operations assumes a new dimension.

TABLE 1

Share of the Major Export-Oriented
Manufacturers in the World Exportation
of Construction Equipment, 1975

Country	Export Value (Million US$)	Share in World Exports
US	3,730	48.8
FRG	1,010	13.2
UK	650	8.5
France	580	7.6
Japan	370	4.8
Poland	300	4.0
USSR	298	3.9

SOURCE: Wojciech Konecki, paper distributed at the Poznan Fair, June 1979.

TABLE 2

Leading North American Companies
Construction Equipment Industry, 1977

	Total Sales ($m)	Sales of Construction Equipment ($m)	Construction Equipment as Percent of Total Sales
Caterpillar	5,849	5,087	87
J. I. Case	1,506	862	57
International Harvester	5,975	731	12
John Deere	3,604	670	19
Clark Equipment	1,309	583	45
Massey-Ferguson	2,805	398	14

SOURCE: "Construction Demand Brings Pack in on Caterpillar's Heels," *World Business Weekly* (November 20, 1978), pp. 5-6.

TABLE 3

Poland's Exports and Imports of Equipment and Machinery, 1976-78
(in millions of foreign exchange zloty)

Product	Year	Exports			Imports		
		Total	Socialist Countries	Capitalist Countries	Total	Socialist Countries	Capitalist Countries
1	2	3	4	5	6	7	8
Earth-moving, construction and road machinery and equipment	1976	696.7	631.4	65.3	703.4	438.1	265.3
	1977	837.4	771.8	65.6	686.1	526.9	159.4
	1978	854.0	778.0	76.0	710.0	554.0	156.0
Including: Excavators	1976	196.9	189.0	7.9	218.9	132.8	86.1
	1977	181.0	173.2	7.8	152.8	149.7	3.1
	1978	191.1	188.4	2.7	140.3	138.2	2.1
Bulldozers	1976	—	—	—	44.0	42.4	1.6
	1977	—	—	—	96.2	93.6	2.6
	1978	—	—	—	89.9	89.9	—
Construction machinery and equipment	1976	87.3	68.0	19.3	—	—	—
	1977	105.0	76.6	28.4	—	—	—
	1978	82.4	58.3	24.1	—	—	—
Road machinery and equipment	1976	—	—	—	60.0	43.5	16.5
	1977	—	—	—	36.2	34.1	2.1
	1978	—	—	—	39.5	34.4	5.1
Transport and handling equipment	1976	286.1	241.5	44.6	487.1	323.1	164.0
	1977	338.6	272.8	65.8	557.1	388.7	168.4
	1978	343.8	278.2	65.6	590.0	415.8	174.2

Including:							
Cranes	1976	141.5	133.4	8.1	86.9	47.8	39.1
	1977	139.7	117.7	22.0	139.7	77.2	62.5
	1978	119.1	94.7	24.4	72.5	40.0	32.5
Fork-lift trucks	1976	55.3	34.7	20.6	152.7	117.3	35.4
	1977	69.9	47.5	22.4	133.4	121.8	11.6
	1978	73.9	51.0	22.9	185.1	168.0	17.1
Parts and components	1976	48.1	39.3	8.8	—	—	—
	1977	77.7	62.3	15.4	—	—	—
	1978	90.0	75.4	14.6	—	—	—

SOURCE: *Foreign Trade Statistical Yearbook 1978*, GUS, Poland.

TABLE 4

BUMAR Union Production and Export, 1978

Product Lines	Production (units)	Export (units)	Percent Export
Excavators	3,730	2,173	58
Loaders	2,190	1,796	82
Cranes	1,475	736	50
Concrete mixers and bodyworks	1,950	1,247	64
Crawler tractors	586	540	92
Assembly lifts	500	215	43

SOURCE: *Ministry of Machine Industry: Poland 1979* (MMI publication), p. 16. Percentage column compiled by the authors.

TABLE 5

International Harvester Sales by Major Product Groups, 1978

Product Lines	Sales ($ million)	Percent
Trucks	3,211	48.2
Agricultural equipment	2,348	35.2
Construction and industrial equipment	852	12.8
Turbo machinery	253	3.8
Total	6,664	100.0

SOURCE: IH 1978 *Annual Report.*

Notes

1. These include Clark Equipment with BUMAR to manufacture heavy duty drive axles; Westinghouse with UNITRA for semiconductors and switchgear circuit breakers; Honeywell with MERA Union for an industrial process control system and other instruments; Singer with PREDOM Union to manufacture sewing machines; Corning Glass and RCA with UNITRA for color television picture tubes; and Koehring with BUMAR for hydraulic excavators (this agreement is now dormant).

2. Council for Mutual Economic Assistance.

3. John Holt, Paul Marer, and Joseph C. Miller, *East-West Industrial Cooperation: The US Perspective.* Report to the Bureau of East-West Trade, US Department of Commerce, May 1976 (unpublished).

4. ECE, *Analytical Report on Industrial Cooperation Among ECE Countries* (Geneva: UN, 1973).

5. W. Burzynski, J. Kozinski, W. Szydlowski, E. Tabaczynski, and Z. Wolowiec, *Some Problems of Industrial Cooperation Between Poland and Other Countries* (Warsaw: Foreign Trade Research Institute, 1976), p. 4.

6. An excellent, comprehensive survey of East-West IC is Carl H. McMillan, "East-West Industrial Cooperation," in *East European Economies Post Helsinki: A Compendium of Studies Submitted to the Joint Economic Committee, US Congress* (Washington, D.C.: US Government Printing Office, August 25, 1977), pp. 1175-1224.

7. See Kossut's analysis on p. 109.

8. The papers in this volume offer a more comprehensive discussion of the development of IC in Poland and of US-Polish economic relations.

9. Paul Marer and Joseph C. Miller, "US Participation in East-West Industrial Cooperation Agreements," *Journal of International Business Studies* (Fall/Winter, 1979), pp. 17-29.

10. Ibid.

11. For these and other trade figures, see Kossut.

12. See Zagorski for details, p. 121.

13. Joseph M. Callahan, "Big Pay Off at Pay Line," *Automotive Industries* (August 1978), pp. 37-40.

14. Indonesia, for example, is presently considering a massive trans-migration project aimed at transforming less inhabited islands into agricultural communities, which would involve clearing millions of acres of land.

15. John C. Noonan, "'78 a Banner Year—How Will '79 Compare?" *Construction Equipment Distribution* 45:1 (January 1979): 13-16.

16. Art Faber, " Don L. Douglass Talks About the Industrial Market," *Construction Equipment Distribution* 34:9 (September 1968): 12ff.

17. Ibid.

18. Stanley Vance, *Industrial Structure and Policy* (Englewood Cliffs, N.J.: Prentice-Hall, 1955), pp. 222-25.

19. Ibid.

20. For example, Bucyrus-Erie manufactured scrapers and bulldozers for mounting on IH tractors, and in fact IH bought those component parts from Bucyrus-Erie over a long period. Vance, *Industrial Structure and Policy*.

21. See Brada's discussion on p. 207. Product technology involves the development of new, unique products that have few close substitutes. Process technology involves the ways of organizing production, of lowering production costs, of motivating consumers to purchase the product, and of servicing the product.

22. Ibid.

23. To be sure, sublicensing is exceptional in the industry, which more commonly relies on a supplier-customer type of arrangement for components.

24. "World Equipment Picture Scanned at Paris Meeting," *Construction Equipment Distribution* 29:6 (June 1972): 25, 28.

25. *BUMAR Revue* (a BUMAR Union publication) (1977), p. 37.

26. Caterpillar's jump from 32nd to 24th on the *Fortune 500* list in 1978 made it the only firm in the construction equipment sector to have larger company-wide sales than IH. IH ranked 28th in 1977.

27. "A Business in Billions, a Profit in Pennies," *Forbes* (June 1, 1972), pp. 19-20.

28. In 1830, 91 percent of the US population lived on farms, compared to 4 percent today.

29. "International Harvester Views Product Support in the USSR," *Business Eastern Europe* (March 4, 1977), pp. 69-70.

30. "Harvester Signs Licensing Pact," *Wall Street Journal* (March 29, 1977), p. 28.

31. "IH Reorders Priorities to Emphasize Asset Management Over Sales," *Business International* (April 15, 1977), pp. 115-19.

32. "International Harvester: Axing the Fat Off a Company Gone Flabby," *Business Week* (June 26,1978), pp. 66, 71. According to the *Wall Street Journal* (January 19, 1979), p. 4, the cost-cutting program saved the company $100 million in fiscal 1978. IH now plans capital spending of about $500 million annually in fiscal years 1980 through 1983, which the company contends can be achieved without increasing long-term debt.

33. By 1975 the new planning process had provided information on the basis of which IH discarded its steel division and shifted its emphasis on light trucks to medium and heavy trucks ("IH Reorders Priorities").

34. IH 1977 *Annual Report*.

35. The new CEO had come from Xerox, where in one year (1975) he had discharged 8,000 employees.

36. The discussion in this section, unless otherwise noted, is based on Joseph M. Callahan, "Big Pay Off at Pay Line," *Automotive Industries* (August 1978), pp. 37-40.

37. The manner in which Pay Line announced the new strategy was unusual, perhaps in order to exert maximum pressure on its suppliers to reduce their production costs and lower prices. Instead of following the industry practice of arranging private meetings with suppliers to improve service and prices, Pay Line Group created a more competitive atmosphere by publicly announcing that it was open to new vendors. The message, which went to the Group's suppliers in 24 states and 8 foreign countries, was an unambiguous threat to current suppliers. See "Harvester Tries New Tactic with Suppliers," *Industry Week* (July 24, 1978), pp. 32-33.

38. Interesting parallels may be drawn, incidentally, with Poland's recent attempts to introduce economic reforms. See Josef C. Brada and Marvin R. Jackson, "Internationalization of U.S. Firms and the Polish Economy: Parallels in Organizational Change?" *Working Paper Series, #78-20,* New York University Faculty of Business Administration (March 1978).

39. This is still the case of the Doncaster plant in England, where Pay Line products are "guests" of the Agricultural Equipment Group.

40. Until July 1, 1979, when HSW and its satellite plants became directly subordinated to the Ministry of Machine Industry.

41. Tadeusz Nowakowski, "BUMAR Specialization Construction Equipment," mimeograph (1979).

42. The FTRI team insists that negotiations lasted only eight months (see Szumski, p. 000). In the opinion of the IU team, the eight months refers only to the final and most intensive phase of negotiations and the actual preparation of the agreement.

43. Both teams noted the importance of the strong commitment at high levels in the respective organizations. On the Polish side a key person in the negotiations was Mr. Sykstus Olesik who, as director of the BUMAR FTO, had the general responsibility. On the US side, the leadership of Mr. Brooks McCormick, President and Chief Executive Officer of the company, played a key role. Mr. McCormick had long known and worked with Polish leaders. He lived in Poland during his formative years when his father was director of the Hoover Relief Commission in that country. In 1973 he became the American co-chairman of the Polish-US Economic Council.

44. A skid is a semi-knocked down machine sent as a shipping package; for a crawler tractor it is about half of the unit pre-assembled, but without the engine, tracks, sheet metal, and so on.

45. See H. Waldemar Niemotko, "International Commercial Arbitration in Poland," *The Arbitration Journal* 29:4 (December 1974).

46. By early 1975, BUMAR was manufacturing 40 percent of the volume of components; 30 percent was purchased from various original equipment manufacturers, 10 percent comprised the engine which, like the remaining 20 percent, was manufactured in various IH facilities. Eric W. Hayden, *Technology Transfer to East Europe: U.S. Corporate Experience* (New York: Praeger, 1976), p. 55.

47. BUMAR welcomed this provision, because the royalty payments are actually REM (research, engineering, and manufacturing) fees, the basic purpose of which is to keep the technology current. They are based on the quantity of machines produced times X percent of the net American dealer's price (from a price list supplied by IH). Yet that percentage descends to zero over a number of years as well as to zero after a certain number of machines each year.

48. For a description of the CMEA and the role of specialization agreements, see Paul Marer and J. M. Montias, eds., *East European Integration and East-West Trade* (Bloomington: Indiana University Press, 1980).

49. For a theoretical model of marketing, see Miller's paper (pp. 259-66).

50. In the original agreement, North Vietnam. Vietnam became a CMEA member in 1978.

51. We have used the term "unrestricted," although the agreement refers to "exclusive" marketing rights. Szumski notes that the term "exclusive" is misleading because IH may compete with BUMAR for sales anywhere. Thus, "exclusive" apparently refers to BUMAR's freedom to sell without using IH distributors.

52. The rationale seems to be the strengthening of IH market position in a foreign country when faced with a relatively weak distributorship there. If Pay Line sells to the

distributor, the relationship between the two is the same as if the product came from Melrose Park. If Pay Line sells directly to the end user, then a servicing fee or commission is reserved for the distributor, who is given servicing responsibility for the unit.

53. See also Szumski's paper on p. 159 concerning quality control procedures.

54. IH also has an administrative manager stationed in Warsaw. This three-man staff will probably be expanded in 1980 in response to the increased volume of activities.

55. See discussion of Polish costing and pricing on pp. 92-97.

56. There are frequent complaints voiced in Poland by those not familiar with the agreement that IH is not meeting its buy-back commitments. Because there are no such commitments, these complaints obviously are based on a misunderstanding. Moreover, IH would like to buy much more from BUMAR than BUMAR has proved capable of delivering.

57. REM (research, engineering, and manufacturing) fees (royalties) keep the technology current.

58. More than 20,000 drawings were involved, according to Mr. Szumski. See p. 159 for his analysis of problems of technology transfer.

59. This was definitely not a question of deception on either side, but rather a question of strict vs. loose interpretation of the technology transfer clauses.

60. "A British Town Faces 3-Day Week With Display of the Old Dunkirk Spirit Plus New Pessimism," *Wall Street Journal* (January 15, 1974), p. 36.

61. This example is not the only case in which, for various reasons, IH has been less than satisfied with westward deliveries. There is, for example, some concern at IH that the production of the jointly developed large crawler tractor will not come on stream as soon as planned, thus causing a loss of revenues for both partners.

PART III
CONFERENCE IN BLOOMINGTON

*Papers by the Polish Team
and Discussion*

The Foreign Trade System In Poland

Jan Giezgala

Poland's present development strategy is based on an outward-looking economic policy, the most reasonable approach in a medium-size economy that is trying to accelerate its growth rate. This policy is based both on the central directives of the Planning Commission and on instruments of indirect management. Where central decisions and initiatives operate successfully, they can be relied upon. Where these central decisions are not effective, they should be supplemented by indirect instruments.

Intensifying the effectiveness of the central planning and management of the national economy is accompanied by a considerable widening of independence and initiative in the economic units. The successive introduction of the so-called "integrated economic system"—the system of large economic organizations (LEOs)—is one means of reaching this end. Therefore, the term "large economic organization" (in Poland, Wielkie Organizacje Gospodarcze [WOG]) came to be associated with changes that have recently taken place in the functioning of the economy.

The term "large economic organization" covers different groupings of plants and enterprises. Unlike other economic units, these units are directly subordinated to ministries. Central economic authorities influence and direct the LEOs mainly by using economic instruments; that is, targets of directive or imperative character do not dominate. The new financial system should influence economic units so that the results of their decisions are compatible with the assumptions of the overall economic plan.

LEOs function on a self-financing basis and, as far as possible, cover the full production cycle satisfying simultaneously the needs of consumers, producers, and exporters. They are responsible for meeting the needs of the branch they represent. At the same time they are allowed to acquire adequate means for its further development through effective economic activity. The implementation of these targets should be followed by a steady improvement in working conditions and wages, as well as in the social conditions of LEO staffs.

Three types of LEOs can be distinguished in the Polish economy:

1. Industrial combines or multiple-plant concerns are the most internally centralized type of LEO. All basic functions connected with management and planning are centralized on the level of the managing board of this organization. Subordinate executive units have no legal status and follow decisions of the board.

2. In industrial unions (corporation type), internal relations between the managing board of the LEO and the member-units are not as tight as in the first type. Only some functions connected with management, such as international cooperation, forecasting, research and programming of the development of the branch, and price policy, are centralized on the level of the managing board. In this type of LEO, subordinate executive units maintain the status of an enterprise. They create separate funds and manage them independently.

3. Independent units, in close cooperation on the level of the managing board, together make decisions about matters that are important to the whole branch, such as development policy for main lines of production, sales specialization, and marketing. In current practice the industrial unions give the most support to the integrated system of economic planning and management.

LEOs, which embrace about 65 percent of Polish industrial capacity, are really a new quality in the economic system of Poland. They are not only directly responsible for current production, but also for investment policy, research, and industrial cooperation as well as home and foreign trade promotion. Decisionmaking in the LEO is based on the principle of maximization of value-added and of profit. The value-added directly influences the amount of wage fund, whereas profit is a basis for a special premium fund for management board members. Value-added and profit are closely connected with financial results of export and import transactions due to the special system of converting foreign prices into domestic costs and revenues. Because this focuses attention on improving efficiency, it should support the expansion of foreign trade and industrial cooperation (IC). Moreover, the real interest in the development of IC with foreign partners results from the very nature of the LEO.

Thus, the LEOs can speed up the transfer of modern technology, increase their scale of production, and earn additional profits from foreign transactions. Moreover, they can allocate some of the foreign exchange they earn, an additional incentive for expanding international relations.

The foreign trade organizations (FTOs) are either a part of the LEOs or they are LEOs themselves. Some of them still follow the old pattern of management. The planning of foreign trade is a multi-level and multi-phase process. There are three substantial levels: the central planner (i.e., the Planning Commission), the sectoral units (i.e., corporations and FTOs), and the executive units (i.e., producers). These levels cooperate closely to establish plan directives. The central planner proposes preliminary targets, which are a basis for a multi-phase discussion with the lower levels. They take into account the changing external and domestic conditions, and they arrive step by step at the confirmation and adoption of the foreign trade plan. There is a dynamic approach to this process whereby the plan can be verified and alterations of proportions can be introduced. Therefore, the planning of foreign trade is a continuous process.

There are different time horizons in foreign trade planning. First, with a long-term approach, covering 10 to 15 years, general trends in foreign demand are predicted and the global strategy of the country's development is formulated. This type of plan deals with large aggregates, where more detailed data concerning prices, production costs, and investment outlays cannot be worked out at an early stage. The meduim-term approach, covering five years, deals with specific costs, prices, and investment choices for exports and imports. Medium-term decisionmaking shapes the future Polish position in world markets, because it directly affects the productive and selling capacities of the Polish economy. The time horizon of the short-term approach is usually one year, and emphasis is on the optimization of the current production and sales program.

Within this framework, it is necessary to point out the nature of planning directives. Previously, all export and import goals were expressed in terms of natural units (in kind). Now, the foreign trade tasks are expressed in two lines: the centralized and the decentralized. The fulfillment of these tasks is obligatory for all respective executive levels under control of the Ministry of Foreign Trade and Shipping. The first line is closely connected with the most substantial fuel and raw material supplies for our economy, which are balanced with essential investment imports at the central planner's level. The second (decentralized) line deals with all remaining industrial exports and imports. The plan targets for import and export are more indicative than compulsory. The targets specify the aggregate balance-of-payments in respective sections of the plan. Enterprises are allowed to increase their imports if they expand exports so that the aggregate planned balance-of-payments will not be affected. All items of the second line (e.g., machinery, equipment, industrial consumer goods, foodstuffs) are expressed at the central and medium levels in terms of value, promoting a better structure and increasing flexibility of export offer and import demand. This significant modification in the Polish methodology of foreign trade planning is an important precondition for a gradual decentralization of decisionmaking. In this way, the FTOs and industrial units have considerable room to maneuver for their concrete sales and production activity. They should adapt their commodity structure and geographical expansion to the changing requirements and circumstances, keeping in mind the fulfillment of plan goals and efficiency criteria. This situation should be regarded as especially important and advantageous for East-West cooperation links, since cooperation agreements are usually long-lasting and can easily be incorporated into subsequent medium-term plans.

The above-mentioned planning system should be followed by a comprehensive and rational system of foreign trade management:

First, steps must be taken in the organization of industrial plants and foreign trade units. Foreign trade agencies are brought closer to industrial manufacturers through organizational fusion (e.g., in ships, machine tools, cars, chemicals, textiles) or they act as commercial agents and commissioners on behalf of their industrial partners. In this way, the responsibility for foreign trade results and real interest in foreign trade operations are moving to and concentrated in the industrial decisionmaking centers.

Out of about 55 FTOs, only 15 are now directly subordinated to the Minister of Foreign Trade and Shipping, corresponding to 40 percent of the general turnover of Polish foreign trade. These 15 FTOs are active mainly in raw material, fuel, and some heavy industry branches where the principles of balanced production and sales requirements dominate. The remaining FTOs are subject either to the respective ministries (CIECH for chemicals, TEXTILIMPEX for textiles), to the corporations (METALEXPORT for machine tools), or even to individual producers (H. CEGIELSKI for ship engines). This new system encourages the direct approach to Eastern and Western producers, which is especially important for the successful development of IC between partners.

In order to strengthen mutual knowledge and to facilitate penetration of the Polish market, foreign firms are invited to establish offices in Poland. There are now about 60 foreign representatives in Poland, whose main sphere of activity is technical information and consulting. Some are American (e.g., International Harvester). Another promising development results from establishing joint Polish-foreign companies outside Poland. We now have about 100 mixed enterprises of this type, both commercial and manufacturing. There is the possibility of setting up such companies inside Poland. Another interesting idea is the proposed establishment of a special FTO for cooperation agreements in some specified industrial sectors.

The most important changes have been introduced in the foreign trade financial system. Until recently, the most important parameters of the financial system—such as domestic and foreign prices, rates, and profits—represented rather passive instruments of control and had no direct influence on the rational allocation of resources. The industrial units supplied their goods for export according to some detailed plans and were paid at fixed domestic prices, quite independent of foreign prices. The same system was applied also on the import side, where prices paid by Polish buyers had no direct connection to the respective import prices in foreign money.

The price differences arising both in exports and in imports were settled through the special State Budget account. In other words, there were no direct links between home and foreign prices and a lack of interest by producers on the level of export-import prices. There is another system within the LEO structure—call it indirect management—where financial results of foreign trade operations have a considerable influence on the balance sheets of the producing and selling organizations. This is due first to the introduction of the "transaction prices," which are in practice foreign trade prices converted into domestic currency.

There is a special significance of transaction prices for Polish producers. The value of export deliveries has a direct impact on the total revenue of an industrial unit with follow-up in profits, value-added, wages, and premiums. Because of this, the representatives of producers should join all trade negotiations with foreign customers and influence the level of agreed upon prices, delivery time, payment conditions, etc.

The only group of products in which the principle of transaction prices does not apply is important raw materials, fuels, and foodstuffs; these remain under the special control of the State Price Commission.

Finally, the new financial system is based on special incentives for workers and executives. These incentives (premiums and bonuses) are a function of financial results of the foreign activity and contribute directly to better staff performance. This flexible system of wages and premiums should raise the workers' concern about the quality and modernity of their products.

Undoubtedly, there is still a great deal to be done in the fields of planning and management of Polish foreign trade, but even achievements to date justify an optimistic view of the development of Polish-US economic relations.

Comment

Robert W. Campbell

Professor Giezgala's paper is an intriguing and tantalizing survey of the institutional setting within which industrial cooperation agreements (ICAs) function. His theme is the interrelationship of strategy and structure; and for someone like myself, interested in socialist planning generally, it is one of the most interesting issues there is.

Giezgala says that Poland has tried to structure its foreign trade system to facilitate an export-led development strategy. This seems very sensible; in the postwar experience of the world such a strategy seems to have been the most successful route to rapid development. It would be interesting to know what makes the Polish version of this strategy different. It must make a difference that Poland is smaller than Japan; that it probably has greater potential for independent technological development than a country like South Korea; that it cannot look to a raw material base for the main export commodities; and that, given its planned socialist economic system, it is cut off from many of the institutional choices that other countries have used, such as direct foreign investment. But the central concern is how effectively Poland has adopted economic structure to development strategy, and specifically in relation to our conference, how the ICAs, one of the major devices in that strategy, fit in with the structure. In discussing this theme, I will take Professor Giezgala's paper as the point of departure, though I rely rather heavily on the experience of the BUMAR-IH ICA, as summarized in the report presented in this volume.

Giezgala's paper passed rather lightly over some very interesting aspects of this central issue. First, he explains that under the new system, the large economic organizations (LEOs) are exposed to the balance-of-payments impact of their decisions by having their exports and imports reflected in their financial statements at foreign prices converted to domestic prices via a special exchange rate. It would be helpful to know more about the exchange rate used in these calculations. Is it uniform for all sectors and classes of transactions? Is it fixed for long periods or does it fluctuate? Is it the official exchange rate or some kind of shadow price? Second, do all the enterprises or LEOs that are engaged in ICAs have foreign trade organizations (FTOs) directly associated with them or under their control, as I gather BUMAR does? If not, what is the rationale for the difference? Can an ICA work when it operates through an FTO under the Ministry of Foreign Trade?

Giezgala describes the decisionmaking criterion for LEOs as "maximizing value-added and profit." But those criteria can be in conflict, as in a make-or-buy decision. If an organization decides to purchase some component rather than making it itself, its value-added is reduced, but its profit might be raised either because of cost reduction or by improving its potential for export sales and profits. But what would be the final criterion in such a case?

Finally, how strong and consistent is the incentive system to encourage ICA expansion? For example, the Indiana study mentions that BUMAR's ICA has generated a negative balance-of-payments position with International Harvester (IH), though for Poland as a whole, this ICA may have a positive balance by strengthening Poland's export posture in the socialist market, enabling it to acquire goods that it would otherwise have to buy for hard currency. In this case, the local and global success measures differ, and I can't imagine that in general the "integrated system of planning and management" has really succeeded in fully reconciling local and global optima. To put the issue in more general terms, there seems to be a rather complacent view of the effectiveness of the current strategy and structure expressed in several of the papers. Professor Giezgala ends his paper with a statement that "a great deal has still to be done in the planning and management of foreign trade," and I should think that one of the goals of our discussions here should be to deal with that issue, as well as with what may need to be done by American corporations to more fully realize the potential of industrial cooperation (IC).

But these specific points are only a prelude to a larger set of isues that have to do with the interrelationship of strategy and structure:

First, there must be a problem of coordinating the central and peripheral authority and responsibility for ICAs. As I interpret Professor Giezgala's paper, Poland has effectively decentralized a portion of its industry to support the strategy and to encourage IC. In this decentralized sector, the LEOs are given a great deal of freedom to initiate and to operate ICAs. The price system has been reformed in its treatment of foreign transactions. The LEO with an ICA is made to feel the impact of its activities on the national balance-of-payments by having its exports and its imports entered into its financial results via a meaningful exchange rate. And these organizations are given additional incentives to improve the national balance-of-payments outcome by being rewarded with some share of the export earnings.

This decentralized sector has some of the characteristics of an export-oriented enclave. The existence of such an enclave always raises an interface problem, and I wonder how the two parts of the economy are coordinated. Success in the development strategy requires reaching backward out of this enclave to react with the other parts of the economy that supply materials, components , and parts.

This may not be possible, as we are told in the Indiana report on the BUMAR-IH ICA; it was necessary for BUMAR to make special investments in producing its own metals to meet IH specifications. There is, in addition, a kind of strategic-tactical division of decision-making responsibility; someone has to make the priority decisions (described by Mr. Tabaczynski, p. 98) as to which sectors are the best bets for export expansion and ICAs. It is not clear what the respective roles of the center and LEOs have been in this respect or how smooth this relationship has been. The same problem may show up as a conflict between current central goals, such as helping the balance-of-payments now or curtailing investment commitments in the economy as a whole versus taking actions to assure the long-run success of an ICA. For example, the Indiana IH-BUMAR study suggests that BUMAR may have lost the opportunity to produce components for the West German affiliate of IH for a front-end loader because it could not meet the need soon enough. I don't know whether this was a result of bad planning by BUMAR or of interference and lack of support from the Center.

In any case, there is an interface problem, and I wonder if our Polish colleagues think they really have it solved. There are two ways to deal with such a problem. One is to bring more of the domestic economy into this enclave; the other is to turn the export enclave more and more to the outside world. As an example of the latter, it might be possible to solve a supply problem or a quality problem by buying a higher share of components from the foreign partner. But this would require altering the division of the output away from the domestic and socialist markets toward the hard currency markets to support the greater dependence on foreign suppliers.

A second question is how these decisions about Western-oriented specialization and technology transfer (TT) are to be coordinated with similar decisions regarding trade with the socialist group. The premises of the Polish development strategy are that as a small country Poland must trade, and that as a country at an intermediate level of development it has the possibility of influencing the role it will be assigned in the international division of labor and in creating its comparative advantage. Successfully choosing the right sectors for IC, their reasonableness in terms of technological potential, and the effectiveness of the structure in motivating management to make ICAs work will dictate whether this export-led growth strategy is a success or not. The problem is that the central planners are making these judgments in two different contexts. On the one hand, Poland hopes to exploit a specialized niche in the non-socialist world market. At the same time it is still going to trade with the socialist countries and is going to earn or be given a specialized role within CMEA through the machinery of the Complex Program. The motivation for ICAs involves *both* these markets.

The Indiana study makes it clear that both BUMAR and IH entered into the ICA because they expected considerable sales in socialist markets. IH will receive royalties from such sales, while BUMAR sees the possibility of creating a special advantage for itself in this market by high quality and the IH trademark. Is the decisionmaking structure adequate for making sure that these two roles are consistent with each other? One speculation in the Indiana BUMAR study is that a situation may emerge in which BUMAR fails to fulfill its plans for capturing the socialist market and turns outside for markets, which might create a conflict with its Western partner. Whether this kind of consistency is achieved ultimately goes back to the antinomy described in my first point, i.e., whether central control over the choice and evolution of individual ICAs needed to maintain consistency between CMEA specialization and ICA-based, Western-oriented, specialization interferes with the kind of decentralized authority that must be given to the LEOs to make the ICA work effectively.

There is a third ambiguity about this strategy. ICAs are intriguing because they seem to be one of the most effective vehicles of TT, including the possibility of *reverse* transfers from East to West. We can think of TT in two ways: On the one hand, the most important goal may be to make the export-driven development strategy work. The reasoning is that it is not possible to expand exports unless one succeeds in matching world standards of modernity and quality and can go through an apprenticeship in developing the necessary marketing and service skills. That is precisely what the Polish firm hopes to get from a foreign partner in an ICA. On the other hand, TT is also sought to upgrade technological and innovational capabilities *throughout* the economy. Surely the planners are counting on significant diffusion of these new capabilities to other sectors as well. They don't just want to learn how to make crawler tractors; they want to create general technological competence and dynamism. There must be an expectation that once these skills are transferred internationally, they can be transferred *internally* to the supplying industries and to those that produce primarily for domestic and socialist markets. It seems unlikely that the architects of Poland's current growth strategy want the ICA-based, export-oriented sector to be an isolated enclave, with a corresponding dualism in economic structure. The hope is to move the interface inward. It may at first be necessary to produce a tractor with 20 percent of its components imported from the partner, but it is surely expected that eventually more of those parts can be produced domestically.

How have the architects of Polish development strategy perceived this aspect of the strategy, and to what extent have they discussed it and worked out a policy line? Suppose there is some ICA-supported export product line in which the Polish producer uses imported electronics. How will domestic electronics producers be moved into the new system, and how would the new system of incentives and pressures be applied to them? For example, as an effort is made to push the electronics industry toward world market standards for import substitution purposes, would that indirect contribution toward export earnings be rewarded with the same kind of exchange rate and incentive system as applied to the main exporter? Professor Giezgala's paper suggests that most of the sectors that would be involved in ICAs or in an ancillary role to ICAs are already in the enclave where FTOs are controlled by LEOs, where the new rules for handling foreign transactions apply, and where the new incentive systems operate. But it is not clear from any of the papers presented by the Polish participants just where the interface is, and I would be interested in having that more carefully explained and in knowing whether there are any problems with the current position of that boundary.

Reply

I share Professor Campbell's doubts regarding the adequacy and advisability of cooperation agreements when the foreign trade organization (FTO) is not directly subordinated to an industrial unit but to the Ministry of Foreign Trade. The very nature of cooperation links demands that the producer be the direct cooperation partner, while the trade apparatus performs only the intermediary or auxiliary functions. This is the case in the majority of existing cooperation agreements.

The zloty conversion coefficient that LEOs apply in export and import settlements is essential for assessing their activities. Professor Campbell is right in supposing that this conversion coefficient has the characteristic of a shadow price and is different than the official rate (31 zloty per dollar in 1978). It is fixed for several years by the government on the basis of statistical data and guidelines for long-term economic policy.

The relation between the conversion rate (zl/$) and the situation in the balance-of-payments is shown in the diagram on page 97.

The horizontal axis represents Polish demand for hard currency, and the vertical axis represents the zloty cost of acquiring one dollar through exports.

The zloty cost level of one hard currency unit is affected by such factors as the import needs of the country, the structure of exports, the cost-of-production level of these exports, and the level of foreign

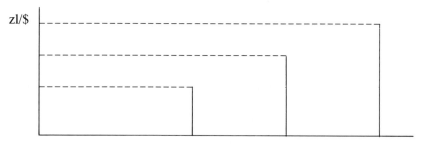

prices for exports. The conversion coefficient is fixed at the same
level for all export and import sectors in Poland.

Professor Campbell draws attention to the possible contradiction of
aims with a simultaneous maximization of value-added and profits in
the enterprise. This may take place in our enterprises as well as in
capitalist ones. If the value-added constitutes the basis for assessing a
firm's performance, the firm may treat the maximization of profits as
less important. If, on the other hand, the enterprise is interested in
reducing taxation on the value-added, it will place all the emphasis on
the maximization of profits.

There is also the possibility of conflicts between the preferences of
the central and executive level. For example, LEOs often require
more investment resources in zloty or in hard currency than the center is prepared to allocate. There may be a disagreement about the
direction of investment allocation because the expansion of a particular branch may not be consistent with the overall development strategy of the whole economy, the tendency of executive levels to
develop excessively their own production potential instead of relying
on cooperation deliveries from other enterprises, and the like. It is
obvious that in a centrally planned economy these problems cannot
be regulated automatically without any difficulties. They require constant coordination of units on different levels and the interference of
the central authorities when the instruments of indirect management
fail or are insufficient.

We are against creating pro-export enclaves in our industry. On the
other hand, we favor the export-orientation of industry since, considering the dimensions of our home market, most branches have no
scope for effective activity. These activities should be coordinated
within associations and branches and between individual enterprises.
Reforming the management system in our country should speak to
these issues. Our enterprises are interested in expanding both CMEA
and capitalist markets. Cooperation with leading Western firms and
the transfer of technology and experience should help us develop this
expansion to the advantage of all partners.

East-West Industrial Cooperation and Specialization in Polish Production

Eugeniusz Tabaczynski

The CMEA countries account for about 30 percent of world industrial production in terms of value while their share of world trade in industrial goods is less than 10 percent. Poland's share in world industrial production and in world trade is 2.3 percent and 1.0 percent, respectively. The socialist countries account for only 7 percent of the value of trade turnover of the OECD countries. These figures indicate the need for a radical improvement in economic relations between the East and the West.

The commodity structure of East-West trade is now obsolete; this applies primarily to exports from the CMEA countries to capitalist countries. This contention is corroborated by the continuously low share of manufactured goods (machinery and equipment as well as consumer goods). The present commodity structure does not reflect existing differences in the available production factors and in their productivity. It is largely of a historical nature, resulting from traditional regional specialization in production and in exports of fuels, raw materials, other production materials, and agricultural and food products. In 1945-77, because of the dynamic development in industry, foundations were built in the CMEA countries for a radical change in the structure of East-West trade. This problem has top priority for Polish foreign trade in the current five-year period, and we hope that Western countries will understand our efforts to achieve this objective.

The tremendous efforts involved in the reconstruction and development of primary and secondary industries would not have succeeded solely on the basis of Poland's own financial resources. Imports of machinery, equipment, and advanced technology, especially in recent years, together with grain imports resulted in a negative trade balance, but enabled Poland to replace and modernize more than 50 percent of her productive capacity.

The deficit in our trade with developed capitalist countries, growing since 1972, is financed by credit; but this cannot last forever. There must be a considerable acceleration of Polish exports to the West in the coming years. This is the basic condition for maintaining a high rate of imports from the West. This is also the basic assumption in current projections of East-West trade. The requirements of balanced trade may influence our policy with respect to the development of total international trade, as well as trade with industrialized Western countries, so that exports will have to be stimulated as much as possible and imports realistically cut down to the level of current basic needs.

The economic relations between East and West are influenced by differences in their socio-economic systems. We are witnessing a confrontation between market economy and planned economy systems. There are not only differences in the main goals of the economic activity of both systems, but also differences in the parameters and economic criteria. Economic planning in CMEA countries is based on prices of raw materials and production equipment that are kept constant for agreed periods, on the bilateral nature of foreign trade, and on domestic currencies, which are not freely convertible. Trading partners should keep these observations in mind. They necessitate a constant search for better understanding and new forms of labor and commodities exchange.

Policies aimed at improving our foreign trade have been supported by a number of major decisions concerning the organization of industrial plants and foreign trade units. In the last few years in Poland, for example, foreign trade agencies have been brought closer to industrial manufacturers either through organizational fusion (e.g., in ships, machine tools, cars, chemicals, textiles) or through ties of a selling-commission type, which helps to increase the manufacturers' interest in the value and effectiveness of their exports. Attention is also devoted to connections of a parametric nature between planning authorities and executives in industry. A flexible system of wages and premiums has been introduced to raise workers' concern about their output.

On the basis of these general statements, it is necessary to ask: What should be the pattern of future Polish exports and imports? Should our penetration of foreign markets take place across a broad range of goods, or should it be concentrated in particular branches, products, and areas?

In order to establish a proper idea of the international specialization approach, let us divide economic activities into the following categories:

1. Activities "neutral" to foreign trade, i.e., production and consumption of a purely domestic nature. These include some commercial activities, different services, contracting, and food processing for regional needs.

2. Activities closely connected with existing natural resources, climatic conditions, agriculture, and energy supply. Examples are coal output and grain production.

3. Activities whose choice and location are not directly constrained by any existing basic natural condition. Under this category are all kinds of processing industries, based on capital, manpower, and know-how. The availability of skilled manpower is a decisive factor. Raw materials may be supplied where necessary. It is simply a matter of cost calculation.

The third category is a proper field for our discussion. Within this field, due to international competition and a tendency toward cost reduction, we face increasing specialization. Only in some essential branches (e.g., military production) are there quite different rules.

Processing industries may be divided into "progressive" (rapidly growing demand) and "regressive" categories. Good examples of the first group are electronic devices, nuclear equipment components, office machines, data processing equipment; to the second group belong, for example, canned meat and fish.

The proper methodology of specialization should take into account existing production factors (manpower, technology, equipment, potential outlets) in deciding which progressive production program should be developed. This ability to select the best kind of activity seems to belong to the most rapidly developing countries in the Western world, e.g., Japan, the Netherlands, and the Federal Republic of Germany.

The process of international specialization is taking place at the commodity level rather than at the branch level, as most industrialized countries retain production in many different branches while at the same time specializing within branches in selected products. In this way it is possible to maximize economies of scale.

The process of international specialization should be dynamic. Today's specialization pattern may become less favorable due to changes in world demand. It is necessary, therefore, to examine the tendencies and trends in foreign markets and to adjust production accordingly.

When advocating the internationalization of production, however, we should be aware of the disadvantages of this type of development. This is of special interest to small and medium-sized countries like Poland. Growing specialization means growing interdependence with foreign economies. In other words, foreign stimuli are likely to affect the home policy of stabilization. Adjustments to the world situation, necessary in a specialized economy, may provoke internal tensions and added social cost.

We are of the opinion, however, that positive advantages— which need not be listed in this paper—prevail. The impact of the specialized development of international trade should have a stimulating impact on East-West economic relations and a more balanced turnover.

The development of long-term industrial cooperation (IC) agreements seems to be an important contribution to international specialization, since from its very nature it means allocating activities between countries at the level of specific products and not at the branch level.

The present degree of specialization in Polish industry does not satisfy our expectations. In the machinery and equipment sector of our exports (Section 7 of the UN Standard International Trade Classification [SITC]), there are about 50 main categories of equipment and investment goods. For Poland, 65 percent of our export value in the section is derived from 17 important groups (e.g., ships, chemical engineering lines, cars, building equipment, machine tools, and power generating units). By contrast, the number of machinery groups, representing 65 percent of export value in Spain, is seven; in the Federal Republic of Germany, six. We concluded that the existing diversification of Polish production should be considerably reduced.

Over time, we should carefully select certain items for production specialization. It is necessary to distinguish between progressive and regressive products for the next five-year program and to make the bulk of our investment and production decisions in the first category. We should start large-scale production for selected products to enjoy all advantages of scale and specialization. The selected products should be compatible with market forecasts and modernity requirements.

The choice and marketing of specialized products is closely connected with international IC. Cooperation agreements enable us to concentrate our research work and investment outlays on specific products and to rely on the technical experiences and subdeliveries of our partners.

Technical and industrial cooperation involves scientific research, design and documentation of new projects, adaptation of existing processes in manufacturing, joint production and subdeliveries, as well as joint selling decisions. It results in a direct relationship between two or more partners in different countries to carry out the above duties according to their agreements. The essential features of these agreements are:

1. A direct relationship between the cooperating producers.

2. Preparing reports, manufacturing products, components, spare parts, or providing services in accordance with the technical, time, and organizational parameters specified and agreed upon by the partners.

3. The considerable frequency of deliveries and a long duration of the agreement.

A mutual, obligatory agreement between two or more interested sides forms the basis for cooperation. The agreement can be a framework, requiring detailed data for the specified subjects of cooperation (such as the Poland-Yugoslavia agreement on the production of cars), or it can consist of a number of specified production agreements (such as a Polish-British agreement on the production of cranes).

On the Polish side, cooperation agreements can be signed by production enterprises, combines or unions, and other industrial units; by way of some competent foreign trade enterprises; or directly, if they have been authorized by the Minister of Foreign Trade and Shipping.

In the past few years, Polish authorities issued bylaws to encourage Polish industrial and trade enterprises to extend cooperative relations abroad to the benefit of both sides. The decisionmaking process has now been simplified, and facilities have been introduced in the field of investments for the correct organization of the cooperation supplies.

One-way or two-way deliveries, which are an indispensable condition for starting or expanding the coproduction of final products, are especially interesting for the growth and development of specialized production. We could mention here the Polish-British production of self-propelled cranes or the Polish-US manufacture of heavy bulldozers. These are positive links between the specialization and cooperation procedures. In our agreements with these foreign partners, we confine ourselves to some selected types of building equipment. But our producers do go deeper and further with our production program. We are able to enter not only the markets of our cooperating partners but also some new ones, due to our improved reputation and better marketing power.

The above mentioned forms of IC are based on a long-term, mutually agreed upon exchange of goods and services offered and rendered by the independent economic units. Each cooperation element (parts of final goods, technological documentation and services, marketing services, organization of selling) is described quantitatively as to price and specified as to the time and place of its delivery or rendering. The cooperating subjects at the same time keep their full autonomy, both economic and legal (costs, internal organization of production), and independently calculate the earned profits. Currently, we meet with this type of cooperation almost exclusively in Polish practice and we count on its further intensive development.

Another type of IC that can contribute to the development of our specialization program is the so-called capital cooperation of two or more partners who undertake a common economic activity (service, production, research, or project) within one organization, giving rise to new legal and economic types of organizations in one or both partner countries.

Considering the place and character of the capital cooperation (the so-called joint ventures), we can distinguish the following:

1. Joint investment and production or scientific research ventures in one of the countries involved or in a third country.

2. Joint trade ventures distributing the production of one or both partners on markets of the third countries.

The most frequent form of joint cooperation is the building of production plants, their exploitation, and the undertaking of scientific research within one of the cooperating countries, the profit being shared according to the contribution.

The main economic difference between the current IC and joint ventures lies in the specification of the effects of the cooperation. In current IC each partner names his own price and specifies his own cost, while in organic cooperation there is the joint selling price and the overall production cost, with neither concept quantitatively specified in the agreement since they depend on the market situation, the organization of production, and the quality of joint management.

This is the new direction of promising development for the future specialization of our industry. It should stimulate our managers to take further steps toward concentration and specialization of production and the further elimination of unnecessary production items.

Comment

Thomas A. Wolf

I've known Professor Tabaczynski for five or six years, and I'm always struck by the balance in his presentations. They are always well thought out and comprehensive; he always seems optimistic, but he also has a sense of proportion. There is very little in his paper that I disagree with. My comments will focus on a few issues he raises, with the hope that our Polish colleagues will in turn elaborate even further.

First, a few words about specialization, one of the important themes of Tabaczynski's paper. When I was in Warsaw in 1977, there was a lively discussion at the Foreign Trade Research Institute about the appropriate foreign trade strategy Poland should follow. I imagine that the discussion continues and is still lively. An interesting distinction was made then between product specialization, the prime emphasis in Professor Tabaczynski's paper, and specialization by geographical market. The discussion tended to dwell mostly on the geographical aspect; that is, should a country like Poland attempt to single out a few important geographical markets for its exports and achieve a high profile in those markets, or should it follow a low profile strategy and remain a residual supplier in several markets? This was right after the Polish golf cart case, and it was felt that perhaps the only way to really prosper was never to become that important an element in a given Western market for fear of being hit with antidumping regulations and protectionist barriers. Would increased product specialization of the type Tabaczynski emphasizes imply to a certain extent a greater geographical concentration of Polish exports?

Tabaczynski does cite the relatively high number of product groups that account for roughly two-thirds of Poland's exports of manufactured products. This is in contrast to West Germany, Japan, Spain, and some other countries, as he notes. What isn't entirely clear is whether he is referring to Poland's total export structure, exports to the industrialized West, or exports to a greater area, perhaps the non-ruble area? Would Professor Tabaczynski expect to find significant difference in this crude measure of specialization among the various large export markets that Poland has, that is, between the industrialized West, the CMEA region, and the developing countries? If there are significant differences, why? And to what extent do the relationships with other CMEA countries really constrain Poland's attempt to increase its degree of specialization in exports, or are the other relationships perhaps a reinforcing influence? We would welcome more discussion about the interaction of different major geographical markets in the Polish export strategy.

Tabaczynski also notes that the products ultimately selected for more intensive development and specialization should be those compatible not only with market forecasts but also with the requirements to update Polish domestic industry. I am not certain whether he is thinking of a kind of tradeoff; that is, in some cases, external market forces might call for specialization in certain areas while domestic demand might call for less specialization and concentration on other products.

The second major point has to do with forecasting future trends. Tabaczynski stresses the ability to forecast with some degree of certainty and notes that there is an attempt in his institute and elsewhere in Poland to try to divide the different products and industries into those that could be considered progressive, with fast-growing demand on the world market, and those that would be regressive. But how can such a distinction be made? Industrial cooperation agreements (ICAs) are often seen in Poland as an important way to obtain information about world market trends. This raises another question: If one must sign an agreement and become a full-fledged partner with a Western firm to obtain some of the benefits of increased information, how does the Polish partner know at the time that it is concluding an agreement (1) that it is in the right industry and (2) that it is looking at the right partner within that industry? This raises the whole question of how forecasts are being made, what kind of information is being processed, and what the coordination is between the micro level—the enterprise level— and the macro level—the planning level.

As to the selection of the industries in which Poland should specialize, Tabaczynski does give some examples of so-called progressive industries and regressive industries. A number of other, especially smaller and medium-sized, countries that do have planning bodies are probably going through a similar exercise, trying to identify their future niche in the world economy. Many of the big corporations, if they are as efficient as we seem to think they are, presumably are engaging in the same process. Therefore, the so-called progressive industries may correspond to those that are labeled as most progressive by these other countries. The question is, if everyone is targeting those particular industries as the industries of the future, what is going to happen? Are we going to have a glut while products in some of the other industries that might not be so progressive (in the sense of having the most advanced technology or even the greatest growth rate in world consumption) may be undersupplied simply because everyone wants to move into the more progressive industries? More specifically, how do economic researchers and planners in Poland see Poland in the worldwide division of labor? Who does Poland see as its competitors in the world economy, and at what technological level? Is it always necessary to have the most advanced technology?

It is very refreshing to hear Tabaczynski stress that "progressive specialization means growing interdependence with foreign economies," which means the potential of greater integration of Poland into the world market. But he also cites that a growing interdependence will create higher risks for achieving a domestic policy of stabilization and that adjustments to changes in the world economy "may provoke internal tensions and some additional social costs." He briefly discussed these in his presentation, and I hope that I am correctly interpreting his conclusions. He seems to be talking about growing tensions or the possibility of greater tensions and costs at both the micro and the macro levels. At the micro level, the need is for more flexible reallocation of resources—labor and capital—among and within different industries as fundamental changes in world market conditions occur. At the macro level, he notes that specialization to some extent may necessitate increased direct linkages with the world market (this also comes out in Giezgala's paper (p. 87) when he talks about the transaction prices, the LEOs, and so forth), and these increased direct linkages should mean that the Polish economy will be more vulnerable in a macroeconomic sense to external economic disturbances. So I interpret Tabaczynski as saying that at both the micro and at the macro level there will have to be more flexibility in the Polish economy if there is to be more interdependence without creating substantially greater internal instability.

How are these different issues perceived in Poland? What are the major potential or actual tensions and costs that are deriving from this increase in interdependence? Is it the problem of labor mobility, of trying to enhance the potential for the actual reallocation of labor among enterprises, within enterprises, and so forth? Is it the fear of imported inflation? Is it the coordination of investments? Or are there other issues? The answers would be very interesting from the standpoint of US firms working in the polish environment.

My final point has to do with the relationship between specialization, interdependence, and IC. One of the questions raised at the end of the case study, as a speculation to be sure, is whether International Harvester and BUMAR interests in the long run will be more complementary or more competitive. Of course, it is not clear that it is always an either/or proposition. But it is interesting whether the strong complementarity that seems to exist in this particular example of IC and in most of the other cases that actually have been implemented will continue over the longer run. If we continue to see sluggish demand on the Western world markets and persisting unemployment and general stagflation in the West, this would suggest to Western firms that they need to push to find new export markets. Of course, the CMEA region—the East—would be a logical place to try to compensate for sluggish demand in the West, one of the main motivations for most IC seen to date. On the Polish side—and more generally on the East European side— a continued hard currency debt problem might suggest that they will try to hold down hard currency imports and will be pushing exports to a very competitive and yet very sluggish Western market. And, as Campbell also points out (see p. 92), another factor might be that over time Poland may find that the CMEA market for products coming out of ICAs might not be quite as attractive as originally thought, maybe because there is increased competition in the CMEA, or perhaps for other reasons. So it does raise the question of whether ICAs might take on a more competitive rather than a complementary relationship.

This is a very complicated issue, to be sure. It depends very much on what is going to happen in the Western world market, what happens within the CMEA, and what the particular strategies are of each country and enterprise involved.

Reply

Professor Wolf and others have raised the issue of Poland's strategy on specialization. The same question has been put to us by our colleagues in Poland. But when our colleagues from the ministries and enterprises come to the Institute and ask what the best commodity is, the best branch on which they should concentrate, our answer is that we can't answer these questions, because it depends on the industrial branch, on the concrete situation, and on the forecast.

It is possible on the central level to take a macro approach to this problem by establishing some general rules of choice making, but it is not possible (or it is extremely difficult) to choose concrete commodities or concrete branches. The fundamental question is: Should we, from above, decide and order which branches or commodities should be chosen for this specialization program, or should we, as an advisory body to the Ministry of Foreign Trade, propose what economic parameters are necessary in order to encourage people and to stimulate people on the executive levels to make decisions by themselves? I believe that the latter course is best, because those people are better acquainted and have more experience with the relevant problems. Our general attitude is that first it is necessary to introduce the appropriate economic rules of the game, and then allow people to make decisions.

In these big LEOs, more people should be educated and made responsible for making these decisions. But this takes time. When a person is accustomed to having someone else think for him, he cannot make a transformation in a day. It is not only an economic problem; it is to some extent a psychological problem.

We should influence the economic parameters; we should establish the new economic climate; and we should wait and see in which branches there are appropriate, ambitious people who are prepared to make forecasts, to go ahead with their proposals. There are already such branches that live up to our expectations, where the executives are prepared, not only from the intellectual but also from the psychological point of view, to carry out their special ambition to enter the domestic and foreign markets.

Furthermore, at our Institute we don't think there should be product specialization for Western *or* for Eastern markets. We speak about specialization in general, specialization of the Polish industry as a whole national industry, not for special customers, not for special countries, and not for special geographical or political directions. The 17 branches mentioned are a general statistic embracing our exports to the West and the East. To be sure, we currently export most of our machinery to the East. We should specialize in general, especially since we are a medium-sized country; we can't afford to produce different commodities for Eastern and for Western markets. Of course, as is customary in business, there are special orders; but that is quite another problem.

As far as geographical specialization is concerned, there are people who are very proud to export to many countries. For instance, our people who are exporting Polish cars (which are almost unknown in the US) are very proud because they export them to many different countries. And we say to our colleagues from this large economic organization, "That is a wrong policy; you should concentrate your sales on selected markets, because for such industrial commodities as cars, the problem of service and spare parts is paramount." So we should concentrate on some specifics and be good at providing those products for selected markets.

The example of exporters in what the UN calls newly industrialized countries (NIC) is instructive. There are 11 countries—Brazil, Spain, Portugal, South Korea, and Taiwan among them—that have made a tremendous increase in exports. But 70 percent of their increase was in 40 commodities, and 40 percent of their increase was in 10 commodities. This is a shining example of product specialization. And as far as their geographical distribution is concerned, 75 percent of their export goes to five countries in the European Common Market and to the US.

Problems of Polish-US Economic Relations

A Polish Perspective

Zygmunt Kossut

At the beginning of the 1970s, the political atmosphere in East-West relations was considerably improved. In 1972, the US President visited Poland. The Warsaw Joint Communique, issued by the President of the United States and the First Secretary of the Central Committee of the Polish United Workers' Party on the first of June 1972, created a new stage of development between Poland and the US and became the turning point of Polish-US contemporary relations. The US made it possible for Poland to receive loans and guarantees from the Export-Import Bank (Eximbank). The purchases of new US technology and investment goods could thereby be realized. New commercial credit possibilities made it easier to import agricultural products, especially grain, from the US. Also some improvements in shipping and in air transport between the two countries were introduced. At the same time, the two parties established the Joint Polish-American Trade Commission to prepare the way for further development of Polish-US economic relations and to provide facilities for doing bilateral business. Every session of this interstate Commission becomes very important in Polish-US relations and creates new forms of promoting economic cooperation. The Commission plays a substantial role in shaping Polish-US economic relations and has already done a very useful job in solving some important trade problems.

A long step toward further development of political and economic relations between Poland and the US was taken during and after the visit of the First Secretary of the Central Committee of the Polish United Workers' Party to the United States in 1974. Two very important documents were signed: the Joint Statement on the Principles of Polish-American Relations and the Joint Statement on the Development of Economic, Industrial, and Technological Cooperation between Polish People's Republic and the United States of America. At the same time, agreements were reached on the following issues:

1. Financing the scientific-technological cooperation.

2. Preventing double taxation and ensuring that firms on both sides would not try to avoid paying income tax.

3. Expanding trade in agricultural products.

4. Mutual cooperation between the Polish Chamber of Foreign Trade and the US Chamber of Commerce.

Agreements on cooperation in the mining industry and on the protection of natural environments were also signed.

The official documents on bilateral political and economic cooperation between Poland and the US signed in 1972 and afterwards made a good framework for development. The confirmation of the Most-Favored Nation (MFN) Clause for Poland by the US Congress was a logical and necessary step toward regulating economic relations. Last but not least, Polish and American businessmen began to cooperate more closely. Among other things, the Polish-US Economic Council was established. It is a useful, nongovernmental advisory body and a good forum for discussing controversial problems.

There is much to be done to improve Polish-US economic relations. In 1977, for instance, the share of Polish exports to the Western developed countries was 31.2 percent and the share of Polish imports from the same group of countries was 43.3 percent. The figures for European Economic Community (EEC) countries were 18.2 percent and 24.0 percent, and the figures for the US were 3.0 percent and 3.7 percent. Polish-US trade in that year reached $910.8 million, exports $365.5 million, and imports $545.3 million. The figures for 1972 were: $238.1 million, $128.1 million, and $110.0 million. In five years, turnover increased 3.83 times, exports 2.85 times, and imports 4.96 times, at current market prices. This relatively fast development of Polish-US trade was possible because of the agreements reached between the two countries. The target for 1980, accepted by both parties, is a $2 billion turnover, or 35 percent of Polish-EEC countries turnover of 1977. The gap between Polish-US trade on the one hand and Polish-EEC trade on the other suggests that more rapid development of Polish-US economic relations is not only possible but necessary. It also means that there is plenty of room to enlarge Polish-US trade. It should be stressed that the share of Poland in US trade is very small. In 1976 it equalled 0.26 percent in imports and 0.54 percent in exports.

But there are some conditions that must be fulfilled in expanding Polish-US trade. Changing the structure of Polish exports to—and Polish imports from—the US is one of the most important conditions. Structural changes of the Polish economy in the last 33 years have made Poland an industrialized country with many modern branches. In 1977, 64.7 percent of Poland's GNP was produced in the industry and construction sectors. These modern branches form the basis of Poland's trade development with other industrialized countries. In 1977 the share of electrical engineering and light industries products was 25.7 percent and 18.2 percent of Polish exports to the US. There is considerable improvement in the structure of Polish exports to the US in comparison with 1972, but it is still far from Polish expectations. Our intention is to export more manufactured consumer goods as well as industrial goods. This is the natural and logical consequence of industrialization. There have also been some changes in Polish imports from the US. Imports of products of both electrical engineering and chemical industries are growing, for instance, and in 1977 reached the level of 24.3 percent and 6.6 percent of total Polish imports from the US. This favorable direction of trade development should be continued.

Structural changes in Polish-US trade do not mean that imports and exports of agricultural produce and products of food industries are unimportant. Poland is interested in importing grain and feed from— as well as exporting Polish agricultural products to—the US. This specific field of Polish-US trade is well known.

The next important objective of Polish foreign trade is to maximize exports. The question now is how to increase Polish exports to the US and at the same time make more use of the international division of labor.

Production of adequate finished goods and services for export is the traditional way of doing international business. At the same time, new types of international economic and commercial relations occur. The following forms of cooperative activities have been identified:
1. Exchange of technical information
2. Licensing
3. Supply or leasing of plants or production lines
4. Contract manufacturing and subcontracting
5. Joint research and development (R&D)
6. Coproduction
7. Specialization
8. Co-marketing and provision of after-sales service
9. Joint tendering and joint projects.

In practice, some of these activities can overlap (for example, licensing and supply of plants), but this list characterizes the possibilities of doing international business in new forms. Poland supports these kinds of international cooperation for good reasons. First, a more permanent division of labor between partners can be established. Second, deeper specialization of production can be organized and economies of scale can be utilized. As a result, Poland supports long-term industrial and marketing cooperation agreements. There are many difficulties that must be overcome before the partners of such agreements will begin to benefit from such forms of international cooperation, but after that the benefits last for a very long time. Industrial cooperation (IC) needs persistent partners. There are some good examples of such cooperation between Polish and American Businessmen; the BUMAR-International Harvester (IH) ICA is one of them.

IC already has a good tradition in Polish-US economic relations and, therefore, can be easily developed further. More precise fields of such cooperation should be elaborated, however, and the Polish and US governments should help businessmen create new projects. Large US corporations can play important roles in realizing major IC projects. IC between Poland and the US has been examined with great care in the papers prepared by the other Polish participants of this seminar. Formation of a consortium for realizing a given project or contract is another form of cooperation between Polish enterprises and foreign partners.

The participation of small and medium-sized firms and organizations in trade and IC is also desirable. There are some small American firms already operating in Poland, but it is too early to make generalizations. Some time must elapse before one can describe what kind of contribution small and medium-sized American firms can make to IC between the two countries.

Joint ventures create another problem. It is comparatively easy to organize such ventures in a country with convertible or hard currency. However, in the case of Poland, the application of a realistic model to such ventures creates many complex problems that must be solved. Some studies on the model(s) of organizing joint ventures in Poland are in progress.

Poland is also interested in other forms of cooperative activities, such as licensing and co-marketing as well as joint research and development.

Gaining better access to the American market is necessary to promote growth of Polish exports to the US. Marketing activities include organization, distribution, and promotion on the American market. Market research is going on constantly, and Polish enterprises regularly partake in international fairs and exhibitions. The distribution network, however, should be enlarged and advertising should be expanded. Polish enterprises and organizations now work to improve the distribution system by using American middlemen or by organizing domestic branches and subsidiaries. But new forms of organization should be developed, such as marketing joint ventures. Polish enterprises have some experience in this field in the US, but much more has been done in Western Europe. Therefore, the organization of further Polish-American marketing ventures in the US seems to be a realistic target. The distribution system for Polish goods is much better in the Eastern part than in the Western part of the US. Establishing a branch of the Polish Chamber of Foreign Trade in San Francisco was an important step toward establishing further commercial activities in that region.

Access to American markets may also be improved by lowering American protectionism. Protectionism is a matter of great concern for Polish businessmen. It is extremely difficult to give access to international division of labor when the tendency toward protectionism exists. Caution must be used in building a highly specialized industry to satisfy a chosen international market and in joining the international division of labor if the exporter can be stopped suddenly by some administrative regulation. In the history of Polish exports, there is the well-known case of bacon exported to Great Britain: After several decades of exporting this product, its sale dropped considerably and suddenly, because Great Britain joined the EEC with its agricultural policy and customs duties system. Another drastic example is the application of the US Trade Act of 1974 in the precedent-setting case of Polish Melex golf carts. The methodology of establishing the relevant fair value based on the price of a similar product sold by a US manufacturer could deprive Polish exporters of the possibility of effective competition in the US, creating a danger of foreclosing the US market.

There are other bottlenecks in Polish-US trade, such as quotas, license requests, and trigger prices. Quotas, for example, currently apply to such items as textiles and steel rods. Trigger prices affect steel products and nails. Trigger prices, quotas, licensing procedures, and other forms of tariff and non-tariff protectionism can kill any idea of participation in the international division of labor.

The following conclusions can be drawn from the above analysis.

First, Poland accepts foreign trade and international cooperation as very important factors of her economic development and looks for improved economic relations with her foreign partners, including the US. Polish-US economic relations have a long and good tradition, which should be cultivated carefully for the benefit of both sides. Continuous public relations activities are needed.

Second, Polish foreign trade, as any other, must be harnessed to the following long-term national objectives:

1. To continue the modernization of the Polish economy.

2. To make more use of international division of labor.

3. To increase Polish exports and imports, remembering that, in the case of Poland, exports are the main source of paying for imports.

4. To change the structure of exports and imports.

Structural changes of the Polish economy need to be reflected in the same changes in Polish foreign trade. Relatively more emphasis should be placed on industrial goods as well as on manufactured consumer goods.

Third, the US market makes enlargement of Polish exports quite possible, and there is plenty of room for US exports to Poland. Modern technologies, know-how, and industrial goods open broad perspectives for American exports to this country. Grain and feed will be important export items to Poland in the next few years.

Fourth, there are many ways of doing business between Poland and the US. Traditional trade of goods is the most important one, but new forms are growing quickly. Coproduction, co-marketing, joint tendering, and joint projects are supported by Poland and can be profitable for both parties. Joint research projects are also useful. The agreement reached by the Warsaw Foreign Trade Research Institute and Indiana University is a good example of this form of cooperation. There are other possible Polish-US research projects that could support economic relations of the two countries.

Fifth, access to the American market for Polish exporters as well as to the Polish market for American ones should be facilitated, marketing activities should be improved and protectionism should be lowered as much as possible.

Last but not least, the human side of business must be stressed. Doing business should not only be a duty, but also a pleasure.

STATISTICAL ANNEX

TABLE 1
Polish-US Trade and Trade Balance 1972-77
(Current prices in mill, US$)

Years	Total	Exports	Imports	Trade Balance
1972	263.4	141.7	121.7	+ 20.0
1973	504.6	190.1	314.5	− 124.4
1974	732.8	259.3	473.5	− 214.2
1975	823.6	234.1	589.5	− 355.4
1976	1114.3	282.0	832.3	− 550.3
1977	910.8	365.5	545.3	− 179.8

SOURCE: "Rocznik Statystyczny Handlu Zagranicznego" of several years and own calculations.

TABLE 2
Polish-US Trade and Trade Balance 1977-78
(FOB. Current prices in mill, US$)

Specification	1977	3 Quarters, 1978
Total	910.8	894.6
Exports to the US	365.5	350.0
Imports from the US	545.3	544.6
Trade balance	−179.8	−194.6

SOURCE: "Rocznik Statystyczny 1978" and current information.

TABLE 3

Polish Exports to the United States in 1977-78 by Branches
(FOB. Current Prices)

	1977	I-VIII, 1978	As Percentage of Total Exports	
	in mill US$		1977	I-VIII, 1978
Total	365.6	304.6	100.0	100.0
of which:				
Fuel and power	11.3	12.6	3.1	4.1
Products and industry:				
metallurgy	23.8	18.3	6.5	6.0
electrical engineering	94.0	95.0	25.7	31.3
chemical	13.5	8.5	3.7	2.8
mineral	6.2	5.8	1.7	1.9
paper and wood	10.7	9.4	2.9	3.1
light	66.3	53.9	18.2	17.7
food	135.7	99.5	37.1	32.8
others	0.2	1.2	0.0	0.3
Agricultural products	1.4	0.2	0.4	0.0
Others	2.4	0.2	0.7	0.0

SOURCE: Current information and own calculations.

TABLE 4

Polish Imports from the United States in 1977-78 by Branches
(FOB. Current Prices)

	1977	I-VIII, 1978	As Percentage of Total Exports	
	in mill US$		1977	I-VIII, 1978
Total	545.3	398.4	100.0	100.0
of which:				
Fuel and power	0.1	—	0.0	0.0
Products of industry:				
metallurgy	19.8	7.3	3.6	1.8
electrical engineering	132.3	56.3	24.3	14.1
chemical	35.7	21.3	6.6	5.3
mineral	1.3	0.4	0.2	0.1
paper and wood	5.6	0.3	1.0	0.1
light	3.9	10.1	0.7	2.5
food	81.9	94.2	15.0	23.6
others	—	3.8	—	1.0
Agricultural products	259.8	204.7	47.4	51.5
Others	4.9	—	0.9	—

SOURCE: Current information and own calculations.

Comment

Josef C. Brada

Professor Kossut's perspective on Polish-American economic relations has two virtues. It is succinct and complete, qualities rarely found in one paper. Moreover, there is little in his paper with which I would take issue. Consequently, since Professor Kossut has given us a Polish perspective on our mutual economic relations, I would like to give a brief American perspective on the points raised in his paper.

I would begin by echoing Professor Kossut's view that, in terms of government-to-government relations and the basis they provide for expanded Polish-American trade, the situation is quite satisfactory. There is, of course, much more that could be done on both sides; I shall return to this later. I also agree that the US-Polish Economic Commission has served as a valuable forum for face-to-face discussions of problems of mutual interest to participants in Polish-American trade. Moreover, it is difficult to foresee circumstances that would, in the future, destroy this fabric of government-to-government, firm-to-firm, and person-to-person relations, which has been the basis of the rapidly growing trade and cooperation between the US and Poland.

Indeed, it seems quite safe to say that any limitations on the expansion of our mutual relations will come from economic forces rather than from politics. Professor Kossut has mentioned the problem of American trade barriers and the specter of protectionism. Although I agree that the rise in protectionist sentiment is a serious problem, and one to be confronted by the American business community and by our trade partners, I do *not* think that it is particularly useful to view it in an East-West context or in terms of specific cases such as Polish golf carts, although I can understand why the Polish government and East European experts may choose to view it that way.

During the 1950s and 1960s, US trade policy toward Eastern Europe was completely divorced from our global trade strategy. While we were busy erecting controls, embargoes, and tariff and non-tariff barriers to minimize our trade with East European countries, our global policy was seeking to promote greater international exchanges of goods, technology, and capital. Within such a policy framework, Poland's natural objectives were to minimize the adverse impact of American East-West trade policies on Polish-American trade. This policy was remarkably successful. Today, therefore, Poland finds itself in new circumstances regarding trade and industrial cooperation (IC) with the US. To deal with this new environment, Poland should recognize that its trade relations with the US will increasingly be governed by America's *global* trade policy and less by our East-West trade policies. This recognition on Poland's part should lead it to realize the limitations of viewing its trade with the US in an East-West framework, and to shift its perception of our mutual relations to a global context, which of course changes the possibilities for influencing American trade policy.

There is another side to the protectionist issue, to which Professor Kossut alludes, but which I would like to examine more closely. This is protectionism on the Polish side, that is, reducing imports from the West in response to continuing hard currency deficits.

Poland's development strategy has led it to run large payments deficits and to accumulate extensive hard currency debts. Poland hopes to resolve these by expanding her exports of manufactures to the West. This solution raises two questions. The first is whether or not such an increased volume of manufactured goods can, in fact, be successfully marketed in the West in the face of slow Western growth, of rising competition from newly industrializing countries, and of past Polish performance in marketing such goods in the West. Second, even if the market for these goods did exist, it is not evident that their supply is assured. Polish development strategy has called for a rapid growth of both investment *and* consumption. It should be obvious that the government cannot increase the availability of exports by reducing domestic consumption, and the 1976-80 plan did not call for a decrease in investment, although since 1977 the decrease in investment has been quite substantial. In view of the fact that Poland's export drive must overcome both demand and supply obstacles, it is not inconceivable that Poland's balance-of-payments problems are likely to be resolved by a reduction in imports rather than, or in addition to, an increase in exports. The implications of such a development for the growth of Polish-American trade are both obvious and undesirable.

IC in its many forms is, of course, a possible solution to many of the problems that face tne expansion of Polish-American trade. However, IC is a long-term proposition, with little relevance for the short-term problems facing us. Obstacles remain on both sides. Since I am taking an American perspective, I might say that the complaints of American businessmen about the difficulty of doing business in Eastern Europe have been met in some cases with insufficient sympathy by East European trade officials. Whenever I have raised this issue in Eastern Europe, I have received two replies: One is that "Americans don't understand the system. They don't know how to get along here the way the West Germans do, for example." The second is that

"Some American firms just cannot cope, so they go away. Those that stay have learned to do things *our* way."

It may be that West German businessmen are more adept at doing business in Eastern Europe, but even they face problems. In a recent article, Professor von Czege reports on a survey of West German firms engaged in IC in Eastern Europe.[1] Sixty-one percent of the firms responded that the East European decisionmaking structure hindered cooperation and 66 percent reported that it hindered innovation in IC projects. I could go on, but I think the point has been made. The problem is not just one of American rigidity or naivete. Moreover, those American firms that do stay and adapt to doing business the East European way often report that they would do more business and undertake more cooperation projects if better and more flexible procedures could be developed.

If my remarks have been unduly pessimistic and negative they should not obscure the overall progress that has been made in Polish-American relations. This conference and the larger project have after all examined the IH-BUMAR coproduction venture, which is, on balance, an example of a successful Polish-American ICA. The lessons to be learned from that case study can help both sides to overcome many of the remaining obstacles to US-Polish IC in the 1980s.

Reply

Professor Brada has made some exceedingly interesting remarks regarding protectionism in the US, alleged protectionism in Poland, and the role IC can play to overcome barriers to commerce. I especially appreciate Professor Brada pointing out that US trade policy vis-à-vis Poland is governed increasingly by US global trade strategy and less and less by US policy on East-West trade. I would like to point out, however, that while there is a tendency for US policy to move in the direction indicated by Professor Brada, several important obstacles do remain that influence, in a discriminatory fashion, Poland and other socialist countries. I am referring to the special anti-dumping and market disruption provisions of the US Trade Act of 1974.

With regard to Poland's access to Western markets, we are dealing much more with West European countries and enterprises than with

---

1. A. Wass von Czege, "Industrial Cooperation and the Transfer of Technology Between the Federal Republic of Germany and Hungary," *ACES Bulletin,* 20.2 (Summer 1978): 13-22.

US firms. If we wanted to discuss obstacles to market access, we would have to discuss first some general rules in a given country and, further, to see the situation product by product. First, the EC countries have very strong protectionist rules for their agricultural goods, which hurt Poland considerably. They have elaborated special rules and we have to accept them. Access to West European countries for our farm products is, therefore, even more difficult than is access to the States. But if we focus on manufactured goods, we sometimes find great obstacles in the US. What we often observe is that after some level of Polish exports has been reached, we have to be very careful. We have invested to create capacity to produce products specially oriented to penetrate the US market but, as was the case with golf carts, our penetration was stopped. If we produce manufactured products for the special US market, we don't know when we will be stopped by some general rules here in this country. And this is not only the case for Polish golf carts. For instance, the new trigger price mechanism practically stopped Polish steel exports to the US. Can we expect the US to implement more of these types of rules?

I want to stress again that the main objective of the Polish side is to facilitate long-term IC agreements with the US. Poland is determined to include IC with Western partners into our long-term economic strategy rather than to rely on IC as short-term business policy.

US-Polish Industrial Cooperation: Achievements, Problems, Prospects

Edwin Zagorski

Industrial cooperation (IC) has in recent years played a growing role in US-Polish economic relations. This is demonstrated both by the results achieved and the many conferences, seminars, and writings on the subject. For this paper, IC is defined as partnership in production, extended to related activities, such as marketing, research and development, transfer of technology, and joint designing of new products.

This kind of IC between Poland and the industrialized West began to grow in the early 1960s. IC with the US did not begin until the early 1970s, when the political climate in East-West relations had considerably improved. The subsequent summit meetings, governmental and other institutional arrangements largely contributed to the building of the confidence and of the infrastructure necessary for the new and creative patterns of cooperation in production.

The largest agreements have been concluded by Polish industrial organizations with such well-known American companies as:

—International Harvester (IH)	Joint manufacture and sale of crawler tractors and loaders
—Clark Equipment	Heavy duty axles
—Koehring International	Hydraulic building machines

—Given International   Machine tools
—Waterbury Farrel   Machine tools
—Singer Corporation   Sewing machines
—RCA and Corning Glass Works   Color television tubes, etc.

Even though US-Polish cooperation links do not have a very long tradition, all of the larger agreements meet the requirements of IC. The agreements cover products with a high degree of processing and ensure the continuous modernization of the products concerned. Most are long-term agreements, usually accompanied by worldwide marketing arrangements. These characteristics can secure a better return on the investment outlays and bring about the necessary infrastructure for cooperation in technology.

Within a relatively short time the US has established a significant position in Polish IC with the West. Of the 200-odd major cooperation agreements operating with Western countries, about 20 are dominant; 4 of these, or 20 percent, have been concluded with American companies. Also the rate of growth of US-Polish cooperation deliveries is quite spectacular in terms of value. Reciprocal turnover (imports and exports) increased from $1.5 million in 1972 to $21.0 million in 1976 and about $16 million in 1978.

In 1976 the US ranked third in cooperation between Poland and the West (in terms of value), after Italy and the Federal Republic of Germany. The US share in cooperation deliveries from Poland to the industrialized West in 1972, 1975, and 1978 was 6 percent, 14 percent, and 7 percent. Cooperation deliveries from the US to Poland didn't begin until 1973, but grew rapidly and reached approximately 22 percent of total cooperation imports from Western countries in 1976 and 14 percent in 1978. From 1972-76 total cooperation deliveries from Poland to the US amounted to $31.6 million, and from the US to Poland totalled $30.8 million during the same period. Consequently, the balance in mutual cooperation deliveries was reached within a relatively short time.

With regard to the branch distribution of cooperation agreements, there seems to be a positive correlation between particular forms of cooperation and branches of industry. For example, coproduction based on specialization of partners is particularly common in the mechanical engineering and transport equipment industry. On the other hand, the supply of plants or complete production lines appears mainly in the chemical industry, metallurgy, and light industries.

In US-Polish IC, the greatest progress has been achieved in coproduction based on specialization. This particular form, which is really the heart of cooperation, has been dominant and explains both the trends in development and the degree of maturity of IC in US-Polish relations.

The next most common form of US-Polish cooperation is the supplying of plants or complete production lines. Other forms, such as licensing in exchange for products or simple sub-deliveries, are far behind in terms of volume.

In practice, all forms of IC are in a process of permanent evolution, by which the contents of cooperation ventures are steadily enriched and diversified. Very often, just by establishing a certain continuity of contact between two partners, simple forms of IC evolve into real cooperation ventures. In addition, particular elements from various types of cooperation are often intermixed and appear together in a single agreement. This explains both the diversity of cooperation contracts and their particular adaptability to different business situations, as well as to different needs and conditions in particular industrial branches.

In the innovative development of IC, a frequently discussed possibility is capital cooperation in the form of joint ventures. So far, Poland has had little experience in setting up such ventures, but the problem is under study and the first steps have been taken by permitting foreigners to invest in Poland. A Council of Ministers decree of May 14, 1976, allows foreigners, both individual and corporate, to invest in such sectors as handicraft, hotels, restaurants, catering, and other services. The regional councils of the provinces have the authority to approve investments.

On May 26, 1976, the Finance Minister issued other decrees spelling out the guidelines for foreign currency investments in Poland. The rules cover such questions as how to open foreign currency accounts and how these accounts may be administered. The guidelines also detail regulations concerning the special rate of foreign currency exchange as well as provisions for repatriating profits.

In the manufacturing industries, there are some serious obstacles to joint ventures. Sometimes systemic impediments are raised, but these are not crucial. In practice, the greatest obstacle to equity joint ventures stems from the inconvertibility of the national currency and, subsequently, from exchange rate difficulties. Because of this, the calculation of production costs and profits is highly complicated. To overcome these inconveniences, various models of joint venture have been considered. One of them involves jointly designed and financed products, manufactured in Polish-owned and -operated factories and marketed by a joint trading company established abroad.

However, some experienced Western businessmen do not think that property ownership is a decisive factor for doing business through IC. What really matters is not so much property but profit, which can be well secured on a contractual basis through long-term cooperation agreements.

From the beginning, US-Polish cooperation in production has been prompted by at least three important factors, among which the policy of détente proved to be one of the most powerful. The long-lasting process of détente is indispensable in providing an atmosphere for long-term and interdependent cooperation links.

The second driving force came from the American side, as US business managers began to realize that Japan and West European countries had outpaced the US in economic collaboration with Eastern Europe by about ten years. It became an economic necessity for the Americans to recapture the lost position and to look for forms of business that would help them get a permanent foothold in the region. One of the significant elements of the new commercial policy of the US toward the East European countries was a reduction of barriers to the transfer of technology, which considerably improved conditions for the development of IC.

A third factor on the Polish side was the outward oriented model of economic growth adopted in Poland at the beginning of 1971, which accelerated the development of trade and IC with foreign partners.

Other factors on both sides also contributed to the further growth of IC. First, Poland belongs to the East European region with more rapid growth potential than other parts of the world. No less important is the country's political and economic stability. This factor is growing in importance, particularly for those American companies that have been facing less stable and deteriorating environments in other parts of the world. Next, the geographical location of Poland facilitates export penetration of American firms to the East European countries and is also a convenient production base for cooperation with Western Europe.

Poland is the ancestral homeland of millions of Americans. This fact, combined with the generally appreciated flexibility and openness of Polish businessmen, contributes to a greater compatibility between American and Polish business partners. This understanding is reinforced by Polish production and technological potential, as well as by the performance standards and professional skills of many Polish industrial organizations. With the development and modernization of many industries in Poland, areas for long-term US-Polish cooperation seem to be growing still larger, for greater complementarity among countries usually arises when they approach similar stages of development.

A third set of factors facilitating IC with Poland is related to the country's outward-oriented strategy of economic growth, which has resulted in bringing end-users and producers closer to foreign trade.

In the new economic structure, industrial organizations have been directly involved in business operations with foreign countries. Hence a substantial portion of foreign trade enterprises have been transferred from the Foreign Trade Ministry to the industrial ministries, and others have been incorporated into the industrial unions and large industrial organizations. Moreover, the Minister of Foreign Trade has permitted some large factories to set up their own foreign trade departments and to operate directly in foreign markets.

At the same time, larger enterprises and industrial organizations have been given greater managerial freedom. They are now responsible not only for current production, but also for investment policy, research and development (R&D), marketing and the development of IC with foreign partners.

According to the case studies of Mary Allen Yacura, most American companies that have successfully established a relationship with Poland are looking for extended long-term involvement, and generally consider IC with Polish partners both feasible and attractive as a long-term option.[1]

On the American side, Polish exports enjoy Most-Favored Nation (MFN) tariff status, which plays an important role in the promotion of cooperation in production and technology. For the Polish partners, the American market has always been attractive because it offers cooperation opportunities, modern machinery and equipment and up-to-date technologies. The huge American market also provides a great opportunity for Polish exports of components or final products cooperatively produced. Large-scale production based on specialization can be highly profitable for both partners.

Since 1972 the US Export Import Bank (Eximbank) has been authorized to support American exports to Poland. Some of the US-Polish large cooperation agreements could be implemented only with the financial support of the Bank. Eximbank credit and guarantees have considerably improved the competitive position of American companies in the Polish market.

A fourth positive factor stimulating US-Polish IC concerns the economic performance of developed market economy countries. In the mid-1970s many Western economies were more or less stagnant, while the US economy continued to grow, although at a lower rate than earlier. As a result, US-Polish IC was not significantly affected by recession; this may favorably influence further cooperation initiatives at the enterprise level. It is also expected that the US, due to its natural and human resources as well as financial potential and technology, will continue to grow and occupy a leading position in the scientific and technical revolution in the West, which encourages Polish industrial organizations to look for cooperation with American companies in many branches of industry.

Which branches of industry are the most promising? The very essence of IC suggests that the best opportunities exist in those industries in which technological progress is of primary importance. This is why the highest concentration of cooperation agreements is in the mechanical engineering and transport equipment sectors. As for future prospects, in Poland's long-term development strategy, preference is given to industries based on natural resource endowments. Prospects seem to be most promising for American firms in coal mining and power generation, coal liquefaction and gasification, and the production of various chemicals based on coal processing. Another promising field is the chemical industry, based on abundant resources of sulfur. Since Poland ranks among the world's largest copper producers, copper-based industries also present great opportunities for cooperation in many branches of the electrical engineering industry. There are good prospects in the steel-making, foundry, and nonferrous metallurgy sectors. Opportunities can also be found in the aviation industry, transport equipment, electronics, petrochemical industry, machinery for agriculture, mining equipment, machinery for the food processing and machine tool industries, and the production of household appliances. Those branches of industry that are expected to develop with the extensive participation of foreign partners do not exclude, however, the growing prospects for cooperation in other sectors, such as light industry, furniture, and tourism.

It should be emphasized that in addition to development prospects in the sectors already mentioned, in each branch of industry one may find proposals that will receive due consideration if the cooperation helps a factory develop a good export product, so that a self-repayment system can be assured.

In the pragmatic approach to IC in Poland, it is essential to distinguish so-called delivery cooperation, which comprises the construction of new (turnkey) industrial plants, from other forms of cooperation based on the extension and modernization of existing facilities. In the first instance, which tends to consist of large-scale projects, these are coordinated by the Central Planning Authorities so that a given project may be incorporated into the medium-term (five-year) and annual plans. Such investment projects were predominant in the previous five-year plan (1971-75), in which about $17.5 billion (in hard currency) was spent on imports of technology, machinery, and installations.[2]

In the present five-year plan (1976-80) investment outlays are even higher, but are concentrated on modernizing existing capacities and completing projects. While new investment projects, coordinated by the Central Planning Authorities, are now developing on a rather selective basis, there is no limit to cooperation initiatives with regard to modernizing existing plants and restructuring the production programs. In the last instance, export-oriented proposals, based on coproduction and specialization, are welcomed, especially by outward-oriented producers in Poland.

The Polish experience permits one to draw certain conclusions about cooperation agreements with the best development prospects in spite of the differences in socio-economic systems. Practice has shown the most successful ventures to be those that involve the long-term complementarity of interests to the greatest possible extent. The community of interests may be seen clearly, for instance, when IC gives the partners a chance to start new lines of production that may have been too expensive for each without cooperation. The unprofitability of individual production may result, for example, from large investment outlays or high R&D costs.

Another point of common interest is the lowering of production costs through application of modern, highly efficient technologies and economies of scale. Lower production costs can strengthen the competitive position of each partner in local as well as in foreign markets. For internationally oriented producers, this is of utmost importance. The benefits from improved competitive power can then be shared by both partners.

A similar approach can apply to export expansion. If, for example, the American partner wants to strengthen his position on the East European markets through licensing and IC, as is the case with IH in its cooperation with BUMAR, the other partner might be willing to have in exchange better access to hard currency markets.

The same principle of mutual benefits also holds with regard to the transfer of technology. Here it is not only the question of one partner wanting to sell technology and the other being willing to buy it. Practice confirms that, for modern products involving advanced production technology, successful cooperation is usually carried out in the context of continued improvements of the products manufactured. The choice of the first technical line is important, because obsolete products have low prices and are difficult to sell, making the whole cooperation business unprofitable. It is also important that both partners be willing to move from simple to more integrated forms of cooperation in designing new products for joint manufacturing and marketing. In order to proceed along this line of cooperation, each partner must be convinced by his calculations that the joint designing and testing of new products would help him save R&D funds, as well as the most valuable intellectual resources, and use them effectively for implementation rather than development.

These stipulations can best be met in cooperation between equal partners or partners having nearly equal bargaining power. To be sure, where there are substantial differences between the partners in technical levels and in production performance, simple forms of cooperation, such as licensing and subdeliveries, may help to close these gaps in a relatively short time. Benefits need not be divided equally. It is essential, however, that the long-term balance of benefits be satisfactory for both partners. For instance, the benefits to the Polish partner from enhanced competitive position on the foreign market may not be equal to those of the American partner. But this lack of balance may be fully compensated for by increased opportunities to enhance one's potential for hard currency earnings.

IC has particularly bright prospects where conditions exist for the two-way transfer of technology. For example, in US-Polish negotiations on cooperation in the coal mining industry technologies developed in Poland and already tested in Polish mines are being considered for use in American coal mines. If successful, this would involve the export of Polish mining equipment to the US. American partners are also interested in Polish safety technology and equipment in coal mining. In return, the Polish side is interested in the application of certain American technologies, as well as machinery and equipment, in coal and copper extraction. Other possible areas for the two-way transfer of technology include environmental protection technologies and equipment.

Considering the goals that are supposed to be attained through IC, the question is sometimes raised as to which American firms, large or small, are more suited for cooperation. Naturally, the large American firms, very often multi-branch and multinational corporations well provided with capital and modern technology, are the first beneficiaries of the advantages offered by IC. Large corporations (MNCs), particularly those with a diversified scope of activities and worldwide marketing ability, are in a position to satisfy most of the cooperation requirements with regard to the long-term stability in business development, two-way flow of goods and services, cooperation in marketing and after-sale service, possibilities of cooperation in R&D, and so on. Due to long-term planning of business development, large corporations appear to be "natural partners" for Polish industrial organizations, particularly in cooperation ventures embracing complex commodity, technological, and financial operations. Large companies tend to have more experience in international relations and greater possibilities of adapting to different economic systems; they are also more resistant to the negative effects of economic fluctuations in the industrialized West. This is why in many cases preference is given to large American corporations, particularly by the large industrial units that are dominant in Poland.

Yet, in searching for a cooperating partner, various considerations are involved, and these differ from one branch of industry to the next. For example, some experts contend that in many instances small and medium-sized firms are more dynamic and can offer more up-to-date technologies than the giant ones. In the electronics industries, it is sometimes possible to cooperate profitably with smaller companies that manufacture products of a quality comparable to that of large firms, but at lower cost. In IC between Hungary and the Federal Republic of Germany, two-thirds of the cooperation agreements have been concluded with small and medium-sized German firms.[3] The structure of Polish industry permits cooperation not only with large but also with medium-size or even small firms. It is essential, however, to choose partners for whom the effects of partnership in IC would also be important. Moreover, much attention and encouragement is being given in Poland to IC by small-scale (usually cooperative) enterprises, which produce a substantial share of the output of medical equipment, garments, furniture, toys, and other products.

Several US-Polish cooperation ventures are developing successfully with the participation of American subsidiaries in Western Europe. On the American side, this kind of arrangement is usually motivated by savings in the cost of transportation, the location of production close to the export markets in Western Europe, the high rate of inflation and rapidly growing costs of labor in many West European countries.

Parallelling the benefits to the American companies the Polish partner may improve its ratio of imports to exports and in some cases generate additional exports to balance the growing imports of machinery from the US as a result of the location of production facilities in Poland within the framework of ICA arrangements. Because Poland enjoys a stable economy and favorable location, prospects are good for specific US-Polish multilaterally oriented arrangements to serve development programs of the American subsidiaries in other countries.

Further prospects for cooperation between American and Polish firms can be found in the emerging field of tripartite IC, which encompasses East-West joint industrial ventures carried out on the territory of developing countries, with the participation of enterprises from those countries. By expanding and diversifying IC, tripartite agreements may foster the development of US-Polish cooperation.

According to world statistics, the US occupies first place in exports of complete industrial plants. This line of exports is also rapidly growing in Poland. Having already accumulated some experience in deliveries of turnkey projects to Poland in cooperation with Polish partners, American companies and the respective Polish export organizations could easily extend this form of delivery cooperation to third markets in developing countries. American companies can act as prime contractors or in various combinations of consortia with Polish partners or with Polish and local enterprises. The first instance would simply constitute US-Polish bilateral cooperation in the third markets, but the last case would create a kind of tripartite IC. This concept of multilateral cooperation is based on the assumption that, in many cases, a small or medium-sized country cannot deliver modern, large-scale industrial plants competitively without cooperation with other countries. The US, of course, can produce everything, but in numerous cases its firms will be more competitive if they bid in cooperation with partners from other parts of the world.

Theoretically, tripartite IC may take as many different forms as can be found in East-West bilateral ventures. However, the most workable form at present is the arrangement known as delivery cooperation, comprising the construction of complete industrial plants in developing countries. Further progress in this field may lead, however, to a complex investment-production business to be run jointly by participants from the three countries. More integrated forms of cooperation are required for package deals embracing joint investment, production, research, and marketing, for which capital cooperation in the form of equity joint ventures would be perhaps the most appropriate.

Practice has shown that tripartite cooperation should always be based on the specialization of partners. Polish lines of specialization, particularly in coal mining, sugar mills (processing beets and cane), chemical plants, and other industrial projects are widely known in the developing countries. Poland can offer many technologies that are most suitable for Third World markets and also has very good relations with many such countries. For this reason suggestions frequently are made that cooperation between American and Polish firms in the markets of developing countries would be attractive to both parties.

The notion of tripartite IC is quite recent and the experience so far is limited, but there is still reason to believe that this kind of international cooperation can play an important role in the development of the world economy.

To conclude, numerous factors on both sides stimulate the development of IC between US and Polish firms. There are, however, some issues that do not encourage progress in this area. Examples are the US export control procedure regarding the transfer of technology and the growing protectionism through non-tariff barriers. Even though most pending cooperation deliveries are not directly affected by protectionism, protectionism contributes to the uncertainty of IC, particularly long-term ventures.

For the sake of better understanding the environment that affects the further growth of US-Polish IC, it would be desirable to clarify some general issues. One is the impact of economic fluctuations in countries with developed market economies on US-Polish cooperation agreements. That is, to what extent do cyclical upturns and downturns in the American and West European markets stimulate or discourage the growth of US-Polish IC?

With regard to the US-Polish cooperation agreements that are multi-country oriented and include US foreign subsidiaries, it seems worthwhile to examine the main factors that foster and hamper such agreements. In the case of new investments, the sensitive problem of financing also calls for attention.

A large unexplored area is tripartite IC. Would American companies be interested in such ventures (as in Polish cooperation with the Federal Republic of Germany, France, Austria, and other countries)? If so, what geographical location and which branches of industry would be the most suitable in the long run? Another problem is the extent to which tripartite IC mirrors the new pattern of international division of labor in the world and how it "fits" the concept of the new international economic order.

In addition, is the promotion of US-Polish IC considered satisfactory; if not, what should be done about it? In this context, it is worthwhile to stress the positive promotional role of US-Polish seminars, such as the one in which this paper is being delivered, which help to clear up many difficult issues and lead to increased understanding of preconditions for developing higher and more efficient forms of US-Polish economic relations.

Notes

1. Mary Ellen Yacura, "Case Studies of US Corporate Experience in Poland" (Paper presented at the Krakow Conference on US-Polish Commerce, August 31-September 2, 1978), p. 18.

2. Zygmunt Krolak, "Financial Aspects of Industrial Cooperation Ventures in Poland and in Third Countries," *Polish Foreign Trade*, 12(1977):23.

3. "Bonn zmierza do zaciesnienia wspolpracy z WRL," *Rynki Zagraniczne* (July 12, 1977).

Comment

Paul Marer

Dr. Zagorski's paper is an excellent overview of the evolution of US-Polish industrial cooperation (IC) during the 1970s. The paper offers a succinct summary of the motives of Polish and American corporations for IC and describes the environment in Poland for IC ventures. Together with Professor Tabaczynski's reply to the comments on his paper (p. 107), Dr. Zagorski presents as much concrete information on opportunities for IC in Poland as American businessmen are likely to receive without submitting a concrete proposal.

Understandably, the executives of American companies interested in Poland often ask, as several have at this conference: Since your economy is planned, what are your strategic plans and preferences; what is the best formula to achieve mutually beneficial commercial ends, either in the simple framework of trade or in a more complex framework of IC? Dr. Zagorski's response, as well as the papers and comments presented by our Polish colleagues, goes something like this: We can describe in a detailed manner what has been done to this point. We can identify several key sectors already that have been developed so extensively that it is clear that they will remain high-priority sectors in which IC will continue to be particularly welcome. The sectors mentioned include shipping, mechanical engineering, transportation equipment, industries based on Poland's natural resource endowment (including coal, copper, and sulfur), and the related machinery and equipment branches supporting these sectors. Dr. Zagorski also mentions other areas of "good prospects" for IC. He stresses repeatedly in his paper that those IC proposals that give firm prospects for the Polish partner to earn hard currency are going to receive high priority. But it is not possible to give more detailed information or to set guidelines as to exactly where the opportunities lie.

We should accept this and understand the difficulties our Polish colleagues face when we ask them to be more specific. As Professor Tabaczynski mentions, IC as such is not really planned or initiated by the central planners or even by the ministries, but is the result of initiatives generated at the enterprise or large economic organization (LEO) level. To be sure, if an *approved* project calls for the construction of new industrial plants that will require a long lead time, so it must be incorporated into the five-year and annual plans, and central coordination of its implementation will be critical.

It was also stressed that opportunities for IC could be created in almost any sector. These are some of the reasons why it is so difficult for Polish experts to state unambiguously which are the priority sectors for IC. By definition, this would mean excluding the other sectors and would surely elicit criticism from the excluded sectors, which would question the judgments at the highest levels. This would occur even if, say, a high-level advisory body such as the Foreign Trade Research Institute felt that it could make an appropriate selection, although it evidently does not itself think so (see reply by Professor

Tabaczynski, p. 107). Furthermore, one might add, "priorities" are not fixed permanently but are continually changing. Low-priority sectors have a way of quickly metamorphosing into high-priority activities. If, for example, a shortage of housing were to create serious economic tensions, an IC proposal that would help Polish firms construct prefabricated housing elements might become a project of high priority and so gain quick approval.

Thus, one understands why we cannot get specific guidelines on IC opportunities even from such knowledgeable experts as our Polish colleagues. Still, I would like to raise several related questions in the belief that the answers would help promote US-Polish IC.

First, what kind of information—or instructions, if you will—is being given to enterprise managers as to why they should consider IC with a foreign partner and, more specifically, how they should undertake a search process for IC partners? Recognizing that many ICAs evolve from simpler forms of economic relations, as Dr. Zagorski points out, what formal or informal guidelines do enterprise managers receive regarding the initiatives they should take concerning IC?

Second, what economic and non-economic motives tend to help or hinder the actions of key decisionmakers (managers, heads of departments, foremen, and worker representatives) at the enterprise and LEO level regarding the enterprise's or LEO's possible involvement in negotiating an IC project? Clearly, there must be economic as well as non-economic inducements promoting a favorable attitude toward IC, just as there must be disincentives discouraging IC at the enterprise level. If US businessmen could better understand these forces, they could empathize with their Polish counterparts. The end result would be to promote such ventures. Also, uncovering the visible as well as the less obvious disincentives at the enterprise level would be an important step toward creating a more effective incentive structure for IC.

Third, what is the internal process of approval of preliminary proposals for IC, and what are the principal considerations involved? What are the differences between what Dr. Zagorski calls large-scale "delivery cooperation" projects, involving the construction of new plants, and smaller-scale cooperation projects based on the extension and modernization of existing facilities? Can we learn something about the process that goes beyond the formal organizational charts?

A key question is how Poland's current balance-of-payments situation influences IC prospects. Will only those proposals which have a quick return in terms of hard currency be approved; that is, is the time horizon of the planners being reduced by balance-of-payments considerations? This leads to another interesting question alluded to by Dr. Zagorski; namely, the calculation of the hard currency contribution of an IC from Poland's point of view. Convertible currency (CC) may be earned by a project *directly,* through exports to the West, or *indirectly.* One possibility is to substitute for hard currency imports; another is to produce inputs that make it possible for other Polish enterprises using these inputs to earn hard currency; still another is to improve Poland's bargaining position within the CMEA or other clearing-currency markets where Poland is able to purchase goods it would otherwise have to import for hard currency. Do all of these considerations enter into the assessment of the potential hard currency contribution of a proposed IC project or is that contribution calculated simply as direct earnings through exports?

My last point refers to what is perhaps the single most significant issue that Dr. Zagorski raises, the question of joint ventures in Poland. This issue is fascinating to businessmen, to academics, to anyone interested in the theory or practice of East-West economic cooperation. Joint ventures involve equity participation, and any country that permits even a minority (up to 49 percent) ownership participation expects to derive two important benefits: an easing of its borrowing burden, since about half of the credits for a project would be shouldered by the Western partner, and acquisition of the strongest possible long-term commitment from the Western firm for the technical, financial, and marketing success of the venture. Because joint ventures would increase the options available to Polish and Western firms interested in cooperation, we are pleased to learn from Dr. Zagorski that "the problem is under study and the first steps have been taken toward joint ventures by permitting foreigners to invest in Poland."

I would like to make a few observations regarding East-West joint ventures that are located on the territory of the Eastern rather than the Western partner.

The attitudes of US (and other Western) companies differ on the principle of participation in joint ventures in Eastern Europe. Some companies take a categorical stand against participating in joint ventures anywhere in the world unless they have majority ownership, i.e., full managerial control. IBM is an example of one such American corporation. Some companies believe that equity joint ventures are not that important, because by and large the same end results can be achieved through a contract. A third group consists of companies that would be interested in joint ventures. The possibility of entering into a joint venture symbolizes for them the strong commitment of the East European country to cooperate with Western firms. It helps explain—and, in a sense, justify—to the stockholders why the firm is so heavily committed in Eastern Europe. It also fits into the corporation's strategy regarding the conditions under which it would be willing to make a strong, long-term commitment to a project and transfer continuously its most advanced technology and managerial know-how.

What are the important issues for a US company interested in pioneering a joint venture, say, in Poland? First, the company wants to make sure that the regulations governing joint ventures are clearly stated. It wants to understand the laws, the regulations, the rules, and the practices of the host country. Stability is also very important. I refer here primarily not to stability of the economic, political, and social conditions in the country, but to stability with respect to the government's attitude toward and the legislation involving joint ventures. Thus, it is perhaps desirable not to experiment too much by frequently changing the rules and regulations. Too much experimentation, even if it tends to make conditions more favorable to the Western partners, may create the impression that the country has not made up its mind about what it wants to do. This can, on balance, discourage Western companies from entering into joint venture negotiations.

There is a great deal of confusion in US business circles about joint venture opportunities and possible techniques in Eastern Europe. The essence of a joint venture is the intermingling of financial contributions—those of initial capital, of inputs, and finally of outputs and profits. Many of even the most sophisticated corporate executives we talked to could not explain how this financial intermingling could be accomplished in a country that has an inconvertible currency. Dr. Zagorski is right, therefore, when he states that "the greatest obstacle to equity joint ventures stems from the inconvertibility of the national currency and, subsequently, from exchange rate difficulties."

Tied closely to the issues of the valuation of contributions, exchange rates, and accounting is the issue of the interface of a joint venture with the rest of the economy, a point raised in a broader context by Professor Campbell in his comments (p. 92). My understanding is that three types of basic models have already been introduced in Eastern Europe. One could be called the "fully integrated" Yugoslav model, in which the joint venture is essentially no different from any other enterprise in the economy. Accounts are maintained in Yugoslav dinars, and the valuation of inputs and so on is determined by the domestic market in Yugoslavia. At the other extreme is what might be called the "enclave system" Romanian model, in which the accounting and settlement are in a foreign currency and the valuation of inputs and so on is by agreement, usually indexed to some world market value reference point. Because even purchases from and sales to domestic Romanian firms are calculated in foreign prices and currency, the joint venture forms an "enclave" in the local currency system. The joint venture determines its own economic plan, which is incorporated into the national economic plan. Otherwise, the joint venture is not integrated into the national economic mechanism; it remains an "enclave." In between the Yugoslav and Romanian models we find the "calculation system" of Hungary, where

> . . . accounting is typically undertaken in both hard foreign currency and local currency. Financial transactions are converted from one currency to the other from time to time. Thus the supply of the joint venture by local enterprises is based on domestic prices, whereas foreign currency is predominant in the prices of exports and imports.[1]

Because the basic approaches to joint ventures appear to be fundamentally different in each of the planned economies that have introduced them, it is particularly important—should Poland decide to go ahead with this form of IC—that the accounting, financial, planning, and other economic interfaces of a joint venture be spelled out clearly. This would reduce the uncertainty and, therefore, the risk that US corporations undoubtedly feel when contemplating joint ventures in Poland.

Reply

IC between American and Polish firms is a recent phenomenon, and one cannot expect to have a fully comprehensive theoretical infrastructure to please everybody. In fact, new questions are still arising, calling for further study. On the other hand, long-term relationships and commitments in ICAs help partners better understand one another and each's economic environments.

It is assumed that differences between the economic systems in both countries will continue, and the prospects or further expansion of IC are determined to a large extent by the willingness and the ability of the partners to make allowances for the system compatibility factor.

Against this background, Professor Marer's extensive comments are particularly appreciated, as are his questions raised "in the belief that the answers would help promote US-Polish IC." Many of these questions have already been answered by Professor Kossut (p. 109) and Professor Tabaczynski (p. 98). In his reply Professor Tabaczynski

---

1. Dietrich A. Loeber, "Capital Investment in Soviet Enterprises? Possibilities and Limits of East-West Trade," *Adelaide Law Review,* 6:3 (1978). A discussion of the various models can also be found in F. Levcik and J. Stankovsky, *Industrial Cooperation Between East and West* (White Plains, N.Y.: M. E. Sharpe, 1979), chapter 6.

has given an exhaustive explanation of how the planning system works in Poland and how a whole range of cooperation initiatives is left to industrial enterprises. It remains for me to add some supplementary remarks of a rather pragmatic nature.

First, the planning system in Poland is bound to our country's development concept. This is why priority tasks in particular sectors are not fixed, but may be changed from one plan to another. Professor Marer rightly states that low priority sectors may evolve into high priority activities. It then looks a bit hazardous to insist on more detail about exactly where the opportunities lie for IC. I believe that everyone here will agree that cooperation options for the near future have been under discussion. The parties concerned have not been asked for any consent, and at least some of them may not wish us to focus our attention on their current business negotiations.

With regard to the relationship between IC and the planning of the economy, various links depend on such factors as the size of the project, scale of additional investments, forms of financing, and marketing arrangements. When ICAs require large-scale investments, as in the production of cars undertaken in cooperation with Fiat or tractors in cooperation with Massey-Ferguson-Perkins, agreements of this kind simply constitute part and parcel of the central plan, or the way of fulfilling the country's development strategy. We may have another approach to ICAs in cases in which the new products are to be manufactured in IC by using the existing premises and other production facilities, or by supplementing them with only a few pieces of additional equipment to cope with new technological processes. It is clear that in each case planning units of different levels are involved and different planning methods are used.

This lengthy explanation has been made to show the obviousness of the existence of a positive correlation between planning system and decision-making processes or approval procedures with regard to ICAs. IC is never the only factor determining development strategy of the enterprise or of the whole branch of industry. Sometimes it is one of the dominant factors. If we say that IC, important as it may be, is only one element of the development of particular industries or one of several available forms of product development or one of the efficient forms of doing business abroad, there is no need to look for a special approval process for such business. It is rather important for the foreign businessmen to know that an export offer submitted with an attractive cooperation proposal may well strengthen the competitive edge of such an offer.

Managers of particular organizational units may make the decisions or they may delegate them to lower levels, depending on the organizational structures in the given branch of industry and on the weight of IC problems to be solved. It is also important to see what coordination is required in each case. If, for example, you want to arrange a cooperation agreement that involves the construction of new buildings, requiring millions in local currency or foreign investment, you must contact the building construction companies and secure construction materials, machinery, etc. A need arises for coordination between many branches of the economy, and acceptance should be obtained at a relatively high level. Otherwise, it would be a rather difficult large-scale project to carry out successfully.

At the opposite extreme, in an agreement involving the manufacture of suits in cooperation with a foreign partner on existing premises using experienced staff, the factory manager faces no coordination problems, no large-scale investments, and no construction of new buildings. In such circumstances his superior would readily tell him to proceed, and he would willingly make decisions for IC. IC would help him to fulfill his main task, which in this particular case is to manufacture good products to boost hard currency exports.

Parallel to the macro-economic considerations discussed in other papers, there are various micro-economic motives that may influence the attitude of industrial management toward ICAs. The strongest incentives appear when the factory is to undergo modernization, which usually brings some changes in production programs and technology. Another important factor is the extent to which a factory is to be export-oriented. Production for external markets and outward-oriented specialization usually provide more incentives for IC than does inward-oriented performance. However, in any case, the success of IC depends mostly on how the long-term community of interests is created between parties and, based on this principle, on the proper selection of partners.

This leads us to another problem which applies specifically to US-Polish relations. We are often told that IC is not an *ad hoc* affair; it must grow out of years of trade or other forms of cooperation between partners, during which time the two sides can get to know and appreciate each other's willingness and ability to stick to long-term commitments. Although this rule may be quite good for cooperation between East and West European countries, it cannot be fully applied to the US-Polish case. Rather, I would expect that most of the future US-Polish ICAs would follow the IH-BUMAR example, in which ICAs are based on common future goals rather than on past experience.

Professor Marer's comments concentrate on explaining the attitude of American companies toward equity joint ventures in Eastern Europe. As mentioned earlier, new regulations are being developed to spell out the rules governing equity joint ventures. The achievements by Yugoslavia, Hungary, and Romania are carefully studied in Poland. As Professor Marer states, they also interest American businessmen and academics. In this context, Professor Marer's information and comments with regard to equity joint ventures in third countries should be highly appreciated as a valuable contribution to our collaborative project.

Technology Transfer in US-Polish Industrial Cooperation

Janusz Kozinski

Technology transfer (TT) is a broad and complex term that means different things to different people. Some think of technology mainly in terms of the machinery, equipment, and products in which it is embodied; others see technology in terms of more intangible carriers, such as patents, licenses, trademarks, blueprints, or product designs. This paper focuses on the intangible elements of technology, transferred between partners from different countries through industrial cooperation agreements (ICAs). The focus is on TT within the context of US-Polish industrial cooperation (IC).

The purpose of the paper is threefold: first, to present some quantitative and qualitative general features of the Polish view of US-Polish IC;[1] second, to identify and discuss those elements of technology that can potentially be transferred through IC, with a view toward creating an institutional framework for optimal TT in an IC; and third, to examine how this potential is being realized in three specific cases of US-Polish IC.

IC with foreign partners is defined in the Polish literature as long-term collaboration between domestic and foreign partners in production, beginning from the research and development (R&D) stage to marketing and after-sale services, carried out according to principles mutually agreed upon by the partners. IC may include licensing agreements with payment in related or unrelated products, supply of complete industrial plants, coproduction agreements where partners specialize in manufacturing different components with final assembly by one or both partners, subcontracting agreements, and joint investment projects. This definition is narrower than that used by some American authors.[2]

Main Features of US-Polish Industrial Cooperation

Although Poland's experience in IC with American partners dates only from the beginning of the 1970s, today the US ranks third, after Italy and West Germany, among Poland's Western IC partners. In 1978, the US accounted for approximately 10 percent of Polish cooperation turnover with Western countries. During 1972-78, the growth rate of US-Polish IC was higher, in terms of value, than the tempo of cooperation deliveries between Poland and the West. In US-Polish cooperation relations, exports and imports combined increased from $1.5 million in 1972 to $16 million in 1978, while in Polish-Western relations IC deliveries grew from $40 million to $169 million during the same period. The shares of IC in Poland's total foreign trade and in its trade of engineering products with all Western countries and with the US are listed in Table 1.[3]

According to Polish data, IC between the two countries is highly concentrated in non-electrical products and machinery in general, and in construction machinery in particular.[4] If the total Polish cooperation exports to and imports from the US of non-electrical machinery is taken as 100, then during 1972-78 the share of construction machinery in these turnovers has fluctuated between 60 and 80 percent. The remaining share was comprised of machine tools, sewing machines, computer equipment, and aircraft pistons (see Zagorski's paper on p. 121).

Six years of experience in this field enable us to identify certain features that differentiate US-Polish IC from IC between Poland and other Western countries:

1. The average duration of ICAs with US firms is more than 10 years; examples are the 15-year coproduction and joint marketing agreements signed between Singer Co. and Universal Foreign Trade Organization (FTO) in 1973 and between International Harvester (IH) Company and BUMAR FTO in 1972. By contrast, one-third of the ICAs in effect between Poland and Western countries in 1978 had been in existence for one to three years, the rest for more than three years, but only a few spanned a ten-year period. Consequently, among the cooperation projects with all Western partners, simple, one-shot contracts predominate; while in US-Polish IC the most im-

portant ones are complex and comprehensive, involving TT production and marketing implemented in the form of coproduction and specialization agreements.

2. The average value of ICAs with American firms is higher than that of a typical ICA between Poland and all Western countries.

3. Poland's American partners in IC activity represent the largest US companies, some of them multinational corporations (MNCs). The reason for the involvement of the giants of US industry in Poland, or elsewhere in the CMEA, relates to their leadership in technology, abundant financing resources, and worldwide marketing systems.[5]

4. Although ICAs are negotiated and signed at the US firms' headquarters, the implementation is usually by the corporation's European subsidiaries (their production facilities and marketing-distribution network). Consequently, instead of US-Polish IC, it is more appropriate to speak of a "cooperation triangle," involving the US corporate headquarters, its West European subsidiary, and the Polish industrial enterprise and FTO.

Polish interest in IC with American companies is prompted by factors similar to those found in ICAs with other Western partners (see Zagorski's paper on p. 121). However, in the case of US-Polish IC one of the strongest motivations on the Polish side seems to be our interest in the effective transfer of intangible elements of modern American technology, while in IC with other Western countries machinery and equipment purchases (i.e., tangible components of technology) seem to predominate. This can be explained in part by the pattern of comparative advantage and in part by transportation costs.

The acknowledgment of TT as the major motive of the Polish partner does not mean that the acquisition of US technology is seen as a self-sufficient end in itself. Technology in the IC context is not "a product," but an indispensable "factor" intended to initiate further effects, such as product quality, economies of scale, and the creation of new markets growing out of active and effective cooperation.

The impact of IC on the Polish economy can be divided into short-term and long-term effects. In Poland's domestic economy as well as in its economic relations with Western countries, attention is mostly focused on short-term effects, i.e., measures related to export expansion and import substitution aimed at improving Poland's hard currency balance-of-payments. IC can improve the hard currency balance-of-payments directly, by getting Western help to produce the kinds of goods that are salable for hard currency and by assistance to Poland with marketing in hard currency areas, or indirectly, by improving Poland's bargaining position among CMEA countries. This last mentioned improvement can improve the hard currency balance-of-payments by getting hard currency directly from other CMEA members or by getting more "hard goods" from them that would otherwise have to be imported from hard currency areas.[6]

IC is considered the most effective vehicle for the transfer of applied production technology. The preference for IC as a channel of TT results from the very essence of IC and its specific characteristics.[7] To underline the relationship between TT and IC, the next section will focus on the potential for TT through ICAs.

The Potential for Technology Transfer Through Industrial Cooperation

Technology, in the broad sense, is the means (i.e., engineering documentation) and the methods (i.e., production techniques and managerial systems) necessary to perform tasks or solve problems, or to manufacture products or render services. The stress in this paper is on disembodied technology; that is, the know-how needed by industrial enterprises to organize and rationalize the production processes.

The successful transfer of technology may be conceptualized as a three-phase process by which a given technology is moved from one organization (enterprise) to another. Table 2 describes the essential features of these three phases and the basic elements of technology that may be transferred through ICAs.

Phase I, "Exploration and Selection," includes choices of appropriate technology and the mechanism of its transfer from donor to receiver. From the recipient's point of view, the selection of a TT mechanism is particularly significant, not only because of economic consequences, but because it determines the scale and scope of foreign involvement and control in the domestic economy. Another critically important aspect is financing. A country's ability to finance technology imports determines, to a large degree, the volume of its imports. In this regard, the choice of a transfer mechanism is also very important.

Phase II, "Duplication and Adaptation to Local Conditions," consists of three basic stages: technology acquisition (i.e., all preproduction operations indispensable to prepare infrastructure for new technology); adaptation of imported know-how to local conditions, including construction and installation works; application of purchased knowledge (i.e., manufacturing and maintenance). This phase is frequently and mistakenly identified as representing the entire TT process. This occurs when the focus is on technology absorption *per se*. But in reality, the critical problem for the Polish partner is how to achieve an appropriate interface among all three phases.

Phase III, "Reproduction and Innovation," concerns the technological upgrading of the original know-how. Technology should be productive not only during its life span, but it should also be reproductive before it becomes obsolete. This may be achieved by choosing among three different variants:

1. The domestic variant: technology improvement is achieved by relying only on domestic research facilities and technical potential.
2. The foreign variant: all upgrading and innovations are transmitted from a donor of original technology.
3. The combined domestic and foreign variant: cooperation in designing and in further R&D is involved.

A vast array of technical knowledge may be embodied in a single transfer of technology.[8] The basic elements of technology can take the form of engineering documentation, production techniques, and managerial systems. The elements of a technology package mentioned only in Phase II can also be found in two other phases, but their role is different (e.g., in Phase I they are decisionmaking factors).

The phases and the elements of TT through ICAs are interrelated. The manner in which all issues in the pre-investment phase in general, and the selection of technology mechanism in particular, are agreed upon predetermines, to a large extent, the economic effectiveness of all phases. For example, if a host country selects a "passive mechanism" of TT (i.e., short-term transfers of technical information that the transferor has already disseminated widely), it will be forced to depend on domestic resources in the implementation of other phases. The choice of the channel for transfer settles questions about the form of the transferred knowledge, costs of transfer, time of technology absorption by the recipient enterprise, or quality of technology.

Three Case Studies

Three case studies have been selected to examine the nature of TT in US-Polish IC:

1. General Motors Corporation (GMC) and Polmo FTO
2. Corning Glass Works with RCA and Unitra FTO
3. International Harvester Company (IH) and BUMAR/HSW.

These cases will present descriptive analyses of technology flows between the partners. Each case focuses on a different phase of the transfer process. This approach allows an exploration of some important issues, such as the role of Polish enterprise in TT, elements of technology usually transmitted through ICAs, or problems each partner has to solve during the TT process. Of several US-Polish ICAs identified, these three cases represent a significant share in overall

Polish cooperation exports and imports from the point of view of their size, value, or complexity of TT. Information and data have been worked out both from the American and Polish sources.[9] Table 3 shows the main features of each case.

General Motors Corporation and Polmo FTO

Any of the three cases of US-Polish IC could have been used to illustrate the first phase of TT. The GMC-Polmo FTO case has been chosen because although the negotiations were discontinued without signing an agreement, the discussions were stopped only at the end of phase I. The proposed ICA between the largest manufacturing corporation in the world and the Polish Engineering Industry would have covered the manufacture in Poland of a family of vehicles ranging from light vans with four-cylinder diesel engines to five-ton, multipurpose trucks.

Selection of the most suitable technology. A unique approach concerning the terms of TT has been agreed to by both sides: The vehicles to be produced in Poland would be based entirely on new designs worked out according to Polish requirements and specifications. Based on Polish concepts and needs, GMC was to develop a whole set of engineering documentation at its Vauxhall, England R&D facilities, with the active participation of Polish engineers and technicians. The American partner was to give Poland complete documentation on production techniques, such as materials specifications, physical dimensions of components and parts, process sheets detailing fabrication steps, tooling and machining requirements, and quality control and testing procedures. Basic managerial activities (planning, decisionmaking, or current operational functions) were to be carried out entirely by the Polish side. The most modern, large-scale manufacturing technology was to be used. FSC Lublin (Truck Factory Lublin), the proposed production facility for the whole series of vehicles, would be expanded and modernized according to GMC's specifications to manufacture 100,000 units annually.

Choice of technology transfer channel. The two sides agreed to utilize what is perhaps the most efficient mechanism for transferring technology: a coproduction and comarketing agreement. Under this approach, the ICA would have had three basic parts: (1) an extended technical assistance contract; (2) the granting of GMC's trademark rights with Poland meeting all the quality and service requirements that a trademark implies; and (3) a long-term product purchase commitment by the American partner.

According to the technical assistance agreement, GMC would be responsible for advice and guidance on specific designs, applications, operations, and manufacturing problems. Company experts would make periodic visits to the Polish production facility to train local technical personnel. Furthermore, a technical assistance obligation would also call for GMC to keep its flow of technology up-to-date throughout the life of the agreement by furnishing all improvements actually put into commercial production, relieving the American firm of the obligation to transfer technology that had not yet passed from GMC's laboratory to the production line. The proposed ICA did not provide for the transfer of technical knowledge from Poland to the US, except during the initial joint designing stage. GMC's granting of trademark rights would be tantamount to a commitment guaranteeing that vans and trucks manufactured in Poland were, in every respect, as good as any product coming off its own production lines. From the Polish point of view, product purchase commitment would enable and facilitate the TT repayment in produced trucks, thereby generating hard currency earnings.

Contract terms. After three years of negotiations, the proposed agreement is now in a "discontinued" status, i.e., discussions about contract terms have been suspended. This was caused by financial arrangements which both sides did not accept until the end of 1976. The decision to suspend negotiations should be analyzed in light of Poland's cautious economic policies of the past three years, resulting in a further narrowing of trade deficits with the West by means of concentrating available labor and capital on a smaller number of selected investment projects.

The total investment expenditures eventually were to reach as high as $1 billion, of which the US component was initially estimated at $30 million. The most significant element of this agreement was that the American corporation would rely on the ICA to create an East European production base, through which GMC would complement and fill out its worldwide production line. The firm was expected to buy from 15 to 20 percent of Polish output annually (i.e., 15,000 to 18,000 vehicles) to be sold in Western Europe via GMC's international marketing network. Poland would have been granted exclusive marketing rights within the CMEA countries.

Corning Glass Works with RCA and Unitra FTO

In mid-1976, two American corporations, Corning Glass Works and RCA, signed separate agreements for the sale of technology and equipment for the manufacture of color TV picture tubes, providing complementary machinery and know-how for start-up production in Poland. Corning Glass's contract was for the sale of a technology package for the production of the glass envelope component of the

21-inch diagonal color picture tube. RCA sold Unitra FTO the manufacturing package to produce so-called "electronic guns," the electronic component of the same cathode-ray color tube. The two contracts cover a 10-year period and their combined value is $124 million. (The contract price for the sale by Corning is about $55 million.) The new production plant, expected to be completed in 1979, is located in Piaseczno, 15 miles from Warsaw. The plant is expected to reach an annual production rate of 600,000 units, although initial production output will be approximately half that figure.

Technology transferred. The two contracts were for the sale of equipment, design, know-how, assistance in purchasing foreign manufactured products, engineering assistance, and technical training of Polish personnel in the US and in Poland. An estimated 60 percent of the contract price was for equipment and machinery; 40 percent was for the intangible elements of technology. There was to be no transfer of managerial techniques.

Although the technology transferred provides Poland with a new and important technology base, it is not unique, and in some respects it is not quite state-of-the-art technology. First, the tube design received by Poland does not meet US and some West European x-ray emission standards; this will hinder the export of the finished products to these markets. Second, the standard tube to be manufactured in Poland utilizes more space and provides a 90-degree angle as compared to the new unit designed and introduced recently by Corning which has a 100-degree angle, a lighter glass bulb, and is cheaper and easier to produce. In addition, the Polish tube is less energy-efficient than the new American design, which is to go into production in the US this year.

Technology transfer channel. The traditional TT mechanisms, in the form of a simple sale-purchase transaction (with American assistance during the plant construction and trial periods), has been chosen. In practice, this means that the responsibility of the American companies in relation to technology is limited and will last only until the last American technical employee finishes his work at the plant site. So the sale, which provides engineering and technical training, is limited to the know-how needed to construct and operate the plant. During the initial period of production, all raw materials needed for the bulb manufacturing will be purchased from Corning-controlled sources. The reason for this provision is that the specialized equipment requires specific tolerances, so that the raw materials must meet particular standards.

Both contracts include a provision for a regular updating of technology related to the design of the glass envelope and of this particular electron gun. The agreements do not include different or new designs and related technology, worked out individually or jointly by the partners. In order to provide a means of checking the accuracy of the royalty payments, which are tied to production output, the American companies have been granted the right to audit the books of the Polish producer when it becomes fully operational, a rather unusual feature. There are no comarketing arrangements or trademark right provisions, and the repayment will be in installments beginning at the end of 1979.

International Harvester Company and BUMAR with Huta Stalowa Wola

The ICA between IH and BUMAR, initiated in 1972 and enlarged since then, encompasses a broad scope of activities and products in the area of earthmoving construction machinery and equipment, produced jointly under several agreements. It includes crawler dozers and loaders (five models), pipe-laying crawler tractors, and front-end wheel loaders (nine models). The duration of the ICA has been extended until 1990. The IC program with IH has been an addition to the production activities in Huta Stalowa Wola (HSW), which has necessitated new investment, such as an assembly plant, additional floor area for the HSW gear plant, and the under-carriage and automatic forging plant. This is the most advanced cooperation agreement between Poland and the US and between Poland and any Western country.

Technology. The technology delivered by IH was mainly in the form of engineering documentation, factory standards, and manufacturing know-how. The technical information had to be converted into the metric system and into the Polish language. The information and data for a single crawler tractor consisted of over 5,000 drawings and designs.

One of the characteristic features of the IH-BUMAR ICA is that it involves an interesting mixture of direct transfer of production techniques and organizational and managerial systems from IH to BUMAR and adaptation. BUMAR and HSW did not universally copy the manufacturing processes and organizational structure of IH production operations, although IH suggestions and requirements were considered. BUMAR and HSW developed their own solutions based on the existing machine-tool park at HSW plus some new equipment that was specified by IH technical documentation. Some organizational adjustments have taken place on the Polish side as a result of the ICA, however, such as a change in the HSW organizational pattern from a vertical to a horizontal structure of decisionmaking, planning, and production.

Technology transfer. According to the initial agreement and its further extensions, the partners have chosen the most complex variant of the TT mechanisms, taking the form of coproduction, specialization, and joint marketing arrangements. In this case, TT has moved resolutely into the third phase of the process. This model of technological cooperation has been possible because both sides are at an approximately similar level of "technological maturity." The complexity of the TT process has been made possible by an unprecedented set of conditions and provisions, including:

1. Fast and continuous enterprise-to-enterprise transmission of production capabilities. With regard to component support from IH to BUMAR, a gradual substitution is planned for imported components by locally produced elements either in HSW's production facility or from other domestic suppliers. It must be pointed out, however, that any or all these changes can be effected only with IH approval.

2. Rights to use the IH trademark on products made by BUMAR. The use of the IH trademark is conditional on successfully meeting the so-called Trademark Approval (TMA) procedure. This must be obtained on individual components and parts as well as on final products and involves very difficult conditions and stringent approval testing of units by IH. If Polish production is to be supplied to IH's American manufacturing facilities, an additional procedure called QA-70 is required, under which parts and components are thoroughly tested and inspected at special IH facilities.

3. BUMAR has sold relatively few machines directly to the US or any other hard currency market, but this will be changed in the near future. In the meantime, HSW is becoming one of the primary sources of components for assembly into new crawler tractors (so-called skids that consist of approximately 40 percent of the value of the complete machine) for IH's West European production facilities (Doncaster, England).

4. The extensive direct contacts among people representing different levels of activity in both firms, mainly in the context of the training program for the Polish partner, have been an important part of the ICA from the beginning. Numerous engineers and technical representatives have been trained in IH works, and IH specialists have frequently visited HSW.

5. The rule of upgrading the original technology sold has been implemented from the beginning of the cooperation. Thanks to this approach, most engineering changes made by IH in the US are incorporated in BUMAR-made construction equipment at approximately the same time.

Joint research and development activities. As a natural outgrowth of coproduction and comarketing activities, the partners decided after five years of satisfactory results, extended experience, and growing confidence, to increase the scope of joint operations and deepen cooperation by joining their financial and technical resources for joint design and construction and then for mutual R&D activities. A new model of a giant crawler dozer has been chosen as the first subject of the new agreement. The program provides for joint designing and engineering of the new model, with IH in the leading role. HSW is to produce prototype units and IH is to test and evaluate the prototypes and issue final approval for production.

In the field of joint R&D activities conducted by research facilities and laboratories of IH and HSW, the partners agreed to concentrate initially on selected technical issues. The first technical questions involve transmission units in construction machines, reduction of the noise level in running machines, and problems relating to the analysis of endurance limits.

Concluding Remarks

The scope of the TT process (i.e., phases of TT mentioned in the Analytical Framework as well as elements of technical knowledge purchased by the recipient) has been analyzed in three selected cases of US-Polish ICAs:

1. GMC-Polmo FTO ICA illustrates the first, pre-investment phase of TT plus a unique concept of comprehensive technology cooperation, with the initial step of joint designing and engineering of new vehicle prototypes to be produced in Poland.

2. Corning Glass/RCA-Unitra FTO ICA illustrates the first and the second phases which take the form of typical sales of technical information with extended technical support, but without continuous interfirm relationships, and engineering guidance by US partners.

3. IH-BUMAR ICA illustrates all three phases of the TT process, with active relationships through sustained interfirm complex cooperation.

Three points are worth noting:

First, there is no real ICA when the TT process stops at phase I or at phase II, as in the case of Corning Glass/RCA and Unitra FTO.

Second, the crucial question is why some ICAs go to phase II of TT and some to phase III. Such factors as the technical tradition, economic policy of the host country, and the nature of technology involved must be thoroughly examined. The longer the technical tradition is, the more advanced the type of ICA can be, with more complex process of TT fulfilled. Satisfactory contract implementation, including TT, depends on whether the receiver of technology is inward-or outward-oriented, or whether servicing of an export or domestic market is a principal motivation when signing an IC contract.

Third, phase III is crucial for each long-range ICA with active and prospective relationships between partners (transferor and recipient). The partners can approach this stage of cooperation through the iterative process of TT, as in the IH-BUMAR ICA: BUMAR requests and receives conventional technology, absorbs it, then develops with IH new findings that result in a two-way exchange of additional specific technical information. As a consequence, joint design of new products, as well as joint research work, seems to be the most significant achievement of the ICA to date, opening the door to the next phase of IC and TT in unique new machines and equipment.

TABLE 1

Poland's Trade with All Western Countries and with the
US and the Share of IC Deliveries in 1978

	Total Trade	Trade of Eng. Prod.	IC Turnover	3 : 1 in %	3 : 2 in %
	In million dollars				
	1	2	3		
West. Devel. Countries					
Exports	4209	832	94	2.2	11.3
Imports	6550	2253	75	1.1	3.3
USA					
Exports	440	120	6	1.4	5.0
Imports	762	114	10	1.3	8.8

SOURCE: Compiled from Polish statistical sources.

TABLE 2

Analytical Framework of Phases and Elements of Technology
Transferred Through Industrial Cooperation Agreements

Phase of Technology Transfer	*Elements of Technology*
Phase I: Exploration and selection (Pre-investment)	From the recipient's point of view, the first stage of TT is the selection of the kind of technology that is appropriate for the conditions in the domestic economy. It also includes the choice of transfer channel, the negotiation of contracts, and all financing arrangements.
Phase II: Duplication and adaptation to local conditions (technology absorption)	This includes acquisition of technology (pre-production), implementation of transfer (adaptation, construction, installation), and application of new technology (production and maintenance). This phase relates primarily to the interaction of the purchased technology with domestic economic institutions (domestic diffusion). The elements of a technology package consist of:

Engineering Documents	*Production Techniques*	*Managerial Systems*
designs, drawings, blueprints	manufacturing processes	planning operation tactics, strategy
equipment requirements	quality control product inspection	production operation
material standards process sheets	personnel training and qualifications	marketing operation

Phase III: Reproduction and innovation	To reproduce the original technology sold, cooperation in designing activities and cooperation in joint research and development are natural continuations in ICA.

TABLE 3
Main Features of Three ICAs Between Poland and the US

US Partner	Polish Partner	Subject of IC	Status	Phase of TT	Nature of TT
GMC	Polmo FTO FSC Lublin	Light vans and trucks	Discontinued	End of the pre-investment phase	Unique concept of TT beginning with joint designing work in Phase I
Corning Glass and RCA	Unitra FTO ZPE Polcolor	Color TV picture tubes	Operating, just before start-up	Middle of the technology absorption phase	One-way flow of technology from US to Poland
IH	BUMAR FTO Huta Stalowa Wola	Crawler tractors and loaders	Operating, being implemented	Third, reproduction phase	The beginning of two-way TT in the form of joint construction and development works

Notes
1. The "Polish view" means that all findings in this part of my paper are presented according to the Polish concept of "international industrial cooperation" and are based on available information and data published in Poland.

2. A broader definition is used, for example, by Paul Marer and Joseph C. Miller in "US Participation in East-West Industrial Cooperation Agreements," *Journal of International Business Studies,* Vol. VIII, No. 2 (Fall/Winter 1977).

3. One should be very careful when using these indicators as a measure of the contribution of IC to Poland for the following reasons: (1) the broad definition of IC, in Polish practice, allows the inclusion of some deliveries that entail very little real cooperative activity (e.g., golf cart production in Poland, sold in US; (2) there appears to be a consensus in Polish literature that the larger the share of deliveries under cooperation, the greater the contribution of IC. But in practice, a decline in a share may be caused by the substitution of domestically made components for imports, made possible by successful IC.

4. Indeed, there is only one ICA outside this sector: Katy Industries Inc. and the Association of Leather Industry and Skorimpex FTO signed in 1976 the ICA on joint production of men's and women's leather shoes.

5. Marer and Miller, "US Participation," p. 21.

6. Commodities traded within the CMEA are implicitly ranked according to the demand for them within the CMEA, either because they alleviate shortages in the domestic economies of the member countries or because they are salable in the West for hard currency. "Hard goods" denote commodities in greatest demand.

7. These characteristics can be stated as follows: (a) the cooperating partners are the direct producers; (b) long duration and regularity of the mutual commitments; (c) gradual and smooth penetration and diffusion of the technological knowledge and organizational know-how to production systems of both partners; and (d) technology penetration possibility to all phases of the production process, including joint R&D.

8. For example, in manufacturing a diesel engine for commercial trucks, there are approximately 750 parts, and each part may require anywhere from 5 to 75 process steps to produce a finished component. Approximately 15,000 manufacturing steps are required to convert materials and castings into final parts for a single engine model. See Jack Baranson, *Industrial Technologies for Developing Economies* (New York: Praeger Publishers, 1969).

9. The first two case studies are based on information obtained from *Business Europe Report,* various volumes and numbers in 1974-78; and Jack Baranson, *Technology and the Multinational* (Lexington, Mass.: Lexington Books, 1978). The third case study is based on work prepared as part of a research project on US-Polish IC by the two teams and from other published sources.

Comment

Robert Campbell

Mr. Kozinski's paper is a stimulating summary of US-Polish ICAs and the technology transfer (TT) activities they involve. Notable features include his explanation of the differences between ICAs that the Poles have engaged in with US companies and with other Western partners. I like the second section of his paper, in which he sets up the analytical framework; his analysis of the successive phases and what is involved in each constitutes a good outline of issues to look at in evaluating and understanding any ICA. He makes one novel point about US-Polish ICAs that I wish he had followed up more fully; i.e., the fact that they really constitute triangular relationships between a US headquarters, a West European subsidiary, and the Polish partner.

But what I find most productive and useful in his paper is that he chose to consider three different examples. As he says, they illustrate in concrete ways the main aspects of each phase of his analytical framework. More important, however, the *differences* among the three cases suggest what I consider some of the most important questions about ICAs and TT. This may not have been Mr. Kozinski's intention; he does not dwell on these differences, go into their implications, or attempt to explain them.

In these comments, I would like to make explicit the questions the differences in experience seem to pose and to offer some interpretation. The main goal of this book, and of the joint research effort it represents, is to understand how to improve the effectiveness of ICA, and Mr. Kozinski's description of these three cases suggests some reflections on what are possible crucial elements in determining the effectiveness and long-term vitality of efforts at industrial cooperation.

The GMC-Polmo FTO case has not yet emerged from the first phase, "Exploration and Selection." One wonders why. At first glance the proposed ICA has some very attractive features. The Western partner would provide a great deal of input in areas where it has great experience, e.g., the detailed design and production engineering of a line of trucks. The fact that TT is a "people process" is fully recognized in the provision for training Polish workers. There is a large foreign exchange benefit through GMC's commitment to buy back much of the output. There is a self-enforcing commitment of continued involvement by the Western partner through its interest in protecting the reputation of its trademark. Why, then, have negotiations been suspended so that the ICA has not moved into Phase II? Mr. Kozinski says only that the two sides could not come to an agreement about financial terms, though it is not clear whether the problem is primarily one of equity or one of long-run advantage being scuttled by short-run financial exigencies on the Polish side.

I wonder, however, if there are not more fundamental difficulties with the whole concept. For example, it may have been too ambitious as a first step, involving too many risks for both sides. Despite the training provision, it may have been a very difficult task to turn the paper documentation into a product, a production operation, and a living managerial process consistent with them. The GMC commitment implied by the grant of trademark rights to the Polish organization might well have entailed the kind of frictive intrusion that would have put intolerable burdens on the Polish partner.

I also wonder about the apparent division of responsibilities. If the product was to be bought back by GMC in appreciable amounts and was to be sold by the Poles in Western markets, it seems a mistake to have given the Polish side full responsibility for specification of the line; that ignores the marketing expertise that the Western side could have contributed. And with the Polish side having independent responsibility for production, it seems to be a mistake to have the Western side design the product and by implication many aspects of the production operation. That would create too many dangers of decisions that did not fit Polish organization, materials constraints, and the characteristics of Polish production equipment and techniques. One element of Phase I is to choose the "transfer channel," and one may hazard a guess that each side came into this process with overly settled ideas, ignoring the fact that one of the tasks of this phase was to explore a wide variety of alternatives.

In the TV picture-tube case as well, Kozinski's summary of the provisions of the ICA points to what would seem to be some features adverse to the objectives of the Polish side. The fact that the technology involved is somewhat behind the current state of the art would seem to make it difficult to achieve balance-of-payments gains through sales in Western countries. Rather than envisaging a dynamic growth into long-range cooperation, the agreement was apparently conceived of as essentially a turnkey plant agreement. One wonders if there is adequate provision for supporting the Polish side in mastering the operation of the plant, or in transferring to the Polish side the skills and experience appropriate to subsequent independent work in the design and adaptation of the production operation. Perhaps these are overly critical judgments based on an inadequate understanding of what the agreement involves, and perhaps the Polish side did consider these issues and still made choices in light of important offsetting advantages. But from Mr. Kozinski's description, these seem to be justified questions.

Both the truck and TV-tube examples seem to contrast sharply with the IH-BUMAR case in the level of ambitiousness involved. I am strongly sympathetic to the point Kozinski makes that the possibilities of success in ICAs depends on the technological and managerial capabilities of the partner receiving the technology. It strikes me, therefore, that in the first two examples the Polish partner accepted overly ambitious responsibilities in areas where they really should have more help from the partner (as in the decisions about the kinds of trucks to be produced in the GMC-Polmo case). In the TV picture tube case, on the other hand, one might say that the concept was *insufficiently* ambitious in terms of the long-range goals to be achieved. It is said elsewhere in this volume that the BUMAR organization was uniquely qualified in experience and facilities to carry out its end of its ICA with IH. Yet it seems significant that the commitments undertaken by both sides in the IH-BUMAR agreement regarding trademark provisions, quality control, and buy-back promises originally reflected a more cautious stance than the GMC-Polmo proposal.

To conclude, I am left with a puzzle as to how to interpret the differences between these three cases. Perhaps there are great differences among the Polish partners. Is it possible that some are simply more aware of the potential difficulties and better able to chart a path to long-range TT that will work? Was the decision for a turnkey plant due perhaps to an inability to find a Western partner who would welcome a more symbiotic and long-range relationship? If so, what kind of effort might be made to explain to Western firms the potentials of more complex interaction? Do the differences perhaps reflect some uncertainty in setting guidelines and controlling the conditions each ICA should satisfy and the long-term goals toward which all should be oriented?

I want to close by commending Mr. Kozinski for having added these two cases to the discussion and thus offering some additional dimensions to the picture of TT provided by the IH-BUMAR case, which has been so thoroughly analyzed in this book.

Reply

I am very grateful to Professor Campbell for his comments on the approach to the subject of IC presented in my paper. He is right that the three cases of US-Polish IC have been chosen to illustrate in concrete ways the main phases and elements of TT shown in my analytical framework. Their additional purpose was to answer some questions beginning with "what" instead of "why": What is the function of TT in these cases? What are the directions of transfer? What are the roles of both partners involved?

Professor Campbell's question about why differences exist among the three cases could be answered from different angles:

1. They depend partly on the situation of the technology supplier, i.e., the US corporation, which is partly conditioned by the US economy, governmental actions, and economic policies.

2. They depend on the nature of the technology receiver, i.e., the Polish enterprise with its motivations, strategies, and technical capabilities, which are also reinforced by objectives of the Polish economy and some activities of the government.

3. The nature, quantum, and complexity of the particular TT between both sides varies from case to case.

4. Trends within each sector of industry where US-Polish ICAs are implemented (electronics, automotive, constructive machinery, etc.) may influence the decisions of both the technology supplier and the receiver.

All these aspects should be taken into consideration in any analysis of technological interaction between firms in general, and potential difficulties and differences in particular.

It seems to me that Professor Campbell emphasizes the second of these factors to interpret the differences between the three cases. I fully agree that the GMC-Polmo and the Corning/RCA-Unitra cases have given some necessary and additional approaches to the discussion about our knowledge of TT within IC between US and Polish firms.

I would like to make one more point. Technology can be transferred through IC in various forms and ways. Some works by the Secretariat of the Economic Commission for Europe of the UN differentiate about 15 forms of IC between Eastern and Western countries recently in force.[1] This wide range of transfer possibilities created by sustained enterprise-to-enterprise relations justifies the significance of IC as a versatile TT channel, and needs careful and individual research not only of each IC form but also of each case of IC.

The joint research project by the two teams focusing on BUMAR-IH ICA confirmed the usefulness of this method.

---

1. See, for example, United Nations Economic Commission for Europe "A Statistical Outline of Recent Trends in Industrial Cooperation," *Trade*, AC. 3/R.8 (August 3, 1977).

The International Harvester-BUMAR Cooperation Experience

Practical Problems and their Solutions

Jerzy Szumski

A. Comments on the Case Study

East-West industrial cooperation (IC), despite the tireless efforts of theoreticians and scientists, has yet to be given a definition that pleases everyone. Pragmatic BUMAR has always viewed its cooperative ventures with Western partners as an efficient vehicle for organizing joint product development, manufacturing, sales, and service in a manner beneficial to both sides and in compliance with the traditions, practices, and modus operandi developed and established by industrialized Western countries, while fully recognizing the socio-economic differences of each of the partners. Sykstus Olesik, Director General of BUMAR Foreign Trade Enterprise in 1970-76 and chief architect of the BUMAR-IH agreement, frequently stressed the need to think and act as though the partners were in a joint venture partnership, although they were just one step short of going this far.

This reasoning and philosophy did not always meet with a positive attitude and favorable response from potential Western partners. Frequently narrowmindedness, a lack of vision or imagination, a fear of today's partner becoming a threatening competitor in the future, or a mere absence of the natural base for such cooperation would reduce the prospects of any meaningful relationship to straight license agreement, with perhaps some sort of a "buy back" commitment, or another limited form. Such cooperation was doomed for extinction at the time the agreement was signed.

But the response from International Harvester (IH) was excellent, with the personal involvement of Mr. Brooks McCormick (the CEO) and Mr. Omer G. Voss, the Executive Vice-president. On September 18, 1972, in Chicago, the "Agreement for Cooperation on the Manufacture and Sale of the International Line of Construction Equipment" was signed and made effective. Richard M. Ogilvie, the Governor of Illinois, witnessed the event. An associated document signed the same day addressed itself to the use of registered IH trademarks in conjunction with the machines manufactured by BUMAR.

Our negotiations lasted only about one year, beginning in mid-1971 and ending in July 1972, the agreement becoming effective in September of 1972. It is true that IH representatives visited BUMAR plants as early as 1969, but serious negotiations did not take place until mid-1971. This disagrees with the Indiana University team report, and it is an important discrepancy. The prospect of having to negotiate for four years may scare away even the greatest enthusiast of East-West IC, especially in times of inflation. In addition, the number of exploratory visits was not very great—perhaps two or three on each side.

One must realize the overwhelming importance of the extremely favorable political and economic climate that existed at the time. On the international scene, East-West détente and cooperation prevailed. The Polish domestic scene was characterized by the drive for expansion and modernization, an open economy, foreign credits, and an invitation to Western technology and marketing techniques. From our experience, industrial and economic cooperation between East and West has yet to prove that it can effectively relieve tensions and help détente to prevail. That it can, I am certain. But in the good political climate of the early 1970s, the decisions were made swiftly. Everyone fully cooperated, and the time for negotiations did not need to be very long. Today, a comparable cooperation might require more time.

The motives of IH and BUMAR have evolved since the implementation of the original agreement. This fact is important, because it supports my belief that each East-West cooperative venture can be a living and growing thing if it rests on a sound foundation and if the partners are right. At the outset of the negotiations, BUMAR's most important motivation was the USSR market. Priorities subsequently changed, as BUMAR could not obtain a long-term commitment from USSR buyers for the expected volume of business, but it was the Soviet interest in large quantities of 300hp crawler tractors that started the wheels turning.

Under the 1972 agreement, BUMAR obtained the engineering and manufacturing know-how and the rights to manufacture and sell three basic sizes (five models) of crawler dozers and loaders: the TD-15C tractor/dozer, the 175C loader, the TD-20E tractor/dozer, the TD-25C tractor/dozer, and the TD-25CS sideboom. The agreement provided for payment to IH of an initial disclosure fee and "Research, Engineering and Manufacturing" fees expressed as a percentage of the value of units produced by BUMAR during the term of the agreement. For all practical purposes this "REM" fee was a license fee, or royalty; but it was purposely labeled so as to emphasize its being a compensation for continuing assistance from IH. It definitely made BUMAR feel better. Much of the agreement was concerned with manufacturing and component support from IH to BUMAR, training of personnel, quality inspection, and approval. While IH was under advisory obligations to BUMAR in matters of manufacturing process and technology, it had neither obligations and responsibility, nor the right, to interfere with the manufacturing. This was entirely at BUMAR's discretion.

Also, IH assumed no specific obligations to buy anything from BUMAR. Indeed, the 1972 agreement does not impose any specific obligation on IH to buy anything from BUMAR. There are many positive statements to this effect, of course, and every such intent on the part of IH is expressed; however, each such expression is so wrapped up in conditions relative to "world demand, the best interest of IH, quality standards, favorable price," that in effect these constitute no commitment whatsoever. The only effective stimulant of IH purchasing was a provision that IH would not collect more "REM" fees than half of the value of its purchases from BUMAR—a minimal requirement indeed. To be sure, the "REM" fees have never been adversely affected by this provision, and today BUMAR has difficulties meeting orders from IH.

Again, a sound foundation and mutual compatibility have proven to be more important than "buy back" commitments smartly written into an agreement. By this I do not mean to say that written commitments to buy from a Polish partner are bad or undesirable. But anyone placed under firm commitment to buy will want to be extra cautious, and this will reflect badly on prices and other terms. There is at least one very substantial cooperative venture that did not materialize because of the US company's unwillingness to commit itself to buy and the Polish company's unwillingness to go ahead without such a commitment.

In 1975, both sides realized the vast potential and advantages in joining their financial and engineering resources for product development. A synergetic thesis that one plus one may be greater than two is at work here, as is BUMAR's firm belief that in the advanced stage of cooperation the flow of technology is not a one-way street. BUMAR and IH now have under practical implementation several agreements for joint development of new crawler tractors, diesel engines, and critical machine components. In these agreements, which will last for at least 20 years, IH basically is responsible for engineering design while BUMAR is responsible for construction of engineering prototypes. BUMAR engineers also participate in the design process, as consultants, in order to ensure that the engineering documentation is truly metric and readily usable in Polish plants. Both sides are involved in testing and future manufacturing.

According to William B. McIlvaine, Jr., IH expert on IC agreements and licensing and a key member of the IH team of negotiators:

Through this arrangement BUMAR becomes, in fact, an integral part of the IH worldwide manufacturing capability. IH is, therefore, totally involved with BUMAR's production to the same degree it would be with one of its own subsidiaries, and we are dependent on BUMAR as the sole source of one of IH's major products.

It might be interesting to note at this point the great importance BUMAR placed on the fact that it would be the source of complete machines to IH and IH's Western markets. BUMAR expects to train marketing and service personnel in the sophistication of Western marketing techniques in the same manner it trains its technical personnel. This arrangement can also be used by BUMAR to upgrade its supplier industry to the specifications of Western markets. An example would be Polish tires or other specialty vendor items. Thus, IH involvement has expanded not only to marketing but to secondary supplier industries. The major advantages of this new agreement to Poland include:
1. No disclosure fee.
2. The prestige of being a co-equal partner.
3. BUMAR is the sole source of a major IH product.
4. Improved level of skills of technical and marketing personnel.
5. Ownership technology.
The major advantages to IH:
1. Shared development expense of a major product.
2. No capital investment.
3. Sales revenue of a major product line.
4. Engineering fees.
5. Competitive component source.
. . . I am convinced that this concept of total involvement by the manufacturer in all aspects of the client's manufacturing and marketing programs is the way in which programs of this type will be carried out in the future."[1]

B. Problems and Solutions

1. Organizational Tools of Implementation

Both BUMAR and IH have realized the importance of assigning the best available personnel and creating suitable organizational structures for implementation of their agreements. The system works satisfactorily, but there is room for improvement. Areas that need improvement most are as follows:

1. Huta Stalowa Wola (HSW) is perhaps too vast an industrial organism. The members of its executive management are not responsible for any particular manufacturing program; e.g., the sales director is for all sales, the director of manufacturing for all manufacturing, the director of engineering for all engineering, etc.

2. We know that IH is somewhat unhappy about BUMAR's not having anyone at HSW fully responsible for all things related to the ICA.

3. The BUMAR-IH cooperation now involves three industrial entities outside of BUMAR Union. The interests of these entities should be better represented and served, and steps will be taken to remedy this situation.

2. Transfer and Absorption of Technical Information

The technical information provided by IH was contained basically in engineering design documentation, factory standards, voluntary manufacturers' standards, manufacturing engineering documentation for items manufactured by IH, and informal know-how. The technical information did not contain detailed data on several and often costly items from outside suppliers, and was all in the American system of measurements. This was a formidable obstacle, considering that the initial release of engineering design documentation consisted of more than 20,000 drawings, all of which required translation into Polish and metric conversion. HSW engineers were not unprepared for such a challenge (remember their previous association with Coles and Jones from the UK), but the volume of work was tremendous, and that it was done in a matter of a few months deserves admiration. The so-called "soft metric conversion" was used, ensuring full interchangeability of parts.

HSW also stays current with most engineering changes introduced by IH for modernization or cost reduction, and Polish crawler tractors incorporate all changes at approximately the same time as IH's own tractors manufactured by the plant in Melrose Park.

Recognizing that considerable manufacturing know-how exists on the shop floor rather than on paper, HSW and IH made extensive use of direct contacts, and numerous Polish technical representatives have been trained in IH works in various areas of expertise. Also, IH engineers frequently visited HSW and other BUMAR works, helping Poles to solve difficult manufacturing problems, often by working on weekends and holidays.

But at no time was there a need for any IH engineering or manufacturing personnel at HSW on a permanent basis—something generally unheard of in such a complex technical venture, and a good testimony to the high levels of technical proficiency of BUMAR's plant and its people. Hayden, in "Technology Transfer to East Europe—US Corporate Experience," states that the "training-in-USA" method was viewed as less efficient and more costly to IH by some unnamed IH executives—as opposed to putting IH's own people in the facility full-time.[2] I strongly disagree with this position.

3. Component Support from IH to BUMAR

Annual shipments of components from IH to BUMAR are substantial, and the list of items is long. Initially, the arrangement was difficult to organize smoothly because of differing systems and procedures on both sides. BUMAR insisted on placing finite orders for sets of components required to build one tractor, and on having them shipped in almost physically separated condition (one case or crate with all the parts needed for one tractor). This was, of course, costly and time-consuming, and in the long term unacceptable to either side. It took, I believe, two years to switch to the more efficient method of having a complete listing of all part numbers (the same part number may often be used for various tractor models) and ordering and shipping the same part numbers in bulk quantities. The component support program and schedules are computer-controlled and seem to be working quite well, assuring flexibility of changes and precise control of inventory.

Penalties for late deliveries *per se* are not used by either side. But a penalty still exists in the form of an obligation to pay air freight by the supplier, if the delay affects the assembly of machines by the partner. We must say that IH periodically has problems delivering on time, mainly because of delays of its vendors, and has always agreed to ship by air, if needed. Components as big as diesel engines have been flown across the Atlantic to Copenhagen, and from there to HSW by truck.

Payment for components to IH is always in cash. BUMAR also gets paid in cash for what it sells to IH. However, lines of credit arranged between Bank Handlowy in Warsaw and Eximbank and US commercial banks are used frequently for shipments from IH to BUMAR.

4. BUMAR's Products Integration Guidelines

BUMAR's policy guidelines for the speediest and fullest possible product integration are as follows:

1. Descend from assembly level to part numbers level in all imported components as fast as possible and where justified by manufacturing considerations.

2. Move from bay assembly of machines to line assembly as fast as possible. Line assembly was introduced in 1975 for the full mix of five models.

3. Because of the priority of economizing on dollar expenditure, substitute locally-made components for imported components as fast as possible and as technically viable (economic cost considerations have secondary importance) from HSW's own production or from other Polish suppliers. This is done only if prior qualification approval of IH has been obtained.

4. In attacking the import substitution problems, concentrate on the most expensive, yet feasible, immediate manufacturing items first, the heaviest and most costly to transport items second, then all remaining items in step with the growth of our own capabilities and availability of specialized equipment and processes.

5. Items not designed by IH that IH normally procures from suppliers are the last to be substituted, and then only to the extent to which they may be approved by IH (hydraulic components, rubber and plastic products, sealants, electrical components). Some items may remain the subject of permanent import.

6. Proceed to develop Polish production of peculiar shapes, profiles, plate thicknesses, and even unique standard fasteners that are not available commercially in Poland. This, of course, is possible only because of the unique capabilities of HSW in steel-making and processing.

These guidelines may seem prosaic and obvious. Yet they require a tremendous effort on the part of the Polish manufacturer and its local suppliers. The program and these guidelines have been quite successfully implemented, always with the full and selfless cooperation of IH. The guidelines encompass the overwhelming priority of the need to save on dollar expenditures, at times even with a disregard for conventional economics. BUMAR's imports at this point represent approximately 30 percent of an average machine (100 percent being all loose components needed to build one machine at the Melrose Park plant); and yet the volume of sales of IH to BUMAR grows from year to year with the growth of Polish production of completed units and shipments of assemblies to IH.

5. Problem of Steels and Other Materials

Engineers and metallurgists on both sides worked hard for several months to draw up a list of Polish equivalents of American steels and other materials. Their purpose was to select an exact equivalent in terms of strength and performance, or a superior material. Of the 158 various steels, cast steels, gray and other irons, the Poles succeeded in substituting 147 from Polish Standard Specifications; 7 types of steels and 4 qualities of iron had to be specially produced in Poland in accordance with American specifications.

6. Development of Manufacturing Engineering and Capabilities

The crawler tractor program, and more recently the program of wheel loaders, was a net addition to the existing manufacturing programs of HSW.

A considerable investment was necessary for constructing buildings, procuring manufacturing, testing, and inspection equipment, and tooling. Naturally, HSW had to utilize existing equipment and process to support the production of crawler tractors to the fullest extent; hence, there was a need to develop HSW's own manufacturing engineering rather than copying the processes and manufacturing of IH. The latter was regarded as supplementary rather than as a reference. In other words, HSW does many things differently, but the final product is the same. As it happens, HSW uses much machinery and many processes that are more modern than those of IH.

New shops and buildings were set up specifically for this project, including the fabrication and assembly shop with 40,000 sq.m. of floor area. The HSW gear shop was increased by an additional 20,000 sq.m. Currently, there is a crawler undercarriage shop nearing completion and a modern automatic forging plant has been imported from Japan.

In selecting manufacturing equipment, emphasis was placed on maximizing the use of the most modern manufacturing methods appropriate for the scale and nature of production of construction equipment, i.e., specialty machine tools, numerically and tape or computer controlled machine tools, and machining centers. HSW also has the unique capability to make its own tooling. By the end of 1973, 6,900 items of fixtures, jigs, tools, gauges, dies, templates, and patterns had been made, involving a total of almost 900,000 toolroom hours.

These facts clearly illustrate the magnitude of the industrial endeavor and deep commitment of BUMAR as a partner in this undertaking. And we have been talking only about the crawler program, not about the wheel loader or other joint programs.

BUMAR's investment in these new facilities and tooling was considerable. Approximately 50 percent involved convertible currency spending, much of it for purchasing US-made equipment. Most of the convertible currency funding was provided by Bank Handlowy in Warsaw under an agreement obligating BUMAR to repay the loan with proceeds from export sales of the very product of the cooperation. Only the convertible currency proceeds qualified for repayment of the principal and interest. These loans have already been repaid. This type of convertible currency financing was very popular in Poland in the early 1970s, and funds were readily available. The Polish zlotys for purchasing these dollars and other currencies were provided by the central planners.

7. Product Quality and Trademark Approval Testing

HSW naturally fulfills the prerequisites for attaining and maintaining the high levels and consistency of quality of parts and machines, thanks to the excellence of the manufacturing equipment, the ability to generate most of the critical materials and semi-fabricates within its own organization, and the high skills of its workers, foremen, and engineers. Notwithstanding these factors, BUMAR and IH devised several procedures for achieving and policing consistent levels of quality and interchangeability of production and service parts. Thus, Polish-made parts may be substituted for US-made parts in BUMAR's own production only after they have met certain quality and test criteria established by IH. For these purposes, all parts are assigned a certain code number, and the entire issue of part qualification is controlled by a computer.

Code A parts: subject to qualification approval by HSW's inspection department, which issues a certificate for IH seconds.

Code B parts: samples of parts or subassemblies made with the use of production tooling must be sent to IH in the US for qualification testing, IH to issue a certificate.

Code D parts: HSW tests the parts dimensionally and metallurgically and establishes the report, which is sent to IH for verification and approval.

Code BD parts: both B and D requirements must be fulfilled.

Code C parts: cannot be substituted.

Currently, 10,807 parts and subassemblies, or 90.5 percent of all parts that could be substituted, have qualified for use in Polish production.

If a part or subassembly is contemplated for supply to IH plants in the US, a different and independent procedure called QA-70 is applied, under which parts and subassemblies are thoroughly inspected and tested by IH laboratories.

The use of the IH trademark in conjunction with the sales of BUMAR-built machines requires prior approval testing of the units at

IH's testing grounds near Phoenix, Arizona. Under stringent conditions, three BUMAR-built machines have already earned the right to use IH trademarks: TD-15C, 175C, and TD-25C.

Celebrating the fifth anniversary of the cooperation agreement in HSW in October 1978, Mr. Brooks McCormick, Chairman of the IH Board, stated:

> We consider our trademark one of our most valuable assets. We are proud of this trademark for it represents the integrity and honor by which our company and its products are recognized worldwide. In our long history we never have shamed it. We never would approve its use by anyone if we felt it would not continue to be so treated and respected. BUMAR and the employees at Stalowa Wola have earned the right to use this trademark, through their outstanding performance over the past five years. I say to you, wear it with pride. It represents the highest recognition we can bestow upon one of our trading partners.

8. Pricing

The pricing formula for IH supplies of components seems to be fair and realistic. BUMAR pays the standard manufacturing cost plus a percentage surcharge (basically IH gross profit), plus the cost of packing and shipping at actuals. As IH relies heavily on outside suppliers, BUMAR feels it could realize some savings in purchasing directly from such suppliers, and BUMAR intends to do this on a larger scale.

It is the pricing of supplies from BUMAR to IH in the US that seems to be a problem now and for the future. The list of people who want, and have the legitimate right, to earn some money seems endless: the ocean carrier, the US Customs, IH, the distributor, and the end-user.

BUMAR, of course, knows its true production costs—in Polish currency or zlotys. The problem is that zlotys are not yet freely convertible into hard currencies. Only certain government guidelines exist as to what is an acceptable export transaction in terms of maximum number of Polish zlotys of cost needed to earn one US dollar, or one D mark, etc. The US dollar has not been very stable lately and, all told, BUMAR sales of complete machines to IH in the US (talking exclusively about prospects of some specialty machines that IH does not build itself) do not look promising now. In the case of components, BUMAR does not seem to have such a big problem.

9. Marketing

Marketing in third countries is another good example of cooperation. To be sure, we are talking about relatively few machines that have been sold by BUMAR with marketing help from IH, but these cases are encouraging as indicators that BUMAR and IH can indeed exploit some sales opportunities which, without their cooperation, would surely be taken by competitors, without any advantage to either BUMAR or IH.

On the other hand, everyone seems to agree that the spectacular entry of IH into some CMEA markets in 1972 probably would not have happened without cooperation with BUMAR. And BUMAR, too, bought a substantial number of IH machines for Poland; none was ever sold before cooperation.

10. Language

Language was no problem during the negotiations. BUMAR Foreign Trade Enterprise has always had a sufficient number of people fluent in foreign languages, including English. But in the process of technology transfer, language problems did come up, causing countless misunderstandings, which were sometimes painful to correct. We have all heard stories about "technicians having a language of their own" and "a picture is worth a thousand words," but this question must not be taken lightly. BUMAR fortunately is past this stage. It is amazing how many people at HSW have learned to understand, speak, and write English in a truly professional manner—in the jargon of trade. On the other hand, our worthwhile colleagues on the IH side have made little progress in mastering the Polish language.

11. Quality

Quality from HSW has been good; HSW is fully capable of delivering a quality product. Lately, however, HSW has met with some criticism from Melrose Park plant quality inspectors in connection with the mechanisms of a new model of crawler tractor that was sent for evaluation and approval before production and quantity shipments from Poland to the US commence sometime next year.

Both sides work together on eliminating these departures from quality, and IH has decided to have its own quality specialist stationed at BUMAR's facility. BUMAR finds some consolation in the fact that there have been cases of IH shipping material of questionable quality to BUMAR, and cooperation did not fall apart just because of this.

12. Balance of Payments

The case study correctly assumes that BUMAR's relationship to IH is one of deficit payments. But both sides do their utmost to improve this, and the scene has been set for a dramatic improvement or even a reversal of the situation. BUMAR will be manufacturing new products that IH is keenly interested in having available for worldwide marketing. BUMAR does recognize this opportunity, but again there is the need to invest heavily in new capacities and facilities.

In the current year, the overall trading position of BUMAR vis-à-vis hard currency markets, I believe, should probably be balanced, with the added advantage of saving the Polish economy tens of millions of dollars on units supplied to Polish end-users, which would otherwise have to be imported from the West.

I would like to pre-empt possible questions on whether this last consideration by itself is a good enough reason for a Polish industrial enterprise to want to establish a cooperative agreement with a Western firm. The answer is definitely "no," unless the product is unique and constitutes an unusual import burden. But for IC with Poland, I believe, the name of the game is "exports worldwide," and all other things, including the elimination of imports, seem to be unimportant. We seem to have developed more effective devices to eliminate nonessential imports. We simply do not import.

In conclusion, my belief, and it may be a very personal belief, is that the basic strength of BUMAR-IH cooperation lies in the mutual compatibility of partners.

C. Recommendations

On the basis of my experience with BUMAR and IH (and BUMAR and other Western firms), I would recommend the following to any potential entrant:

1. See that your firm is compatible with the Polish Industrial Enterprise and Foreign Trade Enterprise.

2. Communicate with people on the other side, not only language, but mentality and basic thinking.

3. Consider products with worldwide marketing capability.

4. Remember that Poland is closest not only to East European, but also to West European markets. Investing in manufacturing capabilities in Western Europe has recently lost a lot of its appeal.

5. Remember that Poland at present confronts some economic problems and is in no position to commit vast capital resources, especially if convertible currency is involved. Therefore, inquire about existing capacities, especially if they remain under-utilized.

6. Be frank and straightforward in your approach and negotiations. Do not try to sell the Poles something under the guise of cooperation. It will backfire, and rather quickly.

7. Industries integrated with a Foreign Trade Enterprise are likely to be more prospective partners. Be satisfied that they work as a team without significant differences of approach and opinion.

8. Shoot for the long term, ten years seems to be a good period for any meaningful cooperation.

9. Negotiations at the operating management level are very important and are a good start (Bureau Director in an FTE, Managing Di-

rector of a manufacturing enterprise). But as the talks progress, and additional investments come into view, make sure that the Director of Industrial Union and the Ministry concerned are also involved, or at least aware of developments.

10. Always see the long-term potential and advantage, and never let it be jeopardized for the sake of a short-term advantage. Polish partners may be slow starters, but they can be loyal and beneficial partners, given the opportunity and time.

11. If possible, offer a cooperation that will or could be global in marketing. Consider that Poland enjoys trading advantages in certain countries that your firm may not enjoy.

12. Bear in mind the potential for joint research and development. Polish engineers and scientists are of a very high caliber, and their skills combined with your firm's expertise in product and markets can accomplish a lot, and for a lot less investment by you.

13. Quality inspection on the spot, if tactfully suggested, will be welcome and may be a good investment.

Notes

1. William B. McIlvaine, Jr., "A Case History of Licensing Joint Ventures in Poland and Algeria," in *The Law and Business of Licensing,* ed. Marcus B. Finnegan and Robert Goldscheider (New York: Clark Boardman Co., Ltd., 1977), pp. 384.431-384.438.

2. Eric W. Hayden, *Technology Transfer to East Europe: US Corporate Experience* (New York: Praeger Publishers, 1976), p. 57.

Comment

John Garland

Mr. Szumski's paper is a particularly welcome contribution. It reminds us that the true determinants of East-West industrial cooperation (IC) are the specific motives and capacities at the level of the cooperating enterprises. In view of the emphasis in the seminar on the macroeconomic considerations influencing Polish production specialization and export structure, it is refreshing to focus on "where the action is."

Mr. Szumski's emphasis on the evolutionary nature of a specific industrial cooperation agreement (ICA) is important in drawing attention to the necessary flexibility of the partners in responding to changing external environmental conditions and their willingness to make internal, strategic organizational changes. Without such flexibility on both sides, neither the long-term commitments nor the community of interests inherent in IC could be effectively realized.

We are grateful to Mr. Szumski for discussing a dozen problem areas that arose during the implementation of the agreement. Although he could not go into a detailed analysis of each problem, his knowledgeable and frank discussion of the issues contributes immensely to an understanding of what he has termed "the Cooperation Touch."[1] It cannot be stressed enough that a mishandling of any of the 12 problem areas mentioned could have destroyed the cooperation agreement. This not only reflects the commitment of both partners to make the agreement work, but also reveals each partner's confidence in the ability and willingness of the other to make the necessary adjustments. In the true spirit of cooperation, the partners have not let short-term considerations or unforeseen technical deviations from the letter of the agreement undermine the implementation and further development of the joint undertaking.

Mr. Szumski's comments reveal the dynamic nature of a successful ICA. He shows that the essence of cooperation is more a flexible and continually accommodating relationship than a contractually agreed upon exchange of goods or technology. It is more a framework for interaction than a blueprint to be followed closely. It is more a foundation on which to build a synergetic relationship than a boundary that confines the partners to limited and specific lines of action. As confidence between the partners grows, so does the complexity of the evolving coproduction.

Having said this, I hope it does not detract from this significant contribution of Mr. Szumski if I present a slightly different perspective on a few of the issues.

First and most important is the question of timely production and delivery of high-quality products for the hard currency markets. Mr. Szumski touches on the problem, but I would like to elaborate on it further. As he mentioned, in 1973 an addition to the ICA was made providing for BUMAR to send tractor skids to the IH subsidiary in Doncaster, England. Everyone benefited from this extension. First, BUMAR increased its hard currency exports, a matter of high priority. Second, the UK subsidiary was able to expand its product line with minimal investment. Third, the extension carried the potential of making IH more competitive in Europe, where the market for construction equipment has been relatively flat and characterized by intense competition among the approximately 800 producers. Unfortunately, after several years, the market for this particular model fizzled

---

1. Jerzy Szumski and Janusz Piotrowski, "The Cooperation Touch," *Eastern Business Magazine* 3:4 (1978):162-65.

out, and the promising arrangement failed to meet Polish expectations—due to conditions largely beyond the control of either partner.

Subsequent efforts by IH to rely on BUMAR as a source of components for IH subsidiaries, however, reveal some basic problems. For example, IH had planned to use BUMAR as a source of components for front-end loaders to be assembled in Germany. But due to BUMAR's other commitments as well as start-up problems, its production of these components has been delayed for several years, so IH had to look for other suppliers. Mr. Szumski mentions that while Polish partners may be slow starters, they can be excellent partners, given opportunity and time. The point is, however, that Western market conditions do not grant such luxuries. BUMAR lost its opportunity for hard currency exports when the German assembler had to find another supplier.

Another problem involving the sourcing of components and machines from BUMAR is their quality standards. It is an indisputable fact that BUMAR has the capacity to produce the quality demanded by Western markets. Yet the delivery of goods from BUMAR to IH units in the United States has been marked by persistent quality shortcomings, whether it be sloppy painting, rusted parts, or similar problems. Whatever the problem—whether it be the incentive system, plant infrastructural activities, or supplier relationships—it seems to be a continuing struggle to keep the workers at HSW producing at the level of quality of which they have already proved themselves capable.

I should also like to raise a potential long-range problem: Will the individual interests of IH and BUMAR become competitive over time? While in some sense competition on third markets is healthy, it may also create friction as long as production by the two partners is not purely complementary, but in some instances parallel. It brings into question the marketing arrangements that characterize East-West IC in general—either implicit or explicit division of markets into exclusive or non-exclusive markets for the two partners. BUMAR's desire for hard currency exports and IH's interest in the CMEA markets might prove to be sources of conflict if the present market division is perpetuated. Should that conflict materialize, it will be a severe test of the commitment to cooperation and of the mutual trust that have been characteristic of the IH-BUMAR ICA. On the other hand, it is possible that the agreement will continue its evolution toward increased partner specialization, in which case the potential problem will be alleviated naturally.

Mr. Szumski seems to have adequately captured the spirit of the IH-BUMAR ICA. And if this specific agreement has any significance for other firms or other sectors, I suggest that it is that very spirit rather than any specific arrangements (which must reflect the nature, capabilities, and philosophy of the cooperating firms) which is most instructive. Systemic differences between East and West can be viewed as an insurmountable obstacle to the creation of inter-enterprise activities or as a challenge for innovative management. Although each problem area must find its own concrete solution, partner compatibility is reflected above all in the method of approach to the problems and in the demonstrated commitment to what can become a mutually satisfying relationship.

Reply

Mr. Garland has expressed concern over three issues: the timely delivery of products by BUMAR, quality standards, and potential competition by the partners on third country markets. In response to the last concern, may I simply comment that in order to minimize competition in third markets and to better capitalize on the potential for joint coordinated marketing, BUMAR and IH recently decided to organize a joint marketing company situated in a third country.

I think also that Mr. Garland has exaggerated the issue of quality, probably because of his lack of full information. BUMAR has not failed IH in quality of any regular shipments to support production at the IH plant in Melrose Park. Our current quality problem relates to prototypes, or pilot units, of very sophisticated machines sent by BUMAR to IH for evaluation, perhaps leading to regular shipments next year. The defects were trivial, because they were simply instances of sloppy workmanship. One thing is certain: they do not reflect any substantial technology problem. BUMAR's record of shipping thousands of units to Great Britain and other Western countries is evidence of the quality of its production.

As I have already said, the set-up is terrific; the important thing is to bring to the cooperation meaningful and timely performance. But I don't want to leave you with the impression that only BUMAR fails to deliver on time, or has delays. To keep things in balance, it must be noted that IH has at times had some material that needed reworking in Poland, and they have had delays with the loader. Also, there have been delays as long as 18 months in releasing some of the documentation. Perhaps it is their business decision; they may have decided that the model currently produced continues to be a good product and sells well. But in spite of all this, I fully agree with the gentlemen from IH that the cooperation is beneficial overall. If I were to start a clean slate, I would do it all over again—perhaps even with greater desire than in 1971.

Summary of the Discussion

The Editors

After presentation of the papers by the Polish team, formal comments by the US team and replies, a general discussion followed, involving members of the two teams as well as other interested participants. The record of discussion that follows is an abbreviated one. The participants' remarks were summarized by the editors, unless reported as direct quotes. We attempted to give an expression to the major ideas and different points of view presented at the conference, even when it was not possible to cite all speakers by name.

The first part of the discussion attempted to clarify how decisions regarding trade and IC with Western partners are made in Poland. Specific cases were mentioned to show that enterprise initiative plays a key role. The discussion then turned to whether and how Poland's economic mechanism guides enterprise managers and planners to make the right export, import, and IC decisions. The second part of the discussion explored the problems Polish exporters face in trying to penetrate the US and other industrial Western markets. The Polish side stressed the problem of US protectionism, especially the discriminatory dumping and market disruption rules. The American side spoke of the difficulty of devising equitable rules of market access for exporters from non-market economy countries such as Poland who, from the American point of view, do not face the usual constraints of a market economy regarding costs, return on investment, and the threat of bankruptcy. This was followed by an exchange of views on the calculation and interpretation of Polish cost of production and exchange rates, and the relevance of these concepts in US dumping investigations. The third part of the discussion concentrated mostly on specific problems relating to the IH-BUMAR coproduction agreement. The Conference sessions were chaired by Howard V. Perlmutter and Josef C. Brada, respectively.

***

Warren Reynolds opened the discussion with a question on Poland's export specialization: "At dinner with a friend the other day, he looked at me and said, 'What do you think of my new suit?' I said it is absolutely beautiful.. And the label said Raleigh Haberdashery, Washington, made in Poland. Now, who made the decision to start exporting suits from your country to the US? What was the role of the central planner vs. the manufacturer?"

Eugeniusz Tabaczynski replied that while he was not familiar with the specifics of the case he would try to answer in a general way. The clothes industry in Poland is organized into a large economic organization,[1] with a special foreign trade organization (FTO) called Textilimpex. This FTO is directly subordinated to the Ministry of Light Industry, not to the Ministry of Foreign Trade and Shipping. Light industry in Poland until 1965 was undercapitalized and obsolete, but in recent years substantial investments have been made in this sector, which includes textiles and clothing.

In this industry there are many examples of initiative. A managerial group that wants to enter foreign markets. The case mentioned illustrates such initiative at work. Another concrete illustration can also be given. A few years ago, the general manager of a Warsaw department store chain went for a private visit to the Federal Republic of Germany (FRG) and came home with a very good order for clothing. The general manager went to the Polish industry and convinced them to produce suits for a West German department store. Poland received models for suits and certain kinds of machines. The cooperation lasted for about five years and earned good hard currency for Poland.

Edwin Zagorski gave a further illustration involving the FRG. Around 1971-73, prosperity in the FRG coincided with the availability of a building and skilled tailors in Poland. Somebody from West Germany said, "I will invest a certain amount of money in Poland to manufacture suits, and you will pay with the suits. You will get your money back in a year or so." Irrespective of Poland's prospects in coal or its emphasis on any other branch of industry, it was argued that such an opportunity must be seized. This example illustrates something about the "rules of IC": a good product and an opportunity can be developed into a successful and profitable industrial cooperation agreement (ICA). *Robert Holubnychi* asked, "I have a ten-year license agreement with a Polish company, Pezetel. I was interested in your comment that the central level sets the parameters to be met by any agreement. Does the center set financial parameters from a return-on-investment point of view, or does it allow the firm itself to take the initiative, say, to spend $2 million for an American license?''

Tabaczynski replied that Pezetel has an excellent tradition in the aviation industry and was one of the most advanced producers in Europe before the war. Today it is responsible not only for aviation but for different types of engines. It even produces golf carts, although the company is known mostly as a manufacturer of modern engines. If Pezetel wants to enter the US market and needs a license, it makes such a proposal first to the Ministry of Machine Building, to whom it is subordinated. There are three ways for Pezetel to obtain money. The first is to utilize part of the investment funds allocated by the state budget to the Ministry of Machine Building. The second source is the credit facilities arranged by the Polish Bank Handlowy, which grants and controls the use of such credit, acting as an intermediary between the Polish buyer and foreign lenders. The third possibility is to obtain the license or machine through leasing or within the framework of IC, i.e., so that there is no direct outlay of hard currency. The proposal must show a rate of return on investment, Tabaczynski added, but the first consideration is the calculation and commitment that Pezetel can export as a result of purchasing the license.

Harry DePledge asked about the kind of advice and information plant executives at the lower level receive: ''What kind of infrastructure do you put in place to make sure that the managers will make the right decisions? We heard several examples of export-oriented IC. The Pezetel example was based on tradition, another one was developed through a chance contact on a private trip. How do you make sure that most executives will acquire the knowledge and then make the right decision?''

Tabaczynski replied that there are different schools of thought on this problem. Some people in Poland are of the opinion that since Poland has some important raw materials, for instance coal, copper, and sulfur, as well as a long agricultural tradition, thses materials and products should be the natural basis for the country's export specialization. This includes to mining machinery and different types of agricultural equipment and related technologies.

Another school of thought contends that Poland should first establish the appropriate economic parameters, use these for the economic evaluation of different solutions, and then let responsible economic units make the decisions by themselves. (To be sure, in many branches, decisions have been made and are being implemented in this way; for instance, in ships and construction equipment.) Central authorities should not say too much to industry because managers are responsible for the financial results of their businesses.

Howard Perlmutter asked, "You say to managers: We let you decide, you should know, we cannot tell you from above. But what happens if the manager is wrong? Is there a reward and punishment system? How are managers educated and rewarded so that they make more right decisions than wrong ones?"

Tabaczynski replied that this is a problem for all producers, in the East and in the West. Anybody can be right or wrong. But what if the manager undertook certain kinds of production and that production was wrong in terms of market demand? This is the problem of risk. Each enterprise has a special fund that covers risks. The point is, however, that there should be more right than wrong decisions made.

Robert McCullough asked how central authorities make sure that the enterprise manager has all the information he needs to make more right than wrong decisions.

Tabaczynski replied that in the 1960s, the financial results of producers were separated from the economics of foreign trade decisions. But since the LEOs were introduced in 1971, managers should be aware of the situation in foreign markets because they have to account for financial results. Moreover, Poland has to some extent solved the problem of the relationship between domestic and foreign financial results by incorporating some FTOs into LEOs and by introducing transaction prices into the balance sheets of producers.

Thomas Wolf approached the question of Poland's international specialization from a different angle. He noted that if one looks at Poland's trade statistics for manufactured products exported to the West, especially to West Germany, its largest market, one finds that between 1965 and 1975 a large proportion of Poland's export success was in clothing products. He wondered where an industry such as clothing fits into the spectrum of progressive and regressive industries mentioned in Tabaczynski's presentation.

Tabaczynski replied that one cannot say that the light industry or the clothing industry is progressive or regressive, only that specific products within them are progressive or regressive.

Perlmutter linked export specialization to IC by noting that the question of specialization for a single country like Poland is going to be more and more difficult to resolve without an increased understanding of how global demand and competitive structures evolve. International division of labor will not take place without some consultation among the actors. The essential question, in hiw view, is: "To what extent are Polish and US companies in various industries around the world ready to ask in global strategic terms what they will do together and what they will not do together in which third markets?"

The discussion then turned to market access in the West for Polishmanufactures. *Zygmunt Kossut* noted that while the EC has erected large barriers to agricultural products, barriers in the US seem particularly large for manufactured products.

Wolf questioned whether Poland's relative lack of success in exporting manufactured products to the US has been determined primarily by the restrictiveness of US trade policy. He argued that other determinants, namely marketing, an exporter's aligning himself with the right partner in a given regional market, and a feel for style and other demand characteristics are more important.

Joseph Miller commented that there are already a lot of sellers with established positions in the US marketplace. Unless a Polish producer has a proprietary or extremely competitive product, it is going to be difficult to gain market access. The experience of the Japanese and others is that initial entry is costly. The price is usually a negative cash flow position for some time.

On the question raised by *Dzikiewicz* about the new US "trigger price system" and its affect on Poland, *Paul Marer* replied that this new system, which unfortunately adversely affects Polish steel and steel-product exports to the US, is not leveled against Poland or against non-market economy (NME) countries, but is an overall US protective measure. In many peoples' view, the measure is justified by the fact that so many countries around the world are protecting and subsidizing their steel industries, whereas no subsidy is given for this essential industry in the US.

Marer then turned to the Polish golf cart case, which had been raised by Kossut and others. He said that it is understandable why Professor Kossut and other specialists in Poland have the same views on this case. Marer summarized these views: "Here is a manufactured product Poland produced specifically for the US market and in which it achieved excellent product quality. We also did a good marketing job and in a few years acquired something like 25 percent of the total US market for golf carts. Just because we were so successful, our hands were slapped, and we were hit with a dumping charge. Does this not indicate that it is dangerous to be so highly visible on the American market and does it not support the argument of those in Poland who say that extreme specialization is not advisable because we'll run into these problems?"

Marer then noted that it is also important to understand the views of Western economists and businessmen on this issue. Our perception is that, for a variety of reasons, producers in Poland (and in other NME countries) do not know precisely what it costs to produce a given product because the price system is to some degree arbitrary and because there are no unambiguously justifiable exchange rates to translate Polish zloty costs and prices into dollars. Therefore, a US producer competing against, say, Polish manufactured imports such as golf carts would typically say: "How are we to compete fairly against the product produced in Poland when it is our perception, right or wrong, that we are competing not against an enterprise that faces the usual constraints of a market economy regarding costs, return on capital, and the threat of bankruptcy if the bottom line stays in the red too long, but in the final analysis, against a government agency that may decide what to produce and how much to charge for exports. We suppose that a Polish producer or his agent can charge whatever low price he thinks is necessary to penetrate our markets to earn the convertible currency the government needs. So how do we protect our employment, our profits, our livelihood, against what we perceive to be unfair competition?"

To answer this question, *Marer* stated, the US (and other Western countries) has rules that try to be fair to consumers, to producers competing against imports, and to the exporters to the US. These rules are not perfect and are continually evolving. But perhaps even more important than the technical details of these rules — which Marer said he will try to summarize in his presentation at the second conference in Warsaw — is that each side must understand the complexity of the matter. Each side must understand the point of view and the reasoning of the other.

Tabaczynski said he could not agree with Marer's statement that Polish producers are not quite aware of the level of their production costs. Polish enterprises rely on so-called transaction prices in their caculations. (The concept of transaction price was discussed briefly in the paper presented by Giezgala.) The transaction price in exports or imports is, generally speaking, a product of the foreign currency price paid or received times the conversion coefficient, which is established separately for trade with Eastern and Western countries (see the diagram in Giezgala's reply on p. 97). To be sure, there are some raw materials whose domestic prices are kept constant, for important reasons. But for foreign trade calculations, transaction prices are also introduced for these raw materilas to obtain the true production cost. Precise production costs are calculated by summing the cost of raw materials, processing costs (technology, wages, overhead), and selling expenses (advertising, packaging, transportation, commissions). The total cost of export production is compared with the transaction prices of the final products for exports. The former, or course, should be smaller.

Szumski said that the Indiana University case study and subsequent comments by the American team said or implied that BUMAR and other Polish producers have no way of knowing their true costs. "I think the key word here is 'true.' I can assure you that every product is individually cost analyzed in a more or less conventional manner, in terms of material, labor, overhead, and other inputs and their zloty costs. Now if someone is saying that bacause of the peculiarities of a planned economy, certain prices or costs are unrealistic, that they are not the result of market forces, then to this extent he may be correct, and we have no disagreeement. But Polish producers know fully what it costs to make a particular product.''

As far as the rate of exchange for the Polish zloty is concerned, *Szumski* concurred with *Tabaczynski's* exposition. He added that for the purpose of determining whether a potential export should indeed be sold, government guidelines state the maximum zloty cost that is acceptable to earn a unit of foreign currency. The cost cannot be more than this; it can only be less. If it is more, then there is no sale, unless an exception is made, as when an exporter can document to the Ministry of Foreign Trade and Shipping that this temporary sacrifice price will in time be improved.

After some further exchange between Polish and American participants on the question of cost, price, and exchange rate calculations in Poland, *Wolf* tried to sort out the apparent inconsistencies among the views by pointing out that there are different ways of defining economic costs, or economic rationality. First, there is the question of whether the cost of an individual product is calculated in the same way in Poland as it is in America. Much depends on how overhead is allocated and on the resolution of other, essentially accounting, problems. A second way of looking at costs is to ask whether they are real costs. The conventional view among Western economists is that while there may be a certain logic in the construction of costs and prices in centrally planned economies (CPEs), these prices may be arbitrary in that they do not reflect fully and accurately relative scarcities within the Polish economy. A third way to look at the cost issue is to focus on the exchange rate, i.e., the conversion coefficient or multiplier. Even if it were in effect an ''equilibrium'' rate, Wolf was not exactly sure what is meant by the term. One problem is that apparently the exchange rate is not uniform. Another problem is that of subsidies. A Polish enterprise may know its costs but it may be willing to take a loss in exports if it knows that it is going to be subsidized by the state, in the national interest. Finally, Wolf added, there is the question of whether Polish producers and exporters may not have to sometimes ignore internal micro-economic profitability in order to meet the world dollar price in the face of world competition.

Robert Campbell asked whether the conversion coefficient is uniform and stable or whether, in the context of an ICA, the Polish producer would have to anticipate its changes when he undertakes commitments about exports and imports. Will the rate continue in force for, say, two or five years?

Tabaczynski, coming back to Wolf's questions, stressed first that countries may have different accounting systems for production costs. For example, in Yugoslavia, wages are not an element of production costs but a component of the financial results of an enterprise. But irrespective of the accounting system, it should reflect accurately whether producers increase or consume the national income. In Poland, economists are always aware of what is and what should be the answer to this question. Therefore, one cannot speak of an arbitrary price system in Poland.

The problem of subsidies may arise, of course, in specific situations as it does in other countries, but it is not a part of Poland's export price system. In general, Poland is against subsidies. Tabaczynski then referred to Campbell's question and stated that the conversion coefficient is uniform for all transactions with Western countries and has remained unchanged for several years.

The discussion then turned to the IH-BUMAR ICA. *H. L. Lehmann* said he became involved in this project just after the initial documents were signed in 1972. The signers of the document had to be visionaries because there was no detailed roadmap; we still don't know the full potentials of the cooperation between IH and BUMAR. The signers of the document had enough wisdom not to try to establish a roadmap showing each railroad trestle and stoplight; instead, they framed the "country" in which they were going to operate. Lehmann pointed out that, "although the Polish partners may sometimes be slow starters, they can be wonderfully loyal and beneficial partners, given the opportunity and time." To be sure, Poland has lost some hard currency sales prospects to IH subsidiaries in Western Europe, Lehmann continued, because of slowness of response or lack of understanding on both sides about how to take full advantage of the opportunities.

Lehmann then explained that the project has imposed a considerable price on IH because there are almost daily problems to be solved. One of the most important is the quality issue, because of a lack of appreciation in the Polish plant of how and why even the seemingly most insignificant aspect of quality is critical. But these and other problems are challenging opportunities. "If you see them as problems, you should not be in the IC business. If you see them as opportunities, you will probably succeed. That has been our philosophy." Lehmann then pointed out that it is often said that a cooperation project abroad will take jobs away from the US. IH's experience has been that every one of its overseas activities, particularly the Polish one, is generating more productivity and jobs in the plants because it allows IH to broaden its product lines and to develop new products at a much faster rate and with higher efficiency.

Marer asked whether any of the products manufactured in Poland under the IH-BUMAR arrangement can or are being sold for hard currency to other CMEA countries.

Szumski replied that this is not really the case, as a rule. In one or two cases that he is aware of, when BUMAR had something another CMEA country wanted badly, a barter transaction was arranged in which both partners recognized the transaction to be in convertible currency, though probably there was no actual transfer of hard currency; it was a bookkeeping operation.

Perlmutter asked what factors each partner considers the most important to assess the present and future success of the cooperation.

Lehmann replied that, in retrospect, there are some significant successes as well as some keen disappointments. "We had hoped by this point to be sourcing a considerable quantity of goods from Poland. I see this sourcing as perhaps 18 months in arrears as far as potential because of quality problems. Even if you have an engine that is made on the best machines and all the parts are there, if the bolds aren't tight, you have got an engine that isn't going to last long. But the larger picture of wanting to attain something in Poland hasn't changed. IH has been operating under an old and a new president; it has gone from a domestic divisional structure to a corporate worldwide group. This hasn't changed our Polish posture one bit; as a matter of fact, it has amplified the opportunities. To be sure, we could be a lot further along than we are now if we had more managerial skill and attention on the Polish side."

Lehmann then tried to rate the success of the ICA with BUMAR on a scale from one to ten. As far as taking advantage of the potentials, he rated the venture at about nine. As far as the bottom line, net profit, is concerned, he rated it about four or five. To be sure, he added, the bottom line is not easily quantifiable because so many intangible and non-collectible expenses are attributable to the Polish project. But so far, those involved have been able to convince top management that it is a good arrangement. Pressed to express what IH considers the single most important measure of net results, Lehmann answered that return on investment is the only single measure that is valid. But, he added, IH's interest in Poland is also motivated by the desire for a peaceful world and a desire to know and understand other countries better. "We have had well over a thousand Polish guests in our office over the last six years, all of whom have returned home with a much better understanding of us. And I know that we are richer for the experience of having them in our homes and in our factory."

Wesley Lee supplemented Lehmann's remarks: "We have short-term and long-range objectives, as all other firms do. I would say that we have accomplished our short-term objective: building a relationship with a business partner in a foreign country and being able to produce five crawler models in three to five years. That is certainly a major short-term accomplishment in anybody's business, and a phenomenal one in a Polish context. Our long-range objective is to develop products jointly. This is a monumental task, another giant step forward in the project. Its simple measuring stick of success is whether we will have started production on time. Without this, the returns on investment cannot be achieved."

Szumski commeted: "I think the gentlemen from IH have put it quite nicely and I agree with them fully. As I already said, the set-up is terrific; the important thing is to fit it in with meanigful performance, and on time. But I don't want you to be left with the impression that only BUMAR doesn't deliver on time, or has problems. IH, too, at times has had components that needed reworking in Poland, and they also have had delays on the loader. There are also delays as long as 18 months in releasing some of the documentation."

Perlmutter asked the representatives of IH whether, given their hindsight and knowing all the opportunities in the world today, they would go after the deal again in Poland. *Lehmann* and *Lee* answered with a definite "yes."

Szumski added: "I would also do it all over again today, perhaps with even greater desire than in 1971. High-caliber individuals on both sides have created a good atmosphere that is absolutley essential for successful IC. Let me illustrate with an example. When the first document was signed in 1972, each page was signed by both sides, so the agreement had more than 100 signatures. On a new agreement signed in 1975, there was only a single signature by each side on the last page. This is significant because in just three years of the partnership, we were able to create trust in each other. Trust cannot be created between organizations, it can be created only between people. The creating and nurturing of trust is one of the key ingredients of successful IC."

Notes
1. See Jan Giezgala, p. 87.

PART IV
CONFERENCE IN WARSAW

*Papers by the US Team
and Discussion*

The Future of East-West Industrial Cooperation

A Social Architectural Perspective

Howard V. Perlmutter

This research is part of an effort to derive new institutional models of the multinational corporation (MNC) that are suitable for the political-economic, socio-cultural, and technological environments of the 1980s and the 1990s. The global strategy of MNCs is increasingly oriented toward permitting non-equity, or less than 100 percent ownership of its affiliates.[1] On the North-South dimension, governmental regulations and increasing nationalism are primary forces for this change.[2] Thus, as they anticipate the 1980s, many firms think that it will be increasingly necessary to take on local partners or host country governments in these ventures. The developing countries' efforts to reduce technological dependencies are being aided by US, Japanese, and West European firms increasingly competing to accept local equity arrangements that will help these firms gain access to the growing Third World markets. At the same time, the firm must accept host country national economic and social objectives, including a quest for increasing technological self reliance.[3]

East-West industrial cooperation agreements (ICAs) have played a lesser role thus far in the development of US MNCs' global strate-

*Research on "Futures of the MNC in the World Economy" has been supported by the General Electric Foundation, American Standard, and IBM. The views expressed are those of the author.

gies.[4] But as East Europeans enter world markets in the 1980s, the development of East European linkages will become increasingly important.[5] The integration of the North-South, East-West, and West-West strategy constitutes the primary task of future MNC global strategists.

What is at issue as a consequence of the proliferation of non-equity or less than 100 percent ownership of affiliates is the model of the MNC as we know it today. The MNC is conceived of as a hierarchical system, whose capabilities in part stem from its capacity to mobilize and utilize the global resources in the system. We have described this attitude and approach as geocentric.[6] A prerequisite of geocentrization has been majority ownership or preferably 100 percent ownership, to avoid the excesses of polycentrism that joint ventures tend to create. Joint ventures were acceptable, if exceptional, and global strategy maneuvered around these exceptions. When the exception becomes the rule, the model of the MNC as a hierarchical system is challenged.

The emerging alternative is a more "horizontal" MNC, composed of linkages with firms that are not wholly owned. New questions are posed about this type of Transnational Network or Global Constellation. A system has definable boundaries, a degree of central control, and a common overall purpose with interlocking objectives among the parts; but the network does not have the same degree of integration and central control as the MNC.[7]

New issues include the concept of corporate stewardship and board responsibility for a Transnational Network over which it has only partial responsibility but more than partial accountability. Thus, the transformation in the concept of the MNC is a major task for the 1980s for senior managements as well as key stakeholders: governments, unions, shareholders, and consumers.

This essay will assess the role of East-West linkages in the global strategy of the MNC, especially the US MNC. While the number of US-East European ICAs is still relatively small, the issues involved in the global strategy are both different and similar to those found in North-South and West-West relationships.[8]

Part I will present a *micro* analysis, consisting in a description of the current constraints and driving forces toward IC experienced mainly by the MNC and the East European firm, with a focus on the US and Poland. Part II will describe what US MNC executives consider to be alternative macro-political-economic scenarios of East-West IC for the 1980s and examine the one they consider to be the most plausible. Part III will develop from the International Harvester (IH)-BUMAR agreement some testable hypotheses concerning the factors that contribute to the success and failure of IC between US

and Polish firms. The profile of "success" attributes will be high-
lighted and considered as a beginning of an East-West institutional
model for the MNC.

The perspective is social architectural; that is, we are seeking a
theory to account for the conditions under which viable (profitable)
and legitimate (publicly, politically, and legally acceptable) long-term
economic relationships can be built between East and West.

While the focus is on *micro* (including behavioral) determinants and
some *macro* factors, the findings may not be equally valid for all industrial sectors. It may be that in an East-West context, ICAs are
suitable only in certain types of commercial and industrial activities.

Part I

Our purpose is to examine the current driving and restraining forces
toward ICAs by US and Polish firms identified by the actors themselves, as a result of their experience of negotiation, establishing, and
implementing ICAs. Thus, the vectors are subjective. The findings
report a current set of perceptions, some of which are already changing and can be expected to change further in the 1980s.

Driving Forces Toward Industrial Cooperation in Poland: The US View

Based on research at the Wharton School of Commerce of the University of Pennsylvania,[9] an examination of the literature on IC,[10]
and the IH-BUMAR ICA, we identify the following set of driving
forces toward establishing ICAs in Poland and other EAst European
countries.

1. *The saturation of existing markets.* For proven technologies,
West Europe and Japan are ceasing to be growing markets for US
MNCs.

2. *Desire to extend the life cycle of a product.* Associated with
market saturation is the interest in extending the life cycle of specific
products in East European markets. Since these products are proven,
there are markets yet untapped.

3. *Long-term market potential of CMEA.* For those US firms with a
longer time perspective, there is a belief that the CMEA will be a
major world market for Western firms in the future. Some form of
present participation is considered necessary to prepare for this even-
tuality.

4. *Need to enter Eastern Europe through a CMEA country.* There
is a belief that a plausible strategy to penetrate the CMEA is to find
the best country through which to gain access to this market and to
lay the foundations for this strategy through that country.

5. *Desire to widen product lines.* For those multidivisional firms

that do not have a full product line, an East European partner can be attractive as a manufacturer of a product that fits into a MNC's worldwide product line.

6. *Need to share costs of development.* To pay the full costs of development in every product division of a multidivisional MNC becomes increasingly difficult, especially if there is a competitor who has a full line or a better product.

7. *Need for lower cost labor.* One way to produce more competitive products and to increase productivity is to produce good or better products at lower prices, for which an ICA in Eastern Europe is one alternative. As inflation becomes a critical factor in Western economies, the attractiveness of this alternative increases.

8. *Need to utilize proven technologies.* Many US MNCs, even though they may have recovered the costs of developing existing technology, seek to generate revenues to afford the next generation of technologies.

These market and cost derived driving forces are generally important and relate to the need to develop a competitive global logistics strategy in each industrial sector.

9. *Good working relationships when negotiating or implementing an ICA.* There is increasing evidence that Polish engineers and managers can learn quickly to communicate effectively with their US counterparts. (See the IH-BUMAR case study, for instance.)

Driving Forces Toward Industrial Cooperation: The Polish View

Research on Polish perceptions of driving forces towards ICAs has involved fewer interviews and has been mainly confined to the IH-BUMAR case. But our impression is that the driving forces on the Polish side are in some respects similar to those found for US MNCs in to reach foreign markets and to be internationally competitive in but in some respects they are different as noted below.[11]

1. *Polish firms need production guarantees.* To the degree that ICAs increase predictability of production and sales, they are welcome in a planned economy.

2. *The need for advanced technology.* Polish firms hope to gain better technology through ICAs. There is, however, a debate about whether they are seeking proven (mature) or the most advanced technology.

3. *Need for market access and hard currency.* Opening up new markets in the US and the rest of the world is attractive and meets an urgent need to earn convertible currency.

4. *Interest in training Polish personnel.* Through working relationships with US firms, Polish management feels it is better able to meet highest world standards on products they produce.

5. *Need to gain foreign trademarks.* Associated with points (2) and (3), success in these areas often requires that Polish-produced products have trademarks of worldwide reputation.

Restraining Forces in US-Polish ICAs: The US View

There are internal and external constraints on a firm that help account for the present modest level of IC activity between US and Poland, and even to a greater degree with other CMEA countries. Whether these constraints will increase or decrease in importance will in part determine the future level of US-Polish IC activity.

1. *The relatively small percentage of sales in Eastern Europe.* Since, on the average, only about 2 percent of total sales and about 10 percent of West European sales are accounted for by CMEA countries, many firms are reluctant to expend a major effort on activities not central to the global involvement of the firm. On the US side, this can be seen in (a) the unwillingness to assign key personnel for long periods of time to develop and ICA and (b) the unwillingness by some firms to share leading technologies.

2. *Technology transfer policies.* The policies of some US corporations regarding licensing, control of trademarks, equity participation, and sale of high technology are rather restrictive, which is a constraint.

3. *US government restrictions.* Controls on advanced technology exports are also cited as a constraint by several firms in our sample.

4. *Organizational structure.* If there is a structure that makes a project in Poland subordinated to the corporation's East European organization, which is in turn subordinated to a European division, it may be difficult to get agreements and long-term commitments.[12]

5. *Fear of creating future competition.* Some US MNCs say they are reluctant to license high technology because they will be creating future competition.

6. *Stress on an integrated global strategy.* Because some firms seek an integrated global strategy, they find it harder to plan when the partner is not affiliated or where equity anticipation and full managerial control is not possible.

7. *Rate of return considerations.* If firms seek a relatively high rate of return on their investment, this can lead to short-term thinking. Since US firms must compare returns on their East European activities with those achievable on other markets, including the US, adjusted to risk (usually perceived as higher outside the US), there is an emphasis on shorter term results. The longer start-up time required in working with East European governments reduces the expected rate of return, which is thus a restraining force.

8. *Unwillingness to do business with planned economies.* There are

still a number of firms (although fewer) that express an unwillingness to do business in countries where the government must be a partner directly or indirectly and where there is a different philosophy of doing business. This position reflects the thinking of the majority of those who serve on the Board of Directors and is considered a constraint which, in some firms, is still difficult to change.

9. *Ethnocentrism*. Those who begin to do business in Poland and other countries often encounter ethnocentric attitudes that create obstacles not only in the negotiation process but also during the operational phases. Specifically:

> a. Lack of understanding is important when in daily concerns the Polish way of thinking seems incomprehensible or undesirable for US businessmen. This lack of mutual understanding may stem, on the Polish side, from an unfamiliarity with US marketing practices and standards of quality control that must be sustained over time to market products in the highly competitive US economy.
>
> b. US lack of experience in doing business in Poland. The structure versus functioning of a planned economy, and the understanding of how and why decisions are made, the role of central planning, the foreign trade organizations (FTOs), and management practices at production facilities are often puzzling and frustrating because they do not correspond to the home country experience.

10. *High entry cost*. This was mentioned as a restraining force, especially if executive time is considered. Since negotiating ICAs tends to require outstanding executives, the entry cost, including time for negotiation, can be substantial in view of the other opportunities the firm may have to make use of the time of its highly paid top managers.

11. *Doubts about the actual size of East European markets*. MNCs distinguish between the nominal size, based on available indicators, and the actual size of the markets to which the US MNC will have access. Since there are government controls on hard currency spending and the population has limited discretionary income to spend on goods imported from the West, there is a perception that the gap between potential and actual market size may be great.

12. *Uncertainties regarding the product-market fit*. Given limited marketing information, there is a question of whether a firm really has products that fit the Polish market, and if so, what the national product priorities are.

13. *Buyback pressures*. This is felt most often in the form of questions about the perceived lower quality of some buyback goods.

14. *Counterpurchase pressures*. The constraints are considerable on US firms when they have to market unfamiliar products.

Constraints on Polish Firms

1. *ICA may be disruptive.* Since a major effort is required and exist-ing patterns must be changed, this introduces uncertainties about meeting current plan directives.

2. *Large upfront capital investments.* To pay for equipment, other technology, and training often requires payment in hard currency.

3. *Domestic market constraints.* While exports are high priority, there are high demands also for many products in the domestic mar-ket.

4. *Buyback may not be guaranteed.* This creates a situation where production may not be purchased because of changes in the world market (for an example, see the IH-BUMAR case study).

5. *Cooperation vs. competition.* In those cases where the Western partner becomes the marketing agent, and hence controls the distri-bution of the product in certain primary markets, the Polish firm is ambivalent about the balance between cooperation and independent marketing in non-exclusive territories.

6. *Multiple commitments.* When some Polish production facilities have several tasks, for instance, to supply domestic, CMEA, and Western markets, often with large excess demand on the first two, the question is how strong a commitment and motivation to any ICA is possible. The overall result of too many tasks may be a lack of strong commitment on those projects demanding most effort.

Assessment of the Future

Looking to the 1980s, US MNC executives are aware that the va-lidity of their current perceptions may be challenged.

Concerning the driving forces, as the respect for the absorptive capabilities of Polish engineers increases and quality control problems improve, more and longer term linkages become possible. Experience is expected to improve working relationships, especially if there is continuity of personnel on both sides.

There are doubts about the premise that any CMEA country can be used as an entry point to the rest of Eastern Europe, given what ap-pear to be increasingly different approaches and aspirations of the CMEA countries. The perception is that the CMEA partner is more interested in world markets outside the CMEA because these are the sources of hard currency.

Some of the present restraining forces may decrease over time, in-cluding those that bear on cultural understanding, US familiarity with doing business with planned economies, and the Polish experience in doing business with US and other Western firms.

The uncertainties are both economic and political and reflect an unclear perception by US corporations regarding the degree of freedom, motivation, and interest of firms in a CMEA country to develop an institutionalized mechanism for legitimizing long-term global strategies with Western firms. This leads us to an assessment of possible future scenarios.

Part II

Macro Scenarios About East-West Relations and ICA Arrangements

In order to assess the future of ICAs in the global strategy of US MNCs, we need to examine East-West relations in a broader context. It is unlikely that any US MNC can assure the political legitimacy and commitment to ICAs in a long-term perspective without taking into account what might become acceptable strategies to the US and Polish governments in the 1980s. We need, then, to know what political-economic scenarios US executives envisaged for the 1980s and to gain some understanding of what scenario would be necessary in order to accelerate the rate of ICAs.

Alternative Scenarios

The previous analysis of driving and restraining forces toward entering into ICAs is a view of the current situation. There is some understandable uncertainty about the long-term political legitimacy of these agreements. Most executives recognize that political considerations can override economic interests.

Many executives are concerned about the fragility of East-West cooperation. Many recognize that direct extrapolation of the growth rate of the East-West trade and IC between 1973 and 1978 is unrealistic, because on that basis, by the end of the 1980s, upwards of 3,000 or more ICAs would be possible. The uncertainty concerns when and why and by what forces the limits will be set on ICAs, as well as trading possibilities. Since everyone recognizes that the status of political relations is very important, we examined US executive perceptions of what they would do in the case of alternative future political situations.

Three scenarios were presented to 20 US executives presently involved in ICAs (See Table 1). They were asked to evaluate each scenario and to estimate what impact each would have on the firm's policies regarding ICAs.[13]

1. *Scenario A*. A divergent-competitive environment, wherein political and economic relations between East and West become increasingly tense; there is strong pressure to increase competition between

the CMEA and OECD countries. There would be strong pressures to abandon current arrangements between Eastern and Western enterprises.

2. *Scenario B.* An emergent-pragmatic environment, wherein pragmatic, relatively short-term considerations take precedence over political and economic differences, and where cooperation is preferred over CMEA and OECD competition. Political interference would not be very great in establishing ICAs. The number of ICAs would increase at a steady but not dramatic rate, but would be limited to a few industrial sectors.

3. *Scenario C.* An integrative-cooperative environment, wherein the long-term view would be legitimized in both East and West. There would be an explicit commitment by both sides to an international division of labor in many East-West industrial sectors, with a wide band of cooperative arrangements in every industrial and commercial sector. This would involve clear political statements on both sides that some form of mutually beneficial long-term economic linkage would be necessary in most sectors.

Corporate Assessment of Scenarios and Impact on ICAs

There was little expectation that the divergent-competitive Scenario A would prevail in the 1980s. While political shocks were expected, the consensus was that "for every three steps forward increasing trade and such arrangements, a political shock would amount to one step back."

US executives saw the emergent-pragmatic Scenario B as the present situation and the most likely to continue in the 1980s. The maintenance of ideological differences between planned and market economies was considered likely, but there would be increasing pressures to rely on each side's comparative advantages through ICA linkages. More cooperation was expected in selected sectors that were relatively free from political constraints, but no dramatic changes were expected.

US MNCs expect to be subject to continued legal restrictions on technology transfer by the US government; few firms expected substantial relaxation of export licensing procedures. But executives did expect new opportunities for equity participation in Eastern Europe to constitute a driving force for IC in this region, although only Yugoslavia ranked high as a country with good prospects for direct investment.

The common reaction of US executives was: "We cannot really plan for the future because we do not have enough information." What the missing information was, was not entirely clear. But we suspect that four questions are at the root of this uncertainty: (a) How much cooperation will be permitted? (b) How long can this cooperation continue? (c) How open will the CMEA countries be to deepening forms of cooperation? (d) What will be the best product-market fit?

US executives believed that because of hard currency shortages, the consequence of Scenario B in the 1980s will be increasing pressure to buy back products produced in the East. They were also concerned about the worsening financial situation of some CMEA countries. But they reacted differently to the resulting pressures for counterpurchase. Some advocated an aggressive counterpurchase policy, including altering existing organizational structures and policies to accommodate a handling of counterpurchased goods.

For those companies viewing counterpurchase agreements under Scenario B, the expectation was that Western firms would learn, some slowly and reluctantly, how to incorporate production agreements into their global logistics, using CMEA as a source for intermediate or finished goods. Many executives pointed out that there are essentially only two choices: (a) to create competition for the firm's products or (b) to cooperate with the Eastern counterpart under long-term arrangements. For firms who preferred (b), shared control of technology and some managerial control would be acceptable without equity.

A major consequence of incorporating an Eastern firm into the US firm's global production and marketing network would be that both firms would have to move to a longer term planning orientation. As long as the US firm remains technologically ahead, it has a strong bargaining position, and Eastern dependence on US (Western) technology is likely to continue. But when the Eastern partner wants to market its own products globally, have its own trademark, and sell in third markets, this dependence is likely to diminish and the ties may be severed unless new, long-term reciprocal agreements are developed. To be sure, it is not necessarily a choice between competition and cooperation, but finding a balance between areas of cooperation and competition, as in the IH-BUMAR case.

The executives of a few firms believed that a reactive wait-and-see approach was not good enough. These executives—we call them the proactivists—believed that the time was ripe for developing a new model for global business planning in the East-West IC arena. For example, in the IH-BUMAR ICA, technology and other inputs have already begun to flow in both directions. But if an effective joint product launch is to be made, there must be coordination in research and development, engineering, manufacturing, and marketing. The cooperation strategy must account for other competitive global firms that are not in the coalition. Thus, a long-term global strategic perspective develops.

Scenario C, an integrated international East-West system, was considered improbable in the short and middle term, but not for the 1990s. There appeared little indication that such a process would be legitimized in the present and foreseeable international political climate, although its prospect seemed more plausible than prospects for the divergent-competitive Scenario A. Many US executives questioned the willingness of the East European planned economics to engage in long-term planning with Western countries and firms and to increase interchanges of information and personnel between the blocs. They saw this process as an enigma for Eastern planners and firms, a problem that will not be easily resolved in the short and middle term.

Part of the concern is with the nature of the reconciliation required between the institutions of planned and market economies. Detailed planning must be carried out by firms rather than by governments. But because Eastern firms are state owned, US executives question whether the East European counterparts can have the independence to engage in long-term strategic planning with Western firms. There is no central planning model that blueprints increasingly comprehensive linkages with non-CMEA economies. But some executives believe that this issue will become increasingly important in the late 1980s and that the chances are good that at least a few CMEA countries will move toward legitimizing this joint planning process.[14] To be sure, everyone recognized that some balance between independence and planning for interdependence must be struck.

So, while Scenario C is tantalizing, it is seen as a distant and less plausible world for the near future. The paradox is that the more proactive the firms become, the more such integrative planning naturally occurs on the micro-level, as illustrated by the IH-BUMAR case.

Part III

Toward an Institutional Model for US-Polish Industrial Cooperation Agreements

A model for long-term ICAs for US-Polish firms can evolve with the assumption that Scenario B is the policy on which the US and Polish governments implicitly agree. This environment permits firms to continue and others to negotiate longer term and relatively complex ICAs.

Choosing a set of parameters that appear critical (see Table 2), one can derive a profile of a US MNC that is likely to be interested and successful in these arrangements. The four main categories are: (1) mission; (2) strategy; (3) character of the organization; and (4) organization structure and functioning. The suggested parameters focus on the managerial and behavioral aspects, although it should be clear that economic factors (e.g., markets, proven technology, size of firm, and distribution systems) are also important.

Our point of departure in selecting the relevant parameters was the experience gained by our team's detailed case study of the IH-BUMAR ICA. The chief merit of the IH-BUMAR case is that it shows how, in practical terms, an East-West linkage can be built. It contributes to the theory and practice of East-West social architecture. Although what happened was in part the outcome of trial and error the key people involved began with an implicit theory of how to build a durable relationship.

The listed attributes of such an ICA can serve as a basis for evaluating (1) the degree to which any given successful ICA approximates this model, and (2) the degree to which those ICAs that have become dormant do not approximate this model.

Developing ICAs in the East-West Context: Some Theoretical and Practical Considerations

Establishing a viable and legitimate ICA is an adaptive-learning process. It takes time to learn to work together over long distances and in cultures with different ways of conducting business. There are language problems, personnel problems, visa problems, and problems of establishing mutually acceptable standards.

The IH-BUMAR case illustrates how this process unfolds over time. The learning and adaptation is mutual. Each side, through specific people, learns how to cope with the unexpected technical and behavioral differences which emerge. There are several stages in this learning process. Clarifying them helps to explain why driving and restraining forces change over time and when and how an ICA grows and becomes more complex.

In *Stage I,* the hierarchical stage, one party (e.g., BUMAR) is dependent on the other (IH). Usually, the Western partner with proven advanced technology is teaching and providing information and the Eastern partner is learning about new technologies, Western markets, etc.

As the learning proceeds, the flow of ideas and products becomes more natural, and the ICA enters *Stage II,* the synarchical stage. The IH-BUMAR ICA has apparently reached the synarchical stage, which is marked by products and people being more or less equally qualified to penetrate world markets. The transition from Stage I to Stage II is usually not simultaneous in all areas of the ICA. There may be a horizontal or synarchical stage in production but not in worldwide marketing, for example.

The synarchical stage implies a shared authority in decisionmaking even though two different organizations are involved. At the end of this stage, a level of integration has taken place in which the two organizations find a durable way of producing and marketing (distributing and servicing) a set of products.

The question then arises: Where do the partners go from here? The direction chosen in IH-BUMAR is to share development costs for a new set of products. This implies a longer term commitment, which gives rise to a new concept of organizational linkage, I call a Global Industrial System Constellation, or GISC. A GISC is a set of interrelated but distinct organizations that share resources to develop a long-term global perspective. It is a joint venture with a world view. GISCing is taking place at a rapid rate in all industrial sectors including the world construction equipment industry.[15]

Dunlop-Pirelli is a GISC, as is General Electric-SNECMA (the state-owned French aircraft manufacturing company) that jointly produce the most advanced low pollution aircraft engine. Similarly for Volvo, Peugeot, and Renault jointly producing automobile engines.

Our experience indicates that when a commitment to global markets has been made, the executives of most firms consider GISCing inevitable in nearly all industrial sectors. Since 100 percent ownership is often not possible, the search is for the best partners with whom to define a market segment on which neither could be competitive internationally without cooperation.

The art of managing GISCs is still in its early stages, but there is little doubt that many multi-industry MNCs will evolve into a set of GISC-like arrangements. In Poland, Huta Stalowa Wola is well on the way to functioning as a GISC.

What is undeveloped is the art of joint planning and implementation of global GISC strategies in order to control the win-lose relationships that may develop at the interfaces. Another new area is to design GISCs that involve advanced, developing, and socialist countries, as suggested by Zagorski.[16]

Recognizing that GISCs are here to stay suggests that managerial training in GISC design will become increasingly important, with explicit attention given to the institutional model on which they are based. Of special importance is government recognition of the nature and character of GISCs and why they succeed or fail.

ICAs are clearly potentially GISCs—when, and only when, there is an explicit attempt to develop a global strategy. Thus, all ICAs are not GISCs.

Conclusions

We suggested at the outset that the MNC is evolving toward a new model of linkage with world markets. MNCs are gradually changing from a hierarchical system to a horizontal set of linkages that must be integrated to some degree in the face of increased international competition.

We further suggest that countries may have to plan or help create the conditions for their firms to plan the set of linkages that will be required to assure exports, the generation of hard currency, and the acquisition or development of competitive technology, capital, and profits. The new rule in the emerging global economy is: Plan for your niche in the world economy or your firm will have your niche planned for you.

Small, medium, and even large nation-states will increasingly find that the viability of their country in the world markets will depend on a judicious choice and support of GISCs. Where 100 percent ownership of subsidiaries is not possible and where more countries are seeking increasing self-reliance, an export strategy that is independent of decisions made by large firms in the same industry in other countries will be precarious in the long term. Going it alone in the global industrial system in the 1980s is a choice reserved, we believe, to very few firms, and to no countries.

Along the East-West dimension of the global economy, an important issue in the 1980s will be: What kind of East-West social architecture for ICAs will be legitimate? Will they be based on Scenario A, B, or C? Once the most likely scenario is identified, what are the implications for each country and firm in their continuing quest for economic and social development?

ICAs thus viewed can be seen as a first, tentative step toward creating a peaceful, durable infrastructure for a dangerous and disorderly world. It may offer more hope for a better world than military security, which still underlies the political climate in East-West relations.

ICAs are, however, only built for the long term if the micro, sectoral, and macro levels of analysis are integrated. In this respect, the research on East-West ICAs is still in its infant stage, and the legitimacy of this form of East-West social architecture is still fragile.

TABLE 1

Key Elements in Alternative Politico-Economic
Scenarios for East-West Industrial
Cooperation in the 1980s

SCENARIO A: *Divergent-Competitive*	SCENARIO B: *Emergent-Pragmatic*	SCENARIO C: *Integrative-Cooperative*
All contacts evaluated in political and military terms	Continuation of present trends: Legal restrictions on trade	Common interests lead to increase in international trade and friendships
High tension while maintaining coexistence	Stable political environment Adaptability of ICA's	Many areas of international cooperation, less competitive, increasing economic interdependence
World industrial system built of isolated economic communities Intercommunity trade limited to a few areas East-West competition	Cooperation in limited areas; competition in more areas Blocs develop mutually acceptable rules	New forms of international industrial cooperation

TABLE 2

Social Architectural Parameters of East-West Industrial Cooperation
(Illustrative)

1. *MISSION RELATED PARAMETERS*
    1. Extent of top management commitment
    2. Degree of global perspective in shared long-term objectives
    3. Intercorporate policies regarding technology transfer and development
    4. Degree of pragmatism
    5. Clarity of joint mission and ground rules (in the contract)
    6. Degree of shared values regarding relationship to customer, end user
    7. Degree of proactivity in future orientation (especially planning)

2. *STRATEGY RELATED PARAMETERS*
    1. Degree of balance between strategic and tactical considerations
    2. Degree of agreement on product-market policy (including pricing, distribution)

TABLE 2 *continued*
Social Architectural Parameters of East-West Industrial Cooperation
(Illustrative)

---

  3. Degree of balance between cooperation and competition in world markets
  4. Degree to which coalition permits partners to occupy a competitive segment in global sector

3. *ORGANIZATION PARAMETERS RELATED TO THE CHARACTER OF THE ORGANIZATION*
  1. Degree of geocentricity
  2. Degree of flexibility and willingness to adapt
  3. Degree of trust and mutual respect at interfaces
  4. Degree of training-learning orientation
  5. Willingness to take risks

4. *ORGANIZATION STRUCTURE AND FUNCTION*
  1. Degree of jointness in decision making
  2. Degree of openness in communication process
  3. Degree of agreement on performance standards, (e.g., quality)
  4. Degree of commitment of capable personnel, for required lengths of time
  5. Degree of incentives for joint improvement in performance

TABLE 3
Proposed Model for a Successful ICA Between a U.S.
Corporation and a Polish Firm
(Abbreviated)

MISSION RELATED

1. Mutual Commitment at the Top
2. Shared Global Perspective
3. Policy of Open Technology Transfer (Two Way)
4. Shared Values on Customer Relations
5. Shared Pragmatism

STRATEGY RELATED

1. Strategic and Tactical
2. Greater Cooperation Than Competition
3. International Competitiveness
4. Acceptable Financial Rewards

TABLE 3   *continued*
Proposed Model for a Successful ICA Between a U.S.
Corporation and a Polish Firm
(Abbreviated)

ORGANIZATION CHARACTER RELATED

1. Geocentricity
2. Flexibility
3. Trust and Mutual Respect
4. Training-Learning

ORGANIZATION STRUCTURE/FUNCTIONING

1. Joint Decision Making and Multilevel Negotiations
2. Two-Way Communication
3. Shared Performance Standards
4. Capable Personnel

Notes

1. This trend is discussed in Howard V. Perlmutter, "The Multinational Firm and the Future," *The Annals of Political and Social Science* (1972), pp. 139-52. (For a Polish translation, see Zarzadzanie, listopad-grudzien 1977-rok V-nr 11-12 [56-57] by Teresa Turczynska.) See also David Heenan and Howard V. Perlmutter, *Multinational Organization Development: A Social Architectural Perspective* (Addison-Wesley, 1979); and M. Casson, *Alternatives to Transnational Enterprise* (University of Reading,1979).

2. The implication that MNCs will disappear is, in our view, mistaken. Our view is that MNCs will proliferate. See United Nations, *The Transnational Corporation in World Development: A Re-examination* (Geneva: UN, March 1978).

3. See Francisco R. Sagasti, "Towards Endogenous Science and Technology for Development," Ignacy Sachs, "Controlling Technology for Development," and Ashok Partaasarathi, "Technological Bridgeheads for Self-Reliant Development," in *Development Dialogue* (Uppsala: Dag Hammerskjold Foundation, January 1979).

4. For a comprehensive view on East-West industrial cooperation, see F. Levcik and J. Stankovsky, *East-West Industrial Cooperation* (New York: M.E. Sharpe, 1978).

5. Raymond Vernon is among the pessimists regarding the future of East-West trade. He has suggested, for example, that because in the future Eastern trading partners, especially the USSR, stand to gain most from East-West trade, this will lead to increasing tensions. R. Vernon, "The Fragile Foundations of East-West Trade," *Foreign Affairs* (Summer 1979). Little attention was given to industrial cooperation in his article, however.

6. Howard V. Perlmutter, "The Tortuous Evolution of the Multinational Corporation," *Columbia Journal of World Business* (January-February 1969).

7. The main contrast at the extreme is between a centrally controlled system of interdependent affiliates and between a loosely controlled constellation or network of largely independent affiliations. My thanks to Mr. Bellamy Schmidt of General Electric for this distinction.

8. See Vernon, "Fragile Foundations," for one view on these relationships.

9. See p. 4.

10. Many of the findings are based on research conducted at the Worldwide Institutions Research Group at the Wharton School by Bruce Karr and Thomas Malknight, "The Current and Future Forms of Industrial Cooperation Between Eastern European

Planned Economies and American Firms,'' (June 1979). See also Paul Marer and Joseph C. Miller, ''US Participation in East-West Industrial Cooperation Agreements,'' *Journal of International Business Studies* (Fall-Winter 1977), and Paul Marer, ''Industrial Cooperation in the CMEA Countries in the Global Strategy of US Multinational Corporations,'' in this volume.

11. My thanks to Miss Teresa Turczynska for her help in preparing this section. See also Jan Giezgala, ''The Present State in the Evolution of the Foreign Trade System in Poland,'' and Zygmunt Kossut, ''Main Problems of Polish-US Economic Relations,'' in this volume.

12. For a general discussion of the impact of organizational structure on IC, see John Garland, ''Organizational Constraints on the Successful Growth of Industrial Cooperation,'' in this volume.

13. These scenarios follow closely those presented in Howard V. Perlmutter, ''Emerging East-West Ventures,'' *Columbia Journal of World Business* (September-October 1969).

14. I infer this also with regard to Poland from the two contributions of E. Tabaczynski, in this volume, ''Thought on the Relationship Between East-West Industrial Cooperation and Specialization in Polish Production'' and ''Today's Approach to Joint Ventures in Poland.''

15. See Heenan and Perlmutter, *Multinational Organization Development,* Chapter 5.

16. Edwin Zagorski, ''US-Polish Industrial Cooperation: Achievements, Problems, Prospects,'' in this volume.

Comment

Eugeniusz Tabaczynski

I want to congratulate Professor Perlmutter for his excellent presentation of so many interesting ideas. In this comment, I wish to be less concerned with the past and focus instead on the future of East-West industrial cooperation (IC). Professor Perlmutter has enumerated the most substantial arguments in favor of and against the development of East-West IC. I fully agree with him as far as the so-called ''driving forces'' are concerned, but I wish to comment on what he defines as ''restraining forces'' to East-West IC.

The fear of creating competition through IC should not be overestimated. First, within the framework of the internationalization of industrial production, which seems to be a long-term trend worldwide, enterprises in a given industry are cooperating more rather than competing. Different technologies are being transferred across national boundaries, and there is now competition among know-how suppliers. Second, there is a growing worldwide trend toward intra-branch specialization in industrial products; that is, an enterprise in one country produces a specific type of machinery, component, or assembly, while another enterprise (in the same country or in another country) manufactures another type of machine, component, or assembly. The two enterprises then supply each other and exchange finished products. IC between US and Polish firms has already begun to serve as a framework and stimulus to the further development of intra-branch specialization. Therefore, instead of creating competition, IC developes new opportunities for expansion, creates new markets, and increases the efficiency for the cooperation partners.

The requirements of counterpurchase and buy-back are not an especially desirable solution. They result to some extent from our payment situation and, on the other hand, depend upon the existing structure of our not fully developed marketing network. For these reasons, counterpurchase and buy-back requirements are and will remain a necessity in East-West relations during the 1980s.

According to the recent findings of the United Nations Industrial Development Organization (UNIDO), about 30% of Eastern technology imports from the West are currently financed under some type of buy-back arrangement; and this share is likely to grow in the future. We hope and expect that our Western business partners will show understanding and confidence in Poland's policy in this area.

Professor Perlmutter's remarks on the possible transformation of the organization and operation of a typical MNC in the 1980s (i.e., the emergence of a more "horizontally-linked" structure within and among the MNC's component units) are very important. This new trend in linkages, both in West and in East, is both a precondition of and a stimulus for a further rapid expansion of ICAs between US and Polish firms.

Joint ventures in an East-West context are closely related to these organizational changes. East-West joint ventures represent a virtually new legal and economic set-up for horizontal-minded partners. So far, there has been only limited experience in the socialist countries in this regard. However, we now contemplate in Poland how to arrange practical workable joint ventures.[1]

Professor Perlmutter has presented the results of a separate study undertaken at his School on the political-economic macro-scenarios about the future of East-West relations. According to most US executives questioned, the maintenance of ideological differences between planned and market economies was considered likely, but these differences should not hinder IC between US and Polish firms. Moreover, there will be increasing pressures on firms in both countries to seek out and to make effective use of each side's comparative advantages through IC-type linkages.

I would like to end my remarks on an even more optimistic note than Professor Perlmutter's contribution. I assume that there will be an increase not only in the number of ICAs, but there will also be a con-comitant expansion of the East-West international division of labor and specialization in a growing number of industrial sectors.

---

1. See Tabaczynski, "Today's Approach to Joint Ventures in Poland," in this volume.

Reply

I am grateful for Professor Tabaczynski's observations, which give more substance to my views of the future of East-West cooperation. We agree on the essentials: the probability of the increasing rate of growth of ICAs and the likelihood of the emergence of a new type of long-term transnational corporate arrangement I call a GISC. We also agree that this kind of structure would prove viable and legitimate through the 1980s.

A long-term organizational model for East-West cooperation is certainly needed, as it is for North-South, South-South, and even West-West economic arrangements.

We may differ on the role that fear of competition will play in different sectors, especially those that are growing at a slower rate worldwide and for whom rising unemployment is a critical concern.

It will be increasingly necessary to conduct a full and open discussion regarding the process by which international division of labor will come about, and how it can be interdevelopmental.

We cannot ignore that the political and economic process must eventually be correlated in the service of the common hopes of peoples in the East and West for peace. Is it not time to consider constructive proposals which relate industrial cooperation to an East-West peace process?

Technology Transfer by Means of Industrial Cooperation

A Theoretical Appraisal

Josef C. Brada

Introduction

It is now commonly accepted that of the possible ways of transferring technology from western firms to socialist enterprises, the most effective in most situations is industrial cooperation (IC).[1] Specifically, the type of IC which we have in mind is one where a long term relationship is established between the two partners, the flow of technology is a continuing rather than a one-time process and a long term commercial relationship based on the exploitation of the technology by both partners exists. Such IC projects are much more effective in transferring technology than are purchases of licenses or turnkey plants because in an IC project the western partner has greater incentives to facilitate the successful absorption of the technology by the socialist enterprise and because the transferred technology is continually updated by new discoveries developed by the IC participants.

While IC is a preferable mechanism for facilitating the transfer of technology, the need for ongoing and intimate relationships between the IC participants may limit the industries and the type of technology amenable to successful transfer by means of IC. This realization appears to have escaped most students of IC and East-West technology transfer. In socialist countries, target areas for IC are established on the basis of domestic development priorities and the desire to acquire technology in "leading edge" sectors of industry where research and development expenditures and the rate of innovation are high.[2] Among Western experts the focus has been on technology gaps as driving forces for the flow of technology and on institutions which act as barriers to such transfers.[3] With a few notable exceptions, the influence of industry structure and the way in which firms in a given industry organize their international operations on the feasibility of technology transfer by means of IC has not been discussed not to mention subjected to systematic examination.[4]

In this paper we argue that the pattern of technology transfer in IC, and in fact the success or failure of many IC projects, can be explained by the economic parameters which determine how the firm organizes its international operations and by the type of technology which the firm employs. A close examination of these factors provides a useful explanation for the existence of technology transfers through IC and thus should serve as a guide for choosing partners and industries most amenable to the successful implementation of IC projects. The general theory is sketched out in Section 1. In Section 2 we illustrate the theory by examining two concrete cases, the pharmaceutical industry where there has been little IC and the successful International Harvester-BUMAR cooperation project for the construction of earth moving equipment, and in the third section we try to broaden the study to other industries. The fourth section of the paper examines the policy implications of the findings.

I. A Theory of Technology Transfer Propensity

In this section we develop the hypothesis that the willingness of a multinational firm to engage in technology transfer through industrial cooperation agreements may be inferred from the way in which the firm organizes and conducts its world-wide production and exploitation of technology. This pattern of international operations, in turn, depends on the type of technology that is responsible for the firm's competitive advantage and on the pattern of technological progress in its industry.

The technology that a firm deploys in support of its market position may be divided into two types, product technology and process technology. Product technology involves the development of new, unique products which have few close substitutes. Although a new product will require a new production process, this process may involve simple adaptations of well understood and easily replicated production technologies; the firm's advantage derives from the exercise of its ownership rights over the technology embodied in the new product rather than from its ability to produce the product cheaply. The exercise of these property rights over a unique product yields monopoly profits for the innovating firm, thus compensating it for its R&D expenditures.

Process technology, on the other hand, may be interpreted as the firm's ability to produce and market a given product. This broad conception of process technology covers ways of organizing the production of the firm's products; of altering the structural (as opposed to the operating) characteristics of the product so as to lower production costs; of motivating consumers to purchase the product; and of servicing the product once it has been sold. A firm with a process technology advantage over its rivals will either be able to produce the same or very similar product at less cost or produce a better product at the same cost incurred by its competitors.

Although every firm employs both product and process technology in order to enhance its competitive position, there are significant inter-industry and intra-industry differences in the proportion of resources that firms devote to each. In some industries competition may be almost exclusively on the basis of the development of new and unique products. In others, competition is based on advances in process technology, such as reductions in production costs, advertising, or product differentiation. The type of technological competition that predominates in an industry will be reflected in the way that the firms in the industry organize and manage their international operations and in the strategies and mechanisms that they employ for the development and intra-firm diffusion of their technologies. Firms that compete on the basis of new products will tend to be centralized, vertically integrated, and unlikely to transfer technology to outsiders. They will also tend to be poor candidates for industrial cooperation with East European enterprises. Firms that compete on the basis of process technology will tend to be decentralized, horizontally integrated, more likely to be willing to transfer their technology to outsiders and also better candidates for industrial cooperation arrangements with East European partners.

Within any economic organization such as the MNC, resources are allocated either by market mechanisms and profit maximization by individual units of the firm or alternatively by central *dirigisme* where resources are allocated so as to maximize aggregate profits without the need for profit maximization by individual units. The advantage of the decentralized mechanism is that it is informationally efficient. The center needs only to establish prices for resources and resource flows are then derived from profit maximizing behavior; no additional information costs are incurred. Market relations are, of course, not only encountered in the intra-firm allocation of resources; they are also the prime mechanism in the inter-firm transfer of resources.

The efficient operation of the market requires many buyers and sellers, low transaction costs, the ready availability of reliable information and relatively homogeneous products. The firm's utilization of technology, however, tends to limit the usefulness of the market not only as an allocative mechanism for technology itself, but also for most of the inputs which embody the technology or cooperate with it. These difficulties in utilizing the market have been amply described in connection with inter-firm transfers of technology.[5] Among the more important consequences of an increase in the use of technology by the firm is a decrease in the homogeneity of inputs, end products, and of technology itself. This decrease in homogeneity segments the market, reducing the number of buyers and sellers; increases the search costs to market participants since they must now examine a number of alternative price-product combinations; and reduces the informational content of prices. Information is also reduced because in many cases the only means available to the firm for protecting its technology is industrial secrecy. Finally, the costs of negotiating transactions increase as both buyer and seller become less certain about the true value of the resources which they are selling or buying. Because the technology, either in its embodied or disembodied form, is difficult to sell to outsiders by means of market transcations the firm internalizes these transactions by exploiting the technology itself.[6] This is of course, one of the principal explanations for foreign direct investment and the existence of the MNC. Since the firm finds it costly to transfer its technology to outsiders or because the price which outsiders are willing to pay yields a lower return to the firm's R&D expenditure than does its own exploitation of the technology, the firm will establish foreign production and thus internalize the costs of allocating technology and the goods which embody it.

The process whereby technology increases the costs of inter-firm transfers of resources and forces the firm to internalize these costs by establishing foreign affiliates is applicable to technology transfers within the firm as well. Some factors, such as the need for secrecy, which are important in inter-firm sales of technology are, of course, irrelevant in intra-firm transfers. However, other factors which raise the cost of market-mediated transfers of technology are exacerbated when the firm internalizes its technology flows. The number of market participants may be reduced to the parent firm and its affiliates. Important externalities may develop. The parent firm seeks to maximize the use of technology by affiliates so as amortize R&D expenses.

Affiliates, on the other hand, seek to acquire the technology as cheaply as possible, or may choose not to adopt certain of the firm's technology out of a desire to maximize profits. Under such circumstances, rational pricing of the product becomes impossible because market prices cannot be determined and "arms length" transactions to outsiders do not take place. Moreover, given the existence of externalities to the parent and affiliates in exploiting corporate technology, profit maximization for the entire firm may not be consistent with profit maximization by the individual affiliates. Consequently, increases in the technological level of the firm should lead to greater information costs in market-type transactions between the parent and affiliates and to suboptimal firm profits from the profit maximizing efforts of individual affiliates. Thus, at some point, a system of central control of corporate operations, despite its higher informational costs, becomes more appropriate than the market oriented model.

Firms whose innovative activities are focused on the development of new and unique products should experience the need to internalize technology transfers more intensely than firms whose innovative efforts are directed toward improvements in process technology. The need to internalize the transfer of technology, in turn, should result in fewer inter-firm transfers of technology and a centralized structure for the firms whose innovative activities are directed toward new products. There are several reasons for this tendency. First, firms which emphasize the discovery of new products in their innovative efforts tend to do so in a structured, formal way, employing specialized facilities and workers. Thus their R&D expenditures tend to be relatively large and highly visible to management. Furthermore, new product development, by its very nature, tends to be risky. A new product may or may not appear as the result of a given volume of R&D expenditures; if it does appear it may not gain acceptance on the market. Consequently the firm cannot, with any precision, allocate R&D costs to successful new products. Rather management must rather arbitrarily spread the firm's large and (in an accounting sense) visible R&D expenditures over the firm's stock of successful product innovations. Thus, the cost of a specific item of technology, such as a new product, is highly ambiguous, both to the firm itself, to individual affiliates, and to any potential purchasers outside the firm. Innovation in process technology is likely to be both cheaper and less visible to corporate management. Process innovation is often carried out by engineers and technicians who may have routine production or design functions in addition to their R&D responsibilities. Thus, their salaries may be viewed as production costs rather than R&D expenditures. Furthermore, to the extent that process innovation takes place on the factory floor, there is no need for research laboratories. Even if the firm were to explicitly recognize such costs, there would be less difficulty in pricing technology for intra-firm transfers because the cost savings of the innovation would simply increase the profits of the individual affiliates.

The uniqueness of new products also complicates their pricing. A new product may have no close substitutes; the components of the product may have no alternative uses. Thus there exist no market prices on which intra- and inter-company transfers could be based. An innovation in a particular process, on the other hand, must, by definition, have at least one substitute; the previous technology for producing the product. Moreover, since the product is not unique, there may be a variety of production technologies for its manufacture. For many mature products there may also exist inter-firm sales of components or firms which specialize in the manufacture of spare or replacement parts. The existence of alternative technologies and of markets for components clearly simplifies the problem of pricing the firm's technology and intermediate inputs.

The uniqueness of a new product makes it difficult to determine the economic benefits which it may bestow on the owner. Since the product is new, neither the size of the potential market nor the long run costs of production can be foreseen with much accuracy. More important, if competition in the industry is on the basis of new products, then the monopoly profits derived from a product's uniqueness are subject to erosion from the generally unpredictable successes of the firm's rivals. In the case of process innovation, the costs are often easier to quantify. A savings in production costs, for example, will generate higher profits whose present value for given levels of production can be readily computed by both the innovator and by potential purchasers of the technology. Moreover, future innovations in the process need not render the process entirely non-competitive.

While we have emphasized, in this section, the informational costs of transferring technology, it is worth while to point out that there are resource costs as well. The informational costs represent the uncertainty which surrounds the transfer of technology and the resource costs of overcoming such uncertainty. These costs interact with the resource costs of physically transferring the technology from the seller to the buyer in that the greater the costs of acquiring the technology, the less risk the buyer is willing to bear. Since studies of technology transfer suggest that the cost of such transfers can be from 19 to 100 percent of the cost of the entire project, it is likely that the pattern of inter-firm transfers should be influenced by the cost of effectuating such transfers.[7] Moreover, the evidence on the resource cost of transferring technology suggests that such costs vary inversely with:

— the number of startups or applications of the technology
— the age of the technology
— the number of firms which employ this or similar technologies.[8]
Such a pattern of costs, however, merely reinforces our findings about informational costs, since product technology, which has the highest informational costs, will also have high resource costs associated with its transfer. Process technology, particularly in mature industries, will have both low informational and resource costs of transfer.

II. Contrasting Patterns of Technology Transfer and Industrial Cooperation: Two Case Studies

In this section we examine two industries in order to show how the theory developed in section I can explain divergence between the involvement of firms in the two industries in East-West industrial cooperation and technology transfers. In order to highlight the differences between industries we have chosen two examples which are, in terms of our theory, polar cases. The pharmaceutical industry relies almost entirely on the discovery of new drugs to promote competition among firms. Because there is, as our theory predicts, little IC between pharmaceutical firms and East European countries, we will treat the industry as a whole so that we can maximize the number of observations about East-West contacts available to us. The contrary case study is of the construction-equipment industry where, as our theory predicts, there is a great deal of IC activity. Since a good deal of information is available about the IC between International Harvester and BUMAR, we will focus on that particular example of IC in the construction equipment industry.

The pharmaceutical industry is both highly internationalized and technology intensive. Most large American firms derive from 30 to over 50 percent of their revenues from foreign operations. The industry as a whole devotes a greater proportion of its sales to R&D activities than any other industry save computers.[9] Despite this internationalization, based on the ubiquitous need for pharmaceuticals, and the research intensity of the industry there has been little IC activity in this sector. This lack of activity, however, is to be expected given the structure and organization of pharmaceutical firms and the pattern of technological competition in the industry.

A pharmaceutical company can be viewed as being built up out of three types of vertically integrated building blocks.[10] The first is the research laboratory where the firm seeks to develop new pharmaceuticals. Pharmaceutical research is carried out by specialized personnel and in all firms is highly centralized. Most large pharmaceutical firms have one or at most two research laboratories. Their activities are centrally funded and carefully supervised to avoid any duplication. Research strategies focus on the development of new drugs which will either cure diseases previously not treatable by pharmaceutical means or supplant existing drugs with medicines of greater efficacy or safety. Once new drugs are discovered, a considerable expense is incurred in the development stage in order to verify the efficacy and safety of the drug, to provide documentation in order to satisfy government licensing requirements and finally to develop a viable mass-production technique for the manufacture of the drug. Not only are overall research costs high, but many drugs which the firm investigates never develop into marketable medicines despite large expenditures on the investigation of their properties. Thus the firm's R&D expenditures must be amortized over a rather small number of products. Moreover, given the element of chance involved in the discovery of new drugs, there is no way of relating the costs of developing a given drug to the total R&D expenditures of the firm. Consequently each product must carry a high, but, in terms of R&D costs, arbitrary markup to compensate the firm for its innovative activity. This markup, however, tends to be related to the characteristics of the market for that product rather than to the costs of bringing it to the market.

Production of the drug takes place in two types of units, bulk plants and dosage plants. Bulk plants are the largest and technologically most sophisticated units in the pharmaceutical production process. They produce, through chemical synthesis, fermentation, etc., the active ingredients for the drugs produced by the firms. The output of the bulk plants is sold, almost exclusively, to the firm's affiliates. Sales or purchases of bulk ingredients outside the firm are rare, one reason being that the firm's exclusive rights to a given drug eliminate any demand for the bulk product by other firms. There appear to be significant economies of scale in the operation of bulk plants. Most large firms maintain one bulk plant in the United States and one abroad, mainly to overcome regulatory barriers against drug exports from the United States. The bulk pharmaceuticals are sold to dosage plants operated by the company's affiliates serving individual national markets. Dosage plants utilize the bulk pharmaceuticals to compound the dosage forms actually consumed by individuals. Here there are few economies of scale because the specific dosage forms required tend to vary from one national market to another.

The vertical integration of the production units of a pharmaceutical firm is an outgrowth of its reliance on product innovation for its competitive advantage. Because of the large price markup over the production costs required to amortize the firm's R&D expenditures, there is a great deal of uncertainty and flexibility in setting prices for intra-firm transfers of resources. The firm may establish high prices for the bulk pharmaceuticals, thus turning the bulk plants into profit centers, or it can set bulk prices to cover the direct production costs and recover R&D expenses from the royalties and profits of dosage plants. The lack of market transactions in the inputs into pharmaceutical production reinforces this tendency; there are no arms-length transactions on which to base intra-firm transactions.

The uncertainty about the costs of developing a given product and about its market life also inhibit inter-firm transfers of technology. Sales of product technology to other pharmaceutical companies are very rare, and usually result from a firm's inability to serve a particular national or regional market.

The lack of inter-firm transfers of technology and inputs evident in the pharmaceutical industry is reflected in the attitude of pharmaceutical firms toward IC in East Europe. In a study of a number of pharmaceutical firms, Holt characterized their behavior as one of limited cooperation.[11] That is to say, pharmaceutical firms are unwilling to transfer their technology to Eastern Europe. In particular cases, country pressures have induced the firms to transfer dosage plant technology to East European enterprises but the firms continue to supply the bulk active ingredients. This strategy of limited cooperation is understandable both from the standpoint of the pharmaceutical firms and of their potential partners. First of all, there is great difficulty in pricing both the firm's technology and its intermediate inputs. Each product is unique—and thus there may be no comparable "technology" with which either buyer or seller could compare their prices. Even if there are alternative technologies (i.e. drugs with similar therapeutic properties) there are not likely to be any inter-firm sales of licenses for these products which could serve as reference prices. Moreover, the pharmaceutical firm will seek to attach as high a price to its technology as possible, since there is, in reality, no objective cost which can be assigned to the development of a given drug. Similarly sales of intermediate inputs will be hampered by similar pricing issues. The final price of the drug must carry some large, but arbitrary, markup to cover R&D expenses. However, this difference between direct production costs and selling price can be captured at either the bulk or dosage stage. In view of the fact that there is a large element of the price of both pharmaceutical technology and bulk pharmaceuticals which is largely arbitrary, negotiations on their sale to East European partners are likely to be filled with great uncertainty and risk to both participants.[12] Consequently, it is not surprising that the strong pressure for internalizing resource transfers within the pharmaceutical firm keep it from intense involvement in IC despite the amount of technology which might be transferred in this field and the potential of the East European market for expanded sales.[13]

In the construction equipment industry, on the other hand, competition is on the basis of process technology. Products of competing firms are close substitutes for each other. The main differences between products are quality, reliability and price. To some extent these characteristics are related to product design. However, firms do not seek to alter products in such a way as to make them capable of performing functions which competitors' equipment cannot, but rather to perform the same functions more economically and reliably. Thus the objective of research is to alter the way in which the product is constructed in order to improve its performance without increasing production costs. Another element of reliability is service; the availability of parts and personnel to keep the company's products in operation.

A second characteristic of the industry is the relatively decentralized nature of the firms and the multiplicity of horizontal intra- and inter-firm relations. As noted in the case study, one part of IH's drive toward profitability was to standardize products and to give individual production units greater autonomy. Standardization is a process innovation which facilitates not only the servicing of equipment but also horizontal integration since standardization permits specialization and intra-firm transfers of components, thus enabling the company to take advantage of potential economies of scale. The pricing of components in intra-company transactions is facilitated by the important role of outside suppliers. In view of the large market for replacement parts, many firms, though they lack the technology to produce the entire product, find it profitable to produce components. Since these are sold both to IH and on the open market there is not much difficulty in establishing a market price. Moreover, when a product is designed many standard or commonly available components are designed into it for reasons of economy. In view of the quasi-market relationship between the various producing units, it seems quite evident that profit maximization, at least relative to production, by individual units is consistent with profit maximization by the firm as a whole. Obviously, important externalities do exist in finance and marketing; the two areas not decentralized during the IH reorganization.

Although the amount of money devoted to R&D is less than in the pharmaceutical industry, large firms in this industry do spend more than the average for US industry.[14] R&D expenditures, however, are often related directly to either cost savings or specific product improvements. Thus expenditures can serve as a more reliable guide to the pricing of technology because there are fewer fruitless expenditures to be amortized by successful innovations. Moreover, with many firms producing similar products, there is a range of technologies available for comparison, thus reducing uncertainty over the value of any one particular technology.

Within this industry then, there are several factors which facilitate

IC. The greater certainty about the price of components and the value of technology greatly aid negotiations and the development of trust between the two partners. Second, the extensive inter- and intra-firm transactions lower the costs of the transfer of technology and promote the incorporation of the products of the cooperation into the activities of the western partner. By means of its dealings with suppliers in western markets, IH has developed important skills in transferring its standards, design needs and technology to suppliers. Thus it is likely to find similar transfers to BUMAR much cheaper and easier to carry out than would a firm which had no experience in inter-firm technology transfer. Also, the IH production process is open-ended in that many of the inputs come from outside suppliers. Horizontal integration also implies that IH's plants are designed to make use of parts from other IH facilities. Thus, unlike a vertically integrated firm which designs its plants to be totally dependent on each other, IH should find it much easier to accommodate the flow of products from BUMAR.

Indeed, the IH-BUMAR cooperation can be viewed as a technological innovation in processing. The production of components and entire products by BUMAR, after all, is a change, not in the function of the products, but rather in the way in which they are manufactured. In this sense, it is important to view the IH-BUMAR cooperation as more than the replacement of higher cost, western suppliers by BUMAR. Rather, the intimacy of the IH-BUMAR relationship represents an internalization of market transactions by the two participants. That is, by means of the cooperation each partner is able to opt out of market transactions for components and rely on (quasi-) intra-firm transactions instead.[15] It is also worth noting that the internalizing of transactions has led IH and BUMAR toward cooperation in the development of new products as well. In this sense we have a two way causality. The greater ability of the two partners to internalize the exploitation of the available technology now makes it feasible for them to increase their development of new product rather than process technology. As the case study shows, IH could not have attempted to develop new technology under its old market oriented relations with suppliers. However, by means of cooperation, the possibility for providing most of the components by the partners makes it sufficiently attractive for them to undertake the design of new products.

IV. Toward Verification and Practical Application

Although the example provided by the pharmaceutical and construction equipment industries serve to put the conceptual framework of our theory into concrete terms, they represent too limited a universe to provide verification for this theory. Such verification will require statistical testing and, more importantly, the conversion of the abstract concepts in which the theory is developed into observable correlates. Such a task will not be easy, because within each industry there will be some process technology and some product technology. Moreover, some technology, such as computer memories and processors, may be unique while other products of the same industry, such as printers and disc-drives, may have many similar competitors. Thus empirical testing will have to go beyond simple categorization on the basis of industry classification. Firm statistics may be similarly misleading. Many firms are made up of several divisions. Some of these divisions may do a large amount of R&D, others very little. Thus, data on corporate R&D may tell us very little about the technological content of any one of the firm's products.

Despite these *caveats,* Table 1 presents those generally available characteristics of firms which are generally available which should be correlated with the participation of MNCs in transfers of technology to Eastern Europe. A test of the theory would relate the positive and negative characteristics of individual firms to their IC experience. While such a detailed effort is beyond the scope of this paper, Table 2 presents some admittedly imperfect evidence. We tabulate the number of IC agreements signed between 1974 and 1976 by industry. Then we present data on the amount of R&D carried out by American firms in that industry and the number of firms in the industry. If the characteristics of US industry, in terms of sectoral R&D expenditure patterns and the number of firms in each sector, are approximately the same as those of West European industry then we can draw some impressions of the validity of our theory. The question we ask is how many East-West industrial cooperation agreements were signed per U.S. firm in a given industry. We recognize that many of the agreements were in fact signed by West European firms, but if their numbers, relative to other West European industries are the same as in Table 2, our conclusions will hold.

The highest ratios for IC agreements per firm are in Cigarettes (1.5) and in Engineering (1.13). Cigarettes represent process technology; making the cigarette and, more important, marketing it to consumers. Engineering involves primarily the construction of turnkey plants or production lines; clearly a process technology. The next group consists of Metallurgy and Mining (0.62), Transportation Equipment (0.54) and Textiles (0.44). Metallurgy again is an industry where processing technology is critical, while textiles tend to compete on the basis of cost and quality. The transportation equipment sector is much like the construction equipment industry and thus needs no further discussion. At a lower level of IC participation is a group of industries consisting of Machinery (0.21), Electronics and Electrical Equipment (0.17), and Chemicals (0.16). In these industries product technology begins to take on some importance. Some electrical products may be unique; nevertheless many standard components such as printed circuits, transistors, and semiconductors are used throughout the industry. Similarly there are both unique chemicals and machines and more standard ones where competition is on the basis of price and quality. Detailed studies of these industries would be required to reveal which types of technology are being transferred by means of IC arrangements.

The industries where firms are least likely to participate in IC are Paper (0.09), Computers (0.08), Food (0.08) and Pharmaceuticals (0.04). The figures for food and paper probably reflect the rather low priority accorded to the development of these industries by many East European countries and the ability to develop adequate indigenous tecnology. Pharmaceuticals and computers, however, do represent sectors where firms compete primarily on the basis of the development of new and unique products.[16] As mentioned at the outset, our data are limited and our categorizations rough and impressionistic. Nevertheless, the results do suggest that the theory presented in this paper does have some predictive ability.

V. Policy Implications

The argument presented in this paper is that certain industries, by virtue of the type of technological competition in which they engage will differ in their ability to participate in IC agreements. To the extent that this argument is valid, both western firms, and, more importantly, East European enterprises should seek IC in those industries where competition is based on prices and service and eschew attempting to develop IC agreements in those areas where competition takes the form of product innovations. This strategy, however, may be at odds with the development plans of East European countries. The industries where new product development is highest may be viewed as being more progressive, and East European countries may perceive a need to participate in such industries in order to maintain a dynamic industrial structure. However, they should be aware that participation in such industries is not likely to be aided by IC but will require, instead, indigenous efforts.

TABLE 1

Firm Characteristics Influencing Participation in
East-West Technology Transfer Via Industrial Cooperation

Characteristics Favoring Participation in IC	*Characteristics Hindering Participation in IC*
ORGANIZATION	
Organized by product divisions	Organized by regional divisions
Autonomy in planning by local affiliates	Planning centralized
Decentralized R&D	Centralized direction and funding of R&D
Lower number of patents, extensive unpatented know-how	High number of patents
ECONOMIC FACTORS	
Horizontal integration of units	Vertical integration of units
Low value added to sales ratio	High value added to sales ratio
Large interchange of components among plants	One-way flow of components among plants
Low parent firm overhead	High parent firm overhead, large royalty payments by affiliates
COMPETITIVE FACTORS	
Products have close substitutes	Products have few or no substitutes
Replacement parts may be purchased on market	No other producers of replacement parts or such parts not needed
Many transactions among firms in industry (components + parts)	Few if any transactions among firms in industry
Many sales of technology and licenses in industry	Few or no sales of licenses in industry
Low or moderate tariffs and non-tariff barriers against products and components	High tariffs and non-tariff barriers against products

TABLE 2
East-West Industrial Cooperation Agreements from 1974 to 1976
by Sector and Characteristics of U.S. Industry

(1) Cooperation Sector	(2) No. of Agreements	(3) Counterpart US Sectors	(4) No. of firms in US Sector	(5) R&D as % of sales, US Sector	(6) IC Propensity Equals (2)/(4)
Chemicals	13	Chemicals	51	2.5	0.16
		Petrochemicals	21	0.4	
		Tires + Rubber	11	1.7	
Cigarettes	3	Tobacco	2	0.5	1.50
Computers	2	Computers	25	5.9	0.08
Electronics + Electrical Equipment	20	Electrical	27	2.4	0.17
		Electronics	39	3.0	
		Instruments+ Measuring devices	37	4.7	
		Semiconductors	10	5.8	
		Telecommunications	4	1.9	
Engineering	17	Engineering Services	15	0.3	1.13
Food	3	Food	38	0.5	0.08
Glass + Ceramics	2	N.A.	N.A.	N.A.	N.A.
Machinery	18	Construction Equipment	12	3.2	0.21
		Machinery	64	1.7	
		Office Equipment	11	4.0	

TABLE 2 continued
East-West Industrial Cooperation Agreements from 1974 to 1976 by Sector and Characteristics of U.S. Industry

(1) Cooperation Sector	(2) No. of Agreements	(3) Counterpart US Sectors	(4) No. of firms in US Sector	(5) R&D as % of sales, US Sector	(6) IC Propensity Equals (2)(4)
Medical Equipment	2	N.A.	N.A.	N.A.	N.A.
Mining + Metallurgy	13	Metals + Mining	13	1.0	0.62
		Steel	8	0.6	
Paper	1	Paper	11	0.9	0.09
Pharmaceuticals	1	Drugs	26	4.9	0.04
Textiles	4	Textiles	9	0.5	0.44
Transportation Equipment	15	Automotive	7	2.6	0.54
		Parts + Equipment	21	1.5	
All industry Average	—	—	—	1.9	—

SOURCE: Columns 1, 2 compiled from Friedrich Levcik and Jan Stankovsky, *Industrial Cooperation between East and West*. White Plains, N.Y.: M.E. Sharpe, Inc., 1979. Appendix 2. Columns 3, 4 compiled from *Business Week* (see note 9 below).

Notes

1. United Nations Economic Commission for Europe, *Analytical Report on Industrial Cooperation Among ECE Countries* (Geneva: United Nations, 1973).

2. See, for example, Margarita Maximova, "Industrial Cooperation Between Socialist and Capitalist Countries: Forms, Trends and Problems," in C. T. Saunders (ed.), *East-West Cooperation in Business: Inter-firm Studies* (Vienna and New York: Springer Verlag, 1977).

3. Stanislaw Wasowski (ed.), *East-West Trade and the Technology Gap* (New York: Praeger, 1970).

4. Joseph LeBihan, "East-West Cooperation in Agribusiness," in C. T. Saunders, *op. cit.*, presents a compelling case for viewing East-West cooperation within the general trends toward internationalization in an industry.

5. See among others, Harry G. Johnson, "The Efficiency and Welfare Implications of the International Corporation," in Charles P. Kindleberger (ed.), *The International Corporation: A Symposium* (Cambridge: M.I.T. Press, 1970), and Stephen P. Magee, "Information and the Multinational Corporation: An Appropriability Theory of Direct Foreign Investment," in Jagdish N. Bhagwati (ed.) *The New International Economic Order*, (Cambridge: M.I.T. Press, 1977).

6. Jean-Pierre Hennart, *A Technological Theory of the Multinational Corporation*, unpublished Ph.D. dissertation, University of Maryland, 1977.

7. D. J. Teece, "Technology Transfer by Multinational Firms: The Resource Costs of Transferring Technological Know-How," *Economic Journal*, Vol. 87 (June, 1977).

8. *Ibid.* Teece summarizes, ". . . the most difficult and hence most costly technology to transfer is characterized by very few previous applications, a short elapsed time since development, and limited diffusion." (p. 249).

9. Typical ratios of R&D to sales for major American pharmaceutical companies in 1977 were Abott Laboratories, .054; Eli Lilly, .082; Smithkline, .079; Upjohn, .090. See "R&D Spending Patterns," *Business Week*, July 3, 1978.

10. For details of the organization and international operations of pharmaceutical firms, see Josef C. Brada, "A gyogyszeripar az Egyesult Allamokban: Attekintes," in B. Bojko (ed.), *Technologia-Transzfer A Kelet-Nyugati Kapcsolatkban* (Budapest: KKI, 1977) and Josef C. Brada, "Government Policy and the Transfer of Pharmaceutical Technology Among Developed Countries," in R. Helms (ed.) *The International Supply of Medicines* (Washington: American Enterprise Institute, 1980.

11. John B. Holt, "Strategies of U.S. Pharmaceutical Companies in Eastern Europe," *ACES Bulletin* Vol. XIX, No. 2 (Summer, 1977).

12. For a discussion of the effects of uncertainty about prices on the success of IC ventures, see Josef C. Brada, "Profit Maximization and Resource Utilization in the Transideological Enterprise," *Rivista Internazionale di Scienze Economiche e Commerciali*, Vol. XXIV, No. 5-6 (May-June, 1977) and Josef C. Brada, "Markets, Property Rights and the Economics of Joint Ventures in Eastern Europe," *Journal of Comparative Economics*, Vol. 1, No. 2 (June, 1977).

13. Holt, *op. cit.*, p. 77 reports that most firms regard conflicts over the pricing of technology as a very serious obstacle to the participation in IC.

14. Typical R&D to Sales ratios are Caterpillar, .038; Clark, .012; Deere, .038; International Harvester, .019. The average for U.S. industry is .019. See *Business Week, op. cit.*

15. As the case study noted, Caterpillar has a significant advantage in being able to produce a large proportion of its components rather than relying on outside sources. The IH-BUMAR cooperation in a sense seeks to duplicate this advantage by different means.

16. Although Computers and Pharmaceuticals also represent the highest R&D to sales ratios, there appears to be no overall relationship between R&D intensiveness and IC participation for the sample as a whole.

Comment

Jan Anusz

The main contribution of Professor Brada's paper is its stress on some little known facts about the influence of industry structure and the way in which firms in a given industry organize and conduct their international operations on the feasibility of technology transfer by means of industrial cooperation. The pattern of a firm's behavior depends on the type of the technology responsible for the firm's competitive advantage and on the mode of technological progress in its industry. Hence the vital distinction between two categories:

A - product technology

B - process technology.

According to Professor Brada's view the product-technology centered firms are markedly less willing to share their technology by means of industrial cooperation agreements while the process-technology centered ones are more likely to engage in this type of international activity. I would not try to discuss all the basic assumptions of Professor Brada's remarkable work which are well supported by the two case studies. Nevertheless, I think that the findings of Professor Brada's paper are, in a certain manner, too restrictive and at the same time too pessimistic in regard to the changing, dynamic realities of the East-West economic relations. The logic of Professor Brada's paper suggests that Poland and other Socialist countries should not count much on the transfer of product technology innovations within the framework of industrial cooperation agreements with Western firms because this kind of innovation is conducted mostly by the corporations themselves in the context of intra-firm relations. What I have in mind concerns two basic facts about East-West economic relations. First of all it is clear that the transfer of technology is the fastest growing single item in East-West trade and that it is becoming a two-way process. Let us bear in mind that Poland is acquiring Western technology in various forms such as license agreements, cooperation agreements, industrial equipment deliveries, other high-technology imports, scientific and technical cooperation, etc. At the same time, we are also increasing our share as active suppliers of some forms of technology embodied in our exports to the West as in the case of ultra-modern special ships, construction equipment and even "pure technology" based on our research and development work. A striking example of the latter is the recent sale of an advanced granulated sulphur production technology to a Canadian corporation. Secondly, industrial cooperation in its developed forms is, for reasons given by Professor Brada himself, the most effective way of transferring technology, including product technology, between East and West. Industrial cooperation agreements create a long-term contractual relationship between the partners and tend to generate a continuous flow of technology which is characterized by a highly favorable ratio of benefits to costs. At the same time the transfer of technology by means of industrial cooperation lessens the financial and technical risk inherent in all R&D-intensive activities.

In the framework of such arrangements even the most product-technology centered Western firms have a certain interest to facilitate the technology absorption by the other side and even to up-date this technology with the help of an Eastern company which has some first-hand experience with the introduction of a given innovation.

Notwithstanding its obvious merits as a means of promoting product and process technology, industrial cooperation between East and West is still a rather marginal activity in the complex web of economic interdependencies that link the world of today. In this respect Professor Brada's rather pessimistic view regarding the propensity of Western firms for the transfer of product technology between East and West tends to overlook some future-oriented factors in East-West economic relations. Nevertheless, in my opinion, Professor Brada's paper leaves room for a positive interpretation that points to the possibilities and not to the limits of industrial cooperation between Poland and Western Countries even in cases when product innovation is a dominant factor.

Among the real possibilities for cooperation in the field of joint research and development activities I would like to stress coal gasification where Polish science and technology has already acquired a worldwide renown. Our contribution could be of interest to many product-innovation minded companies in the West who may be seeking a higher return on their R&D expenditures. Another way to promote technology transfer by means of industrial cooperation agreements concluded with the product-innovative firm could be perhaps a joint venture in a third country or Polish participation in a project realized by a Western company in a third country. A third solution points to the function of industrial cooperation as a means of promoting the transfer of product technology for goods in the second stage of the product life cycle. This stage implies the acquisition by a Polish partner of the know-how and other elements of technology for a product which is modern but not very sophisticated. The Polish side could make further improvements on this "second-stage" of the product cycle by, for example, adapting it to the specific conditions and exigencies of Polish users.

I would like to conclude my remarks by stressing once more the point that in the period of accelerated structural change evident in today's world market, there is a necessity for both sides to spread their product and process technology by means of industrial cooperation implemented to the mutual benefit and advantage of all parties concerned. Evidently, there is a need for several comprehensive studies to be done in order to identify the possibilities for concrete and viable product-innovative industrial cooperation agreements.

Reply

The objective of my paper was to present some hypotheses about the pattern of IC by making use of theories which had proved useful in explaining the operation of multinational firms in western markets. Should careful study show that these hypotheses are also valid in the case of IC, I see no reason for pessimism. Indeed, I would see verification of my theory as aiding IC in two ways. First, it would facilitate the process of partner and project selection for the Polish side by suggesting which types of products and firms would make the best IC partners. Second, the theory identifies quite explicitly what the obstacles to IC are in the case of firms which compete on the basis of unique products. A clear understanding of these obstacles is the first step toward their resolution. Finally, even if my theory is seen not as an explanation of general tendencies but rather as an "iron law" of technology transfer, two points should be kept in mind. First, as Dr. Sulmicki suggests, most innovative activity consists of minor changes in products and processes, and firms which engage in such innovative activity are not competing on the basis of unique products but rather on the basis of differentiated products, prices, quality and service. Thus the negative implications of my theory leave open IC in a broad spectrum of products. Second, while IC is a very useful way of transferring technology, it is not the only way; other means may be worked out for firms and products which do not readily adapt themselves to IC arrangements. Finally, Poland may wish to participate in these product innovating sectors not by means of IC, but rather by means of indigenous research efforts.

The Hungarian pharmaceutical industry is an interesting case in point and bears on the hypotheses raised in my paper. The pharmaceutical industry in Hungary has a long and successful record of innovation and thus has attracted the interest of western firms both as a means of introducing their products into the CMEA market, of which Hungary is the chief supplier, and as a source of new products. Nevertheless, western firms have not been willing to transfer more than the technology for the production of dosage forms. Technology for the bulk production of unique ethical drugs has not been transferred, at least to my knowledge. Interestingly enough, I also understand that the Hungarian pharmaceutical industry has begun to establish facilities for the production and distribution of Hungarian pharmaceuticals in the West. Thus the economic forces which lead western pharmaceutical firms to exploit their technology abroad by means of intra-firm transfers also operate in the same way in the case of the Hungarian pharmaceutical industry.

The Hungarian pharmaceutical industry points up another important determinant of the possibility for successful IC arrangements; the scientific-technical potential of the partners. Just as information costs and the attenuation of market mechanisms discussed in my paper are barriers to IC, high levels of innovation and technical skills on the part of both the western and eastern partner are forces working for IC. Thus, Hungary's high scientific-technical potential in pharmaceuticals is a drawing force for western firms just as BUMAR's technology and skills are a drawing force for IH. To the extent that western firms do not perceive their potential partners in the east as being of equal or sufficient technical ability, their interest in IC decreases.

In closing, let me make a *caveat* inspired by the tone of my discussant's comments and that of the general discussion. I think it is quite fruitless to view the decisions of firms in a voluntaristic way. The willingness of firms to undertake any action, including IC, is to a large extent objectively determined by its competitive position and the technology and material means of production at its disposal. Thus, to hope that the firm will act in a way contrary to that suggested by these objective factors will lead us away from rather than toward an understanding of the potentials and limits of IC.

Import Protectionism in the US and Poland's Manufactures Exports

Paul Marer

The expansion of East-West commerce during the 1980s will be determined largely by the rate of growth of the Eastern countries' exports to the West. During the 1970s, the large increase in the hard currency indebtedness of the East European countries and the USSR made it possible for their imports from the West to grow more rapidly than their exports to the same area. But as we enter the 1980s, the indebtedness of these countries is approaching a limit set in part by the borrowing countries and in part by Western private and governmental lending institutions. Consequently, the ability of East European countries to buy from the West will be tied closely to their ability to export to the West. Thus, even those in the West who are concerned only with exporting to the socialist countries must be interested in seeing these countries expand their exports to convertible currency (CC) areas.

A larger than "normal" share of East European exports to the West has consisted of primary products and semi-processed goods. For East European countries, and especially for Poland, much of the future *increase* in hard currency exports must be in manufactured products. A key question, therefore, is: What determines Poland's ability to export manufactured goods to the West? The determinants may be divided into four sets of explanatory variables: two on the Polish supply side and two on the Western demand side.

On the supply side, the first set of factors relates to Poland's ability to produce high quality goods that are fully competitive on Western markets. The ability to produce such goods—largely an economic weakness up to now—is determined by such factors as the level of development, the country's strategy of specialization, its economic guidance mechanism, and the extent and nature of Poland's organic links with Western enterprises through industrial cooperation agreements (ICAs). Each of these factors was discussed in the papers presented by our Polish colleagues at the First Conference in December 1978 and explored further in the comments, discussion, and replies that followed.

The second set of factors on the supply side relates to Poland's ability to release for export to the West fully competitive, high quality manufactured products. The elasticity of export supply depends on the extent of domestic pressure for absorption of the exportables in intermediate production and final consumption and on commitments to supply such goods to CMEA partners and to developing countries under bilateral agreements.

On the demand side, the first set of factors is Western income and price elasticities of demand for Polish manufactures. Is Poland specializing in manufactures with relatively high income and price elasticities of demand on Western markets?[1] The second set of factors relates to Western discriminatory restrictions and safeguard procedures on Poland's manufactured exports. This paper focuses on this last set in the context of US-Polish economic relations.

Import-safeguard policies and procedures are topical because growing protectionist pressures are being felt in many Western countries, as a consequence of the long recessions or sluggish growth performances these countries have been experiencing since 1974. Given the necessary increase in the share of manufactures in Poland's exports to the West, it must be acknowledged that these products tend to be more subject to protectionist restrictions than are primary products. In addition, the issue of Western safeguard procedures is particularly important in US-Polish relations because of the long and unfortunate controversy over the ability of Poland to export golf carts to the US. The symbolic importance of this complex case greatly exceeds its economic importance. As indicated by Professor Kossuth (p. 000) and by the comments of so many Polish specialists who are concerned with Poland's ability to penetrate the US market, this case still raises many questions on which further discussion would be useful.

Poland and other East European countries are facing especially strong—and growing—protectionist pressures in the European Economic Community (EEC). New members are replacing third-party suppliers; the community is granting more and more special trade preferences to the less-developed non-member West European and

Third World countries; and the community's common agricultural policies continue to discriminate strongly against Poland's exports. Given these trends, Poland might well be correct to conclude that it needs to further diversify its Western exports, that is, to place greater emphasis on penetrating North American markets. One aspect of success is improved understanding of and practice in how to market Polish products in the US (the subject of Professor Miller's paper at this Conference). Another aspect is improved understanding of US import-safeguard procedures such as dumping and market-disruption regulations that could seriously harm Poland's exports. The rules and procedures in this area are extremely complex and continually evolving, and they raise controversial theoretical and practical problems. This paper will describe and illustrate the special US laws, practices, and procedures applicable to imports form so-called non-market economy (NME) countries, and will make some suggestions that could be helpful to Poland to increase manufactured exports to the US.

Overview of US Import-Protective Laws and Regulations: General Observations

Before discussing the specifics of US laws and regulations, some general observations should be made about how US trade policy is formulated:

1. The US is the only Western industrialized country in which the legislative branch plays a critical role in setting trade policy, including the control of imports. Consequently, import policy is even more sensitive to political pressure in the US than in other Western countries. Statistical evidence shows, for example, that the structure of US tariff and non-tariff barriers to trade across industries can be explained in part by the government's intention to maximize voter support for its stand on trade issues, and that voter support generated by industrial interests (producers and workers) tends to be more decisive than that generated by consumer interests.[2]

2. The *Trade Act of 1974* made it easier for import-competing interests to seek legal and administrative relief to lessen competition from imports.

3. Nevertheless, one should not automatically conclude that the US has become significantly more protectionist since 1975. Such an assessment must be based on the way in which laws are administered and on prevailing economic conditions. Mindful of the harmful consequences of protectionism—including retaliation and emulation by other nations, an adverse impact on US foreign policy,

and additional fuel for domestic inflation—the Administration and the independent agencies charged with administering the laws (principally the International Trade Commission [ITC]) have avoided taking protectionist stands. But in assessing their "performance," it must be recognized that they must enforce existing laws, which in some cases severely limit their discretionary powers. Moreover, the President must consider that if he disregards serious economic injury caused by imports, the resulting political pressures could induce Congress to pass new laws that might be more protectionist, leaving him with even less discretionary power. Thus, the Administration's wisest course is not necessarily to refuse to yield when domestic industries clamor for relief against what they perceive as unfair foreign competition.

4. Whether or not a country is becoming more protectionist should be judged not only by the decisions of cases being adjudicated but also by the extent of legal and procedural harassment to which foreign exporters and American importers are subject. The more complaints, charges, hearings, and lawsuits, the more uncertainty for foreign exporters, American importers, and domestic sellers of imports. Defense on many fronts takes time and effort and requires costly legal advisors. Hence, legal and procedural harassment represents a new and sophisticated form of protectionism that is difficult to quantify. Compared to other Western countries, the US apparently has a larger number of highly visible administrative legal procedures that can be invoked by import-competing domestic producers who feel unfairly threatened by foreign competition. West European countries and Japan typically use informal, unpublicized rather that formal and highly publicized procedures to reduce imports. One example is the continued heavy reliance on import quotas for Eastern exports set and periodically adjusted by the West European governments, whereas the US, with a few exceptions, does not rely on quotas to limit imports. Accordingly, casual empiricism is probably not an accurate way to compare US protectionism relative to that of other Western countries in general or in the particular case of imports from NME countries. During the last 20 years, the rapid growth of manufactured imports to the US and the strikingly successful penetration of the US market not only by Japan but also by South Korea, Taiwan, Hong Kong, and other Third World countries suggest that the American market is not overly protected. However, exporters to the US, especially newcomers, must take into account the particular—and peculiar—features of the US market, including its safeguard procedures involving manufactured imports.

Laws and Procedures

Table 1 summarizes US import-protective laws and procedures. The column headings show the types of laws applicable to certain imports, such as tariffs or commodity agreements. The row headings show the procedures that can be initiated by import-competing domestic interests and whether they are applicable to imports from all countries or only to NME countries, in which case they would be of special importance to Poland.

In assessing US trade policies vis-à-vis Poland, Poland faces an entirely different situation today than during the 1950s or 1960s. Professor Brada made this point at the First Conference:

> During the 1950s and 1960s, US trade policy toward Eastern Europe was completely divorced from our global trade strategy. While we were busy erecting controls, embargoes, and tariff and non-tariff barriers to minimize our trade with East European countries, our global policy was seeking to promote greater international exchanges of goods, technology, and capital. . . . To deal with this new environment, Poland should recognize that its trade relations with the US will increasingly be governed by America's *global* trade policy and less by our East-West trade policies. This recognition on Poland's part should lead it to realize the limitations of viewing its trade with the US in an East-West framework, and to shift its perception of our mutual relations to a global context, which of course changes the possibilities for influencing American trade policy.[3]

To be sure, Professor Brada's point must not be overdrawn. There are still areas where Poland, classified as an NME, is treated differently by the US.

Three types of laws and procedures have a special importance for NME countries: the tariff law, market disruption, and antidumping procedures. The tariff law is of no special consequence for Poland because it is one of three NMEs that enjoy MFN status in the US.

US Laws of Special Importance to Poland

Market Disruption

Table 2 summarizes the market disruption procedure. The principle is the same as under the standard "escape clause" provision; the difference is that it is easier to satisfy the conditions under which it can be invoked. (See Table 1, row 1, where the key terms that make market disruption different from the escape clause are underlined.)

After the Trade Act of 1974 was signed on January 3, 1975, many specialists thought there would be a spate of proceedings against imports from NME countries under the market disruption provision. The conditions for obtaining decisions favorable to the complainer appeared easier to meet and a decision quicker to reach than under the more cumbersome dumping procedure. Surprisingly, however, no case was brought until December 15, 1977, when a petition was filed by the Work Gloves Manufacturers Association, charging that the importation of certain cotton work gloves from the People's Republic of China (PRC) caused market disruption in the US.

After holding public hearings on February 7-8, 1978, in Washington, D.C., on March 15, 1978, the ITC found, by a four to two vote, that cotton work glove imports from the PRC were not causing market disruption in the US, even though there had been a marked increase in glove imports over the preceding few years. Commission members who rejected the market disruption charge focused mainly on the PRC's still small US market share rather than on its rapid growth. (In 1977, domestic producers shipped an estimated 21.2 million dozen pairs of these gloves and exported an estimated 7.56 million pairs. Imports in 1977 from all countries totalled 75.6 million pairs, including 868,000 pairs from the PRC.) The case is now closed, as there can be no appeal of the Commission's decision in market disruption cases.

A second market disruption case was brought before the ITC on May 16, 1978, examining the charge that imports of clothespins from the PRC, Poland, and Romania were causing market disruption. After holding public hearings on June 22 in Portland, Maine, on August 3 the ITC determined by a six to zero vote that clothespin imports from the PRC *were* causing market disruption, but they found that on similar imports from Poland (by a five to one vote) and Romania (by a six to one vote) were not.

Wood and plastic clothespins imported from China increased from zero in 1974 to a level in 1977 that was higher than that from any other supplying country, exceeding 828,000 gross and 12 percent of US consumption (nearly double their 1976 levels). By contrast, imports from Poland in 1977 increased at a moderate rate, and Polish imports accounted for less than 8 percent of US comsumption. Imports from Romania fluctuated from year to year and showed no increasing trend.

All five domestic clothespin manufacturers experienced an extremely low and declining rate of capacity utilization (34 percent in 1977) and sharply declining production, employment, and profits. The prices of Chinese clothespins were the lowest among all importers: during the first quarter of 1978 approximately $1.13 per gross, or $1 less than the largest domestic producers. The ITC verified that lost sales by the US producers were directly attributable to China, because many purchasers indicated that they buy primarily on a price basis.

The ITC recommended that the President impose quotas on Chinese clothespins but he decided against such action.

Dumping

Table 3 summarizes US antidumping procedures, applicable to ME and NME countries until September 9, 1978, when the procedures involving NMEs were changed.

The basic US dumping legislation is the Antidumping Act of 1921, as amended, which provides administrative remedy if dumping is found. There is also the Antidumping Act of 1916, which permits criminal prosecution or civil-court remedies, i.e., treble damage compensation, if dumping can be shown to have been motivated by an *intent* to destroy or injure competition. The 1916 law has never been successfully applied because it is extremely difficult to prove intent. But a civil suit under this law was brought in 1977, involving golf cart imports from Poland; the case is currently pending in the District Court of Delaware.

Under the Antidumping Act of 1921, as amended, special dumping duties may be imposed if two requirements are met: Treasury must establish that imports are sold, or likely to be sold, at "less than fair value" (LTFV), and the ITC must determine that a domestic industry is being injured or is likely to be injured. Should both agencies make an affirmative finding, dumping is found. Following such a determination, special dumping duties are levied, in addition to regular duties, in an amount equal to the margin of dumping established by the Treasury during its price investigation.

The purpose of the statute is to prevent the sale of foreign goods in the US at less than their fair *foreign market value* in the country of exportation, or at less than their cost of production there. The intent of Congress was not to impose a penalty but to charge a duty sufficient to equalize competitive conditions.

Foreign market value is defined under the Antidumping Act as:

> . . . the price, at the time of exportation of such merchandise to the U.S., at which such or similar merchandise is sold . . . or offered for sale in the principal markets of the country from which exported, in the usual wholesale quantities and in the ordinary course of trade for home consumption [are too] . . . small in relation to the quantities sold for exportation to countries other than the U.S. as to form an inadequate base of comparison, than the price at which it is sold or offered for sale for exports and to countries other than the U.S., plus . . . the cost of all containers . . . and all other costs, charges, and expenses incidental to placing the merchandise . . . ready for shipment to the U.S.[4]

Foreign market value is thus the price charged by the exporter, preferably on its domestic market, or if for one reason or another that doesn't provide an adequate base of comparison, its export price to markets other than the US. Where there are exports to several third countries, the foreign market value is, at the Treasury's option, either the price to the country that takes the preponderant share of exports or some weighted average of exports to several third countries.

The Act further provides that if neither the exporter's domestic nor the export-to-third-country price can be used to find a fair foreign market value, then a so-called *constructed value* must be used. Section 321 of the 1975 Trade Act, under "Amendments to the Antidumping Act of 1921," states that the Treasury must

> determine whether . . . the purchase price is less, or that the exporter's sales price is less or likely to be less, than the foreign market value (or, in the absence of such value, than the constructed value).

Constructed value is defined under Section 402 of the Tariff Act of 1930, as amended, as the sum of:

1. The cost of materials and fabrication or other processing of any kind employed in producing such or similar merchandise.

2. General expenses and profits usually reflected in sales of merchandise of the same general class or kind.

3. The cost of all containers and coverings and all other expenses incidental to placing the merchandise, ready and packed, for shipment to the US.

The 1921 law does not balance injuries with consumer benefits, nor does it prescribe that dumping charges should be handled differently, depending on the intent of the exporter, i.e., whether sporadic, intermittent, or continuous dumping is involved.

In 1921, NMEs did not exist as they do today, and the basic law did not spell out how dumping charges involving purchases from NMEs should be handled. The difficulty is in establishing the first requirement of a dumping finding; that is, whether imports are sold at LTFV, below the price charged to others, or below the cost of production in the exporting country. Since for an NME neither its prices nor its cost of production calculations can be accepted as a meaningful standard of fair value, an alternative method of calculation had to be devised. The point of departure for any alternative method is: "What would be a fair price if the NME in question were a market economy (ME) country?"

In 1960 the Treasury initiated a method, subsequently incorporated in its Antidumping Regulations, that spelled out how dumping cases involving NME countries should be handled. The regulations state that instead of using domestic prices of the manufacturer as a standard of "fair value," the Treasury would use the prices of comparable merchandise by a manufacturer in an ME country.

After spelling out how it would interpret the antidumping statutes for NME exporters, Treasury's concern was whether its interpretation would stand up in the courts. To forestall any such challenge, Treasury proposed that Congress incorporate into the 1974 Trade Act a provision describing how dumping charges involving NMEs should be handled. The proposal was accepted, and the relevant portion of the Trade Act (the first specifically dealing with imports for NMEs) incorporates, in substance, para. 153.5 of Treasury's Antidumping Regulations. It states that foreign market value shall be determined on the basis of normal costs, expenses, and profits as reflected either by:

1. The prices at which similar merchandise of a NME country or countries are sold either (a) for domestic consumption in the home market of that country, or (b) for exports to other countries, including the US; or

2. The constructed value, i.e., the cost of production, of such or similar merchandise in a ME, after making adjustments, to reflect differences in the quality and the circumstances of sale of the "such or similar" merchandise in the NME and ME countries.

Establishing the second requirement for dumping (that the LTFV imports caused, or are likely to cause, injury to domestic producers) presents no special problem when an NME is involved. As far as the law is concerned, the US petitioner must prove injury and the ITC interprets the evidence. The basic procedures used in such determinations are the same on imports from ME as from NME countries.

From 1960 until the end of 1978 there were a total of 16 cases of LTFV determinations by the US Customs Service on imports from NME countries. Of these 16 cases, the ITC found *no injury* in 11. The most important and famous case involved golf carts from Poland, which between 1972 and 1975 captured 20 percent of the US market at the expense of domestic producers, for there were practically no other importers. Finding a "comparable" ME producer was extremely troublesome. A small Canadian producer was chosen, on the basis of which Poland was found to be dumping by substantial margins and causing injury to domestic producers. The lengthy litigation and the apparent merit the Treasury saw in Poland's bitter complaint about the inherent unfairness of using a Canadian producer as a basis for price comparison were instrumental in introducing a new dumping procedure for NMEs in September 1978.

An interesting case in which no dumping was found involved standard household incandescent lamps from Hungary. On August 4, 1978, the Treasury notified the ITC that an antidumping investigation had been initiated on August 1, 1978, based on a complaint filed by Westinghouse Electric Corporation. The complaint alleged that, on the basis of prices charged by a major West German supplier, the Hungarian producer of light bulbs, Tungsram, was dumping by margins ranging from 234 percent to 357 percent, thereby causing injury to Westinghouse.[5]

The ITC's investigation established that:

1. Between 1973 and 1977, US production and shipments dropped by about 20 percent and then recovered somewhat; but 1977 output was still below the 1973 level. Capacity utilization had changed little, employment had decreased, and there were substantial increases in production, implying that it was automation, not import competition, that displaced workers.

2. Between 1973 and 1977, US producers' share of domestic consumption *increased* from 87.3 percent to 93.4 percent, although Hungary increased its share of the US import market from 16 percent in 1973 to 59 percent in 1977 (representing 2.1 percent and 3.9 percent of total US consumption in 1973 and 1977).

3. Westinghouse cited 11 instances of sales allegedly lost to imported Hungarian light bulbs, but the ITC was able to verify only four accounts in which Hungarian light bulbs were newly bought. Also the accounts continued to place orders with Westinghouse or other domestic manufacturers.

4. The dumping margins alleged by Westinghouse were greatly exaggerated.

On the basis of this evidence, the ITC concluded that:

> The indices we have examined do not reveal any injury within one domestic light bulb industry that may be attributed to imports from Hungary. . . . The increase in [Hungary's U.S.] market share displaced other imports, *not* domestic production.
>
> . . . As for likelihood of injury, the most significant evidence is a report that Hungary intends to expand its capacity . . . [and plans] a 2.4-fold increase in exports to capitalist countries over the next five years. There is no evidence, however, that [this] increase . . . will go exclusively to the U.S. In testimony before the Commission, Counsel for Tungstram stated that imports of incandescent bulbs from Hungary into the U.S. would not exceed 65 million bulbs each year. As long as that objective prevails, . . . imports of light bulbs from Hungary will not injure the domestic industry.

It is important to note, however, that the ITC Commissioners arrived at this conclusion by only a 3-2 margin. Two Commissioners believed that the investigation should continue because "the information developed during the . . . investigation does not warrant a determination that there is no reasonable indication that an industry in the U.S. is likely to be injured," citing Hungary's increasing market share, alleged large dumping margins, and the planned capacity expansion "with increased production available for export to the U.S."

Dumping and Its Application to Non-Market Economy Countries

Issues in definition

Economists define dumping as selling at a lower price in one national market than in another, i.e., price discrimination. But when Western customs authorities apply the concept to exporters from NMEs, they use a different definition: "The NME exporter charges a lower price than what other exporters are getting for the same commodity."

The difference in the definition arises because whereas the costs, domestic prices, and exchange rates of NME countries are determined administratively rather than principally by market forces, they cannot be introduced as evidence in a US dumping investigation. Thus, "dumping" (which normally evokes the pernicious image of an exporter, at best, selling abroad at a lower price than he sells on his home market or, at worst, disrupting someone else's "orderly" markets) is, in the case of an NME exporter, merely an artificial legal construct stating that his competition is being undersold, thereby injuring import-competing domestic interests. Accordingly, the statement that an NME exporter "undersells his competition" should be void of any value judgmemt until the circumstances of a particular case are established. The charge of dumping, when applied to an NME, should be considered a neutral term. At the same time, one must also withhold judgment about whether NMEs are treated fairly in the US and in other Western countries when an import-competing firm brings a dumping charge against an NME exporter. Producers, exporters, governmental officials, and academic specialists in Eastern Europe consider the application of antidumping laws to their exports in the US and other Western countries discriminatory and unfair. But before a judgment is reached, one must examine carefully the theoretical and practical issues involved, focusing particularly on the question of fairness. One must understand the intent of the law, the details and rationale behind the administrative procedures, and the full particulars of typical and important cases. Only then can one discuss what, if anything, should be changed and how a desirable change may be brought about.

A comparison of dumping by NMEs and MEs

Do NME countries, by definition, undersell their competitors on Western markets? In the traditional centrally planned economy, there is reason to believe that the answer may be "sometimes," even though the foreign trade organizations (FTOs) are instructed to sell at as high a price and to earn as much foreign exchange as possible. (In a planned economy of the Hungarian type, where producing enterprises have a direct financial stake in increasing export revenues and if there is no quantitative export plan to fulfill, dumping would be much less frequent.) To be sure, whether underselling occurs occasionally, frequently, or regularly is difficult to establish; the tendency to do so is probably more pronounced for manufactures than for primary products. But even if the evidence compiled in NME dumping cases is disregarded, there are economic and systemic reasons to suggest that an NME exporter may undersell his competitors, for the following reasons:

1. To occasionally unload surplus stocks.

2. To overcome market-entry handicaps that face all "newcomers" in a foreign market, but which are particularly large for NME exporters. These include the frequent absence of trademark or brand name, lack of reliance on sophisticated advertising, and not-fully-competitive distribution and servicing networks.

3. To absorb all or part of discriminatory tariff and non-tariff barriers (NTBs). The former can be particularly significant on the US market for NME countries that do not have MFN status.

4. To fulfill quarterly and annual export plans. The desire by FTOs to meet exports targets set for particular countries or for certain periods may reduce the flexibility required for the FTO to obtain the best price.

5. To re-export some commodities purchased under bilateral trade agreements, often requiring the costly services of a "barter house" intermediary. Such commodities can often be resold only by agreeing to substantial price discounts.

6. To counter cyclical shortages of foreign exchange by an NME. This condition requires that certain exports be sold quickly, possibly at a substantial price discount.

By contrast, dumping by an ME exporter defined more restrictively as exporting at a lower price than on the home market is usually prompted by different considerations:

1. *Sporadic dumping.* Unloading occasional excess inventories at bargain prices in a foreign market.

2. *Predatory or intermittent dumping.* A predatory strategy by an exporter who has a monopoly in his own country or region to gain a foothold in a foreign market by temporarily selling at below full cost to eliminate competition, then raising the price to provide higher than normal profit margins. This is the classic case of dumping and is the principal rationale for antidumping legislation.

3. *Continuous (or persistent) dumping.* Long-run costs can be reduced by increasing the scale of production, but since the domestic market cannot absorb an increased supply without substantial price concessions, prices at home are kept artificially high by exporting the excess production at a lower world market price.

A direct comparison of dumping by NME and ME exporters is not possible because the definitions of dumping are not the same. However, if we view dumping from the point of view of its effect on the producers and consumers in the importing country, then the underselling of competition by NME exporters falls principally into the *sporadic* and *continuous* categories. That is, whether prompted by a desire to unload surplus stocks, to fulfill export quotas, to dispose of unwanted imports purchased under bilateral agreements, or to alleviate critical shortages in foreign exchange receipts, the effect should be the same as *sporadic dumping* by an ME exporter. And when NME exporters attempt to overcome their market-entry handicaps or to absorb the burden of discriminatory tariffs and NTBs, the effect should be the same as *continuous dumping* by an ME exporter.

Who is injured by dumping?

Dumping is injurious to import-competing producers if it disrupts the normal course of production, trade, and markets. Disruption may arise because those who dump may discontinue the process or they may have some unfair advantage over domestic producers. "When dumping is sporadic, the benefit of lower prices would appear to outweigh the marginal harm suffered by local producers."[6] When dumping is intermittent or predatory, however, the substantial injury suffered by local industries would appear to outweigh any benefits resulting from lower consumer prices. The most controversial area is that of continuous (or persistent) dumping. If there is a smoothly-functioning system of adjustment from import-impacted industries, then the importing country can realize a net benefit from the increased efficiency and lower prices for its consumers. If, however, continuous dumping creates or swells unemployment, then it can create a hardship for the receiving country in excess of the benefits its consumers will realize.[7]

Selecting a third country as a standard of fair value

When an NME exporter is accused of dumping, the US Customs Service, which is in charge of the initial phase of the investigation, must select an ME "third country" whose prices are to be used as a standard of fair value. The third country is chosen in a manner designed to give as fair a comparison as possible. Theoretically, the choice is an ME country in the same geographic area and at approximately the same level of economic development as the NME charged with dumping. But practically speaking, the objective is to find, anywhere in the world, a country producing a comparable product. A particular and often narrowly defined commodity usually is produced in only a few countries, so the choice is more apparent than real. The Customs investigators say that the level of development of the third country chosen has not been a guiding factor until now; the selection has been based more on the basis of geographic factors. Geographic proximity takes into consideration that the raw materials and inter-mediate inputs needed to produce the merchandise may be secured from the same or similarly-located suppliers, so that these elements of cost would be comparable in the two countries.

Approximate equality in the levels of economic development (as a criterion for selecting an ME country) assumes that overall cost levels in a given industry are likely to be comparable. But it does not neces-sarily follow that the unit cost of production is always lower in a country with a lower level of economic development. First, key fac-tors of production, such as energy and capital equipment, may be more expensive in a less developed than in a more developed country. Second, because there may be large differences in productivity levels, the less developed country may be forced to use a larger quantity of a less expensive factor input, such as labor, which in turn may offset any apparent cost advantages of this relatively inexpensive factor.

Other important factors considered in selecting a third country in-clude scale of production and the ME manufacturer's willingness to furnish and document information necessary for an impartial investi-gation.

The preferred valuation as the basis of comparison is the domestic "ex-factory" price in the exporter's country. If the amount of sales within the exporting country is too small to form an adequate basis for comparison, the export price to the principal country or countries (other than the US) is used. In either case, adjustments are made, as appropriate, to allow for "differences in the circumstances of sale" between exports to the US and domestic sale or exports to other des-tinations that might legitimately create price differentials, such as transport costs and differences in guarantees and advertising expendi-tures.

If neither the domestic nor the export price to a third country pro-vides an adequate basis for comparison, a so-called "constructed value" is used. In the case of a ME exporter, this approach is pre-ferred when alternative price information is insufficient or inadequate. In such cases, the constructed value used is essentially the cost of production in the country of origin. In the case of an NME exporter, the "constructed value" is the cost of production of comparable mer-chandise in a ME country, i.e., its unit cost of production plus a nor-mal profit margin.[8]

New US procedures

In January 1978, Treasury proposed important amendments to its Antidumping Regulations pertaining to the calculation of "con-structed value" on imports from NMEs: "Based upon the experiences since enactment of the Trade Act of 1974 and in an effort to make comparisons on more equivalent and realistic bases," it will no longer by necessary to accept without adjustment the production cost estimates of a producer in the selected ME country.[9] Two kinds of adjustments beyond those customarily made to account for "differences in the circumstances of production or sale" would be possible. Treasury's thinking has been influenced by the controversy over the dumping determination involving Polish golf carts and by the persuasive recommendations of Poland's brilliant specialist on East-West commercial law, Professor S. Soltysinski.[10]

If it were not possible to find an ME country with a level of economic development comparable to that of the NME under investigation, causing a country at a higher level of development to be selected—as was the situation in the Polish golf cart case when manufacturing costs of a Canadian producer were used to establish "fair value"—then adjustments may be made to the constructed value "for differences in economic factors as reflected by the normal costs in an [ME] country under investigation."

No further explanation of examples is given, but I would interpret the proposal as stating that the weight (i.e., cost) of individual cost components such as labor used in manufacturing the merchandise may be adjusted downward to reflect their hypothetically lower cost in an ME at a comparable level of development to the NME in question. Thus, if manufacturing workers in a Canadian factory producing, say, golf carts, receive $5/hour, which is the average hourly wage for workers in all manufacturing, but Poland's level of economic development approximates that of, say, Spain, where the average manufacturing wage is $2.50/hour, then Poland would be justified in claiming, *ceteris paribus,* that its labor costs should be figured as follows: the number of workers the Canadian manufacturer employs to produce a golf cart multiplied by the $2.50 "adjusted" wage rate.

Alternatively, if the "constructed value" is based on the cost of production of an ME country that is at a comparable level of development to the NME in question, then adjustments may be made for differences between the two economies in the objective physical inputs used to produce the item in question. "Such specific objective factors as hours of labor required, quantity of materials employed, and amount of energy consumed in the [NME] country would have to be verified to the satisfaction of the Secretary [of Treasury] and then could be valued in the more comparable [ME] country or countries where production of such or similar merchandise is not actually occurring." In addition, an amount for general expenses and profits will have to be added to the values thus obtained.

I interpret this proposed new regulation as stating that it should be possible for an NME to calculate and introduce as evidence in a US dumping investigation the objective factors of production it actually uses to manufacture the product. But the cost determination of these factors will have to use the prices in an ME at a comparable level of development.

The proposed amendments appear to be fairer to NME exporters, but important questions were raised about the practicality of their implementation. One critical issue is: will it be possible to obtain reliable documentation from an NME country about the objective costs of production? For example, will an NME permit on-site inspection of its facilities and documents by US Customs agents, which is standard procedure in investigations involving ME countries?

A major conference of legal and economic experts as well as lawyers representing interested parties was organized by the US Treasury and State Departments in July 1978 to discuss the question of the application of dumping and other import-protective procedures to NMEs, including the proposed new regulations.[11] On September 9, 1978, new Treasury regulations on dumping involving NMEs entered into force, containing the following provisions:

1. A new test of constructed value is introduced, making it possible to introduce the "objective factors of production" of an NME into the calculations, provided that these are carefully documented and can be verified through on-site inspection by US Customs agents in the plant and in the books of the NME producer. In such cases, the valuation (costing) of these inputs (materials, electricity, hours of labor, etc.) would have to use the prices of a "comparable free market economy country."[12]

2. Customs agents are instructed to find a comparable ME country on the basis of per capita GNP levels, taking into account the human and natural resources of the two countries as well as the comparability of the industry concerned.

3. US price or US economic data relating to cost of production will be taken into account only as a last resort, that is, if no other comparable ME can be found and if the NME in question refuses to cooperate in the documentation of its production data.

Shortly after the new regulations were introduced, the US Treasury sent a team of specialists to the golf cart factory in Poland where the team verified Polish production data through on-site inspection and access to the producer's accounting records. At the same time the Treasury accepted Spain as a comparable ME country. Poland's cost data were turned over to CREA, a Madrid-based management consulting firm, which established the constructed price. Customs inspectors went to Spain to verify the unit cost and price data in a comparable (motor car) industry, to be used to value the Polish inputs. On this basis, and after taking into account inflation in Spain and recent changes in the dollar/peseta exchange rate, the Treasury has established a "fair market value" price—about $10 more than the price Poland is charging at the factory door.[13]

But the story is still not over. Industry officials and some members of Congress have accused the Treasury of being laggard in penalizing foreign competitors after finding that they were selling unfairly priced or subsidized products in the US. Early in January 1979, Harley Davidson (a division of the AMF that also manufactures golf carts, although it is best known for its motorcycles), filed a complaint with the Treasury challenging both the first Treasury dumping ruling on golf carts in 1975 and the legality of its new regulations involving NMEs.

Conclusions

Given US laws and procedures currently in effect, the following conclusions and recommendations suggest how an NME exporter can avoid dumping and market disruption problems in the US:

1. Dumping *or* market disruption can only be an issue if exports to the US of a certain product from an NME country are increasing rapidly and are causing material injury to domestic producers. Without such an injury, it is unlikely that charges would be brought or, if brought, that the final decision would be against the NME exporter. Does this mean that the NME exporter must remain invisible to avoid injuring domestic producers? Not at all:

a. If an NME exporter wants to rapidly increase its exports to the US, it should select commodities where US imports are already large. In this way, it would be competing not only with US but also with foreign producers. The advantage of this is, first, that the exporter will remain less visible amid other exporters, and second, that other exporters cannot bring charges in the US; only domestic producers can.

b. The NME exporter should watch its market share in total US consumption of the product. No hard and fast rules can be laid down as to what threshold should not be crossed; but based on previous cases, a market share of under 10 percent should not cause any problems, provided that the rate of growth of the market share is not extraordinarily rapid. But additional considerations are also important.

(i) It makes a big difference whether the NME exporter helped to develop a market for a product or whether he entered with a product that is, typically, American invented, developed, produced, and marketed. To illustrate: bottled wines of a given country would be in the first category (OK to aim for a large market share), whereas golf carts would be in the second category (so the exporter must be careful).

(ii) The appropriate market share to watch is not necessarily that of the entire US market; the share of a regional market must also be considered. (A regional market is never smaller than a state; most frequently it is comprised of a group of states.)

2. It may be safe to disregard the above suggestions and really push the sale of a product in the US provided that the NME exporter can defend himself against a charge of dumping. This can be done by finding out which market economies manufacture the same product and how much the product is selling on the domestic market or on the export markets of the country or countries most likely to be chosen as a standard of fair value. As long as rapid penetration of the US market can be achieved at approximately that price, the NME exporter cannot be found guilty of dumping.

3. Under the new regulations, an NME exporter can introduce his own objective physical production inputs, but not his prices and cost calculations, into US antidumping investigations involving products, provided on-site inspection by US Customs agents is allowed. But because the new regulation is being challenged, the outcome of the legal maneuvering must be monitored.

4. The surest and most profitable road, however, for Polish and other NME exporters to avoid dumping and market disruption problems is to export high-quality, up-to-date, and innovative new products, because manufactures with such attributes need not be sold at a price lower than the products of its competitors.

* * *

Author's note: See pp. 330-337 for updated information on US laws.

TABLE 1
U.S. Import-Protective Laws and Procedures

	Tariffs	Antidumping	Counterveiling duty	Escape clause	Market disruption	"Unfair" practices (Sec. 337 of Tariff Act)	Multilateral commodity agreements	Non-tariff barriers (NTB)
When applicable	On goods subject to tariff.	Sales at "less than fair value" (LTFV) causing injury in US.	Foreign government subsidy on exports causes injury in US.	Rapid increase in imports is *substantial* cause of *serious* injury in US.	Rapid increase in imports is *significant* cause of *material* injury.	Unfair competition (not defined) causes substantial injury.	Selected commodities. Eg: Multilateral Fiber Agreement (MFA).	Ex: Quota restriction (QR), health & packaging requirement, orderly marketing arr. (OMA).
Procedures	As detailed in regulations.	Treasury 6-9 mo. for LTFV decision; if yes, ITC 3 mo. to find whether LTFV caused injury.	Essentially the same as for antidumping.	ITC 6 mo. to recommend to President who must decide on type of relief within 2 mo. If President differs from ITC, Congress can override (i.e., agree with ITC) within 3 months.	ITC 3 mo. to recommend to President who must decide on type of relief within 2 months.	ITC (12-18 mo.) orders carried out unless President or courts disapprove.		
Remedy		Antidumping duty = LTFV margin unless export price has been raised.	Counterveiling duty = foreign subsidy.	1. Increase of tariff 2. Tariff rate quota 3. QR 4. OMA 5. Adjustment assistance		1. Cease & desist. 2. Exclude imports. 3. Post bond. 4. Initiate other proc. 5. Other.		

			6. Any combination of above, subject to limitations of Sec. 203 of Trade Act.		
Applicable to which countries?	All countries except those not receiving MFN or granted GSP preference.	All countries, but special procedures for NME countries.	All.	All.	NME countries only.	All.
Important for EE Countries?	Yes, for those not receiving MFN.	Yes, especially Poland.	No.	No.	Potentially very important.	No.

TABLE 2
Market Disruption

When applicable?	Rapid increase in imports is significant cause of material injury, or threat thereof.
Legal basis	Sec. 406 of Trade Act of 1974.
Definition of key terms	Market disruption: a situation generally containing the following elements in combination: (1) sharp and substantial increase of imports of particular products from particular countries; (2) prices substantially below those in the importing country; and (3) injury to domestic producers or threat thereof.

Significant cause: an important cause, but not necessarily the most important.

Material injury: lesser amount of injury than under the provisions of the general escape clause (serious injury) before action can be taken; therefore intended to be an easier test to meet. Injury criteria are the same: significant idling of facilities, unemployment or underemployment, and lower profit.

Threat of injury: declining sales, growing inventory, and downtrend in production, wages, employments, and profits. |
| Cases involving NMEs | Two cases only: cotton working gloves from the PRC. In March 1978, the ITC decided in the negative by a four to two vote, i.e., market disruption was not found. |
| Conformity with GATT? | GATT recognizes need for protection against market disruption, using the same criteria as for escape clause (Art. XIX) but permits simplified procedures and the invoking of it only against NMEs. Thus, US appears not to be in conformity with GATT only with respect to applying a standard easier than under the escape clause. |

TABLE 3
Antidumping

When applicable?	Sales at "less than fair value" (LTFV) causing injury.
Legal basis	Antidumping Act of 1916: criminal and civil (i.e., treble damages) remedies if intent of dumping is to destroy or injure. Apparently these sanctions have never been applied because of difficulty of proving intent, but Polish golf cart case is currently pending in US District Court of Delaware.

TABLE 3   *Continued*
Antidumping

Antidumping Act of 1921 (as amended): administrative remedy if dumping is found; intent is not relevant.

Sec. 321, Trade Act of 1974: essentially codified into law Treasury procedures used since 1960 to implement the Antidumping Act of 1921.

Definition of key terms	"Less Than Fair Value" (LTFV): export price to US is lower than:

For market-economy exporter:	*For non-market-economy exporter:*
1. "Ex-factory" in price to domestic customers in exporter's country.	1. "Ex-factory" price to domestic customers in chosen market-economy producer.
2. Exporter's price to country or countries other than US.	2. Export price of chosen market-economy producer: (a) to third country or countries; (b) to US.
3. Constructed value = cost of production + profit margin in country of production.	3. Constructed value = cost of production + profit margin in chosen market-economy country.
4. — — —	4. Prices of such or similar merchandise produced in the US.

Note: In all cases, adjustments are made to reflect differences in "circumstances of sale."

"Causing injury": no fixed formula but major factors considered important in past affirmative decisions were: (1) large market share or rapid growth of imports; (2) declining domestic output; and (3) declining domestic prices and profits.

Proposed new procedures	Yes, in LTFV investigation to adjust for differences in the level of economic development between the accused NME and the market economy chosen as a standard of fair value.

Cases involving NMEs	1960-1978: 16 cases of LTFV determination, of which injury was found in 5 cases, no injury in 11 cases. The 5 dumping findings were: (1) Czechoslovakia (bicycles in 1960); (2) Poland (cast iron pipe in 1967); (3) USSR (titanium sponge in 1968); (4) GDR, Czechoslovakia, Romania, USSR (pig iron, 1968); (5) Poland (golf carts in 1975).

Notes

1. Thomas A. Wolf, "Effects of U.S. Granting of Most-Favored Nation Treatment to Imports from Eastern Europe: The Polish Experience," *The ACES Bulletin* (Spring 1973). Professor Wolf has examined this question, focusing on Poland's exports to the US.

2. Edward J. Ray, "The Determinants of Tariff and Nontariff Trade Restrictions in the U.S." Unpublished, January 1979.

3. Josef C. Brada, "Comment on Professor Kossuth's Paper."

4. US International Trade Commission, *Clothespins From the People's Republic of China, the Polish People's Republic, and the Socialist Republic of Romania* (Washington, D.C.: US ITC August 1978).

5. This and subsequent information on this case is based on US ITC, Standard Household Incandescent Lamps from Hungary (Washington, D.C.: US ITC, September 1978).

6. Whether dumping of any kind is profitable depends on the interaction of three variables. The *elasticities of demand* for the exporter's product on its domestic and foreign markets: relatively inelastic domestic demand permits high prices on the home market while relatively elastic foreign demand yields increased total revenues as the price is reduced on the foreign market. *Barriers to re-entry* into the exporter's domestic market: insulation of the home market by high transport costs or high tariff and non-tariff barriers prevents the dumped goods from re-entering the home market. The *cost structure* of the exporting firm: high fixed costs characterize dumping producers because marginal revenue will be greater than marginal cost even at the low dumping price. In numerous industries, the Japanese producers are said to be in the best position to undertake continuous dumping because the barriers to re-enter the Japanese market are high and because Japanese firms tend to have relatively large fixed costs, given the high debt/equity ratios of most firms and the guaranteed jobs of the workers with the firm.

7. Peter Ehrenhaft, "Protection Against International Price Discrimination: United States Countervailing and Antidumping Duties," *Columbia Law Review* 43 (1958). Mr. Ehrenhaft currently is Deputy Assistant Secretary of the Treasury for Tariff Affairs and his office is in charge of dumping investigations.

8. Bart Fisher, "The Antidumping Law of the United States: A Legal and Economic Analysis," *Law and Policy in International Business* 5:1 (1973): 91-92.

9. In the absence of an adequate basis for comparison using prices in an ME country, the prices of such or similar merchandise produced in the US may be used. To date, it has not been found necessary to employ domestic US prices as a standard of fair value.

10. *Federal Register* 43:5 (January 9, 1978); 1356-57. The announcement also solicited comments.

11. See, for example, Stanislaw Soltysinski, "The U.S. Anti-Dumping and Countervailing Duty Laws From a Socialist Economy Perspective." Paper presented at the Airlie House Conference on Anti-Dumping and Countervailing Duty Aspects of Imports from State Trading Countries and Government-Owned Enterprises, Georgetown Institute for International and Foreign Trade Law, Warrenton, VA, July 21-22, 1978.

12. Ibid.

13. *The New York Times,* January 28, 1979, p. 1f.

Comment

Adam Szeworski

In his paper on import protectionism in the US and Poland's manufactures exports, Professor Marer has taken a highly pragmatic approach focusing on a careful description of the American import-protective laws and regulations of special importance to Poland and their application to specific imports from socialist countries during the last two decades. Instructive and useful as it may be, it cannot be expected that this approach could be further developed by a Polish discussant, except perhaps for some questions about additional explanations. It seems, however, that the problem of protectionism may be extended for the purposes of this conference by considering it in the broader context of trade relations between countries at different levels of economic development or of changing general business conditions in the importing country. It is on these two aspects that I would like to comment.

Considering the theory of protectionism, in the development of a capitalist economy that policy can be justified, in principle, in two specific situations. The first is the so-called infant industry argument: the principle of educational protection formulated in favor of less developed economies. The other case (much more questionable) falls under the general framework of Keynesian theory that pertains to the advanced stage of monopoly capitalism and the associated distortions in trade relations among countries.

The infant industry argument followed from the correct assumption that, if the levels of economic development of trade partners are unequal, free trade may hamper the economic growth of the less developed country. Consequently, it acknowledged that it may be necessary to apply protectionist tariffs in favor of products of new industrial branches threatened by competition by more industrialized countries until these industries reach a level of costs and productivity that would enable them to compete. The well-known historical examples are the United States and Germany, whose industrial growth was greatly facilitated by the application of that principle, which effectively protected the development of their manufacturing industries against the competition of British products. There is now a common agreement on the application of that principle by developing countries to protect their newly created industries.

The other argument which, strictly speaking, is based on Keynes's thinking rather than on his direct prescriptions, accepts free trade as a means of securing to all partners the benefits resulting from the international division of labor, provided that the economy is at full employment. If this is not the case and, specifically, during business recessions, growth in exports in excess of imports may be considered one means of leading to higher employment and improvement in the country's general economic position. This may justify not only tendencies to promote exports at considerable cost, but also attempts to protect domestic markets against the inflow of foreign products. It would be superfluous to dwell upon the negative effects of such policies—in their most drastic forms leading to the beggar-my-neighbor-policies generally practiced during the Great Depression of the 1930s. Nevertheless, the idea of resorting to such policies, especially at times of poor business conditions, is still alive.

In fact, when we look at the development of international trade during the postwar period, we observe a long-run tendency toward freer trade, although with policy fluctuations generally following the course of the business cycles. That is, a kind of negative association may be observed between the general level of economic activity and the reappearance of protectionist tendencies. When business conditions are favorable, as in periods of cyclical upswing or expansion, there is, in general, more reliance on market forces, and the tendencies toward liberalization or abolition of the still existing trade barriers prevail. By contrast, periods of recession witness a number of setbacks in those tendencies, like temporary raising of tariffs, reintroduction of quantitative restrictions, or the stricter enforcement of other non-tariff obstacles to free trade. Even the US, the country most committed to the promotion of freer trade, was not free from such setbacks. For example, in August 1971 a general surcharge was imposed on imports along with the suspension of gold convertibility of the US dollar.

Fortunately, during most of the postwar period the world enjoyed high levels of economic activity with relatively mild and short-lived business contractions. Setbacks of the kind mentioned occasionally did occur, but did not harm to any important degree the general drive toward freer trade. Only recently has the situation changed in that regard; since the breakdown of the worldwide boom of 1972-73, a general resurgence of protectionist tendencies has been taking place along with the slowdown of the average rate of growth in industrial production and national product, resulting in growing unemployment and low rates of utilization of capital equipment in almost all developed capitalist countries.

Although the US is the only country that, during the five years following the severe recession of 1974-75, not only overcame successfully the recession but enjoyed for more than three years a quite comfortable business expansion (the longest in its history since the

World War II), its protectionist policies do not lag behind those of other developed countries who were painfully affected by the ills of a protracted stagnation. It may even be said that the US is actually in the forefront of the overall revival of protectionist tendencies. Thus, it appears that protectionist tendencies now do emerge not only at times of poor performance of the economy, as in the case until the early 1970s, but also during prosperous periods.

This particular case can be explained by the rapidly growing deficit in the American trade balance and, consequently, in the balance-of-payments on current account, which in turn is partly the result of a higher income elasticity of demand for imports in the US than in its major industrial trading partners and partly the relative cyclical position of the US economy during 1976-80. As stated in official documents (e.g., *The Economic Report of the President* to the Congress, January 1979), the growth of US imports tends to be greater in relation to domestic growth than the growth of US exports in relation to growth abroad. Until about 1975 a rough balance between import and export growth was maintained because growth abroad tended to exceed US growth. From 1976 to 1978, however, growth in the US surpassed the average growth abroad, due mainly to the different time pattern of the business cycle at home and abroad. Business expansion was developing in the US when the rest of the industrialized countries suffered a protracted stagnation, resulting in the US balance of trade shifting rapidly toward deficit. In fact, during 1976-78 the deficit in the US balance of trade reached unprecedented levels in relation to the gross national product. This was due mainly to the long-run increase in the dependence of the American economy on foreign trade. As measured by the percentage shares of exports or imports in the gross national product, this dependence rose by more than one-third during the last decade - from 5.8 percent in 1968 to 7.8 percent in 1978 (in constant 1972 prices).

Putting aside the possible change in the income elasticities of US demand for imports or of foreign demand for US exports (rather a long-term problem), one can be anything but optimistic about the possible improvement, in the near future, of the general climate generating protectionist tendencies in the US. For if it is agreed, in the light of the recent experience of the world-wide boom of 1972-73, that a synchronized business expansion in the US and in the rest of the world is undesirable because that would contribute to an acceleration of the already high rate of inflation, then that would imply that only slower growth in the US than abroad can ever produce a trade balance leading to a manageable current account balance - a proposition that seems hardly acceptable either for American business or government.

But this is exactly what is expected to be a solution to the current

US balance-of-payments problem. An acceleration in the rate of growth in Western Europe is expected to exceed the rate of growth in the US, the latter having already begun to slow down considerably compared with its initial upswing rate three years ago and the US growth is expected to continue its decline. The resulting growth in American exports to the expanding European economies on the one hand and the decline in the growth rate of American imports on the other—both supported by the lagged effects of the recent fall in the exchange rate of the US dollar in relation to other main currencies— should bring the US economy nearer to the desired equilibrium in its balance of current payments. That this would reverse the growing protectionist trend is rather unlikely, especially if the final outcome of the decline in the growth rate would be a recession in this year or in 1980.

Independent of these short-term considerations, the growth of protectionist tendencies has another powerful source: structural changes on the world capitalist markets, such as rapid shifts in relative competitiveness of particular countries and products. The result is that protectionism is no longer intended only to influence the overall level of demand in the given economies, but now affects also, selectively, specific products or groups of products and are aimed against specific countries. These types of measures, hence, are discriminating, contradicting the accepted rules in international trade relations.

The selective nature of today's new protectionist measures resembles the so-called infant industries justification of protectionism in less developed countries. But in fact, that (in principle) valid argument has degenerated into a much less supportable mature industry argument or, better, the aging industry argument. This is the case whatever may be the real factors underlying changes in competitiveness: low real wages on the one side or obsolete techniques, high capital costs, or excessive profit margins on the other.

I would like to end by quoting some excerpts from the 1979 Policy Declaration of the US National Foreign Trade Council:

> Growing unemployment and swollen trade deficits have added to protectionist sentiment in the free world. In the long-run, the rising tide of protectionism threatens to slow world economic growth and add to the problems of inflation and unemployment . . . . The Council believes that the first line of defense against protectionism is a well functioning domestic economy. At the same time, we recognize the sovereign right of trading nations to impose limited safeguards to protect particular sectors of their economy. . . .

In case of severe dislocation, the Council urges that the government rely primarily on the adjustment assistance provisions of the 1974 Trade Act. Finally:

The Council notes with concern the growing resort to orderly marketing agreements among trading nations. While they may have apparent justification in cases where domestic markets have been subject to sudden upsurges of injurious import competition, their proliferation can only have the effect of restricting the growth of international trade. Selective targeting of import relief or safegurad measures against specific countries, such as is inherent in orderly marketing agreements, has the potential for corrupting the most-favored-nation principle on which the inter-national trading rules are based. The 'selectivity' approach should not be agreed to without careful analysis of its potential for disruption, retaliation and increased protectionism.

In view of the rather gloomy picture I painted in my contribution as far as the actual conditions and prospects for freer trade are concerned, it is encouraging to know that not only our American colleagues at this conference table, but also the American business community as represented by the influential Foreign Trade Council, are in favor of freer trade and against protectionism.

Reply

Professor Szeworski's comments, which place the issue of protectionism into its broader theoretical and economic policy context, complement my paper well. I am very impressed by his knowledge of current business conditions in the industrial West and by his logical analysis of the complex relationship between the business cycle, export-and import-elasticities in Western countries, and protectionism.

I understand Prof. Szeworski's argument to be as follows. There are two theoretical justifications for protectionism: the well-known infant-industry argument and the more recently developed full-employment argument, on which his detailed comments focus. A country facing unemployment, Prof. Szeworski notes, wants to create additional demand. One way to do so is to generate an export surplus by subsidizing exports, impeding imports, or both. Although this "beggar-thy-neighbor" policy has been discredited by the experience of industrial countries during the Great Depression, Szeworski contends that protectionism for employment reasons has once again been resurrected. He notes as evidence that protectionist tendencies have become much stronger in recent periods of slow-down or decline of economic activity in Western countries. He then states that the US is "in the forefront of the overall revival of protectionist tendencies." In the final analysis, he attributes this to US attempts to solve its balance-of-payments problems, which have been created in good part by the faster increase in US imports than exports. He then becomes very pessimistic. In his view, this imbalance between US imports and exports can be corrected only by a slowing of US growth rates relative to those of America's major trading partners. But a sluggish US growth rate or a recession will only exacerbate protectionist tendencies, he argues, which will be felt most strongly in the relatively mature, "aging" industries. This, by implication, will create more and more export difficulties for America's trading partners including Poland.

Szeworski's analysis is persuasive because his argument is logical and internally consistent. But whether his final pessimistic conclusions are correct or possibly overdrawn depends on the long-term validity of his assumptions.

I agree that US imports have increased faster than exports and that this has created domestic problems. But I would also argue that (1) this imbalance was to a considerable extent due to special, nonrecurring factors; (2) this imbalance can be corrected by speeding up the rate of growth of our exports rather than by reducing the growth of non-energy imports (either by putting up protectionist barriers or by cutting our growth rate); (3) for improved export performance, much depends on what we do here in the US to become more export oriented rather than on economic conditions in our trade partner countries, so that the export-and import-elasticities of the last decade would not be considered permanent; and (4) the US is not any more protectionist than are the other industrial Western countries. Let me elaborate briefly on these points.

(1) Large and growing dependence on foreign oil has been a key factor in increasing the overall import dependence of the US economy since 1973. But it should be noted that the sharp rise in oil prices in 1973 came at a time when US environmental programs were constraining the use of coal, government regulations were inhibiting an expansion in the availability of natural gas, and domestic production of oil had leveled off. All these factors combined resulted in a sharply accelerating dependence on foreign oil. If we focus not on oil consumption but on overall energy consumption since 1973, we find that the US has made about as much progress economizing on the use of energy per unit of output as have the other major industrial countries. Recent increases in the domestic price of oil and improved prospects for the passage of comprehensive energy legislation suggest that these developments may be translated into a reduced dependence on foreign oil.

(2) It should be noted that during the past 20 years, US exports have grown at only half the rate of other industrial nations and that the US position has deteriorated especially in manufactures. While US agricultural exports have grown nicely, the real volume of our

manufactures exports actually fell between 1974 and 1978. The point is that the problem identified by Szeworski regarding US import- vs. export-elasticities can be solved in good part by reversing the deteriorating US export position in manufactures.

(3) Much has been done during the last few years to improve US export performance, although much remains to be done in the area of improving productivity and reducing inflation. It is important to note, however, that price competitiveness has been restored by the substantial depreciation of the US dollar in the past several years. But it takes two to three years for exports to respond significantly to improved profit opportunities. US concern with export performance is indicated also by President Carter establishing an interagency task force to look into this problem. At the end of 1978 this task force made its recommendations, some of which are being implemented. These include (a) providing increased direct assistance to US exports, mainly in the area of finance; (b) reducing domestic barriers to exports (such as environmental and other regulations, export controls for foreign policy purposes, and stringent antitrust laws); and (c) a strong US stand to reduce foreign barriers to our exports. The recently-concluded Geneva trade negotiations, also approved by Congress, have taken an important step toward implementing this last recommendation.

(4) Although it is very difficult to come up with a comprehensive measure, I would argue that the US is no more protectionist than the European Community (EC) or Japan. The tabulation below shows that average US tariff rates in three major commodity categories are slightly higher than in the EC but lower than in Japan. US non-tariff barriers are probably less numerous and less punishing than those of most other industrial countries. As I stated in my paper, this may not be readily apparent, because while the US tends to rely on highly visible administrative or legal procedures that can be invoked by import-competing domestic producers, West European countries and Japan typically make use of informal and behind-the-scenes procedures to reduce imports.

Country	Industrial Supplies	Semifinished goods	Manufactures
U.S.	2.5%	5.6%	8.8%
Japan	3.4%	6.3%	12.7%
European Community	0.4%	4.8%	8.2%

SOURCE: GATT calculations.

Tariff rates are weighted averages of those on individual commodities within each commodity group in effect since Jan. 1, 1972. These rates were not changed substantially during the remainder of the 1970s.

For these reasons I am somewhat less pessimistic than Szeworski about the inevitability of growing protectionism in the US. He is correct, however, to call attention to the danger of protectionism, whose growth is strongly inimical to the economic interests of the US, Poland, and all other nations.

Marketing Polish Industrial Goods in the United States

Joseph C. Miller

Polish-American industrial cooperation (IC) has a real potential for expanding Polish exports to the United States. Both the motives and mechanisms are present: Polish enterprises can increase their export earnings of convertible currency (CC), and US partner companies can facilitate the export sales through their marketing know-how and organizations. However, the export potential is still largely unrealized. To a large extent, the partner enterprises have concentrated on the development of production capabilities and have marketed primarily to Polish and other Eastern users of their industrial products. Now, some are ready to increase their exports to the United States, and new cooperation contracts can be negotiated to develop further export strength.

There are a number of practical ways to expand exports through more effective export marketing and planning. In particular, a comprehensive marketing plan can develop export capability from the earliest stages of Polish-US cooperative enterprise. As we have learned from BUMAR and International Harvester (IH), IC is a dynamic process that requires continual adaptation by both partners,

The author is grateful to Paul Marer and Robert Campbell for their comments and suggestions on an earlier version of this paper, but is solely responsible for any errors in the final product.

not only to each other's needs but also to changing external circumstances. Accordingly, my suggestions for enlarging export capability are made within the generalized context of this adaptive process.

Each cooperation arrangement follows a different and distinctive pattern of development, but the following process outlines most of the essential steps:

1. *Preliminary screening.* Each partner independently considers the types of products that it will be prepared to produce cooperatively.

2. *Selection of prospective partner.* After informal discussions with a number of possible partners, each side selects one (or a few) prospective partners with whom contract negotiations will begin.

3. *Contract negotiations.* Provisions of the cooperation agreement are hammered out between the two bargainers.

4. *Implementation.* Upon signing the agreement, the partners begin to work together and adapt to the agreement.

5. *Revision.* The partners periodically review their performance and decide whether to modify or expand the basic contract.

It is the thesis of this paper that important marketing decisions are made at each stage of the developmental process, not (as is sometimes assumed) simply at stage 4. An understanding of these decisions enables the partners to plan effectively for export marketing to the United States.

Preliminary Screening

The portfolio of products or industrial processes that the partners examine independently at this stage contains products of high, low and medium-range or uncertain probability of success in US markets. It is often assumed that most if not all of the products in the high probability category are products of US companies, and that the only Polish products are those in which Poland has an obvious comparative advantage (e.g., ham and other specialty foods) or a natural resource lacking in the United States (e.g., copper and other minerals). However, recent research by Grubel and Lloyd[1] has shown that over 60 percent of the ten major OECD countries' imports and exports are accounted for by intra-industry trade, i.e., shipments of differentiated industrial and consumer goods. Even in cases in which the exporting country has no apparent comparative advantage in the inputs used intensively in manufacturing given products, the country can establish an internationally competitive position.

The importance of intra-industry trade has several implications for export-market planning. First, there is an explicit recognition of the trade-creating effects of product differentiation, i.e., the development of product brands that are distributed and advertised to distinguish them from similar products. In contrast to the methods of traditional inter-industry analyses of trade, the new approach suggests that export planning should be brand-specific and take a highly disaggregated view of the costs and demand-generating effects of marketing. Second, the evidence of the rapid expansion of intra-industry trade between the United States, Western Europe, and other industrialized countries indicates that market research information is neither costless nor worthless, as neo-classical models have assumed. Instead, export planning requires that a careful analysis be made of the trade-offs between the cost of additional information about markets and the extra sales revenues expected from the application of the information. Third, the growth of intra-industry trade also emphasizes the importance of brand competition among major manufacturers of differentiated industrial and consumer goods. At the preliminary screening stage, therefore, planning should include the collection and analysis of information on competitors' product brands and marketing methods.

Even though the two partners act independently at this stage, it is essential that each at least begin to develop marketing plans and brand-specific market research information. A solid foundation of marketing research and planning is valuable in many respects, not the least of which is as a corrective to an often exclusive emphasis on production planning. To draw an analogy from econometrics, planning or forecasting needs to take into consideration both supply and demand factors, lest some of the critically influencial variables not be identified. As the partners begin to work together, each will learn from the other, and their joint knowledge will make them more effective.

Selection of a Prospective Partner

As the Polish enterprise and the US corporation approach a decision about mutual selection, each group of executives will have shifted its focus from product-brand screening to the screening of firms or enterprises. In many cases the distinction is practically imperceptible. Intra-industry product screening reveals the relative strengths or weaknesses of various product-brand alternatives as potential exports to the United States, and informal discussions among firms enlarge this information base and make it specific to the prospective partner.

Depending on its need for further information and the range of options it examines, the enterprise or corporation typically conducts these preliminary discussions with several prospective partners. Prior experience with IC negotiations may help simplify this task; but under conditions of ever-changing market conditions and technology, a careful, comparative search can be useful. A large, diversified enterprise such as BUMAR employs a full-time staff to keep in touch with potential partners, to contact new prospects, and to analyze the continual inflow of market-research information. The small newcomer firm does not enjoy the advantages of such experience and specialization, but it can also learn a great deal from the selection process.

During preliminary informal discussions and (especially) in the later contract negotiations, information is exchanged on a wide range of concerns, from advertising policies to technological specifications. Where either or both parties wants to develop the capability of exporting to the United States, one topic of particular interest is the organization of marketing channels of distribution. To be sure, the issue of export channels consists of many considerations, including ocean transportation, US warehousing, and facilities for delivery to the end-user. Because channel arrangements are fundamentally important to any export effort, the parties are usually well-advised to discuss them at an early stage. Indeed, one of the basic criteria on which the partner-selection decision rests is channel capability.

The meaning of channel capability in practical terms varies from one firm or industry to another, and a catalog of its characteristics would fill a book. However, some of the essential elements may be suggested here. First, a high degree of forward vertical integration in the US partner is often regarded as a prerequisite to effective market penetration. In lieu of total forward integration, long-term contracts or other stable relationships with sales distributors, brokers, etc. may provide the needed access to end users. Second, export marketing to the United States is more likely to be successful if both the Polish and US partners are able to achieve economies of scale in transportation or distribution. Efficiency in ocean (or air) transportation may be facilitated through central coordination of Poland's technologically advanced shipping services, and the domestic distributional efficiency of a US firm is often indicated by the size and long-range performance of its specialized subsidiaries or affiliates. Third, in some cases US import barriers may be avoided by shipping the jointly produced goods in unfinished form or under the US product brand name. Where US import protection creates barriers, these marketing channel arrangements may be well worth the additional cost.

Contract Negotiation

By the time the partners have settled down to the serious business of negotiating their cooperation contract, they will have developed relatively definite ideas of the type of product they will jointly produce. If they intend to export to the United States, they will have established a solid foundation of market information and have made plans concerning their channels of distribution. Most of these marketing decisions are discussed again in the contract negotiations and are given formal expression in the contract itself. However, one set of decisions that is often deferred to this stage is the issue of prices.

The effectiveness of an export program may depend on pricing policy. We have seen several West European firms recently lose much of their price competitiveness in the US market because of rapid price increases (resulting, in part, from shifts in the foreign exchange rate). Conversely, setting prices too low may cause problems, e.g., anti-dumping and antitrust suits, as in the golf cart case. Thorough research and monitoring of the market, including analyses of competitors' actions, may not solve all of these pricing problems, but they will help to avoid some difficulties.

At the negotiations stage, there is likely to be more concern with the cost side of pricing. Grubel and Lloyd report that the single most important determinant of cost competitiveness is production economies of scale.[2] In his recent and highly significant paper on multinational corporations, Niehans makes a similar point: the large, diversified corporations enter into overseas production arrangements to supply the home market when economies of scale at the various levels of the vertical system (from raw-materials sourcing to retail distribution) provide sufficient efficiency to do so. The implications of these two studies for Polish-US IC, with the objective of exporting to the United States, is that the partners should apply both their technological and managerial resources to realizing significant economies of scale, in competition with other US firms.

Implementation

Once the partners have signed the cooperation contract, they begin to put into action the intentions and plans that they have developed together. Marketing research and planning are still important, but the emphasis shifts from the information or knowledge to judgment and decisionmaking. Because demand and competitive conditions in US markets are changing continually, executives must keep informed and be prepared to adapt quickly when necessary.

Two types of marketing decisions require special expertise at this stage; sales force management and advertising policies. Both depend on research and planning, but their execution typically requires more frequent and detailed decisionmaking than product, channels, or pricing decisions. Indeed, the advertising and sales force decisions are usually limited to matters of general policy, and the actual day-to-day implementation is delegated to specialists in advertising agencies, sales brokers, etc.

The most basic policy decision to be made concerns the objectives of the advertising and personal selling efforts. If the export product is a new brand name, the primary objective is likely to be to introduce the unknown brand. In the case of most industrial goods, it will also be important to communicate the functional usefulness and quality of the product. Where the brand name is well-established, new features or quality improvements should probably be stressed. Another typical objective is to inform potential users of the after-sales service available.

Advertising and personal selling often complement each other in marketing an industrial product. The advertising message in commercial or business journals arouses the interest of the prospective buyer and provides some basic information about the product brand, but most transactions are actually closed through the personal contact of a sales representative. The organization and management of the sales force are clearly more easily conducted by a vertically integrated firm established in the US market, but many non-integrated companies or firms that lack sales forces are able to reach their industrial customers through independent sales representatives.

Revision

The final but recurrent phase of IC that affords an opportunity to improve export capability is the review of the partners' joint performance. In actuality, many cooperation contracts include provisions for periodic and formal reviews as well as specific control procedures, and each partner usually develops systematic methods of generating information on the performance of, for example, production quality and personnel. Aside from regular checks on performance, however, from time to time the partners also need to review their basic aims and methods of accomplishing these aims.

At least once a year the partners need to set aside a few days to re-evaluate their entire marketing program. Basic issues should be examined, such as, "What kinds of changes are needed in a product or services to better serve the needs of our present or future customers?" All aspects of the marketing program are analyzed, from product design and quality to physical distribution and after-sales service. Emphasis is placed on trends in the market, especially competitors' actions, shifts in demand patterns, and the emergence of possible new customers.

Review also enables the partners to modify the basic cooperation agreement. Many contracts have sufficient flexibility to permit changes in pricing, transportation, distribution, and even advertising or the addition of a product through a supplementary agreement or protocol. However, some basic changes in objectives or methods of cooperation may require rewriting of the contract.

Conclusions

IC between Polish enterprises and US corporations can provide opportunities for the development and growth of Polish industrial exports to the United States. This paper has suggested that IC is an evolving, dynamic process of adaptation between the two partners, and that the development of export capability begins even before the partners sign their contract and continues throughout the life of the cooperation.

Five phases of the development process are identified and suggestions are made for planning or implementing export marketing at each stage. To summarize, the first phase of preliminary screening emphasizes the selection of products and technology. Phase two, selection of the prospective partner, stresses planning for export transportation and channels of distribution. The importance of cost-competitive pricing is the focus of the third phase, contract negotiation, in which the parties closely examine their abilities to achieve economies of scale in production and distribution. Phase four, implementation, brings all previous planning into action, but special emphasis is on management of advertising and personal selling. Finally, we come full circle to the fifth phase, review and revision, in which the partners develop control procedures and re-evaluate their basic marketing objectives.

Notes

1. Herbert G. Grubel and Peter J. Lloyd. *Intra-Industry Trade: The Theory and Measurement of International Trade in Differentiated Goods*.
2. *Ibid.*

Bibliography

Business International. *Managing Global Marketing–The Headquarters Perspective.* Geneva: BI, 1978.

Herbert G. Grubel and Peter J. Lloyd. *Intra-Industry Trade: The Theory and Measurement of International Trade in Differentiated Goods.* New York: Wiley-Halstead, 1975.

Gabor Hovanyi. "Marketing Strategy in Socialist Industrial Enterprises," *European Journal of Marketing,* 6: 42-52, Spring 1972.

J. G. Kaikati. "The Reincarnation of Barter Trade as a Marketing Tool," *Journal of Marketing,* 40: 17-24, April 1976.

Warren J. Keegan. *International Marketing: Text and Cases.* New York: Prentice-Hall, 1974.

G. Peter Lauter and Paul M. Dickie. "Multinational Corporations in Eastern European Socialist Economies," *Journal of Marketing,* 39: 40-46, October 1975.

Paul Marer and Joseph C. Miller. "U.S. Participation in East-West Industrial Cooperation Agreements," *Journal of International Business Studies*, 8: 17-27, Fall/Winter 1977.

Juerg Niehans. "Benefits of Multinational Firms for a Small Parent Economy: The Case of Switzerland," in *Multinationals from Small Countries*, edited by Tamir Agmon and C.P. Kindleberger. New York: MIT Press, 1977.

Howard V. Perlmutter. "Emerging East-West Ventures: The Technological Enterprise," *Columbia Journal of World Business*, 4: 39-50, September-October 1969.

Thomas A. Wolf. "New Frontiers in East-West Trade," *European Business*, No. 39, p. 35, Autumn 1973.

David B. Zenoff and Donald L. Caneo. "Formulating Strategy for U.S. Business with Eastern Europe," *Financial Analysts Journal*, 27: 67-80, 91-94, July-August 1971.

Comment

Jerzy Borowski

My position as Professor Miller's discussant is a bit different from those of my Polish colleagues serving as discussants. It will be perhaps the first time that full agreement is reached between East and West on the basis of Professor Miller's contribution to this program.

Professor Miller develops in his paper marketing strategies for effective market penetration. He points out some very important principles, some universal marketing rules, which should be followed by each enterprise seeking to increase exports by means of a cooperation arrangement. The rules he mentions are so universal that it does not matter what firm—Eastern or Western, Polish or American—is in question.

Any cooperation arrangement between two partners should follow the five steps described in Professor Miller's paper:
1. Preliminary screening
2. Selection of prospective partner
3. Contract negotiations
4. Implementation
5. Periodic review.

These steps are correct and useful for everyone. But as J. Robinson stated, "A model which can take into account the whole diversity of real life would have no greater application than a geographical map made in a scale of one to one."

So, fully supporting Professor Miller's view on the marketing process between East and West, let us follow Professor Perlmutter's suggestion to identify critical points in the cooperation process, to move toward greater knowledge and concreteness, and to formulate some solutions.

Three obstacles can affect the marketing process between Polish and American enterprises. These obstacles influence only the initial step mentioned by Professor Miller; namely, preliminary screening. I shall discuss briefly two of them: the nature of socialist and capitalist marketing and product policy in the East and West, and shall develop more precisely the third, marketing research.

1. When discussing marketing problems between Eastern and Western enterprises, one must keep in mind significant differences in the nature of marketing activities on both sides. They originate from the differences in political and economic systems, targets of the enterprise, and consumers' and producers' decision processes.

The theoretical concept of socialist marketing is carefully explored in Professor K. Bialecki's and my book, *Marketing in a Socialist Economy*. It is worth emphasizing that in its decision to cooperate with a Western firm, the Polish enterprise has to learn export marketing to the West, which at present is quite different from domestic marketing and export marketing to socialist countries. These differences originate from product policy, price policy, channel of distribution policy, and communication with the market policy.

Because of the nature of the markets in the East and the West, export marketing to the US is far more sophisticated and more expensive than domestic marketing and export marketing to other socialist countries. Selling to the West often requires much more effort from the producer, without additional benefits, compared with selling to the home market or to another socialist market.

2. There are also significant differences between East and West in the determinants of the selection of products for export specialization. Without going into details, I would only like to mention that Polish product policy has been mainly designed to satisfy domestic needs; to generate hard currency through export specialization has been a secondary motive. By contrast, American corporations view exports as a means to become larger, to expand their operations.

Looking to the future, one can discern certain trends in Poland and in the US which will bring about more convergence between the product policies of Polish and US firms. In Poland, the growing interest in hard currency export specialization stimulates the development of export marketing skills for application in the Western countries, while in the US there is a growing "centralization" in decisionmaking about product specialization. An article in the March 1979 issue of *Fortune* indicated that the share of total US manufacturing assets owned by the 200 largest companies rose from 46 percent in 1947 to 61 percent in 1972. The implication is that fewer and fewer companies are deciding what goods are to be produced and where factories are to be located.

The two factors mentioned above combined with a third, namely, a radical revision of the US antitrust law (toward fewer restrictions on corporate expansion), may favor the joining of Polish and American efforts to create closer economic cooperation. They may, perhaps become additional forces aiding cooperation.

Coming back to the marketing determinants of partner selection, that is, the branch or the product to be involved in IC, I suggest that before sophisticated marketing research is employed, several initial conditions be met:

1. A tendency to satisfy simultaneously domestic needs and the requirements of hard currency export specialization should grow in Poland.

2. The selection should ensure large-scale production.

3. The selection must take into account the product life cycle. For a given product, the phases in the product life cycle in Poland and in the US should not differ significantly.

4. The marketing costs of entry to the US market should be minimized, and the whole marketing activity in a given product market should be as familiar as possible to the Polish partner.

These very preliminary considerations lead me to conclude that capital goods rather than consumer goods have to be the main focus of market penetration through IC by both sides.

Let me now turn to a brief discussion of the problems encountered in obtaining information for market studies. In spite of the considerable recent improvement in the transfer of economic and trade information between Poland and the US, difficulties still exist. These may be classified into two groups: those that affect the enterprises in both countries and those that are more specific to enterprises of one or the other country.

Difficulties encountered by enterprises of both countries in comparability of statistical data

In the first stages of a market study, the enterprise—whether Polish or American—often encounters a problem of the comparability of the available statistical data. In several fields, each of the two economic and social systems uses its own concepts, definitions, and nomenclature for statistics, and precise equivalents for the terms to which enterprises are accustomed may be difficult to find. This applies particularly in such areas as national accounts and foreign trade statistics. While the US generally uses the system of national accounts, Poland has adopted a different approach based on the material product concept. Similarly, for their foreign trade statistics the Western countries have adopted the Standard International Trade Classification (SITC) while the countries of Eastern Europe use the CMEA Standard Foreign Trade Nomenclature.

While countries publish some statistics in conformance with international standards, most of their data is based on national terminology and classification and thus contributes to the problem of incomparability.

Dispersion of information sources

The further a Polish or US enterprise proceeds in its market research, the more it notes the multiplicity, variety, and dispersion of its information sources. The sources are dispersed in two ways. First is the geographical dispersion of information channels (e.g., trade organizations, research institutes, and governmental departments). Second is the dispersion of specific data among a multitude of more or less specialized published and unpublished sources.

In this connection, it is worth emphasizing that it is not so much the volume of market information that is inadequate but rather its quality. Statistical sources are many, varied, and readily available in the US. It is often found, however, that the data they contain are partial and not always consistent. Furthermore, as mentioned above, the principles and presentation of the data may vary. Non-statistical sources are equally numerous and varied (e.g., specialized journals and periodicals, trade and other bulletins). This diversity is both an advantage and a drawback. The advantage is the volume of material available, the drawback is the amount of time and money required to process it, especially if the research is confined to a single product or group of products.

The high cost of research in relation to the volume of trade

Often an enterprise's sales constitute a small share of the market. In many cases the enterprise is entering a new, relatively unfamiliar market implying a high possibility of failure.

To such newcomers, the cost of market research may be high in relation to the short- or medium-term potential in the markets of the prospective trade partner. Only larger enterprises can readily afford such an outlay; small and medium size firms are at a disadvantage.

Difficulties encountered by Polish enterprises in obtaining market data in Western countries

In certain cases, Polish firms' collection in Western countries of information needed for market studies presents no special problem. Examples are data on general economic conditions in the market under consideration, customs duties, and quota regulations.

In some areas, however, Polish enterprises encounter difficulties; for example, in obtaining specific information on the current situation in a particular market, or in finding sufficient data to forecast the development of the market to prepare a medium- and long-term commercial strategy.

In the first case, the main difficulty lies in obtaining information on administrative restrictions on trade (e.g., technical, sanitary, and veterinary requirements, systems of measurement, quality control, safety and environmental protection requirements, and packing regulations). Such information is often scattered widely among sources, some of which may be difficult to consult. Another difficulty facing East European enterprises is inadequate information on any restrictive trade practices of their actual or potential competitors (e.g., state aid which is sometimes available to domestic producers in the form of direct or indirect subsidies and priority in the allocation of government contracts).

For planning their trade strategies, Polish and other East European enterprises can use Western forecasts of overall economic trends or of trends in particular sectors. But these forecasts are usually very general. Moreover, as experience shows, the actual evolution of the economic situation may not tally with the forecast. Eastern enterprises also face uncertainty in planning their trade strategies due to the almost total absence of information on the future plans of major firms whose activities may greatly effect the market trend.

The impossibility of forecasting the future trend of Western countries' economic and trade policies is another major problem encountered by Polish enterprises in preparing their medium- and long-term strategies. Our enterprises cannot ignore the possibility that their products may be affected by Western countries' protectionist measures directed against all countries and those specifically aimed at the countries of Eastern Europe.

Reply

Professor Borowski's exceedingly perceptive comments compel me to concur that full agreement has indeed been reached for the first time between East and West. He has performed a valuable service to the cause of Polish-US IC by pinpointing three obstacles to the process of cooperation and by suggesting ways to overcome these obstacles. The first obstacle refers to systemic differences between East and West, including divergences in the goals of producers and in the decisionmaking processes of both consumers and producers. The second critical point is the contrast between East and West in product policies, especially the selection of products for export. Professor Borowski rightly calls our attention to differences in the past policies of Polish and US corporations, and he makes a suggestion which is not entirely convincing that future policies may be converging toward a mutual interest in export specialization and centralization in product decisions.

Professor Borowski emphasizes the third major obstacle, difficulties encountered by both East and West in trying to obtain market information. Herein lies his most valuable contribution to our discussion. There can be no doubt that the cost of securing market data must be balanced against the benefits of such information, and every major decision in IC, from preliminary screening of product possibilities through partner-enterprise selection, contract negotiations, implementation, and revision, must implicitly or explicitly analyze such information costs and benefits. I should like to argue, however, for the addition of one further principle; namely, that the development of a valuable and continuing market-information base should be considered an investment for the future.

An investment perspective is altogether consistent with our thinking about scientific and technical information, and it has the advantage of turning the focus toward planning for the future. To be sure, the costs of compiling useful market data can be formidable, as Professor Borowski demonstrates. However, these costs are not for the moment or even for the current period. Properly managed, expenditures on market information will generate income for the next several years. Further, the market-data base becomes a cumulatively valuable investment in both numerical and experiential terms. Executives learn progressively more from such a base as they develop it.

Again, let me say that I appreciate Professor Borowski's highly instructive comments. His insights are positive and forward-looking, and I am sure that the process of Polish-US IC will benefit from his timely advice.

Determinants of Polish Exports of Manufactured Products to the West and the Strategy of Industrial Cooperation

Thomas A. Wolf

In recent years East-West industrial cooperation agreements (ICAs) have emerged as an important ingredient of the Polish strategy of economic modernization and increasing penetration of Western export markets. As stressed in the earlier paper by Professor Tabaczynski, maximum benefits from ICAs are likely to come from judicious specialization: the reorientation of Polish production and the structure of Polish exports toward those branches, and within branches toward those products, in which Poland could have a reasonable expectation of worldwide competitiveness.[1] Furthermore, Tabaczynski emphasizes the need to distinguish between *progressive* and *regressive* products, the former being characterized by relatively rapidly growing world demand.

The author is grateful to David Kemme, Richard Steckel and Jerry Thursby for methodological and programming advice. Heinrich Machowski and Jochen Bethkenhagen have also been of great assistance at various stages of the study. All interpretations and any errors or omissions are the sole responsibility of the author.

Professor Tabaczynski also correctly points out that "the process of international specialization should be envisaged in a dynamic way. It means that the specialization pattern for today may become less favorable over the course of time due to the evolution in world demand. It is necessary, therefore, to examine the tendencies and trends in foreign markets and to adjust production to the new requirements." This suggests that the selection of export activities and ICAs should not be based on just an extrapolation of past trends in demand and competitive factors; indeed, ICAs give Poland and other centrally planned economies (CPEs) the potential for escaping from such a mechanical forecasting approach. Nevertheless, future economic trends are unlikely to represent a complete break with the past, and in any event much can usually be learned from putting the present into historical perspective. The basic premise behind this paper is that it may be useful to understand more adequately the primary determinants of past Polish exports to the industrial West. With this understanding, we should be in a better position to answer such questions as: How important are ICAs in expanding exports? What types of ICAs are most likely to enhance export capabilities? To what degree does the need for ICAs differ across industries, or among products within a given industry?

The focus of this paper is on measurable determinants of Polish exports, such as (1) Western commercial policies, (2) secular income elasticity of demand in the West for Polish exports, (3) pricing policy and the response of export quantities to changes in relative export prices, (4) the relative income elasticity of Western demand for Polish products over the trade cycle, and (5) domestic supply constraints. The non-quantifiable aspects, which may in fact be the most important facet of ICAs from the standpoint of the Polish partner, are not explicitly examined in this study. Rather, by focusing on what *is* measurable, this paper delineates various relationships that help to focus further questions regarding the determinants of Polish export performance in specific products.

In Section I the basic design of the empirical study is briefly summarized. Application of this approach to 17 sample Polish export products is discussed in Section II. Some tentative conclusions and implications of these findings, with respect to the Polish export strategy in general and the role for ICAs in particular, are developed in Section III.

I. Basic Approach of the Empirical Study

The basic approach of this paper is to focus on an important sample of industrial products that Poland has had some success exporting to the industrial West. To the extent that such products are carefully selected and are in some sense representative, some generalizations regarding past Polish export performance should be possible, which might be of use to Polish foreign trade planners and managers in making decisions.

Previous studies of East European export performance on Western markets have been either too limited in scope (e.g., focused only on Western commercial policy, such as US granting of MFN tariff status) or too aggregative (e.g., investigations of total CMEA export performance in the West) to be of much use to policymakers.[2] The present project attempts to remedy these deficiencies by examining Polish export performance at the most disaggregated level possible. It focuses on individual products exported to Poland's largest Western market, the Federal Republic of Germany (FRG).[3]*

Because our study is quantitative, we require that the products examined have some "track record," or *history* of exports. This, of course, biases the study toward *past* Polish achievements, and possibly away from relatively new, progressive Polish exports that may be growing rapidly but which are still too insignificant in volume or history to generate a very long data series.

It should also be noted that ideally we would like to have "supply-side" as well as "demand-side" data regarding our sample of Polish exports. By supply-side variables are meant domestic relative prices facing Polish producers, production capacity, output, domestic consumption and exports to other CMEA countries of the specific products covered in the study. Unfortunately, up to now it has not been possible to obtain such data for Poland. Consequently, the econometric results summarized in Section II (and table 4) undoubtedly contain some biases.

Although we had to focus on Polish exports of manufactured products to just one Western country (the FRG), we attempted to select a sample of products as broadly "representative" as possible of Polish exports to the West. Accordingly, we used a list of Poland's "top fifty" four-and-five-digit SITC exports in 1976 to the West.[4] From this we compiled a shorter list of "manufactured product" groups (SITC 5-8). This list is reproduced in table 1, with 1976 Polish exports to the FRG, the Polish share of FRG imports, the FRG rank as a Western market (by Polish export value), and the rank of each product group among all Polish exports, reported for each of 25 product groups. Polish exports of these products to the FRG amounted to $244.7 million in 1976, roughly two-thirds of total Polish SITC 5-8 exports to the FRG in that year.

Because we wanted a list of products for which Poland had a "history" of exports to the FRG and which could be examined using statistical techniques, we used a minimum market-share criterion (i.e., a one percent or more share of 1976 FRG imports). Also for statistical reasons, we wanted to avoid including a product for which exports are inherently lumpy and erratic (e.g., Polish exports of ships). Consequently, Poland's share of the FRG import market had to be equal to or greater than one percent in *both* 1975 and 1976.

The next step was to select that one seven-digit (BTN)[5] product group within each of the remaining four or five-digit SITC groups for which Poland had (a) the largest export value to the FRG in 1976 and (b) a market share of at least one percent in both 1975 and 1976.[6] If criterion (b) could not be satisfied, this seven-digit product group would be rejected and the next largest group, in terms of export value, would be selected and criterion (b) again applied. For each of these product groups, we then had to see if we could generate a consistent series of quarterly observations on import values and quantities for at least five years (i.e., 20 observations).[7]

As a result of this screening process we ended up with 15 7-digit products, ranging across SITC 5-8. We also added two other products about which Polish foreign trade officials had expressed particular interest. The 17 products investigated on this basis in the broader project are indicated in table 2, along with the value of 1976 Polish exports to the FRG and the 1976 Polish market-share for each product. These 17 products accounted for 35 percent of total Polish SITC 5-8 exports to the FRG in 1976. The Polish share of FRG imports in 1976 ranged, for these products, from 2.9 percent for centre lathes to 46.3 percent for cotton bed linens.

Using econometric techniques, the basic thrust of the study is to examine the degree to which variations in Polish market-share (in quantities) over time can be explained by several *measurable* explanatory variables.[8] These variables are (1) relative price, (2) the long-run or "trend" growth of a relevant FRG *activity* variable (income, consumption, or investment spending), (3) cyclical fluctuations of the "seasonally adjusted" value of this activity variable around the trend value, (4) seasonal fluctuations of this variable around its seasonally adjusted value, and (5) a measure of changes in the relative discrimination of FRG commercial policy (tariffs and quotas) against Poland.[9]

We would expect in general that the Polish share of FRG imports would respond positively to a decline in the relative price of Polish exports. Everything else held constant, we also might expect Polish exports to increase, over time, with increases in FRG income (or consumption or investment spending). Whether Polish *market share* increases, however, depends on whether as incomes increase the *relative* non-price attractiveness of Polish products rises. This would depend on style, quality, packaging, and various other marketing considerations. Consequently, the calculated responsiveness of Polish market-share to secular changes in spending is really a summary statement of a number of "qualitative" considerations. Also, to the degree that relative tariff preferences and FRG quota policies change systematically over time (and we are not able to isolate these effects), the calculated "trend" elasticity could also reflect these trade policy changes.

East European observers frequently complain that their producers are only *residual* suppliers of manufactured products to Western markets. The notion is that as spending increases and Western producers run into capacity constraints, imports from Eastern Europe are sought to fill the gap. By the same token, being only residual, East European exports allegedly fall off more rapidly in a period of economic slackening in the West. The result is a market share that rises and falls with the business cycle. This residual-supplier hypothesis takes on a certain plausibility when the combined share of Bulgaria, Czechoslovakia, Hungary, Poland, and Romania in FRG imports is examined over the past two decades. Combined market share increased from 2.3 to 2.4 percent between 1961-65 and 1966-70, at least in part as a consequence of liberalization of FRG import quotas beginning in 1966.[10] Further gains in market-share occurred until the peak year of 1973 (2.9 percent), but the East European share plummeted in the recession years of 1974-75 to 2.5-2.6 percent, a level at which it has since stabilized.[11] If this fluctuation is the consequence of cyclical demand pressures (and possible changes in Western trade policy discrimination related to unemployment pressures domestically), we would expect to be able to isolate statistically for individual product groups a positive relationship between Polish market-share and a ratio of actual to trend income (or spending) values, holding all else constant.

An additional possible explanation of the *residual* supplier effect, at least in the West German case, is the enormous growth since the late 1960s in the reliance of FRG clothing manufacturers on Poland (and other East European countries) for cutting sewing, and trimming services. Indeed, it appears that this particular form of ICA has been the dominant one in terms of the generation of Polish exports to the West. Polish exports to the FRG under this type of agreement amounted to 31 percent of total exports of finished products to that country in 1972, and 24 percent in 1977, compared to only 5 percent in 1967.[12]

In the late 1960s, faced with growing domestic production costs, FRG clothing producers increasingly sought out relatively low-cost ways of extending production lines in a period of booming domestic demand. A natural complementarity of interests existed between these producers and Polish textile enterprises interested in improving their technology and their penetration of the FRG market. In effect the West German producers exported cloth, technology, and know-how to the Polish enterprises; the latter produced the finished garments, which were then exported to the FRG. West German firms paid import duties only on the value-added accruing to the Polish producers. Should FRG producers tend to reduce their reliance on extraterritorial production during a cyclical downturn, as their own production capacities become underutilized, then we would expect the Polish market share in FRG imports of such products to fall in such periods, holding all else constant. (On the other hand, if these particular imports are relatively inexpensive, they could face relatively greater FRG demand in a period of reduced per capita income in the FRG.)

The issue of seasonal fluctuation in market shares, however, presumably has little relevance to long-range export strategy. Yet, if market shares do vary significantly in a seasonal pattern, this might have implications for shorter-range marketing strategies and programs. Given production constraints in domestic industry, seasonal variation in exports could have additional important ramifications.

Finally, we would expect that Polish market share would be negatively correlated with increased degrees of FRG trade policy discrimination, whether tariff or non-tariff. As for tariffs, Poland has been subjected to increased discrimination vis-à-vis the EFTA countries and the three new EC members since 1973, Yugoslavia and other recipients of the Generalized System of Preferences (GSP) since 1971, Spain since 1973, and the Mediterranean and Lomè Convention countries over the past decade.

Because in this study we examine only the Polish share of total FRG imports, there is no way to take into account explicitly this quite complicated evolving pattern of tariff discrimination. As noted earlier, the effects of increasing tariff discrimination may show up in the relationship between Polish market-share and secular income changes.

To the degree that there are still quantitative restrictions (QRs) on FRG imports, the CMEA countries in particular are affected. It is virtually impossible, however, to gauge changing degrees of relative QR discrimination on the basis of published information, at least for those products still subject to quota. For products whose quotas have been eliminated during the period of investigation, the marginal effect of quota abolition on Polish exports may be tested.

II. Statistical Results

Summaries of the statistical results for each of the 17 products are presented in tables 3 and 4. Table 3 shows the distribution, over the past decade, of peak Polish exports (by value), peak Polish market-share, and highest and lowest Polish relative price, as well as an unweighted average relative price for 14 of the product groups. Maximum annual export values were achieved for 13 of the 17 products in the last two years covered by the study, 1976-77. Peak Polish market-share was attained for most of the products between 1974 and 1977, with more than half achieving maximum market-share in 1976-77. "High" and "low" Polish relative prices were more evenly distributed, however, with only a slight positive secular pattern discernible for peak relative prices. Overall, there is little secular trend in unweighted average Polish relative prices, although there is evidence of an upward movement in the relative prices received by Polish exporters of these products in the period of rapidly growing Western demand in the early 1970s. Roughly three-quarters of the 160 annual Polish relative prices calculated for individual products were less than 1.00, and the median relative price was 0.877.

The econometric results are summarized in table 4. Although the degree of "explanatory power" was statistically significant for 16 of the 17 individual estimating equations,[13] only about 50 percent of the variation in Polish market shares was on average "explained" by the various determinants, such as relative price, included in the equations. The most successful regressions, in terms of maximizing overall explanatory power (high R^2), were those for refined copper, wooden chairs, and wooden dining and living room furniture.

One of the most surprising results is the general lack of significance of the relative price variable in explaining changes in Polish market-share. Statistically significant negative constant price elasticities of substitution were found for only six of the products (casein, cotton printed fabric, cotton bed linens, alloyed zinc, chairs, and centre lathes). Five other products yielded negative relative price coefficients, but these were all statistically insignificant at the 20 percent level.

There are several possible explanations for the apparent lack of systematic price sensitivity. First, there is no reason to suppose that all price elasticities should be constant, or even best approximated by a constant elasticity specification. Therefore, the lack of evidence of a negative constant elasticity of substitution does not mean that FRG importers are not sensitive to relative prices. Other specifications should be tested.

Second, regressions for five products run earlier that estimated the price elasticity of substitution between Poland and different subgroups of competitors (e.g., Poland versus EFTA exporters to the FRG) showed in general a higher degree of price elasticity than evidenced in the more aggregated results presented in this paper. For example, table 4 suggests that relative price plays an insignificant role in explaining Polish market share vis-à-vis its competitors on the West German market for absorption refrigerators. Yet, earlier pairwise regressions yielded statistically significant estimates of price elasticities of substitution in the range of -1.99 to -2.73 between Polish and EEC and Hungarian exports of these products. At the same time, there was no evident price sensitivity of Polish market-share vis-à-vis EFTA exporters, who sold a much higher-priced product on the FRG market. When all these competitors were lumped together, for purposes of this study, as the "rest of the world," all evidence of market-share price sensitivity disappeared.

A third factor is the quality of the "price" data utilized in the study. These prices are actually "unit values" calculated from reported value and quantity data on FRG imports. There is reason to believe that for most of our products the degree of homogeneity is high and consequently the effects of changing product mixes on the unit values are minimal. Nevertheless, these prices are the pre-tariff prices paid by the importer, and in general the relative price paid to Polish exporters will be affected by the pattern and degree of *relative* trade policy discrimination. Thus in general one might expect the relative price received by Poland to be deprssed by the tariff preferences in favor of other exporters and by continued discriminatory quantitative restrictions on FRG imports of Polish products. (Six of the products covered in this study are still subject to QRs). That these prices reflect the existence of discriminatory trade policy also severely restricts the degree to which we can interpret the relative price data summarized in table 3.

Fourth, our estimates of price elasticities of substitution are biased by the lack of supply-side data that would have permitted a proper sorting out of supply and demand price elasticities.

Finally, it is possible that for some products none of the above-mentiond problems are important, and that in fact there is very little substitution by FRG importers among competing exporters on the basis of price competitiveness alone. In this connection, it may be noteworthy that the estimated demand elasticities for the two products in our sample most characterized by industrial cooperation, namely men's coats from synthetic fibers and women's and children's woolen coats, were positive (although only the elasticity for the latter product group was statistically significant). This suggests that ICA's, at least in the clothing industrty, may reduce competition between suppliers on the basis of price alone. Obviously more research needs to be done on this subject, however, before any definite conclusions are drawn. (Interestingly, the relative price received by Polish exporters for both of these products increased quite steadily over most of the period studied.)

If we provisionally accept the relative price elasticities reported in table 4, we also can draw a conclusion on Polish pricing policy. Provided several simplifying assumptions are made, one can derive a precise and simple functional relationship between the normal price elasticity of demand facing Polish exporters in the West German market and the estimated relative price elasticity of substitution. Using this relationship, five of the products may be considered to have price elastic demand in the FRG market (casein, cotton printed fabric, cotton bed linens, alloyed zinc, and wooden chairs). This suggests that over some price range Polish hard currency revenues could be increased by reducing prices, although anti-dumping regulations would have an important bearing on the decision to pursue such a strategy.

Turning to the estimated secular activity variable elasticity (column 3, table 4), Polish market-share was positively and statistically significantly related to the trend value for income (consumption, or investment spending) for eight products. In contrast, a statistically significant negative trend elasticity was found for only two products (men's underwear and centre lathes). For the remaining seven products, there was no evidence of a systematic relationship between Polish market-share and the secular growth of the West German economy.

These results are suggestive of a secular increase in Polish competitiveness on the FRG market in roughly half the products examined. The problem in interpretation is that this increase in competitive strength could be caused by increased non-price competitiveness of Polish products (caused, say, by improved quality, packaging, and marketing services), secular relaxation of Polish export supply constraints, FRG trade policy changes over time, or a combination of these factors. In some cases, however, one or two of these determinants can probably be ruled out. For example, the degree of tariff or non-tariff policy discrimination has clearly not changed at all or only negligibly over the past decade for products such as casein, unwrought silver, and refined copper. More intensive study might also suggest that in the case of relatively homogeneous products such as refined copper, changes in non-price competitiveness on the demand side may be of only negligible importance.

Positive relative business-cycle-related elasticities were estimated for only three products (casein, cotton bed linens, and dining and living room furniture), whereas Polish market share was found to be negatively related to cyclical swings in FRG income (consumption, or investment) in five cases. Furthermore, the two clothing products most subject to processing contracts (i.e., clothing ICAs) showed either an insignificant relationship or, in the case of women's and children's woolen coats, a negative elasticity. These results suggest that the conventional wisdom regarding Poland as a "residual supplier" of manufactures to Western markets is perhaps oversimplified. As with the secular elasticity, interpretation of the relative business cycle elasticity is also complicated by the possible changes in FRG trade policy, at least for those products still subject to quotas, over the trade cycle. But even so, the results in table 4 suggest that holding relative prices constant, there is no systematic evidence of Polish market-share varying positively with cyclical movements in West German economic activity.

The estimated effects of removing quotas on Polish market share are perplexing (see column 6, table 4). For the four products for which quotas were eliminated in the period studied, the impact on Polish market share was found to be either negative or insignificantly different from zero. That QR removal has been important in some product categories, however, seems evident from close examination of the timing of development of Polish market shares.[14] Specifically, the Polish share of FRG imports of rolled steel wire increased dramatically after discriminatory quotas were removed (*de facto* liberalization) in 1975; Polish exports of wire tacks and nails materialized only after *de facto* liberalization in 1970; *de facto* liberalization of refined copper imports preceded the initial Polish exports of that commodity in 1968 by two years; only after *de facto* liberalization in 1970 did the Polish market share in dining and living room furniture rise appreciably; and Polish exports of absorption refrigerators to the FRG began in 1967, one year after that product was *de facto* liberalized.[15] This evidence, admittedly not rigorous in an econometric sense, suggests a need to respecify some of the individual estimating equations to incorporate more sophisticated use of dummy variables.

III. Conclusions and Implications for Industrial Cooperation

As noted at the outset, a basic premise of this paper is that a careful examination of past determinants of Polish exports to the West should aid in devising a dynamic Polish export strategy and an appropriate role for East-West IC. Generalizations based on our study must of necessity still be tentative in nature because supply-side data were not available and some alternative econometric specifications must still be attempted.

Nevertheless, we may hazard a few tentative conclusions. A general conclusion is that we should avoid snap, general judgments as to the determinants of Polish hard currency export performance, at least with respect to manufactured products. For example, this study has found no consistent evidence of the "residual supplier" syndrome which many believe to characterize Polish exports to the West. That the overall Polish share of the FRG import market fell steeply from

1973 to 1974-75 and then rebounded sharply in 1976 is not satisfactorily explained by a simple "residual supplier" hypothesis.[16]

Another instance of perhaps unwarranted generalization is the frequent observation that East European export enterprises, and Polish firms in particular, are unable to keep pace with rapid increases in world market prices for their exports, a phenomenon that allegedly contributes to terms of trade problems in periods of rapidly rising world price levels. As indicated in Section II, there is little evidence that Polish enterprises have difficulty keeping pace with world market price increases in their own product lines. In fact, peak Polish relative prices coincide with periods of rapid Western exporter price rises for several of the products examined. (A more comprehensive, econometric investigation of this issue would be possible using the quarterly data generated in this study.)

The degree of price sensitivity varies enormously across the products investigated. Surprisingly, negative and statistically significant price elasticities of substitution were found for only 6 of the 17 products. For the two (clothing) products exported in recent years primarily within the framework of ICAs, the study found a positive relationship between Polish market share and relative price. As noted in Section II, several methodological problems must make one somewhat skeptical of the general lack of evidence of price sensitivity. But to the degree that these problems may not be controlling, the results suggest that non-price factors may be more important in determining Polish competitiveness than is commonly thought, and that ICAs, presumably by upgrading product quality and securing more reliable marketing channels, may enable Polish enterprises to achieve higher relative prices for their exports.

A frequent claim that is somewhat borne out by the evidence in this study, however, is the tendency of Polish export prices to hover in the range of 80-100 percent of the average rest-of-world export prices. This observation naturally and unfortunately tends to reinforce Western prejudices regarding the alleged "dumping" of East European products. It should be pointed out, however, that *someone* has to sell at "below average" prices by definition. This is particularly the case for some of the products considered in this study, for which detailed relative price calculations across exporting regions suggest considerable style or quality differentials. Moreover, most of the products investigated are subject to some degree of relative tariff or non-tariff discrimination when imported from Poland and most other CMEA countries.[17] This means that in general the prices received by Polish exporters may be artificially depressed below non-discriminatory levels. Consequently, one should not conclude simply on the basis of these relative price data that Polish enterprises are dumping on Western markets.

For roughly half of the products investigated, Polish market-share was found to be positively (and statistically significantly) correlated with the secular growth of the West German economy. To the extent that the calculated "relative trend elasticity of demand" is not primarily determined by Polish supply trends and FRG trade policy changes coincident with secular development patterns, this positive correlation suggests a secularly improving Polish position with respect to non-price demand factors for many of the major Polish manufactured product exports. Significantly, none of the products with positive *relative* income elasticities were importantly affected by ICAs. Thus IC should not be seen as the only way to expand market-share in Western markets. On the other hand, of all these products for which Poland had a strong secular trend in market-share independent of price effects, only half (bed linens, rolled steel plates, wooden chairs, and wooden dining and living-room furniture) were subject to more than average growth in West German import demand. One of the hoped for benefits from ICAs is that such arrangements will assist Polish firms in penetrating, in Professor Tabaczynski's words, the more "progressive" product markets rather than relatively slow growing markets.

With future refinement of the econometric analysis, and additional advice and suggestions from Polish colleagues, it is hoped that further and better substantiated insights may emerge from the author's continuing study of the determinants of industrial exports to the West. While saying nothing about what will be the most "progressive" export products in the future, this study hopefully has provided some insights and has led to new questions concerning the best export strategies for Poland and the proper role for industrial cooperation.

TABLE 1

Leading Polish Exports to the Industrialized West, 1976, SITC Divisions 5-8

(1) Number	(2) Product Description	(3) Polish Exports to FRG, 1976 (millions $)	(4) Polish Share of 1976 FRG Imports	(5) FRG Rank as IW* Market	(6) Rank Among all Exports to IW*
735.30	Ships, boats	$20.7	5.6%	3	2
682.12	Refined copper	55.2	9.2	1	5
841.12	Women's outerwear, not knitted	32.9	3.4	1	9
711.5	Internal combustion engines	9.5	2.2	2	10
851.02	Footwear, leather	3.7	0.5	4	12
841.11	Men's outerwear, not knitted	15.6	2.3	1	13
681.11	Unwrought silver	15.8	9.5	1	14
821.09	Furniture and parts	12.8	3.3	2	15
674.11	Iron or steel plates	13.7	4.4	1	19
732.1	Motor cars	8.6	0.3	1	25
561.1	Nitrogenous fertilizers	7.6	6.6	2	26
715.1	Machine tools-metal working	1.4	0.6	6	27
841.44	Outerwear, knitted	7.9	0.7	1	29
656.91	Linens, etc.	2.9	2.3	2	30
841.43	Undergarments, knitted	5.3	1.5	1	32
686.1	Zinc, zinc alloys, unwrought	2.5	2.5	3	35
675.01	Iron or steel loops & strips	2.6	1.7	2	38
821.01	Chairs, other seats	5.2	2.5	1	39
722.1	Electric power machinery	4.0	1.0	1	40
672.71	Iron or steel coils	1.0	0.6	3	42
694.11	Iron or steel nails	1.6	6.6	2	43

712.5	Tractors	0.6	0.6	6	45
673.11	Iron or steel wire	7.7	4.0	1	47
652.29	Other cotton fabrics	2.8	1.1	2	48
599.53	Casein, etc.	3.1	22.4	1	50

SOURCE: Bureau of East-West Trade, US Department of Commerce.

NOTE: Industrialized West = Austria, Belgium, Canada, Denmark, FRG, France, Italy, Japan, Luxembourg, Netherlands, Norway, Sweden, Switzerland, UK, US.

*IW = Industrialized West.

TABLE 2
Seven-Digit Product Groups Investigated

(1) *Statistical* *Number (1976)*	(2) *Product* *Description* (general)	(3) *Polish Exports* *to FRG, 1976* (millions DM)	(4) *Polish Share* *of 1976* *FRG Imports*
3102-300	Potassium nitrate fertilizer	17.0	7.9%
3501-150	Casein	7.8	32.1
5509-660	Printed cotton fabric (130-200 grams)	2.8	3.2
6004-230	Men's cotton underwear	5.3	8.6
6101-492	Men's coats from synthetic fibers	11.6	13.0
6102-410	Women's and children's woolen coats	24.7	12.6
6202-750	Cotton bed linens	2.8	46.3
7105-010	Unwrought silver	31.7	9.3
7310-110	Rolled steel wire	19.4	4.0
7313-220	Rolled steel plates	34.6	4.4
7331-969	Wire tacks, nails	4.1	8.5
7401-300	Refined copper	120.4	8.8
7901-150	Zinc, alloyed	2.6	14.0
9401-410 450 509	Wooden chairs	8.1	8.0
9403-550	Dining, living room furniture	20.6	3.3
8415-150	Absorption refrigerators	1.1	9.4
8445-220	Centre lathes	1.0	2.9

SOURCE: Calculated from *Aussenhandel Reihe 2, Fachserie G* (Wiesbaden: Statistisches Bundesamt, 1976).

TABLE 3
Summary Data on Polish Exports,
Market-Shares, and Relative Prices

Year	Distribution of peak export values	Distribution of peak market-shares (value)	Distribution of peak relative prices	Distribution of low relative prices	Unweighted Polish relative price (14 products)[1]
1977	6	6			.824
1976	7	4	3	2	.847
1975	2	2	1	2	.827
1974	1	3	4	1	.903
1973			3	1	.839
1972		1		2	.828
1971			1	3	.816
1970	1	1	2	2	(2)
1969			1	1	(2)
1968			1		(2)
1967			1	3	(2)
Total Products	17	17	17	17	

SOURCES: Calculated from *Aussenhandel Reihe 2, Fachserie G* (Wiesbaden: Statistisches Bundesamt), various issues.

1. Polish export price relative to rest-of-world export price.
2. Data not available for one or more of the 14 products.

TABLE 4
Econometric Results

Product	(1) Constant	(2) Relative price elasticity	(3) Relative trend elasticity	(4) Relative Konjunktur elasticity	(5) Relative seasonal elasticity	(6) Relative discrimination elasticity	(7) D.W.	(8) R^2
1. Potassium nitrate fertilizer (n=24)				-12.40[d]	-13.93[a]		2.24*	.39[c]
2. Casein (n=44)	-33.91[a]	-1.46[b]	6.24[a]	7.39[c]			1.97	.64[a]
3. Printed cotton fabric (n=22)		-1.73[d]			-3.29[c]		1.43*	.47[c]
4. Men's cotton underwear (n=19)	36.33[c]		-8.20[c]				2.03*	.57[c]
5. Men's coats from synthetic fibers (n=31)	-16.62[e]				-14.79[a]		2.06*	.49[a]

6. Women's woolen coats (n=37)		-1.35[a]		-4.37[e]	2.66[e]		2.29*	.55[a]
7. Cotton bed linens (n=41)	-20.75[a]	-3.49[a]	4.40[a]	5.87[a]	2.45[e]		2.16*	.65[a]
8. Unwrought silver (n=22)	-87.16[a]		16.02[a]				1.98*	.60[a]
9. Rolled steel wire (n=26)	-145.76[b]		52.87[b]	-23.47[c]	-6.03[e]	17.36[d]	2.00	.49[c]
10. Rolled steel plates (n=46)	-13.51[a]		3.40[a]	-2.83[c]			1.65*	.50[a]
11. Wire tacks, nails (n=28)					.81[e]		2.13*	.34[c]
12. Refined copper (n=32)	-21.51[a]		6.63[a]				1.75*	.74[a]
13. Zinc, alloyed (n=22)	-4.15[a]			-9.40[c]		-3.42[d]	2.08	.49[c]
14. Wooden chairs (n=47)	-18.23[c]	-1.40[a]	3.24[d]				2.23*	.80[a]

TABLE 4 *continued*
Econometric Results

	(1)	(2)	(3)	(4)	(5)	(6)	(7)	(8)
Product	*Constant*	*Relative price elasticity*	*Relative trend elasticity*	*Relative Konjunktur elasticity*	*Relative seasonal elasticity*	*Relative discrimination elasticity*	*D.W.*	R^2
15. Wooden dining, living room furniture (n=35)	−14.21[a]		2.44[c]	11.38[b]			1.71*	.76[a]
16. Absorption refrigerators (n=40)							1.83	.06
17. Centre lathes (n=35)		−0.43[c]	−2.61[d]				2.07	.36[a]

Notes: (1) Only statistically significant estimated coefficients are shown in the table.
(2) D.W. = Durbin-Watson statistic. An asterisk (*) beside this statistic means that the equation was estimated using the Cochrane-Orcutt technique for adjusting to serial correlation.
(3) R^2 = Proportion of variation in market-share "explained" by variation in the explanatory variables.
(4) a,b,c,d,e = Statistically significant at the .01, .02, .05, .10 and .20 levels for a two-tailed test, respectively.

APPENDIX

All the equations for which ordinary least squares estimation results are reported in Table 4 are of the form:

$$\log(q_{it}/q_{jt}) = \beta_1 \log a + \beta_2 \log(P_{it}/P_{jt}) + \beta_3 \log y''$$
$$+ \beta_4 \log(y_t'/y_t'') + \beta_5 \log(y_t/y_t')$$
$$+ \beta_6 \log d_t + \log v_t$$

where: (1) q_{it} and q_{jt} are quantity exports (to the FRG) of Poland and the jth exporting country respectively;

(2) P_{it} and P_{jt} are the respective export prices (actually, unit values);

(3) y_t is actual quarterly real income (consumption, or investment);

(4) y_t' is seasonally adjusted income (consumption, or investment);

(5) y_t'' is the calculated trend value for income (consumption, or investment), the fitted value for each period of the equation $y' = b_2 t + u_t$ where t = time;

(6) d_t is a dummy variable designed to pick up the influence of major changes in relative trade policy discrimination;

(7) v_t *and* u_t are disturbance terms;

(8) subscript t refers to period (quarter) t.

Notes

1. See E. Tabaczynski, "East-West Industrial Cooperation and Specialization in Polish Production," in this volume.

2. A survey of earlier studies is found in T.A. Wolf, "Determinants of East European Exports of Manufactured Products to the Industrial West: Methodological Issues and Data Constraints" (Paper presented at the Fourth US-Hungarian Joint Economics Conference, Budapest, November 1978).

3. Ideally, we would like to investigate Polish export performance for individual products on the entire Western market, not just in the FRG. The incompatibility of the statistical nomenclatures and trade policies of the different Western countries, as well as other problems, make such an approach very difficult, if not impossible, at the disaggregated level considered in this study.

4. This list was made available by the Bureau of East-West Trade, US Department of Commerce. SITC=Standard International Trade Classification.

5. BTN=Brussels Tariff Nomenclature.

6. The most disaggregated published FRG trade statistics are at the seven-digit level.

7. Consistency problems are often formidable, because West German statistical authorities have periodically changed the degree of aggregation at which they publish trade data. In addition, every several years there have been nomenclature changes at the six- and seven-digit level.

8. We were unable to use our model to examine variations in the Polish share of the entire FRG market (i.e., including FRG production for domestic consumption). At the very disaggregated level at which this analysis was conducted, the FRG domestic and foreign trade statistical nomenclatures are not compatible.

9. In further work on this project the behavior of Polish market share vis-à-vis each of its main competitors on the FRG market will be analyzed. Because it would be too costly to examine the competitive position of Poland with respect to *each* competing country, countries will be lumped together according to basic changes in FRG trade policy discrimination over time. Thus the eight competing exporting regions are: (1) the five other original European Community member countries; (2) Denmark, Ireland, and

the UK, which joined the EC in 1973 and for which EC tariffs were eliminated in stages between 1973 and 1977; (3) the remaining EFTA countries, for which EC tariffs on most industrial products were abolished by 1977; (4) Spain; (5) Yugoslavia; (6) all other countries qualifying for the EC's Generalized System of Preferences (GSP); (7) the Mediterranean countries, which now receive a considerable degree of preferential treatment under EC commercial policy; (8) the Lome convention associated African and Oceanic countries; and (9) "third" countries, which in general receive no trade policy preferences, consisting of the CMEA countries and other centrally planned economies, the US, Canada, Japan, Taiwan, South Africa, Australia, and New Zealand.

10. See T.A. Wolf, "The Impact of Elimination of West German Quantitative Restrictions on Imports from Centrally Planned Economies," *Weltwirtschaftliches Archiv* 112:2 (1976): 338-58.

11. See Deutsches Institut fuer Wirtschaftsforschung, *Wochenbericht* 12/77 (Berlin, March 24, 1977), and 13/79 (Berlin, March 29, 1979).

12. See Wolf, "Determinants of East European Exports."

13. As evidenced by an "F-statistic" significant at least at the 5 percent level.

14. For the results of a more comprehensive examination of the effects of FRG quota elimination on imports from Eastern Europe, see Wolf, "Elimination of West German Quantitative Restrictions."

15. Because FRG imports from individual countries in a given year are only reported if their value is greater than some minimum level (e.g., DM 15,000 in 1966), it is possible that negligible amounts of Polish exports of the products mentioned in the text actually occurred prior to the year indicated.

16. The Polish share of total FRG imports increased steadily between 1970 and 1973 to 0.85 percent, fell to 0.78-0.79 percent in 1974-75, and then increased in subsequent years to 0.86 percent in 1976, 0.89 percent in 1977, and 0.87 percent in 1978. (Calculated from Deutsches Institut fuer Wirtschaftsforschung, *Wochenbericht,* 12/77 and 13/79.

17. One CMEA member, Romania, has qualified for limited tariff preferences under the EC's Generalized System of Preferences since 1974.

Bibliography

Deutsches Institut fuer Wirtschaftsforschung, *Wochenbericht* 12/77, 24 March 1977, Berlin.

Deutsches Institut fuer Wirtschaftsforschung, *Die Osteinfuhrstruktur der Bundesrepublik Deutschland und anderer westlicher Laender-Eine vergleichende Darstellung* (Berlin, December 1977).

Deutsches Institut fuer Wirtschaftsforschung, *Lange Reihen der vierteljahrlicher volkswirtschaftlichen Gesamtrechnung fuer die Bundesrepublik Deutschland,* Berlin, January 1979.

Deutsches Institut fuer Wirtschaftsforschung, *Wochenbericht* 13/79, 29 March 1979, Berlin.

Statistisches Bundesamt, *Aussenhandel Reihen,* 2 and 3, Fachserie G (various issues), Wiesbaden.

Tabaczynski, E. "East-West Industrial Cooperation and Specialization in Polish Production," this volume.

Wolf, T.A., "The Impact of Elimination of West German Quantitative Restrictions on Imports from Centrally Planned Economies," *Weltwirtschaftliches Archiv* 112(2), 1976, pp. 338-358.

Wolf, T.A., "Determinants of East European Exports of Manufactured Products to the Industrial West: Methodological Issues and Data Constraints," paper presented at the Fourth US-Hungarian Joint Economics Conference, Budapest, November 1978.

Comment

Zygmunt Kossut

Professor Wolf has examined determinants of Polish exports of manufactured products to the developed capitalist countries and the strategy of IC. He suggests "that a careful examination of past determinants of Polish exports to the West should aid in devising a dynamic export strategy and an appropriate role for East-West industrial cooperation." It is very true that *historia est magistra vitae* (history is the great teacher of life); but in economic life, just an extrapolation of past trends in demand and competitive factors should not be the basis of selection of export activities. New requirements appear each time; therefore, export policy should be future-oriented rather than past-oriented. As I understand Professor Wolf's paper, he has accepted this argument. I am of the same opinion.

There are, however, some questions in Professor Wolf's paper concerning both methodology and his conclusions regarding IC.

First, it seems that a separate study of Polish IC with capitalist countries independent of Poland's relations with socialist countries and from home market requirements would lead to very limited conclusions with short-term rather than long-term meaning. If I am right, we have to change the existing approach to the problem of IC studies. The process of IC of a given country cannot be divided into these three parts if we intend to find out what is really going on in the economy as a whole.

Second, I doubt that Polish-West German foreign trade relations are a good example of Polish exports to all the capitalist developed countries. A generalization on the basis of only one country, in this case the Federal Republic of Germany, is rather hazardous.

Third, the question is whether the relatively few groups of goods examined in Professor Wolf's paper can help us to answer the questions: (1) how important are industrial cooperation agreements (ICAs), (2) what types of ICAs are most likely to enhance export capabilities, and (3) to what degree does the need for ICAs differ across industries, or among products within a given industry. The five groups of goods do not represent in any way Polish IC with industrial capitalist countries, and most of these goods have no connection with IC at all.

Fourth, I agree with Professor Wolf that by focusing on what is measurable we are able to delineate various relationships, and this helps us to focus on other questions regarding the determinants of

Polish export performance in specific products. But I also agree with his view of the non-quantifiable aspects, which may be the most important facet of ICAs—and not only from the Polish point of view. Because these aspects are not explicitly examined in Professor Wolf's study, it is difficult to accept or reject the results. We have to be very careful in adapting any result of this study to practical economic or business life until we also examine the non-quantifiable aspects of IC.

I would like to support this viewpoint by referring to the "1979 Policy Declaration of the National Foreign Trade Council, Inc." (issued in November 1978), which discusses the problem of East-West trade (pp. 45-46). The Council stresses, among other things, that:

> Expansion rather than contraction of East-West trade is advisable for many reasons. Expanding, non-discriminating trade helps create an environment of cooperation and reduced tension in which arms control and other vital national objectives can best be achieved. There is a wide gap between current restrictive East-West trade policies of the United States and world trade practices, as all other developed capitalist countries extend MFN and export credits and avoid unilateral export controls in trade relations with the East. Consequently, the United States, standing alone, is at a trading disadvantage. Unilaterally imposed trade barriers and attempts to link trade to non-commercial concessions will continue to result primarily in increased tensions and depressed United States East-West trade levels.

I have cited this part of the Declaration, not because I fully agree with it—for example, there are some non-commercial barriers in other capitalist developed countries—but because it suggests that examination of only measurable determinants of exports is only a first step.

Fifth, pricing policy of Polish exporters is oversimplified in the paper. We receive only aggregated prices of a group of products, and this is not enough for business purposes. To examine the price factor as an element of marketing policy as well as marketing strategy, we need price information about a single product, and even that is not enough. We also need to know about what segment of the market receives our goods, because we have to form prices of a single product on a given segment of the market. We also need information about the life-cycle of a given product. And we must know who is responsible for providing after-sales service, because this is also a basis for establishing price policy.

Finally, there are the very difficult market and monetary conditions surrounding business with developed capitalist countries. Economic crises and crises of the international monetary system make international trade, at least for socialist countries, a very risky business. Poland tries to adapt to these difficult market conditions through her global foreign trade policy. Also for this reason analysis of only Polish-West German foreign trade cannot be the basis for measuring Polish past export performance. I hope Professor Wolf agrees that the most important current economic problems causing market disruption in developed capitalist countries are inflation and an unstable monetary system. When these two problems are dealt with, other problems will be more easily resolved.

Reply

Professor Kossut's comments on my paper are quite helpful, although I do not agree with them in every instance. I am still uncertain how my Polish colleagues view IC as part of the Polish foreign trade strategy. Is IC seen as a driving force of Polish exports to the West in the next 10-25 years? Is it seen as only a peripheral force? I have yet to hear a very concrete description of how they see IC fitting in, in a quantitative sense. Therefore, one of my reasons for looking at the past is simply to ask why Polish exports have behaved the way they have. Specifically, what detrimental factors is IC intended to eliminate, or at least ameliorate? How important were these factors in limiting Polish exports in the past? If we can better understand the past determinants, presumably we can better understand the appropriate role for IC and see it in proper perspective.

I seriously doubt that IC in and of itself is going to solve all problems. It is my understanding that many existing ICAs have not been export-oriented, but have been undertaken to meet increased domestic consumer demand, for example, cooperation in color TV production. Of course there might be an export potential in many of these ICAs, and presumably that is Poland's hope. But I have little sense of what proportion of signed and partially-implemented has led or is expected to lead to expanded exports. So I see my role as helping to place the issue of IC into a larger perspective.

In my paper there is very little that deals with IC *per se*. In examining past determinants of Polish exports to the West it was difficult to find many individual products that have both been important hard currency earners *and* were at least partially the result of IC. The great exception, of course, is clothing, but we all understand that most clothing ICAs are not really "higher forms" of cooperation. When I began this project I hoped that I would find more products with a history of exports that did incorporate IC.

A significant expansion of East-West IC will probably entail greater integration of a number of Polish enterprises within the logistic systems of large Western transnational corporations. While increasing the potential for both eastward and westward technological and product exchanges, this development will also likely result in a greater dependence of Polish enterprises on these Western transnationals. Furthermore, Polish export enterprises, and thus the Polish economy, may become more vulnerable to world market fluctuations, a point discussed briefly at the Bloomington Conference.

Professor Kossut suggested that one of the basic East-West trade problems is the instability of the capitalist world market system. I am fairly confident that fluctuations will continue to characterize this economic system. So the question is, to what degree do IC or specific forms of IC really ensure against this kind of susceptibility to world economic fluctuations? Will IC on balance be stabilizing or destabilizing? This is a complex issue, and I raise it not because I have an answer but because I think it is an implicit and very important question for both Polish firms and their Western counterparts.

I would like to turn now to several of the specific issues raised by Professor Kossut. He made the valid point that one should not artificially separate, for analytical purposes, the three main Polish markets: internal, CMEA, and Western. In my paper I look only at one of these markets, indeed at only one (albeit very large) submarket, the Federal Republic of Germany (FRG). Ideally, I would like to examine interactions among all important markets. If one really wants to understand the determinants of Polish exports of product X or Y, one has to understand fully where it is being produced, to whom it is being sold, what role prices play internally, what the supply constraints are, and so forth. As far as I can determine, it is very difficult, if not impossible, in Poland to obtain this type of data, at least at a reasonably disaggregated level. If more of this information were available, I would gladly integrate it into my study.

I agree that trade with the FRG is not necessarily representative of trade with the industrial West. But the FRG *is* the largest single Western market for Polish products, accounting for approximately one-quarter of Poland's exports to the West. If that market is not representative, which markets are? One of the problems of statistical work in this area is that there are different trade barriers in different countries. Also, in general they classify many products differently or maintain trade data at different levels of aggregation. It would therefore be extremely complicated and expensive to attempt to examine, in detail, Poland's export performance on *many* Western markets for a wide range of products.

The basic criticism of Professor Kossut regarding the "representativeness" of the products examined must still be answered. Given that each is an important Polish export and that together they account for roughly 35 percent of Polish SITC 5-8 exports to the FRG, and given that these products were selected systematically from different major export product groups, they can reasonably be considered "representative" export products. It follows that to generalize to some degree on the basis of this sample is also reasonable.

Professor Kossut correctly stresses the non-quantifiable determinants of Polish exports. Indeed, this is one of the points I emphasize. He also stresses the importance of political factors, whereas my impression is that Polish relations with the United States are free of severe tensions. Thus, I believe there is a fairly solid basis for abstracting from the political environment and focusing on the economic determinants, which is what I have attempted to do in my paper.

Organizational Constraints on Industrial Cooperation

John Garland

This seminar is part of a collaborative research project to assess the problems and prospects for US-Polish industrial cooperation (IC). The point of departure for this paper is that US-Polish IC creates an institutional linkage between two different and partially incompatible economic systems, one market-oriented and the other centrally planned. To alleviate the problems associated with the incompatibilities stemming from systemic differences, organizational adjustments must be made by both sides. Consequently, an assessment of the problems and prospects for US-Polish IC must deal with the interrelationship between organizational structure and strategy.[1]

Conventional theory of organizations tells us that a firm's organizational structure must be congruent with its strategy; in other words, structure follows strategy. Accordingly, when a new strategy such as IC is adopted, an organization must undergo structural adjustments to implement the new strategy. Otherwise, the success of the new endeavor will be limited, and tension and conflict will characterize intra-organizational relations.

Recently, however, organizational literature has called attention to the reverse causation: the effect of existing organizational structure on the choice and implementation of strategy. In some cases, especially in the short run, the strategy of a firm may derive from its struc-

The author is grateful to Professors Paul Marer and Robert Campbell for comments on an earlier draft. Errors of interpretation or fact are the sole responsibility of the author.

ture; that is, the structure of an organization may effectively restrict the strategic options available to the organization. This causal relationship seems particularly plausible in the case of IC, because IC can be considered a dominant strategy neither for the Western nor for the Eastern partners. Instead, it is a substrategy.

Consequently, it is more appropriate to speak of an interrelationship between strategy and structure than to assert that one follows the other. Organizational adjustments must be made to facilitate IC, yet they cannot be easily fitted into existing structures without potentially disrupting an organization's more traditional activities. Thus, there arises the question of congruency of the new strategy with the entrenched organizational structures within each system (West and East). This paper addresses the issue of organizational constraints on the successful growth of IC.

Because of systemic differences, the specific configuration of organizational constraints will be different for the Eastern and Western partners. This paper focuses on the Eastern partner's organization. Still, one should keep in mind that the Western partner operates within organizational constraints just as the Polish partner does.

Because this paper's author is insufficiently familiar with Polish organizational structure, its findings are tentative. The conclusions reached are based on the available literature and on interviews the author conducted in Warsaw during the summer of 1978, in English. Although the language seemed to pose no obstacle to communication in most cases, some misunderstandings were bound to arise. Another limitation of the paper stems from the fact that organizations are continually evolving. For example, the IH-BUMAR case study reveals that IH is still adjusting to a reorganization that has taken at least five years to implement. The organizational structure of many Polish enterprises is similarly in flux. On both sides, the structural evolution is fostered by considerations of which IC is only a small part. Therefore, it is extremely difficult to determine which adjustments are directly related to IC, either as cause or effect. Consequently, the purpose of this paper is to pose questions rather than to supply answers. I hope that stressing the interrelationship between organizational strategy and structure will stimulate further discussion between our teams in efforts to assess IC prospects.

The strategy of IC can only be evaluated properly in terms of its objectives and environmental context. Section I outlines my understanding of the Polish economic environment and the role IC plays in it. Section II describes my perception of the role played by various Polish administrative units in the implementation of IC. Section III explores the interrelationship between strategy and structure in the implementation of IC. A few tentative observations are made in Section IV.

I. The Economic Environment and Objectives of IC

Poland's foreign trade policy is subordinated to several national objectives: modernization of the economy, the fostering of specialization through the international division of labor, the maximization of exports as a means of increasing imports and reducing balance-of-payments pressures, and changing the structure of exports and imports.[2] But these long-term objectives are sometimes thwarted by short-term considerations such as Poland's relatively high indebtedness.

In 1971 the introduction of the crash investment program relying heavily on capital borrowed from the West seemed sound. First, borrowed Western capital would allow simultaneous expansion of consumption and investment, possibly breaking the "vicious cycle" stemming from competition between consumption and investment.[3] Increased consumption was considered a necessary condition of growth because of its motivational role to increase productivity, on which the new strategy was based. Hence the extent to which investment needs could be met from domestic saving along was constrained. Second, Western capital would facilitate the acquisition of Western technology, to modernize the economy, to stimulate manufactures exports, and eventually to service the debt through exports.

Unfortunately, both external and internal environmental conditions have impeded debt reduction. Externally, the economic slow-down in the West has led to reduced demand for East European manufactures, to increased protectionism by Western governments, and to intensified competition on third markets. At the same time, Western inflation and OPEC actions have increased the cost of imports for Poland. Internally, a series of poor harvests in the mid-1970s, a management system that has been slow in changing from a structure more suited for extensive than intensive development, and lack of economic slack have all contributed to a foreign trade performance less than satisfactory. Moreover, various domestic considerations have delayed the coming-on-stream of investment projects involving Western credit and technology. In addition, the high degree of uncertainty at enterprise levels associated with the introduction of new reform measures has partially undermined the ability of the central planners to effectively implement long-term developmental objectives. The urgency of the situation has forced them to focus instead on short-term goals, which have often been in conflict with long-term strategy.

Given the long-term objectives and environmental conditions, IC with Western firms is viewed in Poland as an appropriate and feasible strategy. IC facilitates the transfer, absorption, and diffusion of technology; provides access to Western markets by helping to improve quality and by making available the partner's marketing channels; and encourages specialization in manufactures, which in turn should lead to an improved structure of exports. In short, it has the potential of serving each of the four long-term national objectives of foreign trade.

From my understanding, a new foreign trade code which reportedly emphasizes IC is being hammered out in legislative committees and is of great interest to us.[4] Similarly, the recent announcement of joint venture guidelines merits our attention. At least, it is desirable to determine the extent to which these new codes are compatible with the system of management in general in order to assess accurately the problems and prospects for US-Polish IC.

II. The Role of Various Administrative Units in IC

A. The Central Planning Body

The basic assumption of CPEs is the subordination of the functioning of the economy to the development strategy as reflected in the central plan. Two factors generally determine the allocation of resources: the structure of preferences embodied in the controls and directives emanating from the center, and the reactions of the people making up the management system. In a purely centralized system, preferences of the center prevail, whereas in a purely market-oriented system, the preferences of individual decisionmakers prevail. With regard to the management system, direct orders from the center imply direct allocation; indirect allocation arises when decisionmaking is systematically delegated to lower levels. The Polish system combines elements of central and market-oriented preferences, and simultaneously uses obligatory central directives and indicative instruments of parametric management. The relative importance of central and market-oriented preferences and of direct and parametric instruments varies from industry to industry. Between the center and executive levels (levels of implementation) are various intermediate levels, each having a defined scope of decision maneuvering.[6]

The central planning body's role in IC decisions varies with the specific nature of an ICA. For example, if an ICA involves the construction of new industrial plants or especially large projects, then it is coordinated by the central planning authorities, and the project is incorporated into the medium-term and annual plans. Such investment projects were predominant during the 1971-75 plan. On the other hand, IC may serve to extend and modernize existing facilities. These projects have been predominant during the current (1976-80) planning period; their coordination is left to industrial ministries, industrial unions, or even to large industrial organizations rather than to the central planning authorities.[7] In all cases, however, the annual plans include a list of cooperation-related imports. It is my understanding that the import schedules proposed by the industrial ministries are usually accepted by the center, but that they cannot be amended once the plan has been approved without special permission by the central planning body.

B. The Central and Foreign Trade Banks

The role of the Central and Foreign Trade Banks in the implementation of IC is usually limited to arranging and providing credit and financing. This is a crucial role, because most East-West IC projects initially require substantial convertible currency expenditures by the Eastern partner. For example, to support the IH-BUMAR ICA, BUMAR was provided hard currency funding by the Foreign Trade Bank (Bank Handlowy) and was obligated to repay the loan with proceeds from hard currency export sales of the resulting product. This type of arrangement was very popular during the early 1970s, but IC must now be extraordinarily export-effective to gain such financing, because some ICAs have not lived up to their anticipated potential for hard currency earnings.[8]

One variation of this arrangement is the case in which, because of CMEA specialization arrangements, an FTO is obliged to sell to another CMEA country machinery which it otherwise could sell in the West for hard currency. In some cases, the central bank may treat these exports as hard currency exports. The revenues earned would work to the FTO's advantage by counting toward its hard currency loan repayment.

C. The Ministry of Foreign Trade and Shipping (MFTS)

The role of the MFTS in the implementation of IC is by far the most difficult to ascertain. The widely differing perspectives on the Ministry's role, possibly due to the frequent shifts in policy, leave a great deal of ambiguity as to exactly what authority the MFTS has *de jure* or *de facto* at any given time. Some people perceive that the MFTS in fact has little power other than to establish general foreign trade policy guidelines, within which the FTOs can do fairly much as they please. Others point out that at times the MFTS has been involved directly in negotiations for IC.

The ambiguity over the role of the MFTS may be related to policy shifts, sometimes encouraging decentralization of decisionmaking and at other times moving toward centralization. For example, the reorganization of the foreign trade structure on January 1, 1976, centralized authority by making all FTOs, including those technically attached to industrial ministries, directly responsible to the MFTs.[9] However, less than a year and a half later, a decentralization drive reversed that policy by delegating even more authority than before to the middle and lower levels of the industrial hierarchy.[10]

Ambiguity is also reflected in policies concerning export specialization. At the Bloomington seminar in December 1978, the FTRI team suggested that export specialization be determined by the industrial ministries and the enterprises rather than by the MFTS, whose proper role was to elaborate general rules.[11] But in 1979, according to a report in *Business Eastern Europe*, the thrust of Polish foreign trade policy aimed at implementing the decision *by the MFTS* to narrow the scope of export specialization to about one-third of the branches enjoying export priority in the past (from roughly 17 to 6), focusing on those proven to be internationally competitive.[12]

The ambiguous role of the MFTS in IC is also reflected in the apparently contradictory perspectives regarding its role in granting export and import licenses. Some people say that this is the only direct control that the MFTS has over IC, whereas others contend that the MFTS licensing merely passively confirms financial arrangements already made. The latter stress the MFTS's facilitating role in approving credit and determining foreign exchange rates, taxes, and subsidies.[13] These varying perspectives suggest that the Ministry's role in IC remains highly ambiguous, probably due to the frequent shifts in policy. Its role is difficult to ascertain, which contributes to the uncertainty faced by IC partners.

D. The Ministry of Machine Industry (MMI)

Among industrial ministries, the MMI has made a unique contribution to IC. IC was officially promoted in Poland by a lengthy government act in 1971. From all indications the MMI was one of the driving forces behind IC in Poland. Today, enterprises under the MMI account for approximately 80 percent of Poland's IC turnover. The stage for IC was set within the MMI through (a) structural changes aimed at achieving a better organizational concentration of the industry (by setting up powerful industrial groups well equipped with the technical and economic means of production, and integrating the full cycle of industrial activity within individual economic organizations); and (b) emphasis on technological and qualitative growth, supported by the creation of special bodies (such as the Quality Control and Testing Center). In other words, the industry was both organizationally and technologically prepared for IC at the beginning of the 1970s.

The MMI supports IC in basically three ways. First, it allocates funds to subordinate bodies. This involves the distribution of state funds for investment based on priorities determined at the ministerial level and closely coordinated with the expressed needs of subordinate units. Second, the MMI determines the feasibility of projects proposed by its subordinate units. This is necessary primarily because some proposed IC projects are of very large scale, requiring the MMI to consider other obligations, such as its CMEA-related commitments, in determining the feasibility of the proposed production capacity, the labor requirements, and so on. Third, once feasibility is determined, the MMI coordinates the activities of groups within its own realm and paves the way for implementation by winning the cooperation of groups outside the industry. Such outside groups include, among others, the Ministry of Construction and Building Materials (in the case of new production facilities) and the Ministry of Chemical Industry (which supplies many products for building projects). Such coordination is crucial because these outside groups have their own priorities. The MMI also confers with local people about the infrastructure for new factories, generally leaving to local authorities the decisions pertaining to new plant location.

E. Large Economic Organizations

The 1972 reorganization of the Polish economic structure identified large economic organizations (LEOs) as the fundamental units implementing economic development. Earlier, such LEOs (or unions) were basically administrative rather than economic units, more closely identified with the industrial ministries above them than with the productive enterprises under their jurisdiction. Now they are basically autonomous units, working under the principle of economic accountability. Although directly subordinated to the industrial ministries, LEOs are controlled essentially by economic (indirect) instruments rather than by administrative directives. In general, the LEOs are highly integrated units, which facilitates the tasks of administration and promotes economies of scale.

The internal structure of LEOs varies considerably, depending on, among other things, the specific sector and technology involved as well as on foreign trade propensities. For those LEOs heavily engaged in IC, however, one might typically find a Department of External Cooperation or a Department of Cooperation Imports (both under the Commercial Director) as well as a Main Specialist on Collaboration and Cooperation Abroad (a staff position directly responsible to the General Director). These offices are organizationally separated from the IC activities carried out by foreign trade organizations, which are in some cases subordinated to the LEO's Director of Foreign Trade.

F. Foreign Trade Organizations (FTOs)

On January 1, 1971, a general reform of foreign trade organization in Poland resulted in the transfer of many FTOs from the Ministry of Foreign Trade to relevant industrial ministries. A main objective of the reform was to bring foreign trade activities closer to the producing enterprises. The reform included a change in the incentive system which introduced "prices of realization" partially aimed at increasing the interest of productive enterprises in foreign trade. However, difficulties involving the correct choice of parameters and unfavorable environmental conditions led to a weakening of the new incentive system through the introduction of price equalization subsidies and taxes on exports and imports, "to compensate the economic organizations for the differences between the domestic and foreign trade prices, or to eliminate extra benefits resulting from these differences."[14]

It is at the level of the FTO that IC has apparently had the greatest effect on organizational structure. A typical departmentalization of an FTO finds four offices or divisions: one for exports to capitalist countries; one for IC with and imports from capitalist countries; a third for exports, imports, and IC with socialist countries; and a fourth for technical service. The division for IC with and imports from capitalist countries contains departments for IC with and imports of specific product lines. Thus, an FTO's IC-related departmentalization often extends even to the types of machinery involved, with coordination at the division level.

What is not so obvious, and will be discussed in the following section, is the reverse direction of influence—through which the existing structure affects the implementation of IC.

IV. Strategy and Structure

This section focuses on certain organizational constraints under which IC has been implemented. Some of those constraints have been overcome, at least partially, through structural adjustments. In such cases, we can refer to the influence of strategy on structure.[15] Other constraints remain firmly entrenched in the organization, so that the dominant direction of influence is reversed. To illustrate this interplay of strategy and structure, let us consider five characteristics of bureaucratic organizations.

1. The *departmental separation of functions,* characteristic of all bureaucratic organizations, is generally aimed at increasing the efficiency, effectiveness, and control of organizational activities. It is based on task differentiation and involves a hierarchical delegation of specific responsibilities to individual offices. But departmentalization can be functional or dysfunctional in regard to IC, depending on

whether or not IC was the main determinant of such departmentalization.

For example, in 1974 one FTO established a special department to deal solely with Western IC partners. This department handles all contractual matters, all direct sales and purchase transactions between the FTO and Western IC partners, and all new negotiations for IC. It also coordinates all joint sales and service activities in third markets. The prime objective of this organizational change was to improve effectiveness in dealing with IC partners. In 1979 another organizational adjustment was under discussion: the probable establishment of the FTO's own company in the US to support its IC activities with American firms.[16]

Closer scrutiny of an FTO's organizational structure suggests certain dysfunctional aspects of its departmentalization regarding IC. For example, the organizational structure suggests that IC is identified more closely with imports from capitalist countries than with exports to those countries. The stronger identification of IC with imports than with exports makes good sense from an organizational perspective if one considers that the basic flow of technology transfer under IC so far has been from West to East. In the long run, however, if a more balanced flow is to be implemented, it might make sense to link IC more directly to the Export Office, or perhaps to combine the entire Office for Exports to Capitalist Countries with the Office for IC and Imports from Capitalist Countries. Many people in Poland are disappointed in IC turnover with the West, and hard currency exports are being given high priority. At least part of the problem might be in the organizational structure, which is more suited to the earlier strategy of technology acquisition than to the current strategic emphasis on exporting to Western markets.

A more difficult dilemma is posed by the existence of a separate Office for Exports, Imports, and IC with Socialist Countries. Given the different nature of Poland's trading relationships with socialist and capitalist countries (plan vs. market orientation), such compartmentalization may be necessary. On the other hand, as I understand it, one of the main motives for Polish IC with the West is to enhance Poland's specialization role within the CMEA; to do this effectively may require closer coordination between IC with the West and exports to the CMEA. As in the problem of identifying IC with imports from capitalist countries, I do not mean to suggest the direction of adjustments that should be made. Rather, my intent is merely to suggest that strategy and structure are interrelated, and that departmentalization necessary for efficient operations causes subsequent problems of coordination and integration.

2. A *bifurcation of interests* inevitably arises in any large organiza-

tion, because what is best for the organization is not necessarily advantageous to all of its individual units. A vertical bifurcation of interests is found when the objective of lower level administrators conflicts with steps taken to achieve higher objectives. A horizontal bifurcation of interests occurs when units at the same level compete for scarce resources allocated from above. For example, one ICA involves at least three industrial enterprises outside the union that implements the agreement. Their interests may not be represented by the FTO as well as those of units subordinated to the union. The FTO must find it easier to deal with units subordinated to its own ministry than with units subordinated to other ministries.

The vertical bifurcation of interests between organizations at different hierarchical levels is far more obvious. The MMI, basically an administrative body, is in a particularly anomalous position. It represents the interests of its subordinate bodies while being responsible for implementing plans, such as hard currency allocations, given to it by higher organs. But IC projects proposed by its subordinate enterprises or FTOs often involve extensive technology imports from the West, placing strains on the Ministry's hard currency allocation. Reportedly, the MMI has often had to reduce the scale of proposed projects by allocating less investment funds than requested by the initiating units, whose projected pay-back capabilities are sometimes considered unrealistic. The reduced scale of IC projects, on the other hand, may hinder a firm's hard currency earning potential and thus exacerbate the very problem it intends to avoid. The MMI must meet its own financial plan indices, and overly optimistic investments resulting in less than anticipated returns might cause a reduction in the Ministry's budget in subsequent years. For these reasons, the MMI's role in fostering IC has not always been fully appreciated by its subordinate units.

There seems to be less conflict of interest between unions and their subordinate bodies, perhaps because of the nature of those links. Although unions have hierarchical authority over their sub-units, it is probably an error to view such links primarily in terms of administrative authority. Instead, economic power (through the instruments of wages, bonuses, other funds, and so on) apparently gives unions most of their control over subordinate units. The principle of economic accountability and the use of parametric instruments of management possibly result in closer goal congruence than would relationships basically administrative in nature. The links between FTOs and the productive enterprises for whom they serve as agents are similarly based on economic rather than administrative criteria.

3. *Growth pressures* are inherent in all large organizations. The problems stemming from such pressures are quite noticeable in a

country such as Poland, whose remarkable post-war industrial growth rate has necessitated continual organizational adjustments. They are also particularly apparent in certain branches, where strong domestic demand pressures are coupled with pressures to export to the CMEA and to hard currency markets.

Some FTOs face problems stemming from rapid growth. Since 1971 the number of employees in one FTO has quintupled, increasing from approximately 100 to over 500. The FTO now exports to more than 50 countries and has sales outlets and service stations in about 30 countries. But having representatives in 30 countries when exports are going to 50 is hardly sufficient in its specific sector, in which after-sales service and the availability of spare parts are crucial. IC has provided an alternative strategy to the possible concentration of sales in selected markets to alleviate the pressures exerted by such rapid growth. IC can provide the Polish partner with the choice of using the sales outlets and service networks of a Western partner. Such marketing arrangements, typical of many ICAs, not only relieve growth pressures, but also make it easier to enter Western markets.

In the present context, however, the main point is that the scarcity of foreign sales outlets and service stations, since they have not grown in proportion to the growth of export activities of the FTO has limited the strategic options available to the Polish partner. In other words, structure has constrained strategy. To be sure, the constraint has enhanced the attractiveness of IC, which, in effect, has made the partner's marketing arm part of the Polish organizational structure. The other side of the coin, of course, is that this constraint also partially dictates the terms under which IC can be mutually most advantageous under present conditions.

A more concrete example of how growth pressures have impeded the implementation of IC can be found at the level of the manufacturing enterprise. As mentioned in the case study (pp. 000), one Polish organization had to forego the opportunity, perhaps only temporarily, to become a source of front-end loader components for the IH subsidiary in Heidelberg, apparently because the manufacturing enterprise simply had too many other commitments.

4. *Integration and coordination* of activities are made necessary by the departmentalization and task differentiation referred to earlier. The problems of integration and coordination are made more difficult when various administrative, trade, and producing organizations are involved in the same project. The problems become more acute when bifurcation of interests emerges, and inter- as well as intraorganizational communications channels become crucial. In this paper, we will simplify the illustration by focusing on intra-organizational coordination at the level of the producing enterprise.

Primarily because the producing enterprise is such a vast industrial organization, its executive managers are not responsible for any specific manufacturing program. Instead, the sales director oversees all sales, the director of manufacturing oversees all manufacturing, and so on. Sometimes this adversely affects the implementation of IC, because no one is in charge of all activities related to specific agreements. For example, it would be desirable to improve intra-plant coordination (such as materials handling procedures and production scheduling) as well as coordination with satellite plants and other domestic suppliers, in view of the quality requirements stipulated in many ICAs.

5. *Uncertainty* plagues all bureaucratic organizations, which is exacerbated somewhat in Poland, where the leaders are trying to find a proper balance between the use of administrative and economic directives. Until that balance is found, there is a strong possibility that dysfunctional behavior will emerge. For example, under conditions of uncertainty, it is perhaps natural for any management, in the East or West, to assume greater central control. However, it is the consensus of organizational theorists in the West that such a move is the least effective response, because uncertainty calls for greater flexibility, particularly at lower levels.

Two sources of uncertainty are an organization's inability to control its environment and its inability to foresee all of the consequences of its actions. Both have important implications for those who have to justify IC to their superiors or to outside organizations. The benefits of IC must more than compensate for the adverse economic, social, political, and organizational consequences involved or believed to be involved. To illustrate this from the point of view of a Western partner, IH's Pay Line Group continually has to justify its ICA with BUMAR not only to the IH hierarchy, but also to the US government (in which there are still pressures to restrict the transfer of technology to socialist countries), to its own stockholders (although this has become less of an issue than when the ICA was first negotiated), and to organized labor (which suspects, probably wrongly, that IC destroys rather than creates jobs in the US).

V. Concluding Remarks

This paper has focused on the interrelationship of strategy and structure and its implications for the successful implementation of IC, which is viewed as an appropriate strategy for achieving Poland's long-term economic objectives. After focusing on the organizational structure through which IC is implemented, we discussed five organizational constraints on the successful growth of IC. The first constraint is a departmental separation of functions (differentiation), which is necessary to increase the efficiency and effectiveness of organizations. But this differentiation creates two new constraints: the subsequent need for inter-departmental integration and coordination of activities, and the bifurcation of interests among the various departments. Constraints also arise from pressures associated with rapid growth and uncertainty.

The interrelationship between strategy and structure is highly complex. In each of the areas discussed, there has been a bi-directional influence rather than an overwhelming dominance of strategy over structure or of structure over strategy. To be sure, structural adjustments had to be made to accommodate the strategy. But, as stressed at the beginning of this paper, IC is a sub-strategy, so that even under the best conditions, organizational adjustments that would be favorable for IC might in fact be detrimental from the perspective of the organization as a whole. Without taking into consideration such potentially negative effects, we would have a case of the tail wagging the dog; that is, structural adjustments favorable for IC might induce suboptimization, which would have a negative impact on an organization's ability to achieve its primary goals. It is not surprising, therefore, that strategy also has often had to accommodate structure.

The point is that the effects of IC reach far beyond the individual implementing unit. This suggests that organizational changes to accommodate IC on the Polish (as well as US) side should be made gradually rather than comprehensively and all at once. In no way should these remarks be interpreted to mean that organizational adjustments should not be made in connection with IC. Unless such adjustments are made by both partners, the full potential of IC will never be realized. On the other hand, it would be as great a mistake to undertake adjustments without considering their full impact on the rest of the organization. Rash or unconsidered actions might create a backlash that could significantly undermine the substantial progress already made.

Notes

1. Structure refers to the organizational design and lines of authority (both formal and informal) through which an enterprise is administered. Strategy refers to the courses of action chosen as the means for achieving the enterprise's long-term goals and objectives.

2. See Kossut's analysis on p. 109.

3. Zbigniew M. Fallenbuchl, "The Polish Economy in the 1970's," *East European Economies Post-Helsinki* (Washington, D.C.: Government Printing Office, 1977), p. 822.

4. "Poland to Update FT Code: Cooperation No Panacea," *Business Eastern Europe* (February 2, 1979), pp. 33-34.

5. The term "bureaucratic" is understood in this paper in a strictly neutral sense, as

reflected in the pioneering works of Max Weber. It is not meant to connote a necessarily inefficient administration.

6. Witold Trzeciakowski, *Indirect Management In a Centrally Planned Economy* (Warsaw: Polish Scientific Publishers, 1978).

7. See Zagorski's paper and reply, pp. 121-139.

8. See Szumski, p. 159.

9. "Poland Launches New Foreign Trade Setup," *Eastern Europe Report* (January 30, 1976), pp. 27, 32.

10. "Poland Reinstates Reform Decentralizing Industry," *Business Eastern Europe* (May 13, 1977), pp. 145-47.

11. See, for example, Giezgala, p. 87; Zagorski, p. 121; Tabaczynski, p. 98.

12. "Poland to Update FT Code," p. 34.

13. It is my understanding that the MFTS has a list of all foreign technology that has been bought by Polish enterprises, and permits no purchase duplication whatsoever. The decision to buy is generally made by a committee composed of representatives of the MFTS, The Ministry of Science and Technology, and the industrial ministry involved.

Specific instances of MFTS influence on IC include the following:

> The MFTS has been known to pave the way for IC not only through its concluding of broad agreements with foreign representatives, but also through its organizing meetings with Polish industrial ministries and FTOs in order to encourage IC.
>
> The MFTS has directed activities to specific countries by "reasoning" with industrial ministers (at the highest levels), suggesting that a comparable technology is available elsewhere (say Finland instead of West Germany); such cases are rare and generally aimed at improving bilateral balances.
>
> An extension of the Fiat agreement involved the licensing of a new engine from Italy to facilitate Fiat exports from Poland. Although the industrial ministry had exhausted all of its funds for the project, the MFTS went to bat for the ministry and helped arrange credit by convincing both the Foreign Trade Bank and the Ministry of Finance that the project was sound because it fostered exports. Another example of the MFTS helping to arrange credit was in the case of hotel construction not then included in the central plan.
>
> The MFTS played a decisive role, I understand, in the Massey-Ferguson (M-F) agreement, which is a coproduction agreement for tractors in the agricultural sector. When M-F wanted merely to sell a license, the MFTS insisted on a buyback type arrangement. The MFTS allegedly won the support of both the relevant Polish industrial union, which felt that the deal would fall through without the export rights, and the British bankers, who were financing much of the agreement and saw guaranteed Polish exports as their best security for getting their loans repaid.

14. Fallenbuchl, "The Polish Economy," p. 842.

15. This is an oversimplification. Although some structural adjustments have been made explicitly to facilitate IC, in other cases IC has been facilitated by adjustments made independently of IC, so that the effects were coincidental or unintended.

16. See Giezgala, p. 87. FTOs offer perhaps the best examples (in regard to IC) of strategy influencing structure, but they are not the only examples. One productive enterprise established a separate office in Warsaw in 1973 specifically to coordinate the IC-related processes of technology transfer and absorption, personnel training, procurement of financing, and development of Polish suppliers who source various components.

Comment

Bronislaw Wojciechowski

The forms of organization and the partners' mutual understanding of these are among the most important factors of economic cooperation between countries of different economic systems. This is particularly obvious in the case of industrial cooperation (IC), which requires lasting ties between the partners.

It is, however, very difficult to discuss organizational forms independently of the economic mechanisms functioning in a given country. This aspect is appreciated by Mr. Garland in his valuable work on organizational barriers in the development of IC. However, it calls for a more detailed analysis.

It is to a certain degree understandable that our Western colleagues are more interested in the question of who makes what decisions in Poland on trade and IC than how the decisionmakers are motivated. For an economist, however, this latter question is essential particularly when he is looking for optimal solutions. I would like to add a few remarks to Mr. Garland's interesting statements.

The organizational changes made in Polish foreign trade at the beginning of the 1970s and in subsequent years were closely connected with simultaneous changes in economic mechanisms. As a result of these changes, organizations and enterprises gained more freedom in decisionmaking. At the same time, it became necessary to supply them with relevant criteria that would ensure the compatibility of their decisions with the interests of the national economy. It was also necessary to create incentives encouraging such decisions.

The new system of settlements in foreign trade was of basic significance in this respect. This system linked foreign prices charged by suppliers and received from foreign buyers with the performance of participating enterprises. In this way, foreign prices began to directly influence the financial results and economic effectiveness of producers, constituting a fundamental break with the earlier period in which settlements with producers of exports and users of imports were made autonomically at internal prices only. Under this old system, producers were completely isolated from the conditions of the world market, and the whole price risk had to be borne by the state budget. Now, it is borne mostly by the producer, a very important factor for decisionmaking in economic cooperation.

The changes introduced in the 1970s put an end to both the organizational and the economic isolation of Polish producers from the world market. They formed an important element of overall systemic changes, the best known of which was the formation of large economic organizations (LEOs).

As a result of the decentralization of the foreign trade apparatus, the majority of foreign trade enterprises (more than 60 percent), previously subordinated directly to the Ministry of Foreign Trade and Shipping, were assigned to industrial organizations or, in some cases, subordinated to industrial ministries. At the same time, the number of such enterprises greatly increased. But in spite of all these changes in organization and economic system, the role of the central level is still considerable in Poland, including in the sphere of international IC. It should, however, be stressed that this role is more promotional than restrictive.

I would like to emphasize the role of the Ministry of Foreign Trade and Shipping. The main task of this Ministry is to determine geographical trade policy and, to a much lesser extent, commodity trade policy. It must be stressed that the foreign trade plans in Poland do not specify tasks according to countries and, consequently, are not a tool of geographical policy, except in allocating trade to the ruble and dollar areas.

The main tools of trade policy are the instruments of monetary and credit policy, as well as the economic instruments and parameters of the financial system. There is also export and import licensing in Poland, but its role as a tool of trade policy by now is rather limited.

The problems of marketing—particularly the establishment of trade networks abroad and coordination of cooperational ventures surpassing the domain of a single economic organization—constitute another important concern of the Ministry of Foreign Trade and Shipping. Obviously, being responsible for economic cooperation with other countries, the Ministry is interested in promoting all forms of cooperation, particularly IC with producers in other countries. Export promotion is one of its basic spheres of interest. However, this Ministry has no direct influence on the decisions made by the LEOs, particularly in the sphere of IC with other countries.

The organizational and economic changes in Polish foreign trade and in the whole Polish economy were not introduced, as Mr. Garland rightly remarks, specifically from the point of view of IC. Nevertheless, this aspect was considered and the changes effected were, it seems, in full accordance with the needs of IC and contributed to its growth.

There are both advantages and disadvantages in bilateral IC with foreign producers. An advantage is the domestic producer's guaranteed access to advanced technology and, usually, to foreign markets. On the other hand, the same producer's independence in his market activities is limited, and he is made largely dependent on the foreign partner in this respect. Fully aware of these consequences, Poland decided to develop IC under the assumption that at the present stage, benefits exceed negative effects (provided reasonable prices and terms of cooperation are secured).

Mr. Garland emphasizes the positive role of industrial ministries, especially the Ministry of Machine (Engineering) Industry, in the development of IC between Poland and the US. This opinion is no doubt justified. However, I must state that among Polish economists the role and functions of industrial ministries in the field of economic cooperation are still a matter of dispute. The concept of the LEO, as the center of economic decisions within the plan, foresaw the narrowing of the role of economic ministries. In fact, these assumptions have not proven correct. The strong position of economic ministries follows from their responsibility for the fulfillment of foreign trade plans and from their having at their disposal substantial technical and material means as well as the possibilities of influencing the financial results of LEOs. I might also add that large Western corporations frequently consider the industrial ministries the most convenient partners in starting economic cooperation with Polish producers.

This does not mean that the role of LEOs should diminish, particularly in the field of IC. Yet their position depends, in my opinion, not only on their legal status, but even more on their economic efficiency and on the nature of the branch in which they function. I believe that the importance of LEOs, which embrace a compact and internally linked scope of activities, particularly in organizations of vertical branch arrangement, will be strengthened. The great advantage of such an organization is improved internal coordination. On the other hand, LEOs of a horizontal nature, associating enterprises that are neither economically nor technologically linked are not likely to become strong and inevitably will tend to become administrative organs. Large combines or enterprises, subordinated to organizations of this type, will seek greater independence, particularly in such matters as IC.

In this connection, some remarks should be made on the so-called export-specialized branches. Mr. Garland over-estimates the importance of this matter when commenting on the alleged reduction of the number of branches specializing in export from Poland. Export specialization on the branch level does not play a fundamental role in Poland's economic strategy.

It is not so much the branch, but a narrow group of products or interdependent activities (which usually corresponds to the activity of a large combine) that constitutes the basic level in the process of export specialization. As of a few years ago, there are no regulations in effect in Poland that give special treatment to branches or enterprises specializing in export. Export specialization is promoted mainly through a concentration of outlays on modern technology in branches having particular importance for technical progress and promising the best prospects for export expansions.

The number of preferentially treated branches must necessarily change depending on many circumstances, but this has nothing to do with changes in the methods of economic management. On the other hand, the question of restoring the previous category of enterprises and combines specializing in export and enjoying certain facilities for this reason is now being discussed but no decisions have been made so far.

Export-oriented specialization is not the only problem requiring a solution and being discussed now in Poland. As Mr. Garland correctly observes, systemic changes in Polish foreign trade are of a continuous character. Nobody expects to create a system solving all of the difficulties. Nor is there a tendency to make quick changes. Rather, step-by-step actions aimed at gradual improvement of the organizational and economic system are foreseen.

Information on the so-called "new foreign trade code" should be assessed in this context. Mainly involved is the question of systematizing the existing legislation and providing certain supplements to the regulations already in force. Recently, for instance, regulations concerning the creation in Poland of companies with foreign shares were issued.* Much attention is also given to improving IC. It is essential for Poland that the development of cooperation contribute not only to the transfer of advanced technology, but also to the stimulation of exports. IC with the West can develop successfully only if it is a "two-way" business, promoting not only imports but also exports from Poland. I am convinced that this requirement, though not always convenient for our Western partners, does not constitute a basic obstacle to business that is profitable for both sides. This assumption is supported by the experiences of several cooperation ventures between Polish and American producers. There are many possibilities for developing both bilateral and multilateral cooperation, for undertaking joint ventures on third markets, and for facilitating and promoting trade through other types of ventures.

The further development of IC is likely to require some systemic and organizational changes in Poland. It may prove beneficial to depart from some routine procedures and give relevant authorization in this domain to those economic organizations, combines, or

*Resolution No. 24 by the Council of Ministers of February 7, 1979, *Monitor Polski 1979*, no. 4.

enterprises that will prove most competent and most interested in developing economic cooperation, regardless of their formal subordination.

On the Western side, however, some adjustments in the organization of cooperating partners are desirable, particularly those that would facilitate the reciprocity of cooperation agreements and the opening up of Western markets to Polish industrial products.

Reply

Professor Wojciechowski has made a valuable contribution by emphasizing the role and nature of economic mechanisms, which in his opinion are inseparable from the strategic and structural dimensions of organizations and are essential to the successful implementation of industrial cooperation (IC). To support his argument, he stresses the systemic changes made in Poland during the 1970s, which involved the simultaneous introduction of organizational changes and changes in the economic mechanisms. His argument is supported further by his clarification of the role of various administrative units in regard to IC. I am in agreement with the general thrust of his comments and appreciate the candor with which they are made.

Professor Wojciechowski's emphasis on economic mechanisms adds a new and crucial dimension to the analysis suggested in my paper, in which five organizational constraints on the successful growth of IC were discussed. These constraints are characteristic of all bureaucratic organizations, such as Western multinational firms or Polish administrative units and enterprises. They are inherent in the bureaucratic structure, and thus exist regardless of the nature or role of economic mechanisms.

Professor Wojciechowski is quite right in viewing economic mechanisms as an essential dimension of organizational structure. The mechanisms were introduced, we are told, in order to ensure the compatibility of decisionmaking at lower levels with the interests of the national economy as a whole. Consequently, they may be viewed as an indirect means of control over the large economic organizations (LEOs), which have become, at least theoretically, the centers of decisionmaking within the centrally determined plans. In other words, although the economic mechanisms make it possible to reduce the number of obligatory, administrative directives, one can view the mechanisms themselves as structural constraints on the relevant organizations.

If one accepts the notion that economic mechanisms represent an indirect constraint on organizations, several questions may be raised.

If the economic mechanisms are the proper ones, most economists would consider them more efficient than administrative directives. This is primarily because reliance on indirect economic and financial levers considerably reduces the two-way flow of information required for controlling and monitoring performance. But during the transitional stage, during which much experimentation takes place to determine the proper balance between direct and indirect control mechanisms, efficiency might suffer. For example, in some cases quantitative foreign trade directives (obligatory) have been replaced by directives determining the balance of trade for given units (indicative). However, this is not necessarily an efficient arrangement, because imports for other users as well as for the enterprise's own needs are not necessarily related to the export capacity of a given producing unit.[1]

Poland was one of the first socialist countries to introduce the system of indicative control in exports on a macro-economic scale.[2] It is a notable achievement, and one which, in the long run, has great potential. During the present transitional stage, however, there must be a great deal of uncertainty and ambiguity for those units engaged in foreign trade, as managers are unsure of the nature of the next incremental changes. Uncertainty itself creates a constraint on the implementation of IC, particularly in view of the long-term commitments that IC requires. Nevertheless, the direction of the changes stressed by Professor Wojciechowski is encouraging. What remains to be seen is the extent of commitment to those changes.

---

1. See Witold Trzeciakowski, *Indirect Management in a Centrally Planned Economy* (Warsaw: Polish Scientific Publishers, 1978), pp. 207-209, for this and other reasons why the linking of imports to exports for given units is a questionable practice.
    2. *Ibid.*, p. 203.

Summary of the Discussion

The Editors

After presentation of the papers by the US team, formal comments by the Polish team and replies, a general discussion followed, involving members of the two teams as well as interested participants at large. The record of discussion that follows this summary is an abbreviated one. The participants' remarks were summarized by the editors, unless reported as direct quotes. We attempted to give an expression to the major ideas and differed points of view at the conference, even when it was not possible to cite all speakers by name.

On some technical and legal questions put to the American team which the editors felt were of wide general interest to readers in Poland and the US, we made it possible for the respondent to develop the answer for this written record in greater detail than the response given orally at the conference. We have also inserted into this summary of the discussion the highlights of a few important developments during 1980 regarding the "Polish golf car" case, which is about a lengthy and controversial investigation of alleged dumping by Poland in the US.

The discussion took place in three sessions. Session I was devoted to specific questions that arose after the papers and the discussant's comments were presented. Session II focused on some broader issues of US-Polish industrial cooperation (IC), dealing with such topics as (1) alternative approaches to the study of the IC phenomena; (2) the International Harvester (IH)-BUMAR case study and the general conclusions that can be drawn from the detailed case studies of US-Polish IC; and (3) the environmental factors that impact on IC. By environmental factors one understands those forces outside the im-

mediate control of firms which can have an important influence on the willingness of firms to participate in IC and on the outcome of the endeavors of the cooperating partners. Session III was devoted to the legal, political, and practical aspects of import protectionism in the US and their implications for Polish exports, which could be simple exports or exports resulting from ICAs between Polish and US firms. The Conference sessions were chaired by Eugeniusz Tabaczynski and Janusz Kaczurba, respectively.

* * *

The discussion in the first session was opened with some methodological questions on the papers presented by the US team. *Jan Sulmicki,* focusing on the paper by Perlmutter, noted that the author has compiled 22 forces that favor and 11 forces that hinder East-West industrial cooperation (IC). With respect to Western firms' IC with Poland only, *Perlmutter* has enumerated many more stimulating than hampering forces. The questioner wondered whether to attach any quantitative significance to the number of supporting and restraining factors listed.

Howard Perlmutter replied that no quantitative significance should be attached to the precise number of deriving and restraining forces he compiled; his intent was, primarily, to identify the most important factors that tend to create difficulties for IC in order to focus our attention on the efforts needed to overcome them.

Zygmunt Kossut sought clarification on the role of transfer prices in transactions between the headquarters and the foreign affiliates of a multinational corporation (MNC); are transfer prices typically used to maximize the profits of the corporation's individual affiliates or that of the corporation as a whole? In his view, that latter is typically the case.

Paul Marer replied that in some circumstances transfer prices are difficult to set objectively because no comparable independent, so-called "arms length" transaction prices exists. But, speaking of transfer prices more generally, *Marer* noted that as a rule there are strong pressures to set infra-firm prices as close as possible to independent "arms length" prices. The main reason is the need by the top managers of a corporation to have a realistic basis for assessing the performance of each of the affiliates. If transfer prices are distorted, an accurate assessment is difficult. Another factor tending to push transfer prices in that direction is the increasingly specific regulations imposed on corporations by the US Internal Revenue Service and also by the tax services of the host countries in which the affiliates are located. Nevertheless, examples have been found in which transfer prices are manipulated, typically to get around overly restrictive profit-remittance regulations. Such manipulation is easier for firms that belong to what *Brada* called "product-based technology" groups.

Czeslawa Szczepanska raised question on Brada's paper concerning the pharmaceutical industry as a negative example of commodity transfer, and as an example of limited co-operation activites. *Szczepanska* wanted to know if the Hungarian example of co-operation with Western countries in the pharmaceutical industry does not contradict this statement.

Josef Brada replied that the pharmaceutical industry in Hungary has had a long and successful record of innovation and thus has attracted the interest of western firms both as a means of introducing their products into the CMEA market, to which Hungary is the chief supplier, and as a source of new products. Nevertheless, it is his understanding, said *Brada*, that western firms have not been willing to transfer to Hungary technology for the bulk production of unique ethical drugs. He also understands that the Hungarian pharmaceutical industry has begun to establish facilities for the production and distribution of Hungarian pharmaceuticals in the West. Thus, the economic forces which lead western pharmaceutical firms to exploit their technology abroad by means of intra-firm transfers also operate in the same way in the case of the Hungarian pharmaceutical industry, *Brada* concluded.

Sulmicki referred also to Brada's paper, noting that there is no doubt that the degree of co-operation between pharmaceutical firms is lower than between engineering firms. Yet, the two discussed industries, even when treated as examples, differ not only in production innovation, but also in the intensity of their research and development efforts. On the basis of the data provided by Brada, it can be concluded, said *Sulmicki,* that research-development expenditures in the pharmaceutical industry are about three times higher than in the engineering industry. Hence, the readiness to cooperate with East European countries may result also from differences in the intensity of R&D efforts. In other words, the most dynamic industrial branches apparently have not been particularly eager to co-operate with the East European countries.

The second question *Sulmicki* touched on was the thesis that, for entrepreneurs, product innovations are more risky than process innovations. Consequently, it may be assumed that in market economies the prevailing part of innovations are process innovations. However, the literature suggests that entrepreneurs tend to seek small technical improvements, not involving much risk, which could be realized within a relatively short time. Estimates by US economist Mansfield show that 55 percent of entrepreneurs carried out innovations whose introduction period did not exceed 3 years. It is estimated that in the US about 90 percent of the funds allocated for R&D are spent on improving the existing or creating new products, and only 10 percent on new production processes.

The first part of *Sulmicki's* comment is discussed by *Brada* in the context of his formal reply to his discussant's comments. With respect to *Sulmicki's* comment, that most innovative activity consists of minor, short-term improvements in products, *Brada* said he quite agrees with this point. However,, added *Brada,* minor, short-lived changes in the structure (rather than function) of products really provide very little monopoly power for the innovating firm. Consequently, a close reading of his paper shows, *Brada* argues, that he has classified these as process changes not product changes. His paper classifies technology on the basis of the competitive advantage which it yields, not on the basis of whether the product or the assembly line has changed.

Wlodzimierz Lenard asked Garland about the organizational structures of American MNCs and the impact of the organization on US-Polish IC.

John Garland relplied that the initial response of the Western firm seems to be a partial centralization of IC-related activities. There are numerous reasons for this, each probably varying in importance from firm to firm and according to the specific nature of the ICA. In general, the decision to engage in IC is a strategic rather than operational (tactical) decision, which therefore tends to be made at highest levels. IC usually represents a significant departure from the firm's more traditional practices, and thus requires higher level monitoring to ensure its coordination with the firm's other activities.

Moreover, like IC itself, the entry on a large scale into the Eastern European market is a novelty for most American firms, according to *Garland.* Unfamiliarity with the economic systems, when combined with the potentially vast markets in Eastern Europe, encourages higher-level corporate involvement than would be the case if systemic differences were insignificant. These reasons are complemented by the perception of many Western managers that the negotiations themselves require top-level presence; in other words, Western managers, rightly or wrongly, often feel that proposals are not taken seriously by the East European partner unless the top executives of the Western firm are involved, even though in some firms middle-level managers in fact have the authority to make the relevant decisions.

But perhaps a more compelling reason for the partial centralization, *Garland* contends, stems from the existing organizational structure of the multinational firm. If its business involves primary products, the firm typically has a functional division of departments (worldwide divisions for finance, marketing, production and so on). If it produces consumer goods, it typically has a geographical division based on differences in marketing practices. And if its key to its success is advanced technology, or if it is involved in several different industries, the firm is likely to base its departmentalization on specific product lines. Each of these arrangements has disadvantages as well as advantages. In *Garland's* opinion, the more complex ICAs require a higher level coordination than is necessary for the firm's more traditional activities because the existing organizational structure might not be compatible with the specific nature of the ICA. For example, the IH-BUMAR ICA (which the two teams have studied) has resulted in efforts, not always successful, to involve three European subsidiaries of IH. To coordinate the IC-related activities of the otherwise relatively autonomous subsidiaries required a high level involvement. The same thing, noted *Garland,* could be said for many ICAs which involve buy-back arrangements or joint marketing. These seem to be some of the reasons why IC-related activities of the Western partners have tended to be relatively centralized.

Several participants raised methodological questions and criticisms on the paper by Wolf, focusing on his sampling methodology, the use of unit values as proxies for prices, and the interpretation of his findings. Since *Wolf's* formal reply to his discussant's comments touched on all these methodological questions, his statments need not be repeated. At the more general level, *Wolf* stressed that even his paper's negative finding, namely, a surprising lack of products among Poland's manufactures exports to West Germany for which IC between the two countries was important, is significant. "For years we have heard of IC but where are the resulting exports?" asked *Wolf.*

> *The persons who commented on my paper noted that there was little said in it on IC. They were right. This results from the fact that I have tried to survey the past determinants of Polish exports to the West but found it difficult to discover groups of really important export products where the share of IC was high. Clothes and textiles constituted the only exception but of course we are more interested in the newer, modern forms of IC.*

Regarding a question by *Anna Turowska* about the relationship between Poland's export prices and IC with the FRG in the area of clothing and textiles, *Wolf* stressed that his findings suggest that, apparently thanks to a subcontracting-type of IC, Poland had managed to evolve from a supplier having a very low share of the West German market where it sold at relatively low prices to a position of having become a very important supplier at prices close to (only slightly lower than) the average prices obtained by other suppliers. *Turowska* noted, however, that so many conditions affect Poland's export prices and market share that, in her view, it is difficult to draw general conclusions of the kind suggested by Wolf.

The second discussion session opened with some comments on alternative approaches to the study of the IC experience, followed by a discussion of the case study completed jointly by the two teams and the general conclusions that can be drawn from case studies of US-Polish IC.

Monika Kaczmarowicz, commenting on Perlmutter's paper, suggested that IC partners should jointly work out a strategic plan for their cooperative venture, which would be consistent with the strategic goals each of the partners wants to achieve, independently, for his firm. A joint plan would build up mutual trust and help them discover new areas for cooperation which would otherwise be left out of their joint activities. Joint planning would also help to stabilize the economic environment in which each of the partners operates. One could go even further, added Kaczmarowicz, and attempt to build a formal model to optimize joint activities so as to enable both partners to derive maximum benefits from their IC venture. One obstacle to building such a model, however, is the natural reluctance of businessmen in every country to reveal information to an outside organization.

Perlmutter replied that he was in general agreement, adding that throughout the world many firms, both state and private, have realized that it is becoming less and less likely for them to remain successful without interfirm cooperation, so that natural coalitions have been evolving. There are many precedents. For example, *Agfa* and *Gevaert* consult each other on their plans. Separate technologies for every product could not be developed by all firms, hence there is a growing awareness that the question is not whether but how to act jointly. As far as Polish-US relations are concerned, the main problem is finding grounds on which Polish enterprises can communicate and link up with Americans partners.

Andrzej Calus commented on his interest in the problem of how the framework, the principles, and the assumptions of IC can be developed in the specific Polish-US context. In his view, the matter may be approached from three different perspectives, each leading to different conclusions. The first is based on the assumption that there are traders with competing interests, and co-operation is viewed as an instrument used by each side to achieve maximum profits, without consideration being given to the interests of the other side. The second is the interview and case study approach, focusing on the experiences of IC between Polish and US enterprises in general, as in

Perlmutter's paper and in the joint case study. That is, IC ventures should be studied to see how co-operation is carried out, what works and does not work, and how to use IC on a wider scale. The third approach focuses on the future. It is based on the assumption that there is a certain model of mutually advantageous co-operation. Based on Anglo-Saxon law, one can say that the essence of IC consists of legal co-operation commitments which for either side become important fundamental obligations.

Calus believes, that at present, one approach seems to prevail in Polish-US IC relations, i.e., the point of view of the traditional commercial competitive assumptions. This approach has been reflected, for example, in some publications by the US Department of Commerce and even—to some extent—in the American papers presented at this seminar. Calus then referred to a US Commerce Department publication on US East-West compensation agreements which did not distinguish between compensation transactions and compensation elements included in many East-West ICAs. From the legal point of view, a compensation transaction signifies that relations between the two sides end upon the fulfillment of delivery commitments. On the other hand, when compensation elements are included in a cooperation transaction, they become critically important components on which the success of long-term cooperation depends. Compensation should then be considered a service rendered within the co-operation process, not an additional difficulty to overcome between enterprises. As a consequence, one of the most important issues to be considered is the many-sided analysis of compensation.

Speaking about future models of co-operation, *Calus* distinguished between what "is" and what "should be" if co-operation is really to fulfill any economic, social, or perhaps even political objectives in relations between Poland and the US. He praised the modest attempt to establish model co-operation contracts by the U.N. Economic Commission for Europe in its "Guide to Concluding Agreements on Industrial Co-operation."

At this point there was a brief general discussion by members of the US and Polish teams of the highlights of the International Harvester (IH)-BUMAR ICA (see Part II of this volume). *Monika Kaczmarowicz* then asked and attempted to answer the question: to what extent is the IH-BUMAR case study representative of Polish-US IC experience more generally?

According to *Kaczmarowicz,* Polish-US IC is quite a new phenomenon: it started in early 1970s (later than with West European firms), at the very beginning of a new chapter in Polish-US economic relations. So far, its scope has not been large. Out of numerous IC agreements signed, only four are of significant importance as far as their complexity, the value of the contract, and the scope of exchange are concerned. These are: BUMAR-IH, BUMAR-Clark Equipment, BUMAR-Koehring International (Moenk, FRG), and Universal-Singer. (The speaker did not include the IC project on producing color television sets in Poland which involves RCA and Corning.) The first three agreements were signed in 1972 by the same Polish enterprise in the same industrial branch and product line (IH—construction machinery, Clark—drive axels, Koehring—hydraulic excavators), the fourth one was signed in 1973. The IH-BUMAR IC is the largest, most important, most complex and is generally recognized as being also the best up to now. The IC with Clark ranks, *Kaczmarowicz* believes, second and the scope of its joint activities have also been expanded since the initial agreement has been signed. The agreement with Koehring started quite successfully but it was suspended in 1975 due to the drop in demand for such type of machine in Western Europe. (Added *Kaczmarowicz:* The Polish partner can use the received technology, produce the machine and market it in CMEA, but deliveries to Moenk were suspended, as was the transfer of updated technological information.)

According to *Kaczmarowicz,* these agreements have in common the following. Except for Clark, the agreements extend over the entire product—which is a certain type of machine. Except for the ICA with Singer (sewing machines), they all operate in the sphere of investment goods. Under each ICA, new, advanced technology has been transfered to the Polish partner. The envisaged duration of the IC was at least ten years. The partners on both sides have long-established positions in their respective industries. The Polish manufacturers involved are the leading producers at home and are experienced exporters; some even have previous experience in cooperating with western firms, such as Huta Stalowa Wola. The American counterparts are well known world-wide, possess advanced technology and organizational know-how, have highly esteemed trademarks, and global sales and service networks. They are, moreover, all pioneers in entering into non-equity IC ventures in the Eastern countries.

The motives of the US firms, according to *Kaczmarowicz,* were approximately similar (see the IH-BUMAR case study for details). All the agreements foresaw cooperation in several spheres of activities. In some cases additional agreements were signed subsequent to the initial agreement that widen the scope of cooperation between the partners, reflecting the deepening of mutual trust and suggesting that the ICA is mutually beneficial.

Basically, *Kaczmarowicz* found, the Polish partner receives the technical documentation and organizes the production at his own facilities (usually involving a substantial investment on the Polish side), while the American partner supplies some of the components and buys components, sub-assemblies or final products. The two-way flow of goods between the partners is not organized on the basis of clearing; rather, the commitment of the US side is to buy Polish-made products either under separate short-term contracts or the buy-back can be set as a percentage of the Polish partner's annual output (as is the case in the Singer-Universal agreement).

The Polish side also obtains the right to use her partner's registered trademark, contingent upon meeting specific quality standards.

In all the cases mentioned, added *Kaczmarowicz,* the partners have divided their market responsibilities, listing the countries exclusive for the Polish partner (these being the CMEA countries and in some cases certain LDCs). The Polish side is, as a rule, allowed to sell products to the West through the partner's sales network or to supply directly the latter's manufacturing plants (often West European subsidiaries) with Polish-made components and sub-assemblies. For sales through the partner's sales network, the Polish side pays a certain per cent commission. The fact that the independent sales of Polish-made machines is usually restricted to the CMEA market only reflects, *Kaczmarowicz* thinks, the stronger bargaining position of the US partner ("possibly perhaps also the limited marketing capability in the West of the Polish partner," interjected a participant from the US). Added *Kaczmarowicz:* The possibility for the US partner to impose such marketing restrictions on, say, a West European firm would not be as easy in the absence of at least part-ownership of the manufacturing plant.

As far as the problems connected with the implementation of the ICAs are concerned, *Kaczmarowicz* contends, they are also of similar nature to those experienced under the IH-BUMAR ICA. Although meeting quality standards is often an issue for the Polish producer, in all four cases mentioned, the Polish side was successful in receiving the partner's trademark approximately at the time envisaged by the contract. There have been delays in production start-up as well as in deliveries. The US partner often complains about the small elasticity of supply on the Polish side in responding to changing Western demand. This is due to the absence of reserve production capacity in Polish plants and to various organizational barriers and incentive problems to introduce rapid modifications according to specific customers requirements. Another reason is that the Western partner sometimes would like to have a short series of production, e.g., this was a specific problem in the IC with Clark. The Polish partner often complains that the US side wants to use him as a mere production capacity reserve for periods of boom in the world market, leaving him with his own problems in times of stagnating demand.

As a rule, concluded *Kaczmarowicz,* the cooperating parties have managed jointly to overcome many problems and seem to be satisfied with each other, on balance. The Polish side cherishes American expertise and the Americans stress the Polish commitment to cooperation.

The conference participants then turned to the environmental forces that impact on IC, i.e., those forces that are outside the immediate control of the firms.

Aleksander Legatowicz's remarks focused on the systemic problems connected with cooperation. He stated that the problem of cooperation cannot be considered in isolation from overall systemic problems in Poland, if only because of the fact that both partners are linked to their domestic subsuppliers. *Legatowicz* then wondered which of the main theories concerning the economy are of importance for IC: optimization theory or game theory. Probably both can be applied. It is known from optimization theory that the fewer the environmental restrictions on the activities of a firm, the better optimum is obtained. IC makes it possible to remove a number of restrictions which could not be removed in the case of other forms of economic activities. On the other hand, IC can also be viewed in terms of the principle of coalition in game theory so that almost all features of IC can be formulated in this language.

Legatowicz suggested, further, that the time may be right for attempting to formulate certain "model" solutions of the remunerative conditions which must be fulfilled by the Polish and Western partners to make IC mutually attractive.

Andrzej Rudka touched on several topics. One of these concerned the financing of American exports and in particular, IC ventures. It seems obvious to him that more liberal government export credits could play a key role in improving US competitiveness against other western countries in the socialist markets. So far such credits have played only a minor role in the promotion of US trade and IC with the East. Rudka also called attention to the problem of a wide gap between current restrictive East-West trade policies of the US and world trade practices, as all other western countries extend MFN status and export credits and avoid unilateral export controls in trade relations with Eastern Europe. Consequently, the US is at a trading disadvantage. Thus, the elimination or relaxation of some restrictions in trade with the East, is—according to Rudka—in the best interest of the US. It means not only import restrictions, but export barriers above all. The Export Administration Act of 1969 was to expire September 30, 1979. Liberalizing the laws regulating the export of American technology would be instrumental for promoting IC involving US firms, *Rudka* concluded.

Several participants picked up the theme of US export control regulations, pointing out how these controls limit the possibilities and prospects for IC with Polish firms. *Wlodzimierz Leonard* for example, referred to a 1977 report of the US Department of Defense which recommended that restrictions on the export of US technology to Western countries be eased while those on exports to Eastern countries be tightened. *Andrzej Burzynski* criticized what he considered ill-advised US proposals to CoCom[1] to restrict the export to the Eastern countries of such technologies as the manufacture of jet engines, cables, bearings, machine tools, elements for finishing off ultra-smooth surfaces, and some of the technology involved in producing gas turbines. If the proposals were accepted, *Burzynski* argued, they would be very harmful to the development of East-West IC.

The discussion then turned to the various types of IC arrangements and the role of IC and of exports in Poland's economy.

Stanislaw Falkowski discussed the possibilities of Polish-American co-operation in the developing countries, i.e., tripartite co-operation. In his view, every country works within a definite framework and creates specific technology best suited for its own environment. For example, American technology is often more capital-intensive and labor-saving than it is appropriate for LDCs and hence may not be suitable for some developing countries. For example, rapid transfer of such technology took place a few years ago to the countries of Black Africa, initiated by private enterprises, which in many cases did not meet with much approval on the part of the officials of the recipient countries. Under tripartite IC involving, for example, US, Polish, and African firms, the US could contribute mainly the finance, the initial pre-investment analysis of the project, and market research, while Poland could offer some of the technology and construction.

Aleksander Krzyminski remarked that one should consider whether IC in its traditional form, that is, firms located in Poland cooperating with US firms, is in fact always the best strategy for penetrating the American market with Polish products. One should consider that in some circumstances other forms of direct export or joint ventures located in the US may be more advantageous. Examples of successful direct exports are the two branch offices of a Polish firm in the US—"Toolmex" near Boston and "Polamco" near Chicago—which import for their own account machine tools and other products from Poland and market these products in the US with the help of a mixed Polish-American staff.

Wiktor Szydlowski commented on the technology imported to Poland under ICAs. The projects often require not only investment imports but also raw material imports, which makes the technology expensive. This is partly the result of some Western partners preferring to entrust to the Polish partner the more material-intensive operations while retaining activities that are more labor intensive. Inappropriate technology and inadequate documentation are other reasons while Poland sometimes has difficulty commencing to the West the export of the intended resulting product.

Karol Brzoska added that while it is true that Poland can provide raw materials like copper or coal, the best prospects for cooperation are likely to be found in those domains where the Polish side can provide not only materials but also skilled labor.

In the third and last session, the participants turned to questions and comments on the legal, political and practical aspects of import protectionism in the US.

Urszula Plowiec asked whether US laws conform to GATT and whether US or GATT regulations are stricter. She was also interested in the US definition of injury: does it cover not only actual but also potential injury?

Elzbieta Kawecka-Wyrzykowska commented that Marer's paper focused only on two trade devices which hamper Poland's access to the American market and called attention to numerous other trade barriers.

Wolf asked who may bring dumping or market disruption charges against Polish exporters: are such actions always initiated by firms or can they be brought also by, say, groups of workers? Wolf wondered also what role ICAs can play to forestall dumping or market disruption charges against Polish exporters.

Sulmicki wondered whether foreign branches and affiliates of US MNCs are treated as US or as foreign producers in import-protection-type litigation, that is, can foreign affiliates bring dumping, etc. charges just like domestic US firms.

Calus wanted some information about the US trigger-price system.

Marer responded to the questions. Regarding the trigger-price system, he said that this mechanism covers steel products only. Its origin can be traced to complaints by the American steel industry that it has a competitive disadvantage vis-a-vis foreign producers because while the US government imposes costly rules on them (such as environmental protection laws requiring the spending of hundreds of millions of dollars on antipollution equipment), most foreign producers are either owned or heavily subsidized by their governments. Consequently, American steel firms are asking: "How are we to compete in a situation where others are generously subsidized while we are heavily taxed by the government?" So, instead of the US government trying to determine in each case how much price advantage foreign competitors might have over US producers because of the subsidy they receive, the so-called "trigger-price system" was introduced.

This fixes a price level for each product (loosely tied to Japanese production costs since the Japanese are among the world's most efficient producers). Imports below that price "trigger" a special duty. The trigger price has been set at a level which allows something like 20% of US consumption of steel products to be imported.

Regarding the question by *Sulmicki, Marer* said that US import-protection laws are only concerned with competition on the US domestic market, hence only firms whose US operations are injured may seek remedy. Re the question by *Wolf:* Legally, a complaint may be filed, *Marer* said, by any group, individual, or organization which is injured by foreign competition, including labor. But practically speaking, most complaints are registered by firms or industry groups. Imports into the US under ICAs in principle, not exempt from formal allegations of dumping or market disruption by those who claim injury. However, as a practical matter, such complaints are much less likely when products are imported under ICAs. To give a hypothetical example: Ford Motor Co. is much less likely to sue General Motors over its foreign sourcing policies than it would, say, be willing to sue a Japanese firm importing into the US components or finished products.

To the second question by *Plowiec, Marer* replied that the US definition of injury does encompass the "likelihood of injury" also. (Note by the editors: See the 1980 ITC ruling on Polish golf cars cited on p. 336 for an illustration of how this concept is applied.) As to the more general question by *Plowiec, Marer* pointed out that both GATT and US laws make the same kind of distinction between fair versus unfair trade practices. The basic idea is that if imports are low-priced because the exporting country has a comparative advantage in a given product, then trade is fair and both countries will be better off by permitting such imports without restrictions even if this causes adjustment difficulties in the importing country. In this case both GATT and US laws allow the erection of *temporary barriers* but *only* if such imports cause *serious injury* to the domestic industry. By contrast, export subsidies and dumping are viewed as causing distortions to international trade, so both GATT and US laws permit retaliation if at least *minimal injury* can be established. The basic philosophy of GATT as well as of US laws is that a determination of whether imports are fair or unfair is crucial for setting the conditions under which relief can be invoked and also for deciding whether the relief shall be temporary (to ease the burden of adjustment to domestic industry) or permanent (to offset fully the alleged distortion to international trade). GATT does not—cannot—set percise standards on how unfair trade should be defined and neither does it prescribe exactly the remedies that may be applied. To sum up: The principles of US laws generally conform to GATT; whether in practice US procedures yield greater protection than those of other major GATT countries is difficult to state *a priori,* since the US, the West European countries and Japan employ different procedures to deal with complaints, as is discussed in his paper, *Marer* said.

His paper has focused on dumping and market disruption only, replied *Marer* to the question by *Wyrzykowska,* because in recent years these procedures were of special concern for Polish exporters to the US. *Marer* said he felt that neither the economic rationale nor many of the practical aspects of these laws were adequately understood in Poland. Although there are many grounds on which US laws and procedures may be criticized, he felt that there is much public and private comment on them in Poland that is not realistic. *Marer* therefore asked that he be given some time to present his views on the philosophical as well as on some of the practical aspects of these US laws and procedures.

Enterprises in the US and in Poland, said *Marer,* operate according to different concepts and "rules of the game," which inevitably cause difficulties when they transact business. A market economy, such as the US, is characterized by much competition among enterprises privately owned; efficiency considerations which loom large in relation to social welfare and noneconomic considerations; market forces of supply and demand which as a rule determine prices; and production that is based in large part upon anticipated return on investment. By contrast, a centrally planned economy such as Poland is characterized by state ownership of enterprises; state control over production and prices of goods; and social welfare or noneconomic criteria that may predominate over efficiency or other economic considerations in investment decisions and the allocation of productive resources.

Of course, the above generalizations oversimplify the differences between the "rules of the game" in market and planned economies, *Marer* admitted. State ownership, control, and subsidization of commercial enterprises, and other forms of government intervention have been on the increase in the US, while economic criteria and efficiency considerations are not entirely absent from production decisions and price determination in Poland. Nevertheless, there are basic differences which give rise to potential problems when US producers are faced with imports from Poland, *Marer* concluded.

To the extent that imports from Poland benefit from government intervention which is inconsistent with American "rules of the game," such imports are alleged to be "unfair," *Marer* continued. To illustrate, an industry competing with imports from Poland will raise questions such as:[2]

—Will Poland's export prices be set by noneconomic criteria, such as the goal to caputre a certain percent of the US market, rather than to attain a certain rate of return or profit?

—Does the accounting system of the Polish enterprise reflect the same types of costs and prices which the US industry is subject to through market forces?

—Can prices and production levels be established by Poland without regard to economic or efficiency criteria, and thus injure US producers who may be more efficient but who do not receive state assistance?

—Does the Polish government make free or subsidized capital contributions to its enterprise and as a result can the Polish exporter effectively undersell an otherwise more efficient US producer?

The crucial point is, *Marer* continued, that for the purpose at hand it does not matter what the answer to these and to similar other questions might be in any specific instance, such as in the case of Polish golf car exports to the US. That is because authorities in the US, as in other Western countries, have concluded that *prices and the costs of inputs in Poland* (and in other centrally planned, or state-controlled, or non-market economies—terms that are used interchangeably) *do not reflect real prices and costs for purposes of comparisons to prices and costs in the US*. This conclusion is based on the observations that (1) there are large and unsystematic differences in relative prices in planned and in market economies; (2) prices in planned economies are fixed by the state and generally remain unchanged for long periods; and (3) exchange rates established by the state do not appear to be meaningful for converting Polish prices or costs into US dollars.

Even if our Polish colleagues would not endorse every statement in the above paragraph, they would probably admit that the reasoning has a certain logic, that at least from the point of view of the West, the position taken is not an unreasonable one. If so, then one has understood much of the logic of US import-protection laws affecting Polish exports and one has also begun to appreciate the practical difficulties of separating "fair" from "unfair" competition by Polish exports on the US market, *Marer* added.

For the reasons mentioned, *Marer* continued, the US statute defines the "fair value" of imports from a state-controlled-economy country such as Poland by reference to prices and costs in non-state-controlled-economy countries. "Fair value" must be established in the first stage of the two-stage dumping investigation. First the US Treasury (note by the editors: since January 1, 1980, the US Department of Commerce) must determine whether Poland's export price represents "less than fair value" (LTVF). If affirmative, the case is moved to the International Trade Commission (ITC) which must decide whether the LTFV imports have caused, or are likely to cause, substantial injury to import-competing producers. If yes, antidumping duties are levied on imports.

The most difficult problem in a dumping investigation involving a state-controlled-economy country is how to select the surrogate producer in a market economy that will produce an equitable result in establishing the "fair value" of exports.

US statutes and regulations require that the Treasury use either (1) the prices of similar merchandise sold by a market-economy country in its *home markets,* or (2) the prices of similar merchandise sold by a market-economy country for *exports to third countries,* or (3) the *constructed value* of similar merchandise produced in a market-economy country, in that order of preference, *Marer* added. (The term "constructed value" refers to the adjustments necessary to establish the hypothetical cost of production, considering the actual circumstances of production and export in the planned economy.)

Marer then turned to the practical aspects of a dumping investigation, focusing on the Polish golf car case, which he said he studied carefully. He first noted that in his opinion, the people at the US Treasury charged with choosing a "fair value" standard had bent over backwards to be objective, given the law's legal and procedural limitations. *Marer* said that this conclusion is based on the many hours of interview he conducted with the key people at the US Customs Office and at the Treasury who were handling the case. Treasury agents literally combed the world to find foreign producers of golf cars whose domestic or third-country-export prices could be used as a "fair value" standard.[3] Unfortunately, outside Poland this specialized product was manufactured only in the US and Canada.

On June 16, 1975, the Treasury determined that electric golf cars from Poland were being sold at LTFV, based on comparisons of the Polish exporter, Pezetel's, export prices to a constructed value based on the price of the Canadian-produced golf car. In its investigation, Treasury examined 100% of the golf car entries from Poland during a 10-month period from December 1, 1973 to September 30, 1974 and found a weighted average dumping margin of 21%.

On September 16, 1975 the ITC determined that LTFV imports were causing injury to domestic industry, *Marer* continued. Although having started production of golf cars only a few years earlier, by 1975 Poland exported about 10,000 golf cars to the US, capturing almost one-quarter of the American market. The extremely rapid market penetration, the LTFV finding, and declining sales, employment, and profits of some domestic US producers were the key factors influencing the decision. Subsequently, dumping duties were assessed ("liquidated" in official parlance) on 1975 and 1976 golf car imports from Poland, finding an average dumping margin of only 3.5% by that time. After that date, the assessment of the duty was suspended because of two circumstances: the Canadian manufacturer stopped producing golf cars and in July 1976 new US Customs regulations went into effect which required that, in the absence of similar merchandise manufactured in a foreign market-economy country, prices or costs of US-manufactured merchandise should be used to determine fair market value (FMV).[4] The Polish exporter naturally became extremely concerned: basing FMV on Canadian prices seemed unfair enough; basing FMV on US prices would effectively exclude Poland from the US market.

One conclusion, *Marer* suggested, is that the circumstances surrounding the golf car case were so extreme as to make the case unique. The coincidence of (1) highly visible rapid penetration of the US market; (2) inability to find a producer outside North America; (3) an interpretation of legislative intent regarding how fair value should be "constructed" that was most unfavorable to Poland; and (4) inadequate initial legal advice all combined to yield a decision that seemed most unfair to Poland. While the case was by no means typical of US reception of Poland's other exports, *Marer* noted, its wide publicity in Poland created the understandable but in *Marer's* view greatly exaggerated impression that the US was a very strongly protectionist country. In any event, Poland's concerns were understandable, *Marer,* added.

Witold Trzeciakowski then took the floor to voice the concern that appeared to represent the consensus of Polish academic and trade specialists participating at the conference. He felt that the golf car case illustrated a certain lack of basic logic in East-West trade developments in recent years. The West is ready to finance Eastern imports on credits but at the same time puts up protectionist barriers that seriously constrain the borrower's access to Western markets and hence impedes the repayment of Western credits. The principal criticism voiced by *Trzeciakowski* was the lack of predictability of US trade laws which undermines Poland's effective long-range trade agreements and planning. This concern looms especially large in transactions where Polish enterprises purchase costly US technology on credit and want to pay for it later with resulting products. There is little assurance how such goods will be treated under any number of provisions of the US trade law. Poland and other East European countries which have been experiencing large trade deficits and severe shortages of convertible currency cannot continue to purchase US exports if the products they attempt to sell in return to the US market are being challenged at every point, *Trzeciakowski* argued:

We can fully respect the right of the American government to determine the list of sensitive goods and exclude from our export expansion program these commodities. But we must be certain that if we develop production capacities in other commodities, these new areas of our export specialization will not become 'sensitive' tomorrow. Some 'fair play' rules should be jointly elaborated and then respected by both sides. Of course we do not expect guarantees from the US government that our exports will be sold, only guaranteed access to the US market on equal terms with other competitors.

This interplay between US import restrictions and the possibilities of expanding US exports was also voiced by several other Polish participants at the conference.

Trzeciakowski recommended, further, that the joint elaboration of "new rules of fair play" would be especially needed with respect to dumping. He felt that the assessment of what constitutes East European dumping has rested up to now on very shaky foundations, creating many possibilities for subjective evaluations. *Trzeciakowski* suggested that an alternative to the existing rules would be to rely on the so-called "calculative approach" to cost determination, whose essence is that the prices of raw materials, labor, and other inputs would be based on realistically calculated "shadow prices" and exchange rates. He suggested that an imaginative joint research project may be designed to prepare new proposals in this area which could serve as a basis for reforming the trade laws of the US and of other Western countries.

Several participants expressed agreement with the basic thrust of *Trzeciakowski's* comments. *Marer* added that an important first step may already have been taken last year in the direction proposed by *Trzeciakowski.* Responding to complaints by East European, principally Polish exporters, and prompted by a desire to find a more equitable solution in the golf car and to similar cases, the US departments of State and Treasury organized an international conference, held in Washington, D.C. in July 1978, to analyze problems of the application of US laws to imports from state-controlled economies and state-owned enterprises, and to consider new policy options. A notable feature of the conference, said *Marer,* was the participation of high-level representatives from all relevant agencies of the US government, of specialist private lawyers representing many of the litigants, of academic experts, of specialists from the EEC and from several Western countries, and of experts from Eastern Europe, including leading ones from Poland.[5] *Marer,* who participated, then related that much of the debate at the Washington conference focused precisely on the issues raised by *Trzeciakowski,* as shown by the statement from the conference's conclusions he quoted:[6]

> Much discussion focused on the Treasury Department's proposed
> amendment to the antidumping regulations which would provide that
> fair value of imports from state-controlled-economy countries be de-
> termined by reference to surrogate producers in non-state-controlled-
> economy countries which are comparable in terms of their level of eco-
> nomic development. Under this approach, the home-market or third-
> country prices of the surrogate producers of similar merchandise would
> be used, but if such prices are inadequate for determining fair value,
> then the constructed value will be used taking the physical volume in-
> puts of the state-controlled-economy producer and valuing these physi-
> cal volume inputs by reference to the costs of such inputs in the non-
> state-controlled-economy country of a comparable level of development
> and verifying the physical volume inputs in the nonmarket-economy ex-
> porting country. . . . It was generally concluded by conference particip-
> ants that, given existing US antidumping laws, this proposal is the most
> effective approach in defining fair value of imports from state-
> controlled-economy countries.

Marer then mentioned that, following the Washington conference,
Treasury promulgated new regulations, effective as of September
1978, which direct that the constructed "fair value" standard shall be
computed using (if verifiable) the actual physical inputs in the
nonmarket-economy exporting country, valued at the costs or prices
of a market economy at a stage of development comparable to the
exporting country. In the Polish golf car case, Spanish costs and
prices are now used as surrogates for Polish costs and prices. Comparisons of import prices of Polish golf cars with standards so constructed have resulted in a determination of no sales below "fair
value."[7] However, Marer added, since the domestic producer which
initially alleged that Poland was dumping objects to this procedure
and has a legal challenge under way to this method of determining
"fair value," the case should be considered as still pending.[8]

Wolf commented that while the "Spanish" formula appears to be a
significant improvement over the method used previously, it too has
shortcomings. Under the new method, the "reasonableness" of the
price of the Polish export product remains quite independent of trends
in costs and prices in Poland and are influenced instead by such factors outside the producer's control as the Spanish inflation rate, the
exchange rate between the peseta and the dollar, and so on.

(Note by the editors: In February 1980, the ITC instituted a new
investigation to determine whether changed circumstances exist
which may indicate that the earlier antidumping finding on golf cars
from Poland should be revoked. On September 16, 1980, the ITC revoked by a 5 to 0 vote, the outstanding antidumping finding. The decision was based on the following reasoning:[9]

(1) The volume of imports. *US imports of golf cars from Poland declined from 9,982 units in 1975 to 5,220 units in 1979, or by 48%. The ratio of imports from Poland to apparent US consumption declined by an even greater precentage during the same period.*

(2) Price effects of imports. *The price paid for Polish cars by their dealers and distributors were consistently lower than the weighted average prices of US-produced golf cars, ranging from a margin of 7 to 1 in 1977 which increased to about 11 to 13% by 1979, depending on model. The ITC noted that the price data used in these comparisons do not reflect either the differing levels of support services (e.g., marketing services, financial assistance, inventory control plans, training programs) or the differing warranties offered by the US and Polish producers. If these factors were considered, the apparent competitive advantage of the imported car would be reduced. Since September 1978 (date of the new method of determining LTFV) the margins of underselling were, however, not the result of dumping.*

(3) Impact of imports on the affected industry. *US production of golf cars increased from 45,000 units in 1975 to 53,000 units in 1979, or by 18%. During the same period the US golf cars producers' net operating profit to net sales increased by over 45%. Thus, there does not seem to be proof of serious injury to the domestic industry.*

(4) Likelihood of materials injury by reason of LTFV imports from Poland. *The ITC concluded that several considerations have diminished the likelihood of material injury by reason of imports which may be sold at LTFV in the future. One is that even though the Polish cars have been priced consistently lower than domestic cars, this was not done by resorting to sales at LTFV. Also, the importer of Polish golf cars has given assurances to the Commission that its annual imports will not exceed an average of 8,000 cars through 1985 and that the importer will not knowingly sell its product for LTFV under the regulation for determining foreign market value. Moreover, the factory in Poland where the golf cars are produced has an annual production capacity of 10,000 units. Thus, "assuming that apparent US golf car consumption during the next few years remains relatively unchanged, the assurance on the volume of imports effectively limits Poland's share of the US market to a level lower than the average market share it held during 1975-79. Moreover, given the maximum production capacity in Poland, the possibility of a sudden influx of imports from Poland is minimized.)*

The discussion then turned to some broader questions of protectionism. Several participants wanted to know whether the US or the European Economic Community (EEC) was de facto more protectionist.

Wolf commented on earlier statements by *Szeworski* (see his formal comments on the paper by Marer) which seems to have placed the main blame for protectionism on the capitalist system. In *Wolf's* view, protectionism may be seen, realistically, from a more philosophical, broader point of view. It is really a feature of human nature. No one who is employed and has worked in some job, say, for 25 years is willing voluntarily to take up a new job, to retrain. Thus, a protectionist mentality is not only a government mentality. It is a fundamental, common feature of all people, both bosses and workers, that they try to keep what they have. Socialist economies have secured full employment since the beginning of their existence. Yet in so doing they have introduced a certain inflexibility into the economy, according to *Wolf*. The fact that once an industry or a factory has been established it keeps on producing regardless of its comparative efficiency can also be viewed as protectionism, *Wolf* added.

Andrzej Olechowski agreed with the consensus that it is very difficult to quantify tariff barriers but cited his own calculations on the importance of non-tariff barriers by commodity groups. Comparing the so-called "means of direct control over producers," he stated that in a recent period in the US, 21.3% of imported commodities were affected; the comparable figure for the EEC was 22.7%. Moreover, in the case of the US, these indices show that 11.8% of imports from the developed countries and 22.9% of all remaining imports were affected, with the highest indices being on imports from the socialist countries. By contrast, in the case of the EEC, the indices ranged from 19.5% of imports from developed countries, 25.8% of imports from centrally planned economies, and 34% of imports from the developing countries.

Jozef Soldaczuk observed that, based on his personal experience, the US is probably among the least protectionist Western countries. Still, Polish exports do encounter various kinds of serious barriers, some of which are less obvious than the golf car case just discussed. For example, he noted, Poland was advised by US authorities not to be too aggressive in its export of ham to the US because the US already had difficulties with its imports of ham from the EEC. It was much the same case with textiles, this time partly because of US difficulties on imports from Korea. In both cases Poland agreed to stabilize its exports within certain limits.

Jolanta Hawryszko elaborated on another dimension of the problem mentioned by *Soldaczuk*. When the US confronted Denmark, which exports large quantities of ham to the US, about the EEC subsidies on this agricultural product, Denmark immediately drew attention to the fact that its main competitors on the US market were the countries of Eastern Europe. This is just one indication, added *Hawryszko*, of a general tendency in the West to treat socialist countries as a separate, less favored group.

Soldaczuk commented:

> We realize only too well that given Poland's indebtedness, we must develop exports to the US, to Western Europe, and to third countries. Additional and longer-term credits will be available to us only if Poland can enlarge its exports. IC is only one of the methods to promote exports.

> . When we are talking about prospects for cooperation between the US and our country, we do not expect our American partners to be philantropists. Cooperation is mainly a form of business and both sides have the right to draw profits from it. We cannot ask our American and other partners to help us because we are in a difficult situation. If I were the manager of a Polish firm willing to cooperate with an American firm I would start from profit. One must know what may be expected from America—advanced technology, investments—but they must also know what they can expect from us.

At the end of the discussion, the Director of the Foreign Trade Research Institute, *Janusz Kaczurba*, summed up the proceedings by saying that it has allowed all the participants to understand better the problems. He noted that when discussing issues as complex as IC and related questions—important for a mutual understanding of both the American and the Polish sides—it is not possible to resolve every issue once and for all. The problems discussed must inevitably remain the subject of future debates also. He then thanked all those who have taken part in the seminar.

Notes

1. CoCom stands for the Consultative Group Coordinating Committee, set up in 1949 to coordinate Western export policies toward communist countries. Its original members were the US, Great Britain, France, Italy, the Netherlands, Belgium and Luxembourg, which were later joined by Norway, Denmark, Canada, the Federal Republic of Germany, Portugal, Japan, Greece, and Turkey. Headquartered in Paris, it is an informal organization which develops lists of technologies and products whose exports to the communist countries are embargoed, controlled, and monitored; holds weekly consultations on applications for exceptions to these lists; and attempts to enforce CoCom regulations (The editors.)

2. The above formulation of differences between American and Polish "rules of the economic game" and the list of questions US firms are asking are based on proceedings of a 1978 conference on the application of US antidumping laws to imports from state-controlled economies. Full reference is cited in note 6, p. 340. (The editors.)

3. Treasury officials who handled the case told him, says Marer, that they cabled US customs agents stationed throughout the Western world to seek information. They also asked the Polish exporter to suggest a third-country producer for that purpose. Should there have been several third-country producers of golf cars to choose from, Treasury would have selected a producer in a country whose level of economic development was most comparable to that of Poland.

4. This decision was based on a legal interpretation of the intent of the relevant sections of the Trade Act of 1974 passed by Congress.

5. A key role was played at the conference by Stanislaw J. Soltysinski, Professor on

the Faculty of Law and Administration at Adam Mickiewicz University, who also serves as advisor to Pezetel. (The editors.)

6. Subsequently, the proceedings of the conference were published. See Don Wallace, Jr., et al., *Interface One: Conference Proceedings on the Application of U.S. Antidumping and Countervailing Duty Laws to Imports from State-Controlled Economies and State-Owned Enterprises* (Washington, D.C.: The Institute for International and Foreign Trade Law, 1980). The quote appears on p. 261, emphasis in the original. (The editors.)

7. According to officials of the US Department of Commerce, which became the administering authority in antidumping proceedings on January 1, 1980, there have been no dumping margins on Polish golf car sales made subsequent to September 1978. (The editors.)

8. The House Ways and Means Committee has scheduled to hold hearings on the regulation toward the end of 1980 in 1981. (The editors.)

9. US International Trade Commission, *Electric Golf Cars from Poland* (Washington, D.C. 1980) USITC Publication 1069, pp. 3-9.

PART V
JOINT VENTURES IN POLAND

Today's Approach to Joint Ventures in Poland

Eugeniusz Tabaczynski

Business relations with Poland are now entering a very interesting phase of development. Since the late 1960s, we have observed a new phenomenon related to technology and the organization of production of respective partners. This phenomenon, known as international industrial cooperation,[1] is more complex and sophisticated than traditional commercial links. Industrial cooperation (IC), rooted in the search for increased production efficiency and improved intrabranch and intraproduct specialization, is and will be an irrevocable feature of Polish economic relations abroad. This is true for both the Eastern and Western links of Polish industry and will become increasingly important for Polish-US relations.

It is generally agreed that international IC contributes directly to the development of trade among the partners. In the "traditional" IC model, known for about 15 years in Poland's relations abroad, the partners retain complete autonomy in decisionmaking and make their own calculations of profits. The only link between them is an agreement specifying the obligations and expectations of cooperating partners. Because such an agreement can serve its purpose only if it is based on mutual trust and understanding, the more interesting cooperation agreements are usually concluded after several years of commercial contacts between partners.

There is more and more evidence, however, that in some cases the "traditional" form of cooperation does not completely satisfy the partners. In the search for ways to further stimulate activity and improve economic effects in the long run, parties investigate new possibilities for closer cooperation. This happens particularly when the partners face difficulties such as a shortage of capital, an unsatisfactory level of technology, or an insufficient demand for their products. In such a situation, the partners can try to tighten their cooperation links and initiate a new form of joint international industrial activity. Consequently, a new economic and legal situation arises. The new activity starts as a result of pooling capital, technological, organizational, and trade know-how, which leads to joint risk-taking and calculation of profits. This new kind of IC is known as "joint international productive ventures."[2]

The objective of joint ventures may be formulated as follows:

1. Partners from socialist countries willing to engage in joint productive ventures on their own territory may obtain: (a) increased exports to difficult markets, especially those situated in the area of activity of the partner; (b) modernization of production and acceleration of the transfer of modern technologies, necessary for increasing competitiveness in foreign markets; and (c) increased profits.

2. Partners from capitalist countries willing to participate in joint production ventures situated in a socialist country may obtain: (a) a greater influence on joint production programs, leading to a fuller satisfaction of their objectives for cooperation, including related subdeliveries. The capital cooperation ensures a more satisfactory synchronization of production, a higher quality of intermediate products, a wider range of production capacity and reduced cost of production per unit of output; (b) the possibility of increased trade with socialist countries, usually one of the main objectives of capitalist partners in their cooperation with socialist partners; and (c) increased profits.

Let us analyze some principal aspects of setting up joint ventures with capitalist firms in Poland. There are several problems to consider:

1. The common ownership of the production capital and the respective rights of the partners.

2. The influence the partners have on fundamental decisions in the joint activity.

3. The calculation of financial effects of joint production and their division between partners.

The joint ownership of the capital implies certain rights and commitments of the partners and participation in the financial gains due to the use of this capital. There are two possible legal links between such partners in Poland:

1. An equity solution based on a purchase of shares (mixed companies). This pattern has been introduced in Hungary and Romania.

2. A non-equity solution based solely on a contract expressing all

duties and rights of both sides. This solution has been introduced in Yugoslavia.

According to the analysis of the existing agreements, the partners in joint ventures wish to influence decisions regarding:

1. Technology, i.e., the choice of the optimal methods of production.

2. Development, i.e., adjustment of production capacities to the existing and expected demand.

3. Sales policy, i.e., methods of sales, marketing, geographical directions of export, and prices on home and foreign markets.

4. Production costs, i.e., optimization of material outlays, wages, and general costs.

Experience gained in Hungary, Romania, and Yugoslavia indicates that the extent of each partner's influence on these activities can be specified both in a mixed company status and in a contractual agreement by stating which decisions are to be taken by the local partner alone. In the case of Polish partners, these decisions include, for example, the responsibility for complying with the directives of the central planning authority; transfer, merger, or liquidation of the productive capital of the enterprise; wages policy; social policy; and the role of the workers' councils. According to the Yugoslav experiences,[3] the so-called advisory committees formed in joint enterprises ensure that the requirements of foreign partners are satisfied without disobeying the recommendations of Yugoslav authorities and partners.

Determining calculation methods of production costs and profits to be divided between the partners presents considerable difficulties that result from the lack of free convertibility of the zloty into currencies of capitalist countries and from the autonomous character of domestic prices in Poland, particularly those of production materials.

In the economic evaluation of the operations of a joint venture, the following issues should be decided:

1. Outlays on fixed capital (land, installations, machines, equipment, and licenses).

2. Current production costs (materials, wages, and general expenses)—profits to be divided (sales less costs and taxes).

In existing joint ventures in socialist countries, these issues are related to the two following approaches:

The " Yugoslav" approach (used on a limited scale in Hungary) is based on the convertibility of local currency and on the relatively flexible scale of domestic prices. All items of fixed capital and current production costs as well as financial effects derived thereof are expressed in local money and are comparable to those in the partners' countries.

In the "Romanian" approach the problem of the rate of exchange of lei is practically nonexistent, since all calculations are made in terms of foreign currencies, including those concerning purchases and payments made in the host country. This is reflected in the so-called internal export and import.

This "hard currency enclave" principle is to some extent a transplantation of foreign economic relations (prices, wages, labor efficiency, and fixed assets) to the territory of the host country. It necessitates dual bookkeeping (in foreign and domestic money) and the extremely difficult evaluation of some domestic inputs in terms of foreign monetary units.

Until 1976 Poland had no experience on its territory in capital cooperation with Western firms. The decree of May 14, 1976, by the Council of Ministers represented the first step toward joint activity (not yet joint ventures) by permitting foreigners to invest in Poland. The decree allows foreign firms, both individual and corporate, to invest in Poland in such sectors as handicrafts, hotels, restaurants, and other services. The regional councils have the authority to grant permission and approve investments. Following the decree the respective Polish ministers issued other regulations spelling out the guidelines for opening foreign currency accounts, conversion principles of Polish and foreign currencies, repatriation of profits and capital, and so on.[4]

The decree of February 7, 1979, extended the scope of activity permitted by the earlier regulations. It allows the setting-up and promotion of mixed stock companies (limited liability companies) based on Polish territory with the partnership of Polish small-scale non-basic state or cooperative industrial units whose main goal is production for the domestic market and for export. Basic small- and medium-scale regional industries usually cover local needs of the population and are under the supervision of local authorities. These regional industries produce mainly such goods as food products, home appliances, furniture, and clothing, or provide various services to the population. It is intended that joint ventures should introduce modern technical and technological processes and the utilization of local raw materials, especially waste material resources. The Polish partner's share of the capital should not be smaller than 51%. The mixed company can effect sales and purchases both in zloties and in convertible currency (CC), subject to some specific regulations. Polish authorities allow the repatriation of profits (after taxation) and capital in CC. The companies can be established for up to 15 years.

Small scale, non-basic industry in Poland covers a wide range of production lines. Some capacities in textile, clothing, electrical, mechanical, chemical, wood, foodstuffs, and other industrial units are still controlled by regional, state, and cooperative authorities which can be put at the disposal of joint US-Polish companies. They can be operated on the basis of the existing production departments of the Polish partners or new industrial units can be installed. These companies are subject to the Polish legal and economic stipulations, follow in principle Polish rules of production organization, and adopt the official exchange rate for all payments and calculations (1979, 31 zl/$).[5]

The Polish Research Institute of Foreign Trade is currently elaborating some new proposals designed to achieve further progress in the areas noted above. On the basis of the principles of joint ventures, it is possible to consider the following models of production and trade partnership as feasible both in small-scale and large-scale industries.

One model is: production in Poland and joint sales abroad. According to this model, the foreign partner puts at the disposal of the Polish partner production capital, know-how, and possibly working capital. This contribution should be described in detail in the contract approved by both partners. Using these means and its own contribution (investments, technical skill, labor, and working capital), the Polish partner starts the production of goods specified in the contract and supplies all or most of them to a jointly owned trading company organized abroad. This company sells the goods and divides the profits between the partners according to rules specified in the contract. The mixed trading company purchases the products with CC. The price should be close to the production costs according to Polish stipulations. This model can be attractive to foreign partners and can be negotiated in accordance with Polish legal, financial, and foreign exchange regulations.

Another feasible partnership model is: joint production by both partners at the lowest possible cost. This production covers the needs of both sides in subdeliveries for further processing, assembling, and completing of final products. This type of venture should be based, however, on a foreign currencies approach, similar to the Romanian pattern, to enable both sides to determine and verify production costs. What does this joint production mean in practice? First, it means a more sophisticated contribution by both partners in the sphere of technology and organization. Second, it means a closer mutual search for lower unit costs. This type of joint venture can be envisaged as a straight development of "traditional" industrial cooperation.

Despite the first positive steps toward establishing a regime for joint ventures in Poland, it is necessary to underscore that we are still at the beginning of this type of industrial cooperation. It will be necessary to answer some questions that remain unanswered and to find reliable, confident partners on both sides with the same policy of long-term development and the same spirit of risk taking and profit making. Let us begin.

Notes
1. See Zagorski, p. 121.
2. Hereafter called "joint ventures." See also E. Tabaczynski, *Wspolpraca inwestycyjna Wschód-Zachód* [East-West investment cooperation] (Warsaw: Polish Economic Publishers, 1981).
3. See Miodrag Sukijasovitch, *Joint Business Ventures in Yugoslavia Between Domestic and Foreign Firms: Development in Law and Practice* (Belgrade: The Institute of International Politics and Economics, 1973).
4. For further details, see "Trading and Investing in Poland," Overseas Business Report, OBR 78-44 (Washington, D.C.: US Department of Commerce, September 1978), pp. 25-27, and the documents which follow this essay.
5. See the enclosed full list and contents of Polish legal documents concerning joint ventures in Poland.

Polish Legal Documents Relating to Foreign Investment and Joint Ventures in Poland, 1976-79

Presented below in chronological order is the unofficial translation of Polish legal documents issued between May 14, 1976, and December 31, 1979, relating to foreign investment and joint ventures in Poland. First is an annotated listing of the 14 documents, followed by the full text of each.

A *decree* by the Council of Ministers creates a new legal situation. A *resolution* by the Council of Ministers further develops or elaborates an existing legal framework. An *order* by a minister implements a decree or a resolution at the executive level. An *information* by a ministry or other executive body interprets the relevance of existing laws for foreign or joint-venture enterprises operating in Poland.

Annotated and Chronological Listing of Documents

1. Resolution of the Council of Ministers of May 14, 1976, CONCERNING THE GRANTING OF LICENSES TO FOREIGN CORPORATE BODIES AND INDIVIDUALS FOR CONDUCTING CERTAIN KINDS OF BUSINESS ACTIVITIES (*Dziennik Ustaw,*[1] No. 19, May 26, 1976, item No. 123). The resolution sets out the general procedures and conditions for investing in Poland. It permits wholly foreign-owned businesses on Polish territory but is silent on the question of joint ventures between foreign and Polish firms.

2. Order of the Minister of Finance of May 26, 1976, CONCERNING GRANTING PERMITS FOR OPENING AND MAINTAINING BANK ACCOUNTS BY FOREIGN HOLDERS OF CONVERTIBLE CURRENCY, CONDUCTING BUSINESS ACTIVITY ON THE TERRITORY OF THE POLISH PEOPLE'S REPUBLIC (*Monitor Polski,*[2] No. 25, June 14, 1976, item 109). This order has been CANCELLED and replaced by the order of the Minister of Finance dated March 28, 1979 (see no. 11 below).

3. Order of the Minister of Finance of May 26, 1976, CONCERNING A PERMIT FOR CERTAIN CONVERTIBLE CURRENCY TRANSACTIONS BY MIXED-CAPITAL COMPANIES (*Monitor Polski,* No. 25, June 14, 1976, item 110).

4. Information of the State Board of Prices of May 31, 1976, CONCERNING PRINCIPLES AND PROCEDURES OF FIXING AND APPLYING PRICES BY FOREIGN CORPORATE BODIES AND INDIVIDUALS CONDUCTING A BUSINESS ACTIVITY ON THE TERRITORY OF THE POLISH PEOPLE'S REPUBLIC. Details for businesses licensed to invest or to participate in joint ventures in Poland concerning when and which prices on what transactions in Poland are fixed by the state and when prices may be set on the basis of contracts.

5. Order No. 21 of the Minister of Foreign Trade and Shipping of June 1, 1976, CONCERNING CUSTOMS DUTY EXEMPTION FOR FOREIGN CORPORATE BODIES AND INDIVIDUALS LICENSED TO CONDUCT CERTAIN KINDS OF BUSINESS ACTIVITY ON THE TERRITORY OF THE POLISH PEOPLE'S REPUBLIC. The order exempts the payment of duty on imports by those licensed to invest or participate in joint ventures in Poland.

6. Order No. 19 of the Minister of Labor, Wages, and Social Affairs of July 14, 1976, CONCERNING THE EMPLOYMENT OF POLISH WORKERS BY FOREIGN BODIES AND INDIVIDUALS. The order summarizes employment and social security regulations.

7. Information of the Ministry of Labor, Wages, and Social Affairs of July 14, 1976, CONCERNING THE EMPLOYMENT OF POLISH WORKERS BY FOREIGN CORPORATE BODIES AND INDIVIDUALS. The information details employment and social security regulations.

8. Information of the Ministry of Finance of August 1976, CON-

CERNING FINANCIAL AND TAX REGULATIONS WHEN ES-
TABLISHING AND CONDUCTING BUSINESS ON THE TERRI-
TORY OF THE POLISH PEOPLE'S REPUBLIC BY FOREIGN
CORPORATE BODIES AND INDIVIDUALS. Details for businesses
licensed to invest or participate in joint ventures in Poland on such
financial regulations as the opening of convertible currency investment accounts in Poland and how such accounts may be used; the
opening of zloty accounts and how these funds may be used; rules of
profit repatriation and disinvestment. Also details tax regulations,
such as cost of obtaining licenses, applicable taxes (i.e., turnover and
income), tax rates, and tax relief arising from bilateral tax treaties.

9. Information of the Ministry of Internal Trade and Services of Sep-
tember 1976, CONCERNING THE PROCEDURE FOR APPLYING
FOR LICENSE FOR OPERATING HANDICRAFTS ENTERPRIS-
ES, RESTAURANTS, CAFES, HOTELS, AND OTHER SER-
VICES ON THE TERRITORY OF THE POLISH PEOPLE'S RE-
PUBLIC.

10. Decree No. 24 of the Council of Ministers of February 7, 1979,
CONCERNING THE SETTING UP AND PROMOTION OF THE
ACTIVITY OF FOREIGN-STOCK COMPANIES IN POLAND
(*Monitor Polski*, No. 4, February 23, 1979). The decree states the new
principles of setting up equtiy-type joint ventures in Poland. Its annex
specifies spheres of activities permitted, legal and organizational
principles, use of convertible and clearing currencies, valuation of
fixed assets, the division of profits, sale or dissolution of joint ventures, taxes, connection with the national socio-economic plan, contracts with other enterprises in Poland, and employment- and wage-
related matters.

11. Order of the Minister of Finance of March 28, 1979, CONCERN-
ING PERMISSION FOR THE OPENING AND MAINTAINING OF
BANK ACCOUNTS BY FOREIGN LEGAL AND PHYSICAL
PERSONS ENGAGED IN ECONOMIC ACTIVITIES ON THE
TERRITORY OF THE POLISH PEOPLE'S REPUBLIC. This order
SUPERCEDES order of the Minister of Finance dated May 26, 1976
(see no. 2) and details the setting up and use of various currency ac-
counts.

12. Order by the Ministers of Finance and Foreign Trade and Shipping
of March 28, 1979, CONCERNING PERMITS FOR CERTAIN AC-
TIVITIES CONNECTED WITH FOREIGN TRADE TRANSAC-
TIONS MADE BY FOREIGN CORPORATE BODIES AND NAT-

URAL PERSONS. The order specifies for foreign persons or businesses licensed to invest or to participate in joint ventures in Poland the foreign trade organizations through which they must conduct specified types of export and import transactions.

13. Order of the Minister of Labor, Wages, and Social Affairs of May 30, 1979, CONCERNING THE PRINCIPLES OF HIRING AND REMUNERATION OF EMPLOYEES OF LIMITED LIABILITY COMPANIES WITH A SHARE OF FOREIGN CAPITAL (*Monitor Polski*, No. 15, June 22, 1979).

14. Order of the Minister of Finance of June 18, 1979, CONCERNING SOME REGULATIONS OF THE FINANCIAL MANAGEMENT OF COMPANIES WITH PARTICIPATION OF FOREIGN CAPITAL (*Monitor Polski,* No. 16, June 30, 1979). The order spells out in detail legal and financial regulations affecting the operation of joint ventures, such as accounting and financial reporting standards, minimum initial capitalization, forms of contribution and payment by the respective partners, sources of credit for a joint venture, depreciation rules, the compulsory creation of special funds and their use, profit repatriation and other currency rules, tax obligations, and sale or liquidation of a joint venture.

Full Text of the Documents

1. Resolution of the Council of Ministers of May 14, 1976, CONCERNING THE GRANTING OF LICENSES TO FOREIGN CORPORATE BODIES AND INDIVIDUALS FOR CONDUCTING CERTAIN KINDS OF BUSINESS ACTIVITIES (*Dziennik Ustaw, Journal of Laws,* No. 19, May 26, 1976, item No. 123).

By virtue of Art. i, subpar. 3, p. 3, of the Law dated July 18, 1974, on conducting trade and certain kinds of activities by the entities of non-nationalized economy (Dziennik Ustaw, *Journal of Laws,* No. 27, item 158) and Art. 1, subpar. 3 of the Law dated June 8, 1972, on the practicing and organization of handicrafts (Dziennik Ustaw, *Journal of Laws of 1972,* No. 23, item 164, and of 1974, No. 27, item 158), it is decreed as follows:

§1. The Resolution defines the terms, procedure, and the authorities entitled to grant licenses for conducting business activities by foreign corporate bodies and individuals in the scope of:

1. handicraft;
2. hotel business;
3. local trade as well as restaurant/cafe/bars and catering business;
4. other services.

§2. The provisions of the Resolution shall be applicable to:

1. corporate bodies residing abroad;
2. associations and social organizations of ethnic Poles residing abroad;
3. individuals domiciled abroad;
4. individuals of foreign citizenship supplied with the permanent residence permit in the territory of the Polish People's Republic;
5. non-corporate companies with shareholders specified in clauses 3 and 4.

§3. The authority entitled to grant a license for conducting business activities specified in §1, hereinafter called "license," is a local state administration authority, depending on the locality of the enterprise.

§4. 1. Individuals, associations, and companies specified in §2 submit applications for granting licenses either directly or through an attorney or Polish diplomatic or consular offices abroad.

2. Corporate bodies, associations, and organizations specified in §2, clauses 1 and 2, are granted licenses after the applications have been approved by the Minister of Foreign Trade and Shipping.

3. A license is granted for a period of 10 years, with the exception of the cases specified in subpar. 4 below; the license is valid until the end of the calendar year in which the term expires. After validity of the license has expired, a new license can be granted.

4. The validity of the license concerning activities in a building or on land of a limited lease cannot exceed the period for that lease.

§5. In granting licenses and conducting business activities, the respective provisions of the Law dated June 8, 1972, on the practice and organization of handicrafts (Dziennik Ustaw, *Journal of Laws,* 1972, No. 23, item 164, and 1974, No. 27, item 158) and of the Law dated July 18, 1974, on conducting trade and some other kinds of activity by entities of non-nationalized economy (Dziennik Ustaw, *Journal of Laws,* 1974, No. 27, item 158), shall be applicable as well as the regulations issued by virtue of these Laws, unless the provisions of the present Resolution provide otherwise.

§6. 1. The bodies specified in §2 registered abroad or domiciled abroad are under an obligation to appoint an attorney to handle matters connected with obtaining a license for conducting business activities, and after the license has been granted, to conduct these activities.

2. An attorney is to be a Polish citizen domiciled in Poland or a foreign citizen supplied with a permanent residence permit in the territory of the Polish People's Republic or the International Trading Company Ltd. "Polimar" SA.

§7. Individuals and attorneys of other bodies specified in §2 are not obliged to possess professional qualifications resulting from the Laws specified in §5 of the present Decree, and the executory provisions issued by their virtue.

§8. Individuals and corporate bodies conducting business activities by virtue of the present Resolution are not under obligation to be members of guilds or associations of private trade and services.

§9. The authorities granting a license shall specify the number of employees to be appointed for conducting business activities.

§10. 1. Before the license is granted, the bodies specified in §2 are under obligation to submit:

1. a cost estimate of the investment;
2. a commitment to defray all capital expenses in convertible currency;
3. a certificate issued by the Bank Polska Kasa Opieki SA stating that the applicant has deposited, in convertible currency, on his investment account, 30% of the sum specified in the cost estimate of the investment.

2. The authority granting a license may, in exceptionally justified cases, set up a lower amount of deposit specified in subpar. 1, clause 3.

§11. Within the scope defined by the Resolution and the provisions specified in §5, the following Decrees shall not be applicable:

1. The Decree of the Council of Ministers of December 20, 1928, on the conditions of permitting foreign stock companies and limited partnerships to act in the territory of the Republic of Poland (Dziennik Ustaw, *Journal of Laws,* No. 103, item 919).
2. The Decree of the Council of Ministers of March 28, 1934, on the conditions of permitting companies of limited liability to act in the territory of the Republic of Poland (Dziennik Ustaw, *Journal of Laws,* No. 21, item 281).

§12. The Decree comes into force as of the date of its proclamation.

2. Order of the Minister of Finance of May 26, 1976, CONCERNING GRANTING PERMITS FOR OPENING AND MAINTAINING BANK ACCOUNTS BY FOREIGN HOLDERS OF CONVERTIBLE CURRENCY, CONDUCTING BUSINESS ACTIVITY ON THE TERRITORY OF THE POLISH PEOPLE'S REPUBLIC (*Monitor Polski,* No. 25, June 14, 1976, item 109).

Since this order has been superceded, its text is not reproduced.

3. Order of the Minister of Finance of May 26, 1976, CONCERNING A PERMIT FOR CERTAIN CONVERTIBLE CURRENCY TRANSACTIONS BY MIXED-CAPITAL COMPANIES (*Monitor Polski,* No. 25, June 14, 1976, item 110).

By virtue of Art. 10, subpar. 1, p. 1, and Art. 16, subpar. 1, p. 1, of

the Convertible Currency Law, dated March 28, 1952 (Dziennik Ustaw, *Journal of Laws,* No. 21, item 133), it is ordered as follows:

§1. 1. The Order concerns certain convertible currency transactions
by mixed-capital companies conducting a business activity in the territory of the Polish People's Republic, whose partners are the Polish
entities of non-nationalized economy or social corporate bodies
authorized to do business, as well as individuals domiciled abroad
(i.e., foreign holders of convertible currency).

2. The provisions of this Order apply respectively to mixed-capital
companies, foreign partners being corporate bodies domiciled abroad,
or societies and social organizations of ethnic Poles domiciled abroad.

3. Individuals supplied with a permanent residence permit in the
Polish People's Republic can be partners in mixed-capital companies,
provided they have been granted the convertible currency permit. The
provisions concerning foreign partners apply respectively to those
persons unless this Order stipulates otherwise.

§2. 1. The agreement of a mixed-capital company should stipulate
that:

1. Foreign deposit (share) must be made in Polish zloties obtained
through the certified convertible currency exchange as specified by
the Narodowy Bank Polski; should, however, a part of the deposit
(share) be of a non-financial character, then the financial deposit
(share) is subject to reduction by the certified value of the non-
financial deposit (share). In any case, the financial deposit (share)
cannot be lower than 50% of the whole deposit (share).

2. At least 20% of net profit is to remain in a reserve fund, with the
remainder of the profits divided among the partners. Net profit is a
profit as determined by income tax regulations; with respect to
limited liability companies, it is profit reduced by the income tax
due from the company.

2. Terms of agreement on mixed-capital companies are subject to approval by the Minister of Foreign Trade and Shipping—within the
scope of agreements on commodity turnover with abroad and related
services—and by the respective Minister (Chairman of a State Administration Office) by agreement with the Minister of Finance—
within the scope of other agreements.

§3. Mixed-capital companies have been permitted to pay foreign
partners the sums of Polish zloties—out of their share in net
profits—to cover living expenses during their stay in Poland. Any
unused amounts thereof may be paid back.

§4. 1. The Bank Handlowy w Warszawie SA and the Bank Polska
Kasa Opieki SA have been permitted to effect payments, in convertible currency, to foreign partners due to their share in net profit distribution of the company, less the income tax due from foreign partners

and sums in zloties withdrawn by them from the company. In a fiscal year, these payments in convertible currency cannot exceed 9% *of the value of the foreign partner's deposit (share).*

2. The limitation on convertible currency payments due to the foreign partner's share in net profit is not applicable if more than 50% of the company's products and/or services are exported through documented sales for convertible currency.

3. Payments, specified in subpar. 1, can be realized in the form of:

    1. a transfer to an interest-bearing convertible currency account of a foreign partner;

    2. a transfer abroad,

    3. a cash payment.

4. Payments, specified in subpar. 1, can be effected after the bank has been supplied with:

    1. a certificate issued by the company in a form required by the bank;

    2. income tax payment orders for a fiscal year issued by local administrative authorities.

5. Authorization to net profit payments in convertible currency expires after ten years starting with the profits of a fiscal year in which a foreign partner was granted a permanent residence permit in the Polish People's Republic. With respect to persons specified in §1, subpar. 3, the right to net profit payment in convertible currency expires after ten years, starting with the profits of a fiscal year following the year in which the persons joined the company.

§5. 1. The Bank Handlowy w Warszawie SA and the Bank Polska Kasa Opieki SA have been permitted to transfer abroad:

    1. In the case where the foreign partner liquidates his interest in the company, the value of financial and non-financial deposit (share) and the part of the company's capital, exceeding the sum of joint shares of all partners, being in proportion to the foreign partner's share in the after-tax profit.

    2. In the case of the liquidation of the company, the value of the financial and non-financial shares of foreign partners, after all the company's debts are paid, and the part of the remaining capital of the company being in proportion to the foreign partners share in the after-tax profit.

2. If in cases, specified in subpar. 1, the value of assets of the company is less than the financial and non-financial shares of all partners, the bank may transfer abroad, to the foreign partners' accounts, the value of financial shares reduced in proportion to their share in the net profit of the company.

3. The bank effects payments abroad, specified in subpar. 1 and 2, after the company or a liquidator presents a certificate of transfer of

the sum to be paid in favor of foreign partners, and furthermore after presenting:

1. a certificate issued by the company and signed by the managing board, specifying the foreign partner's share, in the case mentioned in subpar. 1, clause 1;

2. a report on liquidation of the company after the conclusion of liquidation proceedings, together with the list of assets to be paid in favor of domestic and foreign partners, in the case specified in subpar. 1, clause 2.

§6. With respect to partners supplied with the permanent residence permit in the Polish People's Republic, prior to or during their business activity, transfer of money abroad, specified in §5, is subject to a separate convertible currency permit.

§7. Should the foreign partner's share be heired by, or bequested to, bodies domiciled abroad, the bodies dispose of the share and the profits therefrom to the extent executed by the devisor, after the document proving their rights to the inheritance or bequest has been presented.

2. Should the heirs (legatees) be bodies domiciled abroad along with heirs (legatees) domiciled in Poland, the share and profits therefrom are subject to transfer abroad only in the foreign heir's (legatee's) proportion of his share in the inheritance or bequest.

§8. In all calculations, convertible currencies are exchanged into Polish zloties and vice versa, at the special rate of exchange set up by the Narodowy Bank Polski, with a bonus applicable to foreign tourists.

§9. The Order comes into force as of the date of its proclamation.

4. Information of the State Board of Prices of May 31, 1976, CONCERNING PRINCIPLES AND PROCEDURES OF FIXING AND APPLYING PRICES BY FOREIGN CORPORATE BODIES AND INDIVIDUALS CONDUCTING A BUSINESS ACTIVITY ON THE TERRITORY OF THE POLISH PEOPLE'S REPUBLIC.

Foreign corporate bodies and individuals supplied with the license for conducting certain kinds of business activity, by virtue of the Decree of the Council of Ministers, dated May 14, 1976 (Dziennik Ustaw, *Journal of Laws,* No. 19, item 123) are subject to Polish legal regulations relevant to entities of non-nationalized economy, stipulating principles and procedure of fixing and applying prices. Essential regulations and principles arising from them, relevant for foreign corporate bodies and individuals, are as follows:

1. The authorities within the scope of fixing prices are stipulated by provisions §14 and §22 of Law No. 271 of the Council of Ministers, dated November 25, 1974, concerning the competence and procedure

of fixing prices (*Monitor Polski,* 1974, No. 40, item 233, and 1975, No. 19, item 18) and the provisions of the Orders issued on the basis of the Law. If the above regulations are followed, contracted prices (i.e., prices arranged between a buyer and a seller) shall be applicable in the sale of goods produced by foreign corporate bodies and/or individuals to entities of non-nationalized economy or in the retail network. Contracted prices shall be also applicable to the service trade. The above principle of applying contracted prices is not in force whenever the following exemption takes effect: the Chairman of the State Board of Prices specifies cases justifying the application of state prices to the sale of goods and/or services by entities of non-nationalized economy even if prospective buyers of goods or services are entities of the non-nationalized economy or individuals.

The scope of application of prices set up by the State Administrative Authorities for sale of goods and/or services produced (rendered) by entities of non-nationalized economy has been specified in Order No. 57/74 of the Chairman of the State Board of Prices (*Official Journal of Prices,* 1975, No. 1, item 4). According to the above Order, the prices set by the State Administrative Authorities are applicable in all cases involving nationalized enterprises acting as intermediate sellers. If, however, the sale is made directly by a producer or through entities of the non-nationalized economy, state prices shall be applicable only to the sale of the following goods: baking; confectionery (cakes, sweets); meat, processed meat, and animal consumer fat (except poultry, game animals, rabbits, and rabbit meat); fish and processed fish; ice-cream; soft drinks; vinegar; mustard; and the remaining concentrated foods, flour, and cereals. The prices for the above mentioned articles are set up by the Chairman of the State Board of Prices or its district branches. The prices of services rendered to individuals by entities of non-nationalized economy are set up by District Branches of the State Board of Prices, relevant to the location of the enterprise rendering services, with the exception of prices set up by other State Administrative Authorities for services such as: taxi, TV-set repair and TV aerial installation work, and repair of radio-engineering equipment. The list of services rendered to individuals, common to all district branches, has been specified in Order No. 9/76 of the Chairman of the State Board of Prices, whereas lists of services differentiated according to the territorial competence of particular district branches are included in Decisions of the Chairman of the State Board of Prices. Both the Order and particular Decisions have been published in the *Official Journal of Prices,* No. 7-8, of 1976.

2. Principles defined in pt. 1 concern the sphere of business activity involving, on the one side, a foreign corporate body or individual (as producer or service renderer), and on the other side, an entity of

non-nationalized economy or individual (as a buyer). If, however, the buyer is an entity of nationalized economy, contracted prices are not applicable. The parties concerned shall apply state prices (i.e., prices set up by district branches of the State Board of Prices or other State Administrative Authorities), with the exception of atypical articles, if the value of the order does not exceed 50 thousand zloties; or 20 thousand zloties if the buyer is an entity under a state budget (school, hospital). This being the case, the prices concerning atypical articles are arranged with the buyer.

3. The selling prices of goods and services produced by entities of non-nationalized economy are set up by district branches of the State Board of Prices on the basis of production costs, including turnover-tax rate and producer's profit. The price should be specified before the production has started, i.e., on the basis of preliminary cost calculation. If, exceptionally, the price is set up during or after the production process, the basis is the actual cost of production.

The cost calculation is drawn up by the producer, and allowance is made for labor-hour rate, percent rate of profit, and percent margin for overhead costs with respect to labor costs, to the amount specified by the Minister of Internal Trade and Services.

4. Prices of services rendered to individuals are set up by district branches of the State Board of Prices on the level securing profitability of the enterprise rendering the service. The prices in question, included in price lists, are in force territorially for all entities of the non-nationalized economy.

5. Concerning tourist/hotel services rendered by foreign corporate bodies and/or individuals, the prices shall be applicable as specified by the Chairman of the Chief Committee for Physical Culture and Tourism, by virtue of §10, subpar. 13, of Law No. 271 of the Council of Ministers, dated November 25, 1974.

6. The procedure of applying for price specification is stipulated by the provisions of Order No. 1/75 of the Chairman of the State Board of Prices, dated January 10, 1975 (if the authorities concerned are the Chairman of the State Board of Prices, minister/chief of central Office or manager of economic entity), and Order No. 4/75 of the Chairman of the State Board of Prices, dated January 25, 1975 (the authorities concerned being district branches of the State Board of Prices).

7. Where foreign corporate bodies or individuals conduct a restaurant/cafe/bar business, the prices of cooked products and commercial goods are set up by the manager of the restaurant/cafe/bar according to the detiled principles of price specification applicable to gastronomic establishments and entities of food producing industries, as stipulated by Order No. 5/74 of the Chairman of the State Board of Prices, dated February 1, 1974, amended by Order No. 13/76, dated

March 19, 1976. By virtue of the provisions of this Order, the prices set by the managers of restaurants/cafes/bars are differentiated depending on the category of the entity concerned.

Therefore, for entities of Lux/1 category and special "A" category, the sale prices are set according to individual cost calculation, covering the costs of the entity and providing secured profit, relevant to the standard of rendered services.

As to the entities of II-V categories and special "B"/"C" categories, the prices of cooked products and commercial goods are set on the basis of the joint estimate composed of the cost of raw materials, or goods, and the profit margin.

5. Order No. 21 of the Minister of Foreign Trade and Shipping of June 1, 1976, CONCERNING CUSTOMS DUTY EXEMPTION FOR FOREIGN CORPORATE BODIES AND INDIVIDUALS LICENSED TO CONDUCT CERTAIN KINDS OF BUSINESS ACTIVITY ON THE TERRITORY OF THE POLISH PEOPLE'S REPUBLIC.

By virtue of Art. 19, subpar. 4, of the Law dated March 26, 1975, Customs Law (Dziennik Ustaw, *Journal of Laws*, No. 10, item 56), it is decided as follows:

1. The Central Customs Office is under obligation to apply certain principles in the implementation of Order No. 85, dated November 18, 1975, of the Minister of Foreign Trade and Shipping, on authorizing the Central Customs Office to discharge from permit obligation and exemption from customs duty within the scope of non-commercial turnover with abroad (*Official Journal,* No. 9, Ministry of Foreign Trade and Shipping, item 72, and No. 4, item 18, 1976):

    a. exemption shall be granted to foreign corporate bodies and individuals entitled to conduct a business activity in Poland on the basis of licenses granted by virtue of separate regulations;

    b. exemptions shall be granted on importation of machinery and equipment being a part of the capital input for the enterprise set up in Poland, as well as materials and raw-materials necessary for production.

2. In case the customs duty exceeds 100.000 zloties, the Central Customs Office is under obligation to relegate the applications concerning matters specified in subpar. 1 to the Minister of Foreign Trade and Shipping for approval.

3. The Decision comes into force as of the date it is signed.

6. Order No. 19 of the Minister of Labor, Wages, and Social Affairs of July 14, 1976, CONCERNING THE EMPLOYMENT OF POLISH

WORKERS BY FOREIGN CORPORATE BODIES AND INDI-
VIDUALS.

By virtue of §4, subpar. 1, of the Decree of the Council of Ministers, dated June 23, 1972, concerning the detailed scope of activity of
the Minister of Labor, Wages, and Social Affairs, it is stipulated as
follows:

GUIDING RULES define principles concerning employment of
Polish workers by foreign corporate bodies and individuals, hereinafter called "foreign enterprises," covered by the Decree of the
Council of Ministers, dated May 14, 1976, concerning licenses granted
to foreign corporate bodies and individuals for conducting certain
kinds of business activity (Dziennik Ustaw, *Journal of Laws,* No. 19,
item 123), within the scope of:

1. Employment:
   1. Candidates for a job in a foreign enterprise are exempted from
      the employment exchange regulations supervised by the local
      authorities of the state administration.
   2. The principle specified in subpar. 1 is not applicable to:
      a. adolescents (i.e., persons under 18);
      b. university graduates, within 3 years from graduation, and
         vocational school graduates;
      c. persons who quit their previous jobs without notice, or lost
         the job through immediate dismissal.
   3. The relevant local administrative authorities conducting em-
      ployment exchange are under obligation to be of assistance in
      case of underemployment in a foreign enterprise, at the request
      of the interested enterprise.

2. Social Security:
   Workers in foreign enterprises are subject to social security on
   general principles, the exception being sickness and accidents benefits, as well as occupational diseases benefits, which—with respect to employees of these enterprises—are covered by the funds
   of the Social Security Administration Board.
   To profit from other social security benefits, as well as their financing, the principles applicable to employees of non-nationalized
   economy shall be in force.

7. Information of the Ministry of Labor, Wages, and Social Affairs of
July 14, 1976, CONCERNING THE EMPLOYMENT OF POLISH
WORKERS BY FOREIGN CORPORATE BODIES AND INDI-
VIDUALS.

Polish Labor Laws Provisions

1. Polish Labor Laws (i.e., Code of Labor provisions, Acts issued on their basis and Acts effective through the Code, stipulating the rights and duties of employees) are applicable to all labor relations in enterprises conducted in the territory of the Polish People's Republic, including labor relations between Polish citizens and foreign employers.
2. Observance of the Labor Laws by foreign employers is subject to a control by Labor Inspectors, cooperating with Trade Unions. In the case where the violation of employee's rights has been ascertained, Labor Inspectors are entitled to inflict a fine, up to 1500 zloties, upon managers (owners of the enterprises and persons managing work teams), or to propose a motion (in an administrative court) for inflicting a higher fine, i.e., 5,000 zloties (art. 284-286 of the Code of Labor).

Employment

1. Within the scope of accepting employees, the foreign employers are at liberty to choose the workers. The candidates for a job are exempted from the employment exchange regulations.
2. Exemption from the employment exchange regulations does not apply to:
   a. persons under 18;
   b. university graduates, within 3 years from graduation, and vocational school graduates, within one year from completing school;
   c. persons who quit their previous job without notice or lost the job through immediate dismissal.
   In principle, it is not recommended that offices of Labor and Social Affairs refer the above persons to be employed by foreign employers.
3. Offices of Labor and Social Affairs are under obligation to be of assistance in case of underemployment in a foreign enterprise, at the request of the interested foreign employer.

Social Security and Other Benefits

Workers employed by foreign employers conducting a business activity in Poland are subject to regulations (within the scope of social insurance) applicable to workers employed by Polish employers in non-nationalized enterprises.

The basic principles concerning social insurance are as follows:

1. Every employer conducting a business activity on his own account is under obligation to notify the Social Security Administration Board of all his employees and pay the relevant insurance premiums.

2. Social insurance provides the employees with the full range of social security benefits in case of illness, maternity, disablement, and old age, as well as accident on the job and/or occupational disease.
3. Social security benefits are implemented by the Social Security Administration Board. Having paid the insurance premium, the employer is free from any other financial liability to an employee or to the Social Security Administration Board.
4. The insurance premium is subject to differentiation with respect to the kind of business activity conducted by the employer. The premium is computed on the basis of wage percentage and amounts:
   a. for workers employed in handicrafts shops (in production or service activity):
   22%—in service rendering entities,
   27%—in remaining entities.
   The part of the premium amounting to 4% of employee's wages goes to the social security activity conducted by the Trade Unions;
   b. for workers employed in trade, catering, transport, hotel businesses, matrimonial agencies, office services, as well as incubative poultry production, the premium amounts to 30% plus 6% of worker's wages to be paid for social security activity conducted by the Trade Unions;
   c. for workers employed in horticulture or livestock production, the premium amounts to 30%;
   d. for workers employed in housekeeping and other private house services, 10%-22%.
5. Work places conducting a business activity are subject to control by the Social Security Administration Board when necessary, in order to specify a number of employees subject to social security, their wages (incomes and other essentials concerning social security realization).
6. These principles are not applicable to workers employed by enterprises sharing at least 50% of the capital due to Polish entities of non-nationalized economy; this being the case, social security is subject to application of principles concerning workers employed in Polish entities of nationalized economy.

8. Information of the Ministry of Finance of August 1976, CONCERNING FINANCIAL AND TAX REGULATIONS WHEN ESTABLISHING AND CONDUCTING BUSINESS ON THE TERRITORY OF THE POLISH PEOPLE'S REPUBLIC BY FOREIGN CORPORATE BODIES AND INDIVIDUALS.

Proceedings and conditions of granting licenses for conducting a business activity in Poland, by foreign corporate bodies and individuals, are regulated by the Resolution of the Council of Ministers, dated May 14, 1976, on granting licenses to foreign corporate bodies and individuals for conducting certain kinds of business activity. The Resolution was published in the Dziennik Ustaw, [*Journal of Laws*]of the Polish People's Republic, No. 19, dated May 26, 1976, item 123. According to the Resolution, both corporate bodies and individuals domiciled abroad, as well as individuals of foreign citizenship supplied with the permanent residence permit in the territory of the Polish People's Republic, associations and organizations of ethnic Poles residing abroad are permitted to establish and operate in Poland enterprises in the field of various crafts, retail trade, hotel and restaurant business, and other undefined services by virtue of the license granted by the respective local administrative authorities. The license can be granted for a ten-year period, subject to renewal. Applications concerning the license are received by the local administrative authorities. In order to precipitate the formalities, it is recommended that applications of foreign bodies be submitted through the Embassy or the Polish Consulate in the country of the foreigner's residence.

Foreign bodies are to appoint an attorney to handle the formalities connected with obtaining the license and, after the license has been granted, to conduct the business. The attorney is to be a Polish citizen domiciled in Poland or a foreign citizen supplied with the permanent residence permit in the territory of the Polish People's Republic, or the International Trading Co. Ltd. Polimar SA, Stawki 2, 00-193 Warszawa.

The license is granted with the following strings attached:
1. submitting the characteristics and cost estimate of the investment;
2. commitment to defray all capital expenses in convertible currency;
3. submitting the Bank PKO SA certificate of payment to the applicant's convertible currency account, 30% of the sum specified in the cost estimate of the investment.

The authority granting a license may, in exceptionally justified cases, set up a lower amount of the obligatory deposit.

FINANCIAL REGULATIONS

Financial problems connected with investment-business activities of foreign corporate bodies and individuals in the territory of the Polish People's Republic are regulated by two Orders of the Minister of Finance, dated May 26, 1976, published in *Monitor Polski*, Official Journal of the Polish People's Republic, No. 25, dated June 14, 1976, item 109 and 110:
1. the Order on the permit granted for opening and maintaining bank accounts by foreigners conducting business in the territory of the Polish People's Republic.

2. the Order on the permit for certain convertible currency transactions by mixed-capital companies.

The first of the above Orders concerns establishing and operating the enterprises wholly owned by foreigners. Establishing of the enterprise requires certain investment expenses connected with purchasing or leasing, adaptation or building of the enterprises and costs of machinery, equipment, and accessories enabling the exploitation.

Therefore, the contractor opens a convertible currency investment account—at the Bank Polska Kasa Opieki SA—which may be alimented with bank or postal transfers, as well as cash or cheques evidenced in an import declaration certified by the Customs Office. By way of the owner's order, the account may be used for covering all investment expenses, such as import of machinery and equipment from abroad through the relevant Polish foreign trade organizations; the purchase of materials, goods, and real estates through the Polish convertible currency retail network; and payment to meet obligations to Polish enterprises whose services are payable in convertible currency.

The account may not be used for payments to Polish citizens (e.g., costs of labor and services due to a Polish enterprise), whose services are to be paid in zloties.

The company's business must be accounted in Polish currency, and a zloty account must be opened for this purpose, also with the Bank Polska Kasa Opieki SA. The account is to be alimented with incomes made on sales or services, and shall be used to cover expenses resulting from the business operation. The Bank Polska Kasa Opieki SA has been permitted to effect payments in convertible currency, to and by order of the owners of enterprises, the part of net profit made in a fiscal year through business activity, i.e., the after-tax profit. Following the provisions of the Order, up to 50% of the net profit can be repatriated in convertible currency, however, not more than 9% of the total investment. The limitation on payments in convertible currency up to 9% of the total investment is not applicable if more than 50% of the company's products and/or services are exported through documented sales for convertible currency. The document issued by the relevant foreign trade enterprise shall be considered a document of export sale for convertible currency. The document has to specify the value, in zloties, of products or services for export, and confirm their sale for convertible currency.

In the case where an owner of the enterprise is residing in Poland on the basis of the permanent residence permit, he will be entitled to convertible currency transfer of the part of the profit for ten years starting from the date the residence permit was granted.

Further provisions of the Order regulate the financial bases for the sale of an enterprise to a foreigner or home resident.

Where the enterprise is sold, in full or in part, to a foreigner, the Bank Polska Kasa Opieki SA bas been authorized to transfer abroad the entire after-tax profit made on the sale, provided that the sale was made for convertible currency and payment is made in convertible currency through a Polish bank. Furthermore, certain formalities must be fulfilled: the sales contract is to be made in the form of a notarial deed; the buyer is granted a license to carry on the enterprise, if the enterprise is sold in full; and the seller has to pay all taxes.

The sale of the enterprise to a Polish entity (i.e., persons domiciled in Poland) can be made on condition that a prospective buyer has been granted a permit for the transaction. An equivalent of the sales price may then be transferred abroad in convertible currency, up to the amount of investment deposit increased by 50% of net income made on the sale, provided that: the sales contract was made in the form of a notarial deed; the proceeds from the sale have been paid in zloties to the bank account of the seller; and the seller paid all taxes. With respect to the owners of enterprises, supplied with the permanent residence permit in the territory of the Polish People's Republic, prior to or during their business activity, transfer of money abroad is subject to a separate convertible currency permit.

The second Order of the Minister of Finance concerns mixed-capital companies dealing with business activities in the territory of Poland, the Polish partners being entities of the nationalized economy or social corporate bodies authorized to do business; the foreign partners being individuals domiciled abroad and corporate bodies and associations/social organizations of ethnic Poles domiciled abroad. Terms of agreements on mixed-capital companies are subject to approval by the Minister of Foreign Trade and Shipping, or other Ministers concerned, by agreement with the Minister of Finance. The foreign share must be made in zloties obtained through the convertible currency exchange in Polish banks. A part of the foreign participation can be realized in the form of a certified non-financial share (i.e., machinery and equipment).

As to the company's profit (after-tax profit), at least 20% of annual net profit must remain in a reserve fund, with the remainder of the profits divided among the participants. Following the provisions of the Order, mixed-capital companies are permitted to pay foreign partners the sums in zloties—out of their share in net profits—to cover their personal expenses during their stay in Poland. Any unused amounts thereof may be paid back.

Mixed-capital companies can open bank accounts at the Bank Handlowy SA and the Bank Polska Kasa Opieki SA. These banks have been authorized to effect payments, in convertible currency, to foreign partners, due to their share in profits of the company. Payments can be effected after the bank has been supplied with certificates issued by the company, in the form required by the bank, and income-tax-payment orders for a fiscal year issued by the local administrative authorities. Payment in convertible currency, due to the foreign partner's share in the company's profits, are to be effected up to 9% of the total participation. This limitation is not applicable if more than 50% of the company's products and/or services are exported or sold through documented sales for convertible currency.

In the case of a liquidation of the foreign partner's interest in the company, the banks are authorized to effect payments, in convertible currency, of the value of the foreign partner's investment, plus his share in capital gains, after all the taxes have been paid. If, in the case of the liquidation of the company or the liquidation of the foreign partner's interest in the company, the value of the company's assets is less than the financial and non-financial shares of all partners, the bank may transfer abroad—to the foreign partner's account—the value of financial and non-financial shares reduced in proportion to the partner's share in the net profit of the company.

The provisions of the two Orders equally regulate the rights of foreign hiers, stipulating that in case the foreign partner's share is hiered by or bequested to persons domiciled abroad, the persons dispose of the share to the extent executed by the devisor, after the document proving their rights to the inheritance or bequest has been presented.

In all calculations, convertible currencies are exchanged in Polish zloties and vice versa at the special rate of exchange set up by the Narodowy Bank Polski, with the bonus applicable to foreign tourists (i.e., $ US = zl 33.20).

TAX REGULATIONS

Foreign corporate bodies and individuals conducting business activities in Poland are under obligation to pay taxes in the form of fiscal charge, connected with license granting, as well as turnover tax and income tax, connected with the business activity.

Fiscal charges amount to:

— for application concerning license	300zl
— for the license to practice handicraft	500zl
— for the license to conduct retail trade (depending on the kind of trade)	500-5000 zl
— for the license to conduct restaurant/cafes/bars (depending on the town and number of employees)	600-5000 zl
— for the license to conduct hotel businesses	300zl
— for the agreement on company (value of shares)	5%
if the share is of a non-financial character	10%

Business activity results in the obligation to pay the turnover and income taxes.

Turnover tax concerns the capital gains made on business transactions, and amounts to:

— for handicraft turnover	3.5% or 4%
— for restaurant/cafe/bar business turnover:	
sale of food and up to 18%-alcohol drinks	3%
sale of over 18%-alcohol drinks	8%
— for hotel business turnover	15%
— for trade turnover	2.5% or 3.5%
— for service turnover	
— for commission turnover	

Income made on a business activity results in the income-tax-paying liability.

The residual of capital gains (turnover) made on business activity and the costs of this income is subject to income tax.

Income tax assessment is based on accounting records, or valuation by way of percent ratio to turnover, relevant for a given branch of a business activity. A depreciation charge concerning fixed assets is being considered in income tax assessment.

Taxation of income for foreigners is lower than for Polish citizens.

Foreigners are subject to taxation at a progressive rate. However, the highest rate amounts to 50% of income and equalization tax (supplementary assessment) is not applicable. If foreign persons are shareholders in corporate companies, dividend tax (30% of dividend) is applicable.

These reduced taxation principles shall be also applicable to persons of foreign citizenship, supplied with the permanent residence permits in the territory of the Polish People's Republic, and conducting business by virtue of the license, for ten years starting with the year following the year of granting the permanent residence permit. (It practically means that a person residing in Poland and granted the permanent residence permit is subject to a reduced taxation rate for the next ten years.)

It is worth noting that Poland has entered into agreements on preventing double taxation with many countries, including the United States of America, the Federal Republic of Germany, Austria, and Pakistan. The same agreements with France, Sweden, and Denmark have been already signed but not effected yet; and with Belgium, Great Britain, Finland and Norway, they have been initialled.

The agreements regulate the tax-paying liability applicable to persons domiciled in one country and conducting a business activity and/or making profits in the other. Therefore, if persons domiciled in the country which entered into the agreement in question establish an enterprise in Poland, it is subject to taxation in Poland but remains free from tax-paying liability in the country of residence.

In case these persons make profits by virtue of their share in corporate companies (companies of limited liability), the profit is subject to taxation in Poland; however, a lower ratio shall be applicable (for example, to persons domiciled in the USA, 15% instead of the 30% mentioned above), and tax assessment in the country of residence shall be reduced by the tax paid in Poland.

In case these persons are domiciled in Poland (by way of the permanent residence permit) and make profits, subject to tax assessment, in the country of previous residence (the country of their citizenships), the profits in question shall be free from taxation in Poland.

As mentioned above, establishing and conducting a business activity in Poland results in turnover tax and income-tax-paying liability. These taxes can be subject either to so-called "general principles" or "lump form," in case of a small-scale activity. The former is assessed on the basis of accounting records specifying turnover and income to be taxed. (The person conducting a business activity is under obligation to keep these records.) In case of lump taxation, the record documentation is limited.

After the license for conducting a business activity has been granted (and before the business is started) the tax-paying liability must be declared to respective local authorities relevant for the business location. The fiscal charge concerning this declaration is to be paid, the amount equalling 60-300zl, depending on the scale of activity.

The local authorities give all the information concerning tax-assessment, relevant to the kind and scale of business activity, and stipulate further formalities connected with taxation.

9. Information of the Ministry of Internal Trade and Services of September 1976, CONCERNING THE PROCEDURE FOR APPLYING FOR LICENSE FOR OPERATING HANDICRAFTS ENTERPRISES, RESTAURANTS, CAFES, HOTELS, AND OTHER SERVICES ON THE TERRITORY OF THE POLISH PEOPLE'S REPUBLIC.

During the last few years, economic expansion has been a vital point in the development of Poland. The simultaneous increase of wages resulted in the growth of demands for various kinds of industrial goods, commercial articles and services, particularly those connected with tourism and the development of motor transport.

Polish regulations in force stipulate the possibility of operating various small-scale plants and service companies in the form of private workshops.

It has been regulated by the Law dated June 8, 1972, on the handling and organization of handicraft, whereas private trade, catering, and hotel business can be conducted by virtue of the Law dated July 18, 1974, on conducting trade and certain other kinds of activity.

Issued on May 14, 1976, the Decree of the Council of Ministers stipulates considerable facilitation for persons of foreign citizenship wishing to establish handicrafts enterprises, restaurants/cafes/bars, hotels, or other service companies in the territory of the Polish People's Republic. The above concerns both corporate bodies, individuals (irrespective of citizenship), and joint companies as well as associations and organizations of ethnic Poles domiciled abroad.

Particular prominence is given to those who are emotionally and economically connected with Poland through their Polish origin, interest, and personal or economic contacts.

In order to obtain the license for conducting a business activity in the territory of the Polish People's Republic, an investor is to meet the following requirements:

1. An inquiry about:
   a. whether the prospective business activity is permitted to be conducted in Poland by individuals of foreign citizenship or their companies, by associations and/or organizations of ethnic Poles, or by corporate bodies;
   b. whether the prospective activity constitutes handicraft, restaurant/cafe/bar services, hotel businesses, or other undefined services, subject to good terms.

The information in question can be given by: the Ministry of Internal Trade and Services, Plac Powstańców Warszawy 1, Warszawa, Chief Committee for Physical Culture and Tourism, Litewska 2/4, Warszawa (concerning hotel business and tourist services), Central Union of Handicraft, Miodowa 14, Warszawa, Chief Council of Private Trade and Services Associations, Piekna 66a, Warszawa, and the local authorities of State Administration.

2. Preliminary arrangements with the relevant local authority concerning objections (if any) as to the location of a prospective business activity in the particular town and suggested place.

3. Submitting the application for a license to be granted for conducting a business activity. Application forms are available in all local administrative offices.

4. The following documents must be enclosed with the applications:
   a. a cost estimate of the investment (building expenses, machinery, and equipment necessary to conduct a business activity) together with the characteristics of the investment;
   b. a commitment to defray all capital expenses in convertible currency (i.e., building expenses, machinery, and equipment) if the license is granted;
   c. a certificate issued by the Bank Polska Kasa Opieki SA stating that the applicant has deposited, in convertible currency, on his investment account, 30 percent of the sum specified in the cost

estimate of the investment (i.e., building expenses, machinery, and equipment). The certificate can be submitted later than an application;

d. an extract from the identity card (passport or any other document), legalized by a notary, Polish Diplomatic or Consular Offices abroad, including name and surname, permanent address and place of birth, and the citizenship of the applicant.

5. The following documents must be enclosed with the application submitted by companies, corporate bodies, and Polonian associations and organizations:

a-c. documents specified above, subpar. 4abc;

d. a copy of the power of attorney (subpar. 7), translated into Polish, legalized by Polish Diplomatic or Consular Offices abroad;

e. a partnership agreement or the Articles of the company;

f. a certificate issued by the relevant foreign authority stating that the company (corporate body, association, organization) has been established according to regulations effective in the country of its residence and its conducting activities specified in the agreement (the Articles);

g. a copy of the resolution by the general assembly of partners or relevant statutory authority (corporate body, association, organization) on extending the company's activity to the territory of the Polish People's Republic, and on capital input engaged for that purpose;

h. a written statement of the company (corporate body, association, organization), in the form specified by the agreement (the Articles), that the regulations effective in Poland shall be followed in the company's activity in the territory of the Polish People's Republic.

6. The application, together with the essential documentation (see subpar. 4 and 5), is to be submitted to the administrative authority relevant for the location of the prospective activity. In order to avoid delay, the application can be submitted through the attorney (see subpar. 7) or Polish Diplomatic or Consular Offices abroad.

7. Individuals domiciled abroad, corporate bodies, associations, and organizations permanently residing abroad are under obligation to appoint an attorney.

The attorney should be authorized to:

a. handle matters connected with obtaining the license to conduct a business activity,

b. conduct a business activity after the license has been granted.

The attorney may be authorized to accord substitution to a person qualified for handling the manufacturing or service enterprise in question.

The attorney is to be a Polish citizen domiciled in Poland or a foreign citizen supplied with the permanent residence permit, or the International Trading Company Ltd., "Polimar" SA, Stawki 2, Warszawa (within the scope of handling matters connected with granting the license and operating the enterprise).

8. Arrangement with the relevant local authorities as to the way of obtaining:

    a. detailed localization of the prospective investment (i.e., establishing the place where the investment is to be built);

    b. license for fruition of the investment project. For this purpose, the authorities have to be supplied with the materials specifying:

    i. general characteristics of the investments, including technical and operating specifications (i.e., the description of its destination for the certain kind of business activity)

    ii. the number of employees wanted;

    iii. general requirements to be met by the plot of land where the investment is to be located;

    iv. electric energy, gas, and water needs as well as amounts and kinds of industrial wastes to be expected;

    v. the burdens and disadvantages for the neighborhood to be caused by the investment (i.e., required protection zone, sound level, kinds and amount of contamination as a result of technological processes, etc.);

    vi. suggestion (on a plan or a lay-out in a scale arranged with the authorities) as to the detailed localization of the investment, including borders, existing buildings in the plot of land in question and neighboring areas, lines of ownership or the developing of the territory, list of names and addresses of owners or users of the area concerned.

9. Within 7 days after the building has been completed, the investor is obliged to submit the report on the forthcoming operation of the investment to the relevant authorities in the area.

    The Declaration should include:

    a. name and address of the investor

    b. address of the investment;

    c. nature of the investment.

    The basic technical documentation and work specification of the investment are to be enclosed in the report.

    Depending on the nature of the investment and its destination (particularly if persons' or property's security is in danger) the beginning of the operation (i.e., launching of the business activity) might be conditioned by the license granted for this operation.

10. The license being granted for a ten-year period is valid until the end of the calendar year, i.e., until December 31 of the year in

which the validity expires. The license is subject to renewal at the request of the interested investor.

The local authorities specify the maximum number of employees to operate the enterprise when the license is granted.

11. Foreign bodies, both corporate and individual, conducting a business activity in the territory of the Polish People's Republic are not obliged to be members of handicraft guilds or associations of private trade and services.

12. In view of the present economic needs, it has been recommended that foreigners build and/or operate the following kinds of business activity:

a. in the field of handicraft:

i. car servicing, i.e., all kinds of repair shops maintenance services, car washing, etc.;

ii. production and repair of precision tools and instruments;

iii. production and repair of machinery and technical equipment for service shops (particularly handicrafts enterprises);

b. in the field of restaurant/cafe/bar business: all kinds of restaurant/cafe/bar entities, particularly quick service ones, located on motor-roads, in tourist holiday resorts, etc.:

c. in the field of hotel business: hotels (maximum employment is 50 persons), pensions, motels, adaptation of historic premises into hotels or restaurants in areas where they are in shortage.

LIST OF RELEVANT BASIC LAWS

1. The Law dated June 8, 1972, concerning the practicing and organization of handicraft (Dziennik Ustaw, *Journal of Laws*, No. 23, item 164, and of 1974, No. 27, item 158).

2. The Law dated July 18, 1974, concerning conducting trade and certain other kinds of business activity by entities of the non-nationalized economy (Dziennik Ustaw, *Journal of Laws*, No. 27, item 158).

3. The Law dated March 24, 1920, on buying fixed assets by foreigners (Dziennik Ustaw, *Journal of Laws*, No. 24, item 202).

4. The Decree of the Council of Ministers dated December 20, 1928, on admitting foreign stock companies and limited partnerships to conduct business in the territory of the Republic of Poland (Dziennik Ustaw, *Journal of Laws*, No. 103, item 919).

5. The Decree of the Council of Ministers dated March 28, 1934, on admitting foreign limited liability companies to conduct business in the territory of the Republic of Poland (Dziennik Ustaw, *Journal of Laws*, No. 31, item 281).

6. The Decree of the Council of Ministers dated May 14, 1976, on

granting license to foreign corporate bodies and individuals for conducting certain kinds of business activities (Dziennik Ustaw, *Journal of Laws*, No. 19, item 123).

7. The Order of the Minister of Internal Trade and Services, dated September 30, 1972, on specifying the kinds of handicraft and defining authorization and qualifications for their operation (Dziennik Ustaw, *Journal of Laws*, No. 45, item 290, and of 1976, No. 8, item 441).

8. The Order of the Minister of Internal Trade and Services, dated October 28, 1974, concerning conducting trade and certain services by entities of the non-nationalized economy (Dziennk, Ustaw, *Journal of Laws*, No. 44, item 265, and of 1975, No. 38, item 205).

9. The Decree of the President of the Council of Ministers, dated February 27, 1975, concerning operating hotel business by entities of the non-nationalized economy (Dziennik Ustaw, *Journal of Laws*, No. 7, item 37, and of 1976, No. 27, item 157).

10. The Order of the Minister of Finance, dated May 26, 1976, concerning permits for opening and maintaining bank accounts by foreign holders of convertible currency conducting a business activity in the territory of the Polish People's Republic (*Monitor Polski*, No. 25, item 109).

11. The Order of the Minister of Finance, dated May 26, 1976, concerning a permit for certain convertible currency transactions by mixed-capital companies (*Monitor Polski*, No. 25, item 110).

12. The Decree of the President of the Republic of Poland, dated June 27, 1934, code commerce (Dziennik, Ustaw, *Journal of Laws*, No. 57, item 502), together with introductory regulations concerning the code (Dziennik Ustaw, *Journal of Laws*, No. 57, item 503), takes effect in the parts concerning provisions on general partnerships, companies of limited liability, and stock companies, with the regulations on firms, the procuration and the commercial register being in force with respect to the above companies (art. 4 of introductory regulations concerning civil code, Law of April 23, 1964, (Dziennik Ustaw, *Journal of Laws*, No. 16, item 94).

13. Decree No. 24 of the Council of Ministers of February 7, 1979, CONCERNING THE SETTING UP AND PROMOTION OF THE ACTIVITY OF FOREIGN STOCK COMPANIES IN POLAND (*Monitor Polski*, No. 4, February 23, 1979).

Para. 1. 1. State and cooperative firms in Poland are allowed to sign contracts with foreign corporate bodies or natural persons for the setting up of limited liability companies based on the territory of the Polish People's Republic, hereinafter called "companies." The activity of those companies should concentrate on production for the domestic market and export goods.

2. The companies should operate on the same scale and along the same lines of production as medium-size and small (locally or territorially based) industrial factories and cooperatives.

3. The companies are incorporated in agreement with Polish legal regulations, and their activity is subject to Polish law.

4. The decree defines as a "foreign corporate body" or "natural person" a foreign based organization or person living permanently abroad that has established the right to pursue economic activities with other foreign bodies in accordance with the laws of the country in which he lives or is incorporated.

Para. 2. 1. Appropriate Polish administrative units will issue foreign currency permits for foreign corporate bodies or natural persons being the partners of those companies:

a. to transfer abroad a part of their profits, after deducting appropriate taxes and duties and fulfilling their obligations in view of the law and any other agreements:

b. to transfer abroad monies to the equivalent of the returned monetary outlays and assets in-kind in the instance of the selling out of the company—in agreement with the conditions specified by the contract.

2. The permits mentioned in para. 2, p. 1, will be issued within the company's own foreign currency resources and foreign currency means granted by the Minister or the Central Managing Board of the cooperative which made the decision on the setting up of the company within its own foreign currency limitation.

Para. 3. 1. The shares of a Polish state enterprise (a Polish cooperative) in the company should not be less than 51% of the operating capital.

2. The shares of the company are registered and cannot be transferred to a third party without the consent of all other partners; also, the Polish partner is given the right to acquire the foreign partner's shares before any other purchaser.

Para. 4. The company can be established for up to 15 years. In certain justified instances the period of its activity can be prolonged, with the proviso that the partners reserve the right to retire from the partnership in agreement with the binding regulations and under the terms stipulated by the contract.

Para. 5. 1. A permit to sign the contract will be issued on the following basis:

a. a proposal by the Director-in-Chief of a state enterprise or the Chairman of the managing board of the cooperative concerned with the signing of such an agreement with the foreign corporate body or natural person specifying the character and scope of activity of the intended company and the purpose for its establishment;

b. a declaration from the foreign trade organization concerning the possibilities of exporting the intended corporation's production to free currency markets in the event of entering into export production.

2. A decision on signing the contract must be issued by the appropriate minister or the Board of the Central Cooperative Union after it is approved by the Chairman of the Committee for Domestic Market Affairs in agreement with the Chairman of the Planning Committee at the Council of Ministers and the Minister of Finance.

Para. 6. The activity of the companies will be subordinated to the national socio-economic plan in a specific way, i.e., apart from the system of unions and ministries.

Para. 7. The company will be aided by appropriate units of the Polish state administration system in the implementation of their production and co-production tasks.

Para. 8. The guidelines concerning the principles of the setting up, the organization, and functioning of limited liability foreign-stock companies in Poland are introduced in the form of an annex to the Decree.

Para. 9. The Ministers of Finance, Foreign Trade and Shipping, Labor, Wages, and Social Affairs, everyone within his own scope of activity will specifically detail, as defined above, the principal quantities of these companies by April 15, 1979.

Para. 10. The resolution takes effect as of the day of its announcement.

Annex to Decree No. 24 by the Council of Ministers of February 7, 1979 (item 36).
Guidelines Concerning the Principles of the Setting Up, Organization, and Functioning of Limited Liability Foreign Stock Companies in Poland

I. Sphere of Activity

1. Limited liability foreign stock companies, hereinafter called "companies," can be set up:

a. in medium and small (locally or territorially based) industry;

b. in the cooperative movement.

2. The range of activity of the companies should cover mainly processing industries, based on the principles of developed co-production, the main goals of which would be:

a. the production of sought after goods for the domestic market;

b. production favorable for export.

3. While setting up the companies, the following circumstances should be taken into account:

a. the assurance of the introduction of modern technical and technological processes and work organization by a foreign corporate body or natural person;

b. the possibility of using raw material and especially waste material resources in this country for production and processing.

II. Legal and Organizational Principles

4. The contract can be signed on the basis of a decision issued by the appropriate minister of the Managing Board of the central cooperative union, after it has been accepted by the Chairman of the Committee for the Domestic Market in agreement with the Chairman of the Planning Committee at the Council of Ministers and the Minister of Finance.

5. The company should be incorporated in agreement with Polish regulations, and its activities should be subordinated to Polish legal regulations and in compliance with the terms of the conditions specified by the contract.

6. The company can be set up for up to 15 years; however, in justified instances, this time may be prolonged.

7. The shares of the initial capital of a Polish state enterprise (a Polish cooperative) in the company should not be smaller than 51%.

8. In principle, that member of the managerial board who will direct its activity should be a Polish citizen.

9. The contract must stipulate the participation of the foreign partner in checking financial operations made by the company, as well as participation on the board of supervision, or audit commission, if such is the case.

10. In the sphere of exports and imports the company should obtain a favorable trade balance in the convertible currency payment zone.

III. Clearing Accounts

11. The company should settle its accounts in the domestic market in zlotys according to the principles specified by regulations of the Ministry of Finance.

12. In trade transactions with Polish socialized economic units, the company may effect sales and purchases:

a. in zlotys, providing that the purchases are made directly from wholesale dealers in goods or services according to the prices specified by price catalogs and paid by Polish socialized economic units or the prices negotiated by the company with wholesale dealers if there are no catalog prices (consumer goods), or with the central procurement boards or offices (production means);

b. for convertible currency through a foreign trade organization or directly from domestic suppliers or recipients entitled to carry out foreign trade activity.

13. In clearing the transactions made in convertible currency, a special exchange rate fixed by the National Bank of Poland must be used.

14. The company is obligated to spend a part of the profits on the setting up of a capital reserve and a guarantee fund, together with a factory fund for the staff, in agreement with Polish legal regulations.

15. Neither foreign currency credits nor guarantees will be granted to the comapny by the Bank Handlowy SA in Warsaw.

IV. Valuation of Fixed Assets

16. Fixed assets and property as well as floating assets in kind deposited by the partners are valued in terms of zlotys by experts, applying a special exchange rate fixed by the National Bank of Poland to evaluate the elements of foreign assets purchased in Poland or abroad for convertible currency.

17. The monetary assets brought in by the Polish partner will be in zlotys.

18. The monetary assets brought in by the foreign partner should be paid in zlotys obtained through the exchange of convertible currency at the appropriate Polish bank and paid into the running account of the company.

V. Financing of Turnover

19. Foreign currency transactions of the company with its foreign and Polish counterparts are financed exclusively by its bank account at a Polish bank.

20. The transactions of the company with socialized economic units and financial operations connected with the payment of salaries are financed in zlotys from its running account. The detailed principles of financial operation and paying of salaries will be settled by order of the Ministry of Finance.

VI. Profit and Its Division

21. The profit gained by the company can be divided into gross profit, net profit, and distributed profit.

22. Gross profit constitutes a surplus between the amount of receipts due to all kinds of transactions made by the company and its potential time-fixed deposits in the banks, the receipts from sold patents, and receipts from licenses and the operational costs of its activity. These costs also include the depreciation allowance calculated in agreement with the regulations binding in this country, the charges for the land under lease, and other duties paid to state administration units.

23. Net profit is calculated after deducting from gross profit the obligatory funds set up by the company and potential investment expenditures which have not been paid from the depreciation allowance.

24. Distributed profit is calculated by means of deducting all taxes from net profit. Distributed profit is divided among all partners in proportion to their share in the capitalization of the company (shares owned).

25. At his request, a part of the distributed profit accruing to the foreign partner can be transferred abroad in convertible currency to his bank account, and the part accruing to the Polish partner paid into his running bank account in a Polish bank. The Ministry of Finance will issue an order specifying the use of those receipts by the Polish partner.

26. In the event of a loss at the end of the fiscal year, the amount of that loss will be placed to the debit of the risk fund. If the risk fund proves insufficient to cover the loss, then the partners must cover it in proportion to their shares in the company.

VII. Financial Aspects of Dissolving and Selling the Company

27. After the company is dissolved and sold as a result of the termination of the time stipulated by the contract, the fixed assets of the company will pass into the possession of the Polish partner (as stipulated by the contract). The turnover fund is divided in proportion to the shares of the partners and the foreign partner maintains the right to transfer those funds abroad at his request.

28. When the company is dissolved and sold due to reasons other than those mentioned in item 27, through no fault of the foreign partner, the latter maintains the right to transfer abroad a part of the company's assets accrued to him after the selling-out account is drawn and all financial obligations and duties are met.

29. The share of the foreign partner in the net assets (after deducting the duties) of the sold-out company is calculated in terms of their value at the moment of selling the company. The agreement should specify the procedures covering other than financial assets of the company in the event of its sale.

VIII. Taxes

30. The activity of the company is subject to taxation in agreement with tax regulations binding in Poland. The tax on profits gained by the company does not exempt it from other payments specified by the detailed regulations.

31. The Ministry of Finance will specify the conditions under which the company can be completely or partially exempted from paying taxes on profit during a period of three years from the moment of setting up the company (or launching production).

IX. The Principles of the Delivery System

32. If the company makes any purchases for foreign currency in Poland, it has the right to buy directly from the producers without the intercession of wholesale dealers or balancing-distribution units, in the event that the producers have the status of a foreign trade organization, or through foreign trade organizations. In the latter instance, the settling of accounts takes place in terms of the prices in effect at the time of the transaction with foreign trade units. If the company purchases zlotys, it can place orders with wholesale dealers and other balancing-distributing units that make room for the deliveries for the company in their sales plans. A need should be anticipated to sign contracts on the delivery of definite products through provision and sales organizations.

33. The company is entitled to invite tenders for the delivery of intermediate materials and semi-products from Polish companies and through foreign trade organizations and foreign partners. The allocation by tender should be left to the decision of the managing board. When similar terms are offered by Polish and foreign tenders, priority should be given to the Polish tender.

34. The company can set up consignment warehouses of semi-products and spare parts on the basis of contracts signed with Polish suppliers and through foreign trade organizations with foreign suppliers.

X. Connections with the National Socio-Economic Plan

35. In the sphere of planning we should distinguish:

a. the production of the company;

b. the production of Polish co-producers providing supplies for a firm.

The activity of the company should be subordinate to the national socio-economic plan in a specific way (apart from the system of ministries and unions). The company can be exempted, at a request from the Polish partner and as a result of the decisions stipulated by the contract, from certain planning requirements, such as production growth rates, the limiting of the wages fund, the limiting of floating assets and standard stocks. These figures should be viewed according to the principle: implementation—the plan. On the other hand, the total amount of profits should be regarded in the part accrued to the Polish partner in agreement with a rough estimate. The difference in plus or minus would be one of the elements available for assessing the company's activity. The most general planning principles should be applied to products supplied by Polish co-producers.

36. In the sphere of investment planning, the investments made by the company in Poland should be regarded as "off limits"; nevertheless, certain commissioned work and deliveries should be carried out in agreement with the regulations of item 35.

37. The plan for commodity turnover should be specified by the national socio-economic plan in a similar way as the basic activity.

XI. Co-Production

38. The company can:

a. sign contracts on co-production deliveries with Polish socialized units under a strict rule that the co-producers will ensure appropriate quality of products, punctuality of delivery, and size of production. Every legal consequence will be borne by the guarantor, with the proviso, however, that the imposition of these provisions (together with any penalties) be settled in zlotys;

b. sign co-production contracts on the basis of given licenses or through foreign trade organizations with other foreign corporate bodies, particularly if dictated by reason of modern technology.

XII. Employment, Wages and Workers' Affairs

39. In general, the company should employ Polish personnel, and foreigners only if they are highly qualified specialists.

40. The wages of the Polish and foreign staff are fixed and paid in zlotys.

41. The system of payments used by the company should be in compliance with the binding regulations.

42. The wages of the foreign staff are fixed by means of a contract signed between the company and the foreign partner or the employee directly involved. It is possible to use a different scale of wages for foreign personnel as opposed to the Polish staff. The payments can have a permanent character (a monthly or annual wage) or can be

divided into two parts: a stable and a variable one depending on the financial results achieved by the company. The scale of wages earned by the foreign staff will be determined by their actual wages in the foreign based firms.

43. Foreign personnel are given the right to transfer 50% of their earnings abroad into currency used in the company's settlements, or into his native currency, and the company must ensure foreign currency means for that purpose.

44. Social affairs of Polish employees are settled in agreement with Polish regulations.

45. Social affairs of foreign employees should be settled the same way as those of the Polish staff.

46. The issue of retirement fees paid by foreign employees should be settled by the company's contract or individual employment contracts.

11. Order of the Minister of Finance of March 28, 1979, CONCERNING PERMISSION FOR THE OPENING AND MAINTAINING OF BANK ACCOUNTS BY FOREIGN LEGAL AND PHYSICAL PERSONS ENGAGED IN ECONOMIC ACTIVITIES ON THE TERRITORY OF THE POLISH PEOPLE'S REPUBLIC.

The following order is based on Art. 10, para. 1(1), of the currency law of March 28, 1952 (*Dziennik Ustaw,* no. 21, item 133), para. 4(1) of the Council of Ministers' resolution No. 172 of August 6, 1976, on interest rates on bank accounts for the population (*Monitor Polski,* No. 35, of 1976, item 151, and No. 17, of 1977, item 96), and para. 2(3) of the Council of Ministers' resolution No. 98 from July 5, 1977, on interest rates on bank accounts (*Monitor Polski,* No. 17, item 96).

Para. 1. The foreign legal and physical persons described in para. 2 of the Council of Ministers' order of May 1976 on the granting of permissions to foreign legal and physical persons for running some types of economic activities (*Dziennik Ustaw,* No. 19, of 1976, item 123, and No. 31, of 1978, item 135), later called "order of the Council of Ministers of May 14, 1976." These persons are allowed to open foreign currency accounts in Bank Polska Kasa Opieki SA to finance the following activities:

1. investments in the territory of the Polish People's Republic, accounts "F";

2. exports and imports, accounts "EI."

Para. 2. 1. Payments into accounts "F" and "EI" are made in the convertible currencies specified by the National Bank of Poland.

2. Payments into the "F" and "EI" accounts may come in the form of:

1. money remittances (bank and post office remittances) from foreign countries;

2. foreign currencies and sums obtained from the realization of foreign currency letters of credit made out to bearer and to name, up to the sums described in written customs declarations certified on entering Poland by a Polish customs office at the border or in a certificate issued by this office;

3. sums transferred from interest-bearing foreign currency accounts of foreigners.

3. The sums deposited according to para. 10, section 1(3), of the Council of Ministers' order of May 14, 1976, may also be paid into accounts "F."

4. The bank also accepts payments into "EI" accounts, apart from the payments mentioned in section 2, of sums obtained from the export of goods and services conducted through Polish foreign trade organizations and from payments made by socialized economic units authorized to engage in internal export trade. All sales for convertible currencies to these units are treated as export sales.

Para. 3. 1. Owners of "F" accounts are allowed to make withdrawals in convertible currencies for the following purposes:

1. for the purchase of goods in foreign countries through Polish foreign trade organizations;

2. for the purchase of goods within the internal export scheme;

3. to effect payments to Polish enterprises, provided that respective regulations allow these enterprises to sell goods or provide services for convertible currencies.

2. The sum on "F" account may be withdrawn in part or in total and also taken to a foreign country without any separate customs permission. The owner's right to take the money out of the country is certified in all cases by the bank concerned.

3. Withdrawals from "F" accounts to effect payments to Polish citizens with foreign currency accounts who have no right to sell goods and services for convertible currencies may only be made in zlotys.

4. The sums deposited in "F" accounts, according to para. 10, section 1(3), of the Council of Ministers' order of May 14, 1976, may be used in a way described in the order after 50% of the estimated value of the investment has been carried out. In justified cases, however, the voivodship administrative authority concerned may issue permission, after obtaining consent from the Minister of Internal Trade and Services and the Minister of Finance, to use the deposit for the realization of an investment whose 50% of estimated value has not yet been carried out.

Para. 4. 1. Owners of "EI" accounts are allowed to make withdrawals for the purchase of materials and raw materials, spare parts and tools necessary for production and the provision of services when:

1. the purchase is made abroad through a Polish foreign trade organization;

2. the purchase is made within the internal export scheme;

3. the purchase concerns Polish commodities and is made with a Polish enterprise authorized to sell for convertible currencies.

2. Owners of "EI" accounts are also allowed to make withdrawals in convertible currencies to cover:

1. dues to Polish foreign trade organizations resulting from their intermediary services in the export or import of goods;

2. dues for services provided by Polish enterprises authorized to provide services for convertible currencies;

3. the costs of business trips to foreign countries, necessary for the foreign-enterprise to conduct its economic operations in Poland, made by their employees living in Poland.

3. The owner of the account needs no separate permission to use interest accrued on his "EI" account and the sums he pays into the account that are not connected with the operation of his enterprise.

4. The year-end balance sheet excess of export incomes over expenditures for the import of raw materials, semi-manufactured goods, spare parts, tools, and services and the expenditures described in section 2 is transferred from account "EI" to the account described in para. 5.

Para. 5. 1. The foreign legal and physical persons described in para. 2 of the Council of Ministers' order of May 14, 1976, are allowed to open zloty accounts in Bank Polska Kasa Opieki SA to make settlements connected with the running of their enterprises, investments, and modernization ventures and their own personal expenses. From these accounts they may also make zloty withdrawals, according to the regulations set out in para. 7, with the right to exchange them back into convertible currencies, which are later called withdrawals in convertible currencies.

2. Deposits on zloty accounts may also be used for investments mentioned in section 1, providing the person running the enterprise gets separate permission on terms described in para. 10, section 1(1 and 3) and section 2 of the Council of Ministers' order of May 14, 1976, with a reservation that the sum must be used for a specific investment.

Para. 6. Deposits on "F" and "EI" accounts and zloty accounts all bear a 3% annual interest. The interest is added to the deposits in the currency of the account.

Para. 7. 1. The owners of foreign enterprises are allowed to instruct the bank to effect payments in their name from accounts specified in para. 5, section 1, up to a sum representing 50% of the net income they obtain from economic activities in any given fiscal year, but not higher than 9% of their investment spending in convertible currencies. The net income in a fiscal year is that amount described in income tax regulations less the tax.

2. By the value of investment spending in convertible currencies, we understand the value of fixed assets and non-durable objects necessary for running the business, used in the given year, and purchased for convertible currencies or for zlotys obtained from the exchange of convertible currencies and documented with an appropriate document.

3. If the company practices the whole or a part of turnover by means of the documented sales for convertible currency, it is allowed to make payments in convertible currency from the accounts mentioned in para. 5 for and at the request of the owners of the companies not more than 50% of the surplus mentioned in para. 4, section 4, transferred on that account in zlotys. The amount of the money paid in convertible currency from the accounts in zlotys cannot exceed 50% of the net profit. The payments can only be made transferring whole surplus specified in para. 4, section 4, to the account in zlotys.

4. Cash payments are made on the basis of a request made by the company and a certificate issued by the appropriate territorial state administrative organ specifying:

1. the size of the documented investment deposit in convertible currency;

2. the size of export receipts in convertible currency;

3. the size of expenses from the "EI" account in convertible currency made on the imports of raw materials, semiproducts, spare parts, and instruments used in production and rendering services throughout the year;

4. the size of expenditures from the "EI" account made in convertible currency for the benefit of Polish foreign trade companies due to exports and imports mentioned in item 2 and 3;

5. the size of income and an appropriate income tax levied on it.

The above certificate is issued by the territorial state administrative unit on the basis of record books which should bear the items mentioned in item 1-4.

5. Payments can be made in the form of:

1. a transfer to the interest bearing account of the company owner;

2. a transfer abroad.

6. The payments that were not made in a given year, although the conditions enlisted by the order have been fulfilled, can be made during the following years, but no later than a year after the permit for running business activity expires.

Para. 8. If the company owner sells his company, a part or the total amount of money minus the profit tax on sales can be transferred abroad if it was sold to a hard currency foreigner, provided that;

1. the sales contract was drawn before a notary;

2. in the event of selling the whole of the company or a part of it working as an individual unit, the vendee has the right to run this kind of business in a given voivodship or has been ensured by the voivodship state administrative units that he will be granted such a permit in the event of purchasing the company;

3. the money obtained from the sales has been transferred in foreign currency to a Polish bank;

4. the vendor has paid all taxes connected with the running of investment and business activity.

Para. 9. The money obtained by the company owner from the sale of the company to a Pole having foreign currency means can be transferred abroad up to the amount of investment foreign currency outlays plus 50% net income obtained from the sale of the company (gross income minus an appropriate tax on profit from the sale of the company) provided that:

1. the sales contract has been drawn before a notary;

2. the money obtained from the sale has been transferred to a Polish bank to the account of the vendee;

3. the vendee has paid all taxes connected with the running of investment and business activity.

Para. 10. A separate foreign currency permit is required for:

1. the signing of an agreement on the sale of the company mentioned in para. 8 and 9;

2. a transfer abroad of the money obtained by means mentioned in item 1 made by the vendees who have a permit for a permanent stay in Poland or have obtained such a permit while running the company.

Para. 11. 1. In the event of the acquisition of title to a legacy or heritage in the form of the company's assets by people permanently living abroad, these people can manage their property in the same way and to the same extent as the testator (devisor), after they have produced a document confirming their right to the heritage or legacy.

2. In the event that the inheritors include, apart from people permanently living abroad, people also living in Poland, then the company assets and its profits can be transferred abroad only up to the amount payable to the foreign inheritor in proportion to his share in the legacy (heritage).

Para. 12. The rate of conversion of convertible currency into zlotys and vice versa is specified by the special list of exchange rates issued by the National Bank of Poland.

Para. 13. Investment foreign currency accounts and accounts in zlotys that have been opened before the issuing of this order should be run according to the rules specified by the order.

Para. 14. The order by the Minister of Finance of May 26, 1976, on a permit to open and run bank accounts for foreign currency foreigners involved in business activity in People's Poland (*Monitor Polski,* No. 25, item 109) is no longer valid.

Para. 15. This order takes effect on April 15, 1979.

12. Order by the Ministers of Finance and Foreign Trade and Shipping of March 28, 1979, CONCERNING PERMITS FOR CERTAIN ACTIVITIES CONNECTED WITH FOREIGN TRADE TRANS-ACTIONS MADE BY FOREIGN CORPORATE BODIES AND NATURAL PERSONS.

On the basis of art. 10, passage 1, item 1, and art. 16, passage 1, of the foreign currency law of March 28, 1952 (*Dziennik Ustaw,* No. 21, item 133), and paragraph 2, passage 1 and 2, para. 3, passage 1, item 4, of the order by the Council of Ministers of April 24, 1974, concerning the detailed range of activity of the Minister of Foreign Trade and Shipping (*Dziennik Ustaw,* No. 17, item 93), we order as follows:

Para. 1. Foreign corporate bodies and natural persons mentioned in para. 2 of the order by the Council of Ministers of May 14, 1976, on issuing permits for foreign corporate bodies and natural persons to pursue certain business activity (*Dziennik Ustaw,* 1976, No. 19, item 123, and of 1978, No. 31, item 135), who are hereinafter called "foreign persons," are allowed to sell goods and render services in foreign trade turnover on the scale and according to the rules specified by the order.

Para. 2.1. The sales of goods and the rendering of services by foreign persons in foreign trade turnover can be done exclusively through:

1. the Polimar Foreign Trade Company Ltd. if the company acts as a proxy for those persons;

2. the "Remex" Foreign Trade Office, in every other instance.

2. The units mentioned in passage 1 are the only ones entitled to make purchases in foreign trade turnover for such items as: raw materials, semi-products, spare parts, and instruments paid for from bank accounts mentioned in para. 1 of the order of the Minister of Finance of March 28, 1979, concerning a permit on the opening and running of bank accounts by foreign corporate bodies and natural persons involved in any kind of business activity in People's Poland (*Monitor Polski,* No. 10, item 67). The purchases may be made without bidding.

3. Foreign persons can purchase Polish-made products for convertible currency at appropriate foreign trade organizations. The sales of

these products by foreign trade organizations is included among the export results to the convertible currency payment zone.

Para. 3. Socialized economic units authorized to run internal exports can buy products and services rendered by foreign persons directly from those persons at previously set prices.

Para. 4. The sales of goods and services mentioned in para. 1 and the purchases mentioned in para. 2, passage 2, are carried out on the foreign person's account.

2. The principles of paying the companies mentioned in para. 2, passage 1, for the sales of goods and services and the purchase of raw materials, semi-products, spare parts, and instruments in foreign trade turnover will be specified by separate regulations by taking into consideration the costs and the customary profit gained by foreign trade agencies.

Para. 5. 1. The settling of accounts between the companies mentioned in para. 2, passage 1, and in para. 3, and foreign persons is made in convertible currency.

2. The companies mentioned in para. 2, passage 1, will sign contracts with the Bank Polska Kasa Opieki SA, on the principles of cooperation in squaring accounts on the deals specified by the order.

Para. 6. The order takes effect on April 15, 1979.

13. Order of the Minister of Labor, Wages, and Social Affairs of May 30, 1979, CONCERNING THE PRINCIPLES OF HIRING AND REMUNERATION OF EMPLOYEES OF LIMITED LIABILITY COMPANIES WITH A SHARE OF FOREIGN CAPITAL.

On the basis of section 9 of Decree No. 24 of the Council of Ministers made on February 7, 1979, concerning the creation and operation of businesses with a share of foreign capital (*Monitor Polski*, No. 4, item 86), the following instructions have been made:

Section 1. 1. Polish citizens can be employed by limited liability companies with a share of foreign capital (referred to henceforth as "companies") in accordance with the regulations of labor exchange.

2. A list of foreign personnel employed by the company, accompanied by a statement of their professional qualifications and the anticipated length of their employment in the company, should be determined in the company's contract. This list should be previously agreed upon with that local State administrative organ (at the country level) which is appropriate considering the company's location.

Section 2. 1. Polish workers employed by a company should be remunerated and also receive other testimony of their work according to the rules operative in State or cooperative businesses of the appropriate industrial branch. These rules should be stated in the contract.

2. Inclusion of the company in the appropriate business category

with the aim of adopting a salary table for workers in management and administration is carried out by the appropriate minister or headquarters of the cooperative association after coming to an agreement with the headquarters of the appropriate trade union.

Section 3. 1. For the Polish worker employed in a company, the period of previous employment by a State or cooperative business establishment is added to the period of employment that establishes the right to a bonus for continuous work if that worker took the job in the company as a result of an agreement of the business establishments and if in these establishments bonuses are given for full terms of service.

2. For the worker in (1) above, the period of employment is added to the period of employment that establishes the right for jubilee awards according to principles generally in force.

3. Periods of employment in a company are treated on a par with work in a State or cooperative business establishment of the respective branch.

Section 4. The creation at business establishments of funds for compensation (welfare and housing), as well as their utilization, takes place according to the regulations in force at the respective State businesses.

Section 5. 1. Regulations—in the domain of national insurance in the case of sickness and maternity, family insurance, pensions and annuities, as well as claims of job-related accidents—that apply to workers in the units of the State-controlled economy also apply to Polish workers employed by the companies.

2. Regulation (1) above also applies to foreign workers in the company if the provisions of the agreement with the government of the foreign partner do not state otherwise.

Section 6. In the domain of tax exemptions and pension funds, the same regulations apply as for the appropriate State-controlled businesses, with the exception of cases where the foreign worker is a citizen of a nation with which People's Poland did not conclude an agreement about the avoidance of double taxation.

Section 7. These instructions go into effect on the day of their publication.

14. Order of the Minister of Finance of June 18, 1979, CONCERNING SOME REGULATIONS OF THE FINANCIAL MANAGEMENT OF COMPANIES WITH PARTICIPATION OF FOREIGN CAPITAL (*Monitor Polski,* No. 16, June 30, 1979).

On the basis of article 10, regulation 1, pt. 1, and article 16, reg. 1, pt. 1, of the foreign currency regulations of March 28, 1952 (*Dziennik Ustaw,* No. 21, item 133), section 2, regulation 3, Decree No. 96,

Council of Ministers, July 5, 1977, concerning interest on monetary means in bank accounts (*Monitor Polski,* No. 17, item 96), as well as section 9 of Decree No. 24 of the Council of Ministers, February 7, 1979, concerning the creation and operation of businesses with shares of foreign trade capital (*Monitor Polski,* No. 4, item 36), the following instructions have been made:

Section 1. Whenever there is mention in the instructions of:

1. the Polish partner, by this is understood a State-controlled cooperative business unit,

2. the foreign partner, by this is understood that legal or physical person who has an abode or place of residence abroad, authorized in accordance with the laws of that State, on whose territory he has the abode or place of residence, to execute business operations outside the territory of this State as well, with legal persons abroad.

3. company, by this is understood a company with limited liabilities with shares of foreign trade capital, established in accordance with Decree No. 24 of the Council of Ministers of February 7, 1979, in connection with the creation and operation of businesses with shares of foreign capital (*Monitor Polski,* No. 4, item 36).

4. share in the company, by this is understood the value in *zloty* of the monetary and non-monetary investment of one of the partners.

5. decree, by this is understood Decree No. 24 of the Council of Ministers of February 7, 1979, in connection with the creation and operation of businesses with shares of foreign capital (*Monitor Polski,* No. 4, item 36).

Section 2. A company acts in accordance with the regulations of economic accounting, taking into consideration the regulations specified in the instructions.

Section 3. Settlement of accounts on the Polish market is carried out by the company in *zloties* in accordance with the regulations governing the forms of account settlements with respect to sales agreements, delivery agreements, orders, and other agreements between units of the collectivized economy.

Section 4. 1. The company conducts its bookkeeping in accordance with the regulations specified for units of the collectivized economy.

2. The board of directors is responsible for the correct and up-to-date bookkeeping for the company. The board of directors is obliged to appoint the head accountant for the company, who is to be a Polish citizen.

3. The company conducts its bookkeeping in Polish with Polish currency. The fiscal year is the calendar year.

4. The company draws up the financial accounts according to the regulations and models in force among the units of the collectivized economy.

5. The annual financial report of the company should be signed by all the members of the Board of Directors and made available to the partners as well as submitted to supervisory organs of the company. Grounds must be given for a refusal to sign the report.

6. The annual financial report of the company is subject to audit and approval according to procedures specified in separate regulations as well as in the company's contract.

Section 5. 1. The initial capital of the company should total, at the time of the company's establishment, at least five million *zloties* and cannot go under this quota for the duration of the company.

2. The initial capital of the company determines the multiplicity of its shares. One share in the company cannot be less than 250,000 *zloties.* Even as a result of a further division, one share cannot be created whose value is less than the minimum specified above.

3. The foreign partner ought to own at least four shares in the company.

4. Payments into the initial capital of the company by the Polish and foreign partners are to be made in *zloties* into the company's current account with the National Bank of Poland (Narodowy Bank Polski).

Section 6. 1. Monetary payments of the foreign partner, by way of shares in the initial capital of the company, are to be made in *zloties,* proceeding from the documented exchange of foreign currency specified by the National Bank of Poland (Narodowy Bank Polski).

2. The amount of the monetary payment of the foreign partner, in the initial capital of the company, cannot be less than 50% of his total share. In specified cases, to permit the negotiation of a company contract, the investment of the partner from abroad may be set at a lower amount.

Section 7. 1. If the partner makes up part of his share in the company by non-monetary investment, the object of investment as well as the amount and quantity allocated in exchange for shares should be cited in the company contract.

2. The Polish partner's input to the initial capital of the company as non-monetary payment may take the following forms in particular:

1. State lands that are in use by the Polish partner; in this case, as investment is considered the payment for the use of these lands which is owed for the duration of the company.

2. Buildings and structures; as investment may be considered the value of these buildings and structures, taking into account the cost of reconstruction, minus depreciation.

3. Durable means other than those designated in (2) above; as investment may be considered the value of these resources based on their purchase price or the cost of production, or—in the case of

previously used resources—the cost of their reactivation minus depreciation.

4. Circulating resources; as investment can be the value of these resources based on their purchase price or production costs.

3. The basis for ascertaining in *zloties* the value of the durable resources, properties, and the working-capital resources paid in kind by the foreign partner into the company, is the documented and verified by (experts) purchase price of these resources and goods in the country from whence they originated.

4. The company contract should specify the conditions under which the foreign partner may retract his non-monetary investment in the event of the dissolution and liquidation of the company or the foreign partner's quitting the company.

5. In the assets of the company are also included sums due but not paid by the partners, supplementing the initial capital of the company.

6. The sums due in (5) above should be indicated by separate entries appended to the balance sheet of the company.

7. The costs of the establishment of the company cannot be counted as assets; these costs are entered as debits in the financial tabulations for a period of two years from the date on which the company contract was negotiated.

Section 8. The company may get foreign currency credit in banks abroad upon receiving permission to do so from the *National Bank of Poland* (Narodowy Bank Polski).

Section 9. The National Bank of Poland will determine the procedure for granting, guaranteeing, and paying of credit in *zloties* for the business operations of the companies.

Section 10. 1. The company deducts amortizations in *zloties* according to rates operative in the units of the collectivized economy.

2. From deductions for amortization is created the amortization fund of the company.

3. The resources in the amortization fund are kept in a separate account in *zloties* in the National Bank of Poland (Narodowy Bank Polski).

Section 11. 1. The company finances its investments with:

1. initial capital;

2. the amortization fund;

3. the gross receipts of the company, in the event of a shortage of funds in the amortization fund.

2. That portion of the gross receipts of the company that is designated for investments is subject to refund from the resources in the amortization fund in a period of up to three years.

3. In the event of the liquidation or dissolution of the company,

the balance of the account of the amortization fund will augment the reserve fund of the company.

Section 12. 1. The company creates a risk fund. The initial amount in this fund will equal 20% of the gross receipts of the company gained in its first year of operations. The risk fund is increased yearly by 25% until the time it reaches at least 10% of the value of the durable assets and stocks of the company.

2. The resources of the risk fund are to be kept in a separate account in *zloties* in the National Bank of Poland (Narodowy Bank Polski).

3. The resources in the risk fund are set aside for:

1. covering losses on the balance sheet;

2. security on payments of obligations of the company, especially obligations in the form of approved warranties on goods sold or services rendered by the company.

Section 13. 1. The company creates the reserve fund from gross receipts.

2. The company contract should anticipate the allocation of at least 20% of the gross receipts for the reserve fund.

3. The resources in the reserve fund are to be kept in a separate account in *zloties* in the National Bank of Poland (Narodowy Bank Polski).

4. The resources in the reserve fund are set aside for:

1. covering losses on the balance sheet in the event of a shortage of resources in the risk fund;

2. financing the durable and floating resources of the company;

3. covering expenses for sick benefits and liabilities in the form of job-related accidents and illnesses that are subject to financial coverage from the resources of the company.

Section 14. In the event of the dissolution or liquidation of the company, the balance of the accounts of the risk and reserve funds is counted toward the gross receipts of the company.

Section 15. The company covers insurance premiums for social services and deducts funds for housing, welfare, and bonuses for personnel according to regulations specified in separate rules. These premiums and deductions are entered as a debit against gross receipts of the company.

Section 16. Permission is given to the companies to open current accounts of foreign currency with the National Bank of Poland for the purpose of financing their business operations, as well as opening deposit accounts of foreign currency in authorized Polish banks.

Section 17. 1. Settlement of accounts involving foreign currency is carried out through the National Bank of Poland on the company's current foreign currency account.

2. Settlement of accounts in *zloties* is carried out on the company's current account in *zloties* through the National Bank of Poland.

Section 18. 1. Receipts into the company's foreign currency account can be made in convertible foreign currency as specified by the National Bank of Poland.

2. The current foreign currency account of the company may be supplied with supplementary funds by the foreign partner, in accordance with the provisions of the company's contract, or by payments carried out by the Polish partner from foreign currency resources secured, within the framework of foreign currency limitations, through the appropriate minister or board of the central cooperative union that issued the decision allowing the Polish partner to negotiate the company's contract.

3. Supplementary funds from the foreign partner may be acquired in the following forms:

1. a bank remittance from abroad;

2. payment of foreign monies as specified in the written declaration of imports, certified by the Polish customs office or in a written attestation by this office;

3. payment of sums from the realization of letters of credit, personal checks, or checks to the bearer, written out for foreign currency denominations;

4. remittance from foreign currency accounts of foreigners.

4. Besides the payments described in items (2) and (3) above, the current foreign currency account of the company can be supplied by sums in convertible foreign currency in the amount of 50% of receipts gained in the form of exports of goods and services brought about through the mediation of Polish trade firms with businesses abroad, as well as Polish units of the collectivized economy authorized to conduct external exports. The remaining 50% of receipts in this form is subject to conversion into *zloties* and transference to the current account of the company in *zloties*. However, before the division of these sums, which were received in convertible foreign currency by the company, the company may transfer to the current foreign currency account the whole or part of the sum of these receipts up to the cost, in convertible foreign currency, of the company's purchase of goods and services designated for utilization in conducting business operations. This does not apply to cases of resale to a domestic consumer of goods purchased with convertible foreign currency, even if they were in part produced by the company.

Section 19. It is permitted to make payments in convertible foreign currency from current foreign currency accounts of the companies for the following:

1. the purchase of goods and services connected with production operations and services rendered, brought about through the mediation of Polish trade firms dealing with businesses abroad as well as Polish units of the collectivized economy authorized to conduct foreign trade;

2. covering the costs of international transport of goods with Polish and foreign means of transportation as well as the insurance of these goods;

3. covering charges of Polish foreign trade firms incurred through their exporting or importing of goods and services;

4. covering of costs of a company's participation in international fairs and exhibits as well as other costs of a promotional nature;

5. covering of costs of travel abroad for heads of a company and workers in matters connected with the business activities of the company, in accordance with regulations specified in separate rules;

6. payments to the foreign partner of sums owed to him as shareholder in the company, minus income tax as well as sums taken by him from the receipts in *zloties;*

7. remuneration for foreign personnel employed by the company, up to 50% of the amount of remuneration.

Section 20. 1. Payments referred to in Section 19 items 6 and 7 above may be made in the following forms:

1. remittance into the foreign currency account of the foreign partner or foreign employee of the company, and

2. remittance abroad,

from the foreign currency resources of the company, and in the event of insufficiency of funds, from foreign currency resources secured, within the framework of foreign currency limitations, through the appropriate minister or board of the central cooperative union that issued the decision allowing the Polish partner to negotiate the company's contract.

2. Payments are made after prior presentation to the National Bank of Poland (Narodowy Bank Polski) of certificate delivered by the company attesting to the sum owed by the foreign partner as his share of the profits or the amount of remuneration paid out to foreign personnel. These certificates are verified by the appropriate regional tax board dealing with State income and fiscal controls, ascertaining that the company pays the income tax it owes as well as the correctness of the company's calculations of the sum owed to the foreign partner. The standard for the certificate will be determined by the National Bank of Poland (Narodowy Bank Polski).

3. Payments not realized in a given year can be made in coming years, but no later than in the course of the year following the completion of business operations of the company.

4. Payment in convertible foreign currency to the foreign partner in the form of shares in the company cannot take place after a lapse of ten years from the tax year following that year in which the foreign partner received a card of permanent residency in the People's Republic of Poland or moved his residency to the People's Republic of Poland.

5. In the event that the foreign partner obtains a card of permanent resident status in the People's Republic of Poland, or of transfer of his residency to the territory of the People's Republic of Poland, the remittance abroad of sums paid out in convertible foreign currency to the foreign partner as his share in the company requires separate permission concerning foreign currency.

Section 21. Companies are permitted to pay the foreign partner out of the profits due to him as share-holder in the company sums in *zloties* for his personal needs during the time of his stay in the People's Republic of Poland as well as to receive back from him payments from collected but not utilized sums in *zloties*.

Section 22. 1. From the foreign currency accounts, remittance can be made in *zloties* of the Polish partner's share of the profits to his account in a Polish bank.

2. Remittance in *zloties* of the Polish partner's share of the profits to his account in a Polish bank increases the profit of the Polish partner.

Section 23. 1. In the event of the dissolution and liquidation of the company, the balance of the foreign currency accounts, after estimating the settlement of accounts and payment of the company's debts, is subject to settlement between the Polish and foreign partner according to their shares in the company. Part of the balance owed to the foreign partner may be remitted abroad without a separate foreign currency permit, upon prior presentation of the certificate to the appropriate regional tax board dealing with State income and fiscal controls ascertaining the proper collection and payment by the liquidator of the company of income taxes owed from the income of the foreign partner. Part of the balance owed to the Polish partner is subject to payment in *zloties*.

2. The National Bank of Poland (Narodowy Bank Polski) can make the payments, referred to above in item (1), abroad after prior remittance by the liquidator of the company to the current foreign currency account of the company in the National Bank of Poland of the sums owing to the foreign partner and after presentation of the final financial report together with a list of payments falling to the Polish and foreign partners.

3. In the event of insufficiency of funds in convertible foreign currency in the foreign currency accounts of the company, the payments referred to in item (1) above are made from foreign currency

resources secured, according to other regulations, through the appropriate minister or board of the central cooperative union that issued the decision allowing the conclusion of the company's contract.

Section 24. In the event of the withdrawal of the foreign partner from the company, payments made to him from his share in the company are made after prior remittance by the company to the current foreign currency account in the National Bank of Poland the sums owing to the foreign partner and after presentation of a certificate of the board of the company concerning the amount of payment in foreign currency made to him, verified by the appropriate regional tax board dealing with State income and fiscal controls.

Section 25. Payment abroad of the sums referred to in sections 23 and 24 to the foreign partners who hold cards of permanent residence status or residence in the territory of Poland requires separate foreign currency permission.

Section 26. The foreign partners are permitted payments abroad of sums in convertible foreign currency, received from the sale of shares in the company, minus income tax resulting from the sale, under the condition that:

1. the sale was made to the Polish partner;
2. the sale was made to a foreigner or a native if the Polish partner did not take advantage of his right of pre-emption;
3. the sale to the Polish partner or to another native was made after the acquisition of a separate foreign currency permit;
4. the sales agreement was drawn up in the form of a deed executed and authenticated by a notary;
5. the sum acquired from the sale was paid in foreign currency to the seller into a Polish bank;
6. the seller met his tax obligations.

Section 27. 1. In the event of the taking over of shares of the company through inheritance or bequest to individuals residing or having a residence abroad, these individuals exercise control over the assets in the capacity of a devisor (legator), after presentation of documents affirming the acquisition of the inheritance or bequest.

2. If the heirs (or legatees) are also persons who are natives, the assets of the company and profits from the company shares are subject to transference abroad only in the share relating to the heirs (legatees), proportional to their share of the inheritance of bequest.

Section 28. 1. The resources of the company in convertible foreign currency in the current foreign currency account in the National Bank of Poland do not pay interest.

2. The convertible foreign currency resources of the company which are accumulated in foreign currency deposit accounts in authorized Polish banks pay interest in the following amounts per annum:
1.   6 month term — 4.5%

2.   12 month term — 5.0%
3.   24 month term — 6.0%
4.   36 month term — 7.0%

3. In the case of investments justified by amount and length of term, authorized banks in Poland may use a higher percentage than that set forth above in item (2) on the basis of individual applications submitted by the banks and approved by the Minister of Finance.

4. Interest from the resources in foreign currency deposit accounts are compounded in the foreign currency of that account.

Section 29. 1. Resources of the company in *zloties* that are kept in a current account in the National Bank of Poland do not pay interest.

2. Resources of the company in *zloties* kept in the account of the amortization fund and the risk and reserve funds do pay interest according to rates specified in separate regulations.

Section 30. The conversion of convertible foreign currency into *zloties* and of *zloties* into convertible foreign currency is made according to a special rate of exchange fixed by the National Bank of Poland and announced in the list of rates of exchange of that bank.

Section 31. The instructions of the Minister of Finance from May 26, 1976, concerning the carrying out of foreign currency payments by mixed companies is now invalid (*Monitor Polski*, No. 25, item 110).

Section 32. These instructions go into effect on the day of publication.

Appendix 1

QUESTIONNAIRE ON US-POLISH
INDUSTRIAL COOPERATION*

Part I General Overview

The purpose of this overview is, for the US side, to gain an improved understanding of how specific industrial cooperation (IC) opportunities might be created for US firms in Poland and, for the Polish side, to gain an improved understanding of how IC with CMEA countries in general and with Poland in particular fits into the global strategy of US multinational corporations as well as those of medium-sized and smaller firms.

A. The process of generating IC opportunities for Western firms in Poland may be divided into three phases:
   1. Generating the initiative
      (a) How are priority sectors determined in Poland?
      (b) To what extent are acceptable initiatives limited to priority sectors?
      (c) To what extent is the high concentration of existing ICAs in a few sectors a good guide as to where future IC opportunities might lie?
      (d) Are there limits to the number of IC projects in a given industry or priority sector?
      (e) What is the relationship between Poland's participation in the CMEA division of labor and the selection and implementation of particular IC projects with Western countries?
   2. Searching for Western bids or proposals
      (a) Assuming that the characteristics of two or more Western firms and the details of their proposals are the same, under what conditions would Poland prefer to enter into an ICA with the firm of one country versus the firm of other countries? How do European-based US MNCs "fit" into the Polish preference scheme?
      (b) What are the general characteristics of Western firms that Poland seems to prefer and are there identifiable

*Developed jointly by the US and Polish teams as a guide to their research.

differences among industries in regard to preferred characteristics?

3. Approving or denying a preliminary agreement

    (a) Describe the process whereby preliminary or tentative ICAs are approved

    (b) What considerations are involved at various levels in a decision to approve or deny a proposed ICA?

B. How do ICAs with CMEA countries in general and Poland in particular fit into the global strategy of US MNCs? We will examine the hypothesis that attitude toward entering into an ICA in a CMEA country in general and in Poland in particular might be determined by such variables as:

    (a) size of firm

    (b) rank in industry and degree of competition in industry

    (c) share of foreign assets/sales/earnings in the total

    (d) perceptions about the IC experience of other US or West European corporations in the CMEA host country

    (e) product/technology life cycle period

    (f) business cycle period

    (g) preliminary factual basis for assuming that Poland is seriously interested in an ICA

    (h) attitude of US government (licensing, credits)

    (i) ethnic background of top executive in US corporation

Part II Case Study Questions

1. Cooperation partners: summary description of the cooperative project and characteristics of the partner firms

2. Detailed description of partner enterprises

    (a) Multi-country involvement of US firm. Industry position of the US firm. How is the company organized and what is the division of responsibility between headquarters and participating units (profit centers)? What is the role of subsidiaries in Western Europe in implementing the ICA with Poland?

    (b) Organizational status of the Polish partner: No. of plants, position in branch, industry; relationship with planning organs and other enterprises.

3. Motives of selecting cooperation partner. What were the specific arguments in favor of selecting this particular partner for cooperation venture?

4. Previous experiences in mutual trade/and other relations.

5. Initiator of cooperation deal/American or Polish partner.

6. What were the reasons/motives leading to the specific form of industrial cooperation?

(a) motives of American partner

(b) motives of Polish partner

7.   Subject of cooperation venture:
     (a) in the infant stage of cooperation
     (b) in further stages of development

8.   Legal basis for cooperation:
     —long-term agreements (describe their contents)
     —short-term contracts (describe their contents)

9.   Negotiations and preparation of the agreement:
     (a) How long did the negotiations and preparation of the agreement last? Indicate possible impact on the effectiveness of technology transfer.
     (b) Duration of the contract: initial contract period, provisions for extension.
     (c) Does the contract contain provisions regarding the transfer of contract obligations?
     (d) Have reorganization and changes of people responsible for negotiating and overseeing the implementation of the contract caused any difficulties?

10. Implementation of cooperation venture.
     (a) Extension of the initial agreement (with respect to products covered or time period)
     (b) Were new final products introduced into the cooperation subsequent to the initial contract?

11. Does the cooperation venture include elements of higher and more integrated phases of cooperation, e.g., joint designing of new products?

12. How is the division of output and marketing assignments agreed upon and implemented? Describe some common marketing problems encountered and how they were handled, such as:
     (a) finishing and packaging
     (b) erratic demand
     (c) need of special authorization for exports
     (d) inflexibility in sales credit terms
     (e) minimum quantity stipulations
     (f) other factors (please list)

13. Connection of license and know-how buying with production program. Were there difficulties in the introduction of new technology?

14. License costs. What are the principles of payment for the licence and know-how?

15. What indispensable investments were undertaken by both sides in order to start production?

16. What difficulties were encountered during the implementa-

tion of the cooperation venture and what workable solutions were found?

17. Financing: What were the difficulties in this field and ways of solving them?

    (a) Barter payment arrangements in related goods: What proportion of the total value is covered by payment in related goods? Has this proportion changed over time? What is the incidence of payment in resultant products on the overall cost of the transaction? Discuss specific problems encountered with this type of transaction.

    (b) Is leasing used for financing?

    (c) Credit arrangements: usual standard enterprise credit arrangements; existence and role of government and bank support for partner credit arrangements and problems (e.g. collateral; restrictions on the discountability of commercial paper; credits for hard-currency imports, etc.). Have overall balance-of-payment considerations influenced payment arrangements, if so, how?

18. Are there or were there difficulties connected with government regulations, fiscal laws, customs duties, taxes, embargo, quantitative restrictions, and other laws or regulations during the development and implementation of the cooperatation venture? If yes, did they affect the cost of this venture?

19. How were the prices of elements, components, and final goods determined: Methodology. What is the formula for the price adjustment clause?

20. Describe the two-way flow of goods and services, i.e. the export/import ratio in consecutive years of cooperation and changes thereof. Planned quantities and their realization.

21. What was and is the influence of cyclical fluctuations in industrial Western countries on the implementation of the cooperation venture?

22. Discuss the trade-mark arrangement. What proposals and solutions were considered in respect to partners' countries and other markets?

23. What were the agreements concerning quality control procedures and how do they operate in practice? At which stage of production is control being affected by the foreign partner? What are the positive and negative aspects of quality control by the foreign partners? Costs of quality control.

24. What sort of product guarantees are provided for in the agreement? Comment on any advantages or disadvantages experienced in this area.

25. Describe the range of technical, commercial, and financial risks involved in the venture. (Technical risk % transferred technology is too difficult to absorb and manage; commercial risk = resulting product will not be salable; financial risk = costs and sales price relationships will be less favorable than planned.)
    (a) as discussed during the negotiations
    (b) as realized during the cooperation venture
    (c) What ways have been found to minimize these risks?

26. What future possibilities might be found for undertaking joint US-Polish ventures with third countries, such as new forms of cooperative sales efforts in third countries as well as tripartite IC projects?

27. Describe proposals concerning the further development of industrial cooperation between the partners.

28. What are the main determinants of the smooth realization of the existing contracts in Poland?
    (a) management and incentive system
    (b) vertical and horizontal inter-dependencies/both foreign and domestic
    (c) system of setting up short- and long-term goals, i.e., the system and stages of planning

29. What is the influence of institutional factors on venture's success (e.g., joining working groups, governmental commissions, seminars, and so on?)

Appendix 2

LIST OF CONFERENCE PARTICIPANTS

BLOOMINGTON, DECEMBER 1978

1. Andrzej K. Blicharz
   Executive Vice President
   Polikee Inc. Technology Export-Import
   Chicago, Illinois

2. Josef C. Brada
   Associate Professor of Economics
   Arizona State University
   Tempe, Arizona

3. Robert Campbell
   Chairman, Department of Economics
   Indiana University, Bloomington

4. Harry DePledge
   International Contracts Administrator
   Schwitzer Engineered Components
   Wallace Murray Corporation
   Indianapolis, Indiana

5. T.A. Dukes
   Executive Vice President
   Ingersoll Rand

6. Lech Dzikiewicz
   Commercial Attache
   Embassy of Polish People's Republic
   Washington, D.C.

7. Gabriel Eichler
   International Economist
   Bank of America
   San Francisco, California

8. Thomas S. Fedor
   Professor of Geography
   Indiana University-Purdue University
   Indianapolis, Indiana

9. Steve Gaal
   Chief Engineer
   Cummins Technical Center
   Columbus, Indiana

10. Robert Galbraith
    Director of Sales
    Gleason Works
    Rochester, New York

11. John Garland
    Research Associate
    School of Business
    Indiana University, Bloomington

12. Jan Giezgala
    Deputy Director
    Foreign Trade Research Institute
    Warsaw, Poland

13. Robert Gosende
    Center for International Affairs
    Harvard University
    Cambridge, Massachusetts
    formerly:
       Cultural Attache
       US Embassy
       Warsaw, Poland

14. Michael D. Harsh
    Professor of Economics
    Indiana State University
    Terre Haute, Indiana

15. James Huebner
    International Market Development
    Service
    Allis Chalmers
    Milwaukee, Wisconsin

16. Harry W. Jones
    Vice President and Director
    Overseas Affairs
    Westinghouse Electric Corporation
    Pittsburgh, Pennsylvania

17. James Kampmeier
    Director of License and International
    Agreement Activities
    Sunstrand Corporation
    Rockford, Illinois

18. Zygmunt Kossut
    Dean
    Central School of Planning and
    Statistics
    Warsaw, Poland

19. Ireneusz Kubiczek
    Commercial Consul
    Commercial Consulate of Poland
    Chicago, Illinois

20. Janusz Kozinski
    Research Associate
    Foreign Trade Research Institute
    Warsaw, Poland
    Currently (1978-79):
        Fulbright Scholar
        Indiana University, Bloomington

21. Joseph Kramer
    Economic Analyst, Eastern Europe
    U.S. Department of State
    Washington, D.C.

22. W.D. Lee
    Manager of Programs
    Special Operations, Pay Line Group
    International Harvester
    Schaumburg, Illinois

23. H.L. Lehmann
    Director, Special Operations
    Pay Line Group
    International Harvester
    Schaumburg, Illinois

24. George Logusch
    Director, Institute of International
    Business
    Graduate School of Business
    Administration
    Fordham University
    New York, New York

25. Christine L. Lucyk
    Bureau of East-West Trade
    U.S. Department of Commerce
    Washington, D.C.

26. Paul Marer
    Professor of International Business
    School of Business
    Indiana University, Bloomington

27. Robert F. McCullough
    Manager, International Coordination
    F.M.C. Corporation
    Chicago, Illinois

28. Joseph C. Miller
    Associate Professor of Marketing
    Indiana University, Bloomington

29. David Nooyen
    Supervisor of International
    Administration
    Construction Machinery International
    Rexnard Inc.
    Milwaukee, Wisconsin

30. Conrad Pawlowski
    Director of International Sales
    Arthur G. McKee & Co.
    Chicago, Illinois

31. Howard V. Perlmutter
    Professor of Business
    Wharton School
    University of Pennsylvania
    Philadelphia, Pennsylvania

32. Sylvester Pieckowski
    Legal Advisor
    Ministry of Foreign Trade and
    Shipping
    Warsaw, Poland
    Currently with:
        Metzger, Shadyac & Schwarz
        Washington, D.C.

33. Warren H. Reynolds
    Senior Program Officer
    Office of External Research
    Department of State
    Washington, D.C.

34. Andrzej Rudka
    Research Associate
    Foreign Trade Research Institute
    Warsaw, Poland

35. D.K. Shukur
    Director, International Market
    Development Services
    Allis Chalmers
    Milwaukee, Wisconsin

36. Kiprian M. Skavinski
    Special Assistant to the General
    Sales Manager
    Foreign Agricultural Service
    United States Department of
    Agriculture
    Washington, D.C.

37. Roger Stechshulte
    Director, Trade Development
    Assistance Division
    Bureau of East-West Trade
    U.S. Department of Commerce
    Washington, D.C.

38. Carl V. Stride
    Manager of Marketing and
    Technology Services
    USS Engineers & Consultants, Inc.
    Pittsburgh, Pennsylvania

39. Jerzy Szumski
    Commercial Officer
    Polish Consulate General
    Chicago, Illinois

40. Eugeniusz Tabaczynski
    Senior Scholar and Associate

Professor
Foreign Trade Research Institute
Warsaw, Poland

41. Myron Uretsky
    Director, Management Decision
    Laboratory
    New York University
    New York, New York

42. Thomas A. Wolf
    Associate Professor of Economics
    Ohio State University
    Columbus, Ohio

43. Edwin Zagorski
    Senior Research Fellow
    Foreigh Trade Research Institute
    Warsaw, Poland

WARSAW, MARCH 1979

FTRI = Foreign Trade Research Institute
CSPS = Central School of Planning and Statistics

1. Jan Anusz
   Senior Research Fellow
   FTRI, Warsaw

2. Zofia Balczewska
   Research Associate
   FTRI, Warsaw

3. Boguslawa Barankiewicz
   Research Associate
   FTRI, Warsaw

4. Alicja Bielecka
   Senior Research Fellow
   FTRI, Warsaw

5. Wojciech Bienkowski
   Scholar
   CSPS, Warsaw

6. Jerzy Borowski
   Associate Professor
   CSPS, Warsaw

7. Jerzy Boniuk
   Head of Division
   Ministry of Finance
   Warsaw

8. Karol Brzoska
   Professor, Institute of Finance
   Warsaw

9. Michal Bukowski
   Chief Economic Analyst,
   US-Polish Chamber of Foreign
   Trade
   Warsaw

10. Andrzej Burzynski
    Senior Scholar
    Polish Academy of Science
    Warsaw

11. Andrzej Calus
    Professor
    CSPS, Warsaw

12. Antoni Cichocki
    Head of Division
    Foreign Trade Organization
    "Unitra"
    Warsaw

13. Jerzy Cieslik
    Scholar
    CSPS, Warsaw

14. Jerzy Czopinski
    Deputy Director
    Industrial Plant "Stalowa Wola
    Steelworks"
    Stalowa Wola

15. Mieczyslaw Dabroski
    Head of Division
    PWE-Polish Economic Publication
    House
    Warsaw

16. Ewa Drewnowska
    Research Associate
    FTRI, Warsaw

17. Barbara Durka
    Research Associate
    FTRI, Warsaw

18. Tadeusz Epstein
    Expert and Economic Advisor
    Polish Chamber of Foreign Trade
    Warsaw

19. Stanislaw Falkowski
    Senior Research Fellow
    FTRI, Warsaw

20. John Garland
    Research Associate
    School of Business
    Indiana University, Bloomington

21. Donald Grabenstetter
    Commercial Attache
    U.S. Embassy
    Warsaw

22. Jan Grabowski
    Senior Research Fellow
    FTRI, Warsaw

23. Aleksander Granowski
    Head of Division
    Foreign Trade Organization
    "Metalexport"
    Warsaw

24. Eugeniusz Harasim
    Deputy Director and Senior Scholar
    FTRI, Warsaw

25. Jolanta Hawryszko
    Research Associate
    FTRI, Warsaw

26. Aleksander Jung
    Director
    Foreign Trade Organization
    "Metalexport"
    Warsaw

27. Monika Kaczmarowicz
    Scholar
    University of Lodz
    Lodz

28. Janusz Kaczurba
    Director
    FTRI, Warsaw

29. Elzbieta Kawecka-Wyrzykowska
    Scholar
    CSPS, Warsaw

30. Krzysztof Klinger
    Deputy Editor
    Monthly Magazine *Handel Zag-
    raniczny* [Foreign Trade]
    Warsaw

31. Zygmunt Kossut
    Professor and Dean
    CSPS, Warsaw

32. Marek Kulczycki
    Senior Scholar
    CSPS, Warsaw

33. Janusz Kurylo
    Head of Division
    Foreign Trade Organization
    "Pezetel"
    Warsaw

34. Aleksander Krzyminski
    Associate Professor
    Warsaw University

35. Ryszard Lange
    Chief Editor
    Monthly Magazine *Handel Zag-
    raniczny* [Foreign Trade]

36. Julian Lech
    Head of Division
    Ministry of Foreign Trade and
    Shipping
    Warsaw

37. Aleksander Legatowicz
    Associate Professor
    University of Lodz
    Lodz

38. Wlodzimierz Lenard
    Senior Research Fellow
    FTRI, Warsaw

39. Stanislaw Lipinski
    Head of Division
    Foreign Trade Organization "Uni-
    versal"
    Warsaw

40. Zenona Litnik
    Economic Analyst
    "Inter-Polcom" (Polish-Polonian
    Chamber of Industry and Com-
    merce)
    Warsaw

41. Jerzy Mandat
    Scholar
    University of Lodz
    Lodz

42. Paul Marer
    Professor of International Business
    Indiana University, Bloomington

43. Boleslaw Meluch
    Foreign Relations Officer
    FTRI, Warsaw

44. Miroslaw Mirecki
    Head of Division
    Industrial Plant "Stalowa Wola
    Steelworks"
    Stalowa Wola

45. Waldemar Niemotko
    Legal Counsel
    Foreign Trade Organization
    "Bumar"
    Warsaw

46. Marcin Nowakowski
    Research Associate
    FTRI, Warsaw

47. Andrzej Olechowski
    Senior Research Fellow
    FTRI, Warsaw

48. Henryk Olszewski
    Professor
    FTRI, Warsaw

49. Jozef Olszynski
    Senior Scholar
    CSPS, Warsaw

50. Eugeniusz Ostrowski
    Deputy Director
    Consulting Organization "Bistyp"
    Warsaw

51. Howard Perlmutter
    Professor of Business
    Wharton School
    University of Pennsylvania
    Philadelphia, Pennsylvania

52. Urszula Plowiec
    Associate Professor
    FTRI, Warsaw

53. Iwona Radomska
    Research Associate
    FTRI, Warsaw

54. Milton Rose
    Economic Attache
    U.S. Embassy
    Warsaw

55. Andrzej Rudka
    Research Associate
    FTRI, Warsaw

56. Ewa Sadowska-Cieslik
    Research Associate
    FTRI, Warsaw

57. Ludjan Sender
    Technical Advisor
    Central Technical Organization
    "NOT"
    Warsaw

58. John Simpson
    Technical Representative
    International Harvester Office
    Warsaw

59. Jozef Soldaczuk
    Professor
    CSPS, Warsaw

60. Boguslaw Sosnowski
    Senior Scholar
    CSPS, Warsaw

61. Stanislaw Stala
    Director
    Polish Chamber of Foreign Trade
    Warsaw

62. Kazimierz Starzyk
    Senior Scholar
    CSPS, Warsaw

63. Bronislaw Sulimierski
    Senior Scholar
    FTRI, Warsaw

64. Jan Sulmicki
    Senior Scholar
    CSPS, Warsaw

65. Tadeusz Szczepanek
    Associate Professor
    Polytechnic of Lodz
    Lodz

66. Tadeusz Szczepaniak
    Professor
    University of Gdansk
    Gdansk

67. Czeslawa Szczepanska
    Editor
    FTRI, Warsaw

68. Adam Szeworski
    Professor
    Warsaw University

69. Bogdan Szuszkiewicz
    Head of Division
    Foreign Trade Organization "Universal"
    Warsaw

70. Wiktor Szydlowski
    Senior Scholar
    FTRI, Warsaw

71. Marcin Szyszkowski
    Head of Division
    Industrial Development Consulting
    Office "Promasz"
    Warsaw

72. Eugeniusz Tabaczynski
    Associate Professor
    FTRI, Warsaw

73. Maciej Tekielski
    Deputy Editor
    Economic Magazine *Rynki Zagraniczne* [Foreign Markets]
    Warsaw

74. Witold Trzeciakowski
    Professor, FTRI and
    University of Lodz
    Lodz

75. Teresa Turczynska
    Research Fellow
    Institute of Organization and Management
    Warsaw

76. Anna Turowska
    Research Associate
    FTRI, Warsaw

77. Jerzy Urjasz
    Promotion Officer
    Central Technical Organization
    "NOT"
    Warsaw

78. Tomasz Wasilewski
    Research Fellow
    Institute of Finance
    Warsaw

79. Jerzy Wnuczek
    Head of Section
    FTRI, Warsaw

80. Bronislaw Wojciechowski
    Associate Professor
    FTRI, Warsaw

81. Thomas A. Wolf
    Associate Professor of Economics
    Ohio State University, Columbus

82. Jan Woroniecki
    Head of Division
    Ministry of Foreign Affairs
    Warsaw

83. Edwin Zagorski
    Senior Research Fellow
    FTRI, Warsaw

84. Eugeniusz Ziarkowski
    Head of Division
    Foreign Trade Organization
    "Pezetel"
    Warsaw

85. Krystyna Zoladkiewicz
    Senior Scholar
    University of Gdansk
    Gdansk